At-Risk and Handicapped Newborns and Infants

At-Risk
and Handicapped
Newborns and Infants
*Development, Assessment,
and Intervention*

Anne H. Widerstrom
*Professor of Special Education
San Francisco State University*

Barbara A. Mowder
*Professor of Psychology
Pace University*

Susan R. Sandall
*Assistant Professor of Individual
 and Family Studies
University of Delaware*

Foreword by Diane Bricker

Prentice Hall
Englewood Cliffs, New Jersey 07632

Library of Congress Cataloging-in-Publication Data

Widerstrom, Anne H.
    At-risk and handicapped newborns and infants : development,
  assessment, and intervention / Anne H. Widerstrom, Barbara A.
  Mowder, Susan R. Sandall.
        p.   cm.
    Includes bibliographical references.
    Includes index.
    ISBN 0-13-612144-6
    1. Handicapped children--Development. 2. Infants (Newborn)-
  -Development. 3. Infants--Development.   I. Mowder, Barbara A.
  II. Sandall, Susan Rebecka. III. Title.
    [DNLM: 1. Child Development Disorders--diagnosis. 2. Child
  Development Disorders--prevention & control--United States.
  3. Handicapped. 4. Infant, Newborn.]
  RJ137.W35 1991
  618.92--dc20
  DLC
  for Library of Congress   90-7594
                                                                CIP

Editorial/production supervision: Mary McDonald
Interior design: Karen Buck
Cover design: 20/20 Services, Inc.
Prepress buyer: Debbie Kesar
Manufacturing buyer: Mary Anne Gloriande

Printed in the United States of America
10 9 8 7 6 5 4 3 2 1

ISBN 0-13-612144-6

Prentice-Hall International (UK) Limited, *London*
Prentice-Hall of Australia Pty. Limited, *Sydney*
Prentice-Hall Canada Inc., *Toronto*
Prentice-Hall Hispanoamericana, S.A., *Mexico*
Prentice-Hall of India Private Limited, *New Delhi*
Prentice-Hall of Japan, Inc., *Tokyo*
Simon & Schuster Asia Pte. Ltd., *Singapore*
Editora Prentice-Hall do Brasil, Ltda., *Rio de Janeiro*

Contents

SECTION III   ASSESSMENT AND INTERVENTION

Preface

During the past decade, disabled or at-risk newborns and infants have become an important focus of attention for service providers in education, health, psychology, and related fields. This book was written to address the need for current information about these babies that would be useful to various professionals representing multiple disciplines involved in early intervention. It is our experience that, while many professionals have been working with infants for lengthy periods, their knowledge base is unidisciplinary, primarily restricted to their own particular field of training. In order for professionals from diverse fields to become conversant with the literature, research, and intervention premises associated with other relevant disciplines, a general book such as this was needed. While intended for graduate-level study and beyond, it can fill in the gaps for educators and psychologists in health care, for example, and for health care professionals in education and psychology.

Chapter 1, *At-Risk and Handicapped Newborns and Infants*, introduces the topic by means of a brief historical review of early intervention. Following this overview, there is a discussion of legislative mandates relevant to disabled and at-risk babies, and attention to some of the ethical issues currently involving these infants and their families.

In Chapter 2, *Typical Infant Development*, the development of nondisabled infants is examined from conception through the second year of life. Major theories of development are briefly reviewed, and current infant developmental research is presented. Chapter 3, *Determinants of Risk in Infancy*, presents the major factors that place a newborn at risk for disability. Included are both congenital and environmental factors, with particular attention to those associated with the mother's behavior. Attention is given to substance-exposed babies and babies with AIDS.

The primary disorders seen in newborns and infants are the subject of Chapter 4, *Developmental Disorders in Infancy*. These include health-related problems, congenital disorders, and those problems of development specifically related to motor, cognitive, communicative, and social/emotional domains. Attention also is given in this chapter to primary modes of treatment. In Chapter 5, *Preterm and Low Birthweight Infants,* the specific problems of infants born too soon or too small are examined. This chapter reviews causes of these problems, the characteristics of preterm and low birthweight newborns, and the primary techniques of intervention. The neonatal intensive care unit is examined as an environment for promoting optimal physical and psychological development of the infant.

Chapter 6, *Family Dynamics,* addresses the role of the family in early intervention, including a rationale for family-focused programs, the family as a system, and research related to families of at-risk and handicapped newborns and infants. Chapter 7, *Screening and Assessment,* provides a comprehensive review of the evaluation process, with attention to major techniques currently available for screening and assessment. Specific topics such as family assessment, play assessment, and arena assessment are discussed, and timely information is provided concerning specific screening and assessment instruments.

In Chapter 8, *The Individualized Family Service Plan,* the rationale for the IFSP is given, and the components are discussed. This chapter links the IFSP to both the assessment process described in Chapter 7 and the intervention process described in Chapter 9. Case management, an important IFSP component, is discussed as a potential means for helping families with at-risk or handicapped infants to obtain more appropriate services.

The intervention process is the subject of Chapter 9, *Intervention for At-Risk and Handicapped Infants and Their Families.* This chapter presents a review of important issues in early intervention, including curriculum design, intervention techniques, and the role of adults. A variety of methods and resources is provided. In Chapter 10, *Early Intervention Program Models,* the reader is given an overview of best practices in the field of early intervention. Program models are reviewed that have received national recognition due to their effectiveness in serving infants and their families.

The final chapter, Chapter 11, *Future Trends and Issues in Early Intervention,* presents a discussion of certain issues that the authors believe will define early intervention into the next century. Included in this chapter, for example, are directions for policy analysis and development, as well as areas of future research, related to service provision.

Throughout the book, a primary theme is the role of professionals working together for and with families to enhance the development of infants with handicaps or at risk for developmental problems. Further, current research and best practices in the delivery of services are a major theme. Effective services require that professionals be knowledgeable and skilled in their own discipline, knowledgeable in related disciplines and open to the expertise of others, flexible in thought and action, and sensitive to the strengths, needs, hopes, and desires of families. As a whole, the text should provide the practicing professional or the graduate student in education, health, or psychology a current, comprehensive overview of early intervention.

One of the most pleasant tasks an author performs is thanking those who helped bring the book to fruition. All of the authors would like to thank the reviewers who contributed important insights and thoughtful suggestions as this book was being prepared. Special thanks are owed to Diane Bricker, who provided us with an in-depth and comprehensive review of the book during its early stages, and kindly consented to write the foreword. Her insightful comments and attention to detail have undoubtedly contributed much to the quality of the book.

We also wish to acknowledge the assistance of Lou Landry of the Colorado Department of Education, who contributed to the case management section of Chapter 8. We are grateful for his help.

Additionally, thanks must go to Carol Wada at Prentice Hall and Mary McDonald for the care taken in producing a readable, attractive text. We also appreciate Linda Wertheim, a graduate student at Pace University, for her valuable assistance in preparing the references.

Finally, each of us has special thanks for friends, colleagues, and students who have been especially helpful to us during the writing of this book. Anne Widerstrom completed most of her work on the text during sabbatical leave at the University of London Institute of Education, and is grateful for assistance offered by colleagues and staff. Particular thanks go to Professor Klaus Wedell, Department of Educational Psychology and Special Educational Needs at the Institute, whose friendship and support have been invaluable. Barbara Mowder would like to thank Pace University Psychology Department graduate students, faculty, and staff for their support and various efforts regarding this project. In addition, appreciation is extended to Florence Denmark, Joe Houle, and Joe Pastore at Pace University, and to Mary Kay Braccio, Bill and Sarah Kelly, and Joe Prinster. Much of Barbara Mowder's work on this project was supported by a Pace University research award. Susan Sandall acknowledges the assistance of three graduate students: Georgia Athearn, Vicki Halliday, and Kelli Maestas. Their work is greatly appreciated.

Foreword

In our nation, as well as other parts of the world, professionals and the general public are becoming increasingly concerned about infants and toddlers who are at risk for medical, biological, and environmental reasons. This concern for babies who are at risk parallels already established efforts for infants and toddlers who are handicapped. Public awareness of and professional involvement with very young populations who have problems or a significant likelihood of developing problems have been stimulated, in part, by media attention to medical technology that increases survival in infants who are seriously disabled, and to the growing impact of poverty on children—in particular, the biological and environmental effects of substance-abusing parents. Growing interest has also been due to the many professionals speaking out about the need for increased resources and services for infants who have or may develop problems. Finally, the passage of the 1986 amendment to the Education of the Handicapped Act, P.L. 99-457, has provided a particularly strong impetus for improving professional and public awareness. This law, and in particular Part H, offers incentives to states and territories for the development or expansion of an array of services for infants and toddlers who are handicapped. In addition, Part H permits states and territories to develop eligibility guidelines for including at-risk populations in these services.

Although public and professional awareness of young at-risk and handicapped populations has been increased, it appears at present that most states and territories will not choose to expand their eligibility definitions to include at-risk groups. The failure to expand state eligibility requirements results primarily from financial constraints. Most administrators, perhaps all interventionists, and large segments of the public support conceptually and practically the need to provide programs for infants and toddlers who are at risk; however, adequate federal or state funds to include at risk infants in early intervention programs are generally not available. Until adequate financial resources are developed, it is likely that most early intervention programs will have to limit services to infants who have diagnosed disabilities and their families.

The inability of states to expand their eligibility guidelines is unfortunate, for it is clear that many babies who are at risk will develop mild to serious disabilities. Early identification and intervention can often do much to counter or attenuate the effects of a disability on a child. As public awareness continues to grow and as professionals assemble empirical evidence on the importance of early intervention, the garnering of financial resources to provide services to infants and toddlers who are at risk and handicapped should grow. As the number of programs increases, the field faces several major challenges: the development of appropriate screening, assessment, and evaluation tools, expansion of curriculum efforts, improvement of family involvement, increased integration into community programs, and, most critical, the preparation of quality personnel to deliver services.

As we move into the 1990s, the significant shortage of trained early intervention personnel including OTs, PTs, communication specialists, nurses, pediatricians, and special educators has been amply documented. Equally troubling is the fact that many of the personnel providing early intervention services have had no formal training in early intervention. The quality of services offered infants and their families is often poor because personnel lack appropriate experience and training. Developing solutions to the shortage of well-trained personnel has been a topic of concern for professional organizations, governmental agencies, institutions of higher education, and local program administrators who find themselves unable to hire appropriately experienced and prepared personnel. Topics frequently addressed by these groups and individuals include: whether to prepare infant specialists, how to prepare them, who should prepare them, what competencies should be identified, and what type of licenses or certification should be required. It is not likely that uniform solutions will be agreed to or that satisfactory solutions will be developed soon. Nevertheless, increasing numbers of institutions of higher education are recognizing the need to prepare personnel who can provide quality services to infants and their families. To assist these programs, quality training materials such as this book are needed.

In a growing market of textbooks focused on infants, this volume has much to recommend it for use in introductory classes or for use by individuals new to the field or for those whose formal training has been minimal. First, this volume provides a comprehensive coverage of early intervention populations and services. Second, readers will find the chapters straightforward and pragmatic. Each chapter concludes with a list of follow-up resources for students wishing more information. Third, this text juxtaposes typical and atypical development, which will assist the reader in understanding normal developmental phenomena and how they can be derailed. Finally, this volume addresses the major issues and trends confronting those who are or will be working with infants and their families. This volume has assembled and synthesized information that will be of great use to the infant practitioner.

Although there is much we do not know, the authors of this text have assembled, in large measure, what we do know and presented it in a clear, readable fashion. The reader of this volume will be better equipped to understand and intervene with infants and toddlers who are at risk and handicapped and their families.

Diane Bricker, Ph.D.
Professor, Special Education
Director, Early Intervention Program
Center on Human Development
University of Oregon

Chapter 1

At-Risk and Handicapped Newborns and Infants

The past decade has seen a growing interest in intervention programs for infants considered at risk for developmental delays. The interest was fueled in 1986 by the emphasis placed on the infant and toddler age group in federal legislation (Public Law 99-457), but in a larger sense it reflects a commitment to early intervention based on years of efficacy research. Currently there exists a substantial body of research from education, psychology, medicine, and related fields, including longitudinal and cross-sectional studies of children from birth to age 5 with a variety of disabling or potentially disabling conditions, that presents evidence for intervening early in life with multidisciplinary, family-focused programs. At the same time the research on typical and atypical infant development continues to expand at a very fast rate, with several hundred new studies published each year. The result is a greater understanding of what infants need for optimal development and what kind of intervention best provides it.

The educational and economic benefits of early intervention for infants and young children at risk for handicaps has been well documented by research to date (Lazar, Darlington, Murray, Royce, & Snipper, 1982; Meisels, 1984; Simeonsson, Cooper & Schiener, 1982; Smith & Strain, 1988). Smith (1989) summarized the House Report accompanying PL 99-457 as acknowledging that early intervention accomplishes the following:

1. Intelligence is enhanced in some children.
2. Substantial gains are made in all developmental areas, including physical, cognitive, language and speech, psychosocial, and self-help.
3. Secondary handicapping conditions are inhibited or prevented.
4. Family stress is reduced.
5. Dependency and institutionalization are reduced.
6. The need for special educational services at school age is reduced.
7. The nation and society are spared substantial health care and education costs.

Another indication of the current interest in infant development and intervention is the number of journals devoted to infants and toddlers currently available to professionals in psychology, medicine, special education, and related fields. A list of some of the major journals in each field is at the end of this chapter.

In summary, a distinguishing characteristic of the field of infant assessment and intervention at the present time is its multidisciplinary nature, as reflected in the research literature.

NEW TRENDS IN INFANT INTERVENTION

The problems of newborns and infants and their families have been of concern to professionals from various fields for some time. There are, however, several

The infant curriculum has concern for the infants' overall optimal development.

differences between the traditional infant intervention programs established in the 1960s and early 1970s and the programs that are being implemented today.

First, most current programs are working toward a *transdisciplinary team relationship*: team members have as a shared goal to work together as a closely knit unit, sharing roles and responsibilities in assessment and program implementation.

Second, the infant curriculum has grown from a narrow focus on the child's motor or health problems to a concern for the infant's overall optimal development, including cognitive and communication skills, emotional well-being, and parent/peer interactions.

Third, the focus of programs in recent years has become the family rather than the child, in recognition of the greater benefits to be gained from intervention that takes into account factors affecting the child but originating in the family.

Fourth, programs for infants tend to be located in the community and of longer duration than previously. While the need for short-term, hospital-based followup programs continues, particularly for medically fragile and severely impaired infants, the trend is to provide intervention services during the first two years of life in community-based settings that include professionals from many disciplines outside medicine and nursing.

HISTORICAL PERSPECTIVE

According to Smith (1989), early intervention for infants and toddlers became an important focus of federal policy in the 1960s with the passage of PL 88-156 in 1963 and PL 89-313 in 1965. The first of these laws expanded maternal and child health services to include expectant mothers from low-income areas as a preventive measure against mental retardation. The second provided federal monies to state-operated schools for the handicapped, a funding source often used since then by states for early intervention services.

A major milestone for early intervention occurred in 1965 when Project Head Start was first funded, with the goal of helping preschool children from low-income families to overcome the effects of poverty on their development and on their school achievement. From the beginning, an important characteristic of Head Start was its comprehensive and multidisciplinary focus; it provided education, health, nutrition, and parent support services. At first only 4-year-olds were eligible for Head Start, but in 1972 the first Parent-Child Centers for infants and parents were established.

Another landmark was the establishment by Congress in 1968 of the Handicapped Children's Early Education Program (HCEEP). Through this program federal funding has been provided during the past two decades for efficacy research in early intervention, development of model programs, dissemination of assessment tools and curricula, and technical assistance (Smith, 1989). The result has been a vastly increased knowledge base as well as over 500 model demonstration projects, many developed for infants. The knowledge base proved particularly important in providing a rationale for the passage of PL 99-457 in 1986.

Although only a few states presently mandate early intervention from birth, the historical perspective would indicate that it is only a matter of time before we achieve universal access to services from birth for all children and their families. An interesting aspect of the evolution of policy in the field is the uniting of parents and professionals in a common purpose. While we have taken for granted public education of nonhandicapped children from age 5 in this country, the same has not been the case for young children with handicaps. The efficacy of primary school, for example, has not been subjected to the same scrutiny as programs for infants and toddlers, nor have parents of school-age children been forced to fight for publicly funded services. As we enter the last decade of the century, it is encouraging to see the progress that has been made and the present high level of interest and activity related to the well-being of infants.

Three trends currently appear to dominate the field. First, recent federal legislation requires states to provide a variety of early intervention services to infants, toddlers, and their families that were heretofore required only after age 5. Second, advances in medical technology during the past decade have made possible more effective but at the same time more intrusive procedures to save infant lives and remediate serious medical problems. The result of the new technology is an increased number of infants receiving early intervention who present serious medical management problems not typically dealt with in the past, primarily because these babies did not survive. Third, due to these some- times conflicting advances and mandates, serious ethical issues emerge for parents, professionals, and others to consider. Let us examine in more detail each of these trends.

Legislation Affecting Service Delivery to Infants

The most comprehensive legislation governing services to at-risk and handi- capped infants is PL 99-457, which Congress passed in 1986 in the form of an amendment to PL 94-142, the Education for All Handicapped Children Act. This relatively new law extended the mandate of PL 94-142 down to age 3, and gave states the option to provide services to their birth-through-2 populations as well. Under the law each state that decided to participate was required to establish a comprehensive system for the identification, assessment, and treat- ment of infants with handicaps and their families. The system was to be developed by an interagency coordinating council in each state whose members were appointed by the governor and who were representative of both clients and service providers. At the time of writing, 13 states already were mandating services for the birth-through-2 age group, and all states had agreed to par- ticipate in implementing the new law (Smith, 1989).

Under the law services are provided to infants and toddlers who have one of the following:

1. Developmental delays in one or more of the following areas: cognitive, physical, language, psychosocial or self help
2. A physical or mental condition that has a high probability of resulting in delay (e.g., Down syndrome)
3. Risk medically or environmentally for substantial developmental delay if early intervention is not provided (Smith, 1989).

In order to implement the infant/toddler portion of PL 99-457 (Part H), the comprehensive system developed by each state must include, among others, the following components:

1. A definition of the term, developmentally delayed.
2. Multidisciplinary evaluations of the functioning of all eligible children and the needs of their families to assist in their child's development.
3. An individualized family service plan for all eligible children and their families.

4. A comprehensive Child Find system which includes primary referral sources such as hospitals and day-care providers.

5. A central directory of resources available in the state for early intervention services.

6. A comprehensive system of personnel development, including preservice and in-service training for providers, and establishment of standards for their certification or licensing.

7. Procedural safeguards for the parents' right of due process (e.g., rights of appeal and confidentiality, right to examine records, communication in parents' native language).

Two unique aspects of the new law require special comment. First, an Individualized Family Service Plan (IFSP) is required for each infant found to be eligible for services. Similar to the Individualized Educational Plan mandated by PL 94-142 and PL 99-457 for children ages 3 through 18, the IFSP contains a statement of present functioning levels, a statement of goals and objectives, and detailed plans for achieving those goals, including resources to be provided and a timeline for completion. The difference is that for infants and toddlers the focus is on the family rather than the individual child, resulting in a more comprehensive and multidisciplinary plan.

Second, a case manager must be assigned to each family for whom an IFSP is developed to oversee the implementation of the plan. The case manager may belong to any of several disciplines involved in the family's intervention program but must be a professional with whom the family is familiar and comfortable. The case manager's primary responsibility is to take an advocate's role

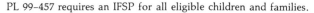

PL 99-457 requires an IFSP for all eligible children and families.

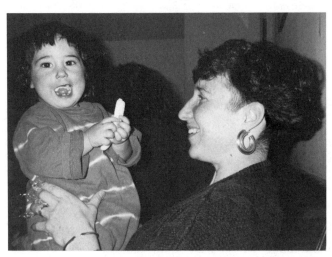

for the family in interactions with service delivery agencies. Both of these aspects of the law are discussed in greater detail in Chapter 8.

Technological Advances in Newborn Care

An incentive to develop new programs for infants comes from the advances in the care of newborns born at risk or with handicaps. Many more infants survive traumatic birth conditions than previously, and many spend considerable time in intensive care and followup hospital programs as a result. The need for long-term, community-based programs to continue the care of these infants has increased proportionally.

Many of the infants born at risk are preterm or small for gestational age (SGA). Causes vary from genetic or biologic disorders to lack of prenatal care and other environmental factors. Prenatal care is particularly lacking in teenage and low-income pregnancies. Although the new technology can be effective in saving very small and very young infants, it cannot effect preventive measures such as better prenatal care for mothers from low-income families. For that, a change in national policy is needed, together with a realization of how expensive intensive care is compared to good prenatal care.

During the past 25 years neonatologists have developed many new and effective means for all newborns, including full-term, preterm, and SGA infants. The result has been a substantial increase in the number of at-risk infants who survive the neonatal period and who reach childhood without serious developmental disabilities. According to several studies, the number of infants with birthweights less than 1500 g who survived the newborn period approximately doubled in the United States between 1960 and 1980 (Bennett, 1987). Seventy-five percent of those who survived in 1980 were normal, whereas in 1960 75% of the survivors had developmental disabilities. The statistics for infants with birthweights under 1000 g are even more striking: about 50% survived in 1983 as compared with 10% in 1960. Of the survivors, 25 percent had developmental disabilities compared to 75% in 1960 (Bennett, 1987). In a study of outcomes of very low birthweight (VLBW) infants (500–999 g), 30% survived in 1980; of those, over half had no developmental disabilities (Kitchen et al., 1984).

Nevertheless, numerous long-term followup studies are indicating that while major handicapping conditions are being prevented in these at-risk infants through improved care in neonatal intensive care units (NICUs), the prevalence of minor neurodevelopmental and neurobehavioral delays is increasing. These delays are manifested at school age in a variety of academic and behavioral problems. According to Bennett (1987), they include mild mental retardation, mild communication and attention disorders, minor neuromotor problems, and emotional immaturity. As with major handicapping conditions, these minor conditions increase as birthweight and gestational age decrease.

They are also more prevalent in male survivors. Thus, VLBW infants currently have a 20% rate of major handicapping conditions, and a 15% to 25% rate of minor problems. This means that between 35% and 45% of these babies may be expected to have developmental delays of some kind that affect their age-expected function (Saigal, Rosenbaum, Stoskopf & Milner, 1982).

The above statistics, the most recent currently available, were collected in the mid-1980s. It must be assumed that current statistics would reflect recent improvements in care. These improvements include an increase in the number of NICUs (Level III) and special care nurseries, better access for pregnant women to good prenatal care, and more effective neonatal care in regular (Levels I and II) nurseries.

For premature and low birthweight infants, different complications lead to different prognosis. Complications associated with good developmental outcomes include respiratory distress syndrome, hyperbilirubinemia, hypoglycemia, and hypocalcemia. Those associated with a poorer prognosis include intraventricular hemorrhage, bronchopulmonary dysplasia, sepsis, and periodic apnea. The prognosis is less good in all cases for SGA infants who are both low birthweight and preterm, or infants from low socioeconomic backgrounds (Guralnick & Bennett, 1987b; Parmelee, 1989). In Chapter 5 we examine more extensively topics related to preterm and low birthweight infants.

Ethical Issues in Newborn Care

As new federal legislation and new technology coincide to promote neonatal developmental intervention, two major debates have influenced the rationale and direction of that intervention (Bennett, 1987). The first debate involves the way in which a preterm neonate should be perceived. Is the newborn essentially an extrauterine fetus in need of interventions that simulate the womb? For example, should the NICU seek to recreate the warm, quiet, peaceful atmosphere of the intrauterine environment? Or does the premature infant differ significantly from the fetus of similar gestational age because that infant has undergone the birth process, which automatically triggers independent functioning of major organ systems? If so, should NICU interventions simulate the extrauterine environment experienced by full-term infants? At the same time, is there a danger in treating preterm infants as though they were deficient and full term? (Als, Lester, Tronick & Brazelton, 1982) These difficult questions pose ethical issues for early interventionists who wish to facilitate the optimal development of all newborns.

The second debate concerns the nature of the NICU as an extrauterine environment. Does this unusual medical setting constitute a source of sensory deprivation, requiring supplementary stimulation for the neonate; constant overstimulation, requiring less handling and more time for uninterrupted sleep; or an inappropriate pattern of interactions rather than simply too much or too little stimulation? (Bennett, 1987) Recent evidence seems to support the third supposition, that infants receive much stimulation in the NICU, but it may be of the wrong kind, administered by the wrong person (Gottfried & Gaiter, 1984; Heriza & Sweeney, 1990). Infants in NICUs are often deprived of social interactions, particularly interactions with their mothers that are necessary to later development (Gottwald & Thurman, 1990).

This fact raises an important ethical issue concerning the role of the family in the treatment of at-risk newborns. During the 1980s there has been a shift away from exclusively infant-focused intervention toward more family-centered interventions that facilitate parent–premature infant interactions and communications (Bennett, 1987).

In a discussion of at-risk newborn and infant care, the issue of controversial and unsubstantiated therapies is pertinent. According to Guralnick and Bennett (1987b),

> an ever-increasing array of controversial therapies, dietary hypotheses, and biomedical approaches continue to be advocated and advertised for at-risk or handicapped infants and young children. These unproved, and frequently unusual, interventions often attract widespread media interest and acclaim despite their total lack of investigative support or even research effort. (p. 376)

Parents of at-risk infants must attempt to distinguish sound, effective interventions from questionable, possibly detrimental ones. Guralnick and Bennett (1987b) state that primary health care providers and infant specialists can play an important role as scientific consumer-critic for these families.

Controversial, unproven therapies include Doman and Delacato's patterning (Harris, S.R., 1987), Ayres' sensory integration (Ayres, 1986), and developmental optometry consisting of visual tracking exercises. Each of these approaches aims at the reorganization and retraining of the central nervous system by means of simple, repetitive body movements that have not been proven effective.

Parents who have a handicapped infant often do not know where to turn for help. In their search for a cure for their child's problem, they are potential victims of these sorts of unproven programs.

A related issue concerns the opposite problem, that parents may be pressured into accepting interventions that they neither want nor for which they see the need. Many current interventions available for at-risk and handicapped newborns and infants are intrusive. Parents may be expected to give over their lives and those of their other children to the care and well-being of the infant at risk. Additionally, the procedures prescribed for the infant may be painful, require long-term hospitalization or difficult surgery, and have doubtful outcomes. Although these interventions represent the best that modern technology presently offers, they are not automatically the best for every child and every family, as many early interventionists realize. To assert that they are is to deny the parents any role in making the decisions about their child that most closely affect that child and their own family. The ethical issue here is a very difficult one, with legal implications for health care providers who would deny intervention. The recent Baby Doe case illustrates this dilemma very well.

The Baby Doe case began in April, 1982, when a baby boy was born with Down syndrome and accompanying respiratory and digestive complications which required major surgery. The family directed that food and treatment be withheld, and they were supported by their family doctor and Indiana's highest court (Shearer, 1985). Within six days the baby died. When pressure groups complained, then-President Reagan instructed the Departments of Justice and Health and Human Services (HHS) to apply civil rights regulations, previously applied to persons with handicaps, to newborns and infants. As a consequence, approximately 7,000 hospitals receiving federal funds were reminded that Section 504 of the 1973 Rehabilitation Act considered it an offense to "withhold from a handicapped infant nutritional sustenance or medical or surgical treatment required to correct a life-threatening condition if (1) the withholding is based on the fact that the infant is handicapped and (2) the handicap does not render treatment or nutritional sustenance medically contraindicated" (Shearer, 1985, p. 194).

HHS went even further with this issue. In March 1983 they required that hospitals receiving federal funds post a notice in delivery wards, maternity units, pediatric wards, nurseries, and infant intensive care units restating the law and providing the number of a 24-hour hotline where HHS could be notified of anyone suspected of violating the law. Subsequently, the regulation was ruled invalid on procedural grounds, and finally in 1984 a new version of the regulations was established. In this version the government saw itself as the protector of last resort, with the primary responsibility being placed with hospital review committees. What these experiences highlight is "a shift in opinion towards the notion that life and death decisions should be made within a more clearly stated ethical framework and that they cannot be properly left to either doctors alone or to doctors and parents together" (Shearer, 1985, p. 196).

Whenever a seriously ill infant is born, serious decisions must be made. Historically the decisions revolved around those newborns with very poor chances for survival. Today increased technology and available sophisticated treatments have increased our abilities to establish a diagnosis and prognosis for at-risk newborns, thereby making decisions complex and subject to judgment (Raye & Healy, 1984). The traditional model of decision-making with the physician as the benevolent paternal figure has been replaced by an alternative view emphasizing collegial sharing of power (Barber, 1976) and a demand for increased parent responsibility (Hatch, 1984; Raye & Healy, 1984).

The current prevailing opinion appears to be that decision-making must center on the best interests of the infant, with the parents acting as the critical decision-makers. Expanding on this general idea, Raye and Healy (1984) outline three specific circumstances when hospital committee involvement may be helpful in the decision-making process:

1. The parents choose a course of action that the attending physician judges to be clearly against the child's best interests.
2. The parents disagree to consent to potentially efficacious treatment.
3. The parents are incapacitated and unable to make a decision regarding medical treatment.

Ethical issues concerning newborns and infants are significant and complex. Ethics refers to morals and relates to right and wrong behavior (Turnbull & Turnbull, 1986). Therefore, any action concerning an at-risk or handicapped baby involves ethics. Many professional organizations provide professional codes of conduct for their members to follow, such as the Code of Ethics and Standards for Professional Practice adopted by the Council for Exceptional Children and the Ethical Principles of Psychologists held by the American Psychological Association (1981). Other organizations such as the American Psychiatric Association, American Speech-Language-Hearing Association, the Association for Persons with Severe Handicaps, National Association for School Psychologists, and the National Association of Social Workers have similar ethical codes of behavior.

As parents and professionals strive to make decisions in the best interest of newborns and infants, many factors must be considered. The wide range of medical, legal, ethical, and political factors involved point to the need for a general societal policy regarding seriously ill infants (Raye & Healy, 1984). Additionally, issues related to quality of life, including education, residence, relationships, access to services, and technology, must be addressed (Powell & Hecimovic, 1985). As stated by the President's Commission for the Study of Ethical Problems in Medicine (1983), ethical decisions must center on the best interests of the child. Potential negative effects on parents, siblings, or society have no place in the decision-making process.

THE INFANT/TODDLER TEAM

A corollary to the multidisciplinary interest in infant development described at the beginning of the chapter is the emphasis placed on multidisciplinary delivery of services. As mandated by PL 99-457, services to at-risk and handicapped infants, toddlers, and their families must be provided by professionals from several disciplines who need to work cooperatively for the benefit of the child and family.

The number of professional disciplines represented in an early intervention program varies according to the needs of the children, the approach taken, and the financial constraints under which the program operates (Mowder, Widerstrom & Sandall, 1989). Nevertheless, certain disciplines are designated

The speech/language pathologist, a member of the infant/toddler
team, works on feeding skills.

in PL 99-457 to provide such services; included are special educators, speech
and language pathologists and audiologists, occupational therapists, physical
therapists, psychologists, social workers, nurses, and nutritionists. A brief
description of each specialist's role is presented in Table 1.1.

In all stages of planning, implementation, and evaluation of the intervention program, the parent is considered to be an integral part of the team. In
fact, the intent of PL 99-457 is to bring a family focus to early intervention,
replacing exclusive emphasis on the child with disabilities with a more global
view that includes the child as a member of the family system. For this reason
the law requires that the IFSP be developed by the multidisciplinary team
together with the parent or guardian, and that it contain goals and objectives
for the entire family based on multidisciplinary assessment.

Thus, the roles of team members in programs for infants and toddlers differ
somewhat from those in programs for older children, which often lack the family
focus. In infant programs there is typically more contact with parents on a daily
basis. Team members must be able to give support to parents on an informal
and as-needed basis; often they are the professionals parents come to know best
and trust most. Additionally, members of the infant/toddler team must perform family assessments in order to develop appropriate IFSP goals for the
parents, siblings, and perhaps extended family members. They must conduct
these assessments in a manner that is both supportive and nonintrusive to the
handicapped child's family. Finally, from the infant/toddler team comes the
family's case manager, a professional who acts as an advocate for the family
and a link to community resources. These aspects of the multidisciplinary team
are discussed in greater detail in Chapters 7 and 8.

TABLE 1.1 Roles and Functions of Service Providers Under PL 99-457

ROLE	FUNCTIONS
Infant special educator	Generally takes responsibility for the child's overall educational growth and development. Planning and educational programming, monitoring infant development, educational assessment, child and family advocacy, and referral to ancillary services (Ensher & Clark, 1986).
Speech/language pathologist and audiologist	Has primary responsibility for the child's development of communicative abilities. In working with infants, this specialist is concerned with oral-motor facilitation, feeding therapy, and development of preverbal communication (Hanson & Harris, 1986; Mueller, 1972).
Occupational therapist	Takes primary responsibility for the child's sensory development and integration. The motor focus overlaps with communicative development, thus necessitating the close working relationship with the speech/language pathologist and audiologist (Mather & Weinstein, 1988), yet the emphasis on sensory information processing distinguishes the functions of this professional (Jenkins, Fewell, & Harris, 1983).
Physical therapist	Focuses on the neurologic functioning underlying gross motor development (Harris, 1981). With the occupational therapist, the physical therapist takes primary responsibility for the child's positioning, handling, and movement; the emphasis is on the facilitation of normal movement and the suppression of abnormal movement (Bobath & Bobath, 1972).
Psychologist	Responsible for the child's behavior, cognitive, and social-emotional development. As such, the psychologist has a strong interest in the family's psychological climate. Primary responsibilities include psychological assessment, child and family counseling, and consultation with other team members concerning the child's behavior and development.
Social worker	Provides a close link between home and program, which is critical to successful intervention. Knowledge of the family's dynamics, information about siblings and grandparents of the handicapped young child, and an understanding of family stresses.
Nurse	Takes responsibility for the medical well-being of the child and family. This may involve both general preventive measures, such as regular physical examinations and routine innoculations, as well as more specific treatment of medical disorders, such as supervising prescriptive medication for a seizure disorder (Peterson, 1987).
Nutritionist	Works with the parents or other caregivers to ensure optimal nutrition for the handicapped infant or toddler. Provides guidance in food purchase, preservation, and preparation to help ensure proper diet and treat dietary problems (Thurman & Widerstrom, 1990)

From B. A. Mowder, A. H. Widerstrom, & S. R. Sandall, 1989. School psychologists serving at-risk and handicapped infants, toddlers and their families. *Professional School Psychology,* 4(3), p. 161.

Suggestions for Further Reading

The following journals publish articles related to infant behavior and development, infant assessment, and early intervention and programming.

Typical and atypical child development

Child Development
Infant Behavior and Development

Psychology

Journal of Abnormal and Social Psychology
Journal of Counseling and Consulting Psychology
Journal of Pediatric Psychology
Professional School Psychology
Psychology in the Schools

Health

Developmental Medicine and Child Neurology
Journal of Behavioral Medicine
Journal of Behavioral and Developmental Pediatrics
Journal of Pediatrics
Pediatrics

Special education

American Journal of Mental Retardation
Journal of Early Intervention
Journal of the Association for Severely Handicapped
Journal of Special Education
Topics in Early Childhood Special Education

Interdisciplinary

Child: Health, Care and Development
Infants and Young Children

Not included in this list are the many journals concerned with a special field such as speech, occupational or physical therapy, or nursing.

Chapter 2

Typical Infant
Development

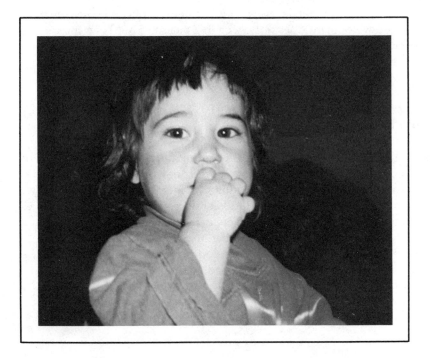

The field of infant development has a long and distinguished history, and much of what is known about how and why infants grow and develop is due to systematic observation, theoretical developments in psychology, and the utilization of experimental techniques. Scientific interest in infant development can be traced to the 1800s when, in 1877, Charles Darwin made a scientific, systematic observation of a child's behavior (Kessen, 1965). This event is usually pointed to by child developmentalists as the beginning of the study of child growth and development (e.g., Bornstein & Lamb, 1988).

Chronologically, other milestones in the evolution of infant and child development include the early theoretical formulations of G. Stanley Hall (e.g., 1891, 1904), particularly his contributions on adolescent growth and development, and the extensive psychoanalytic writing of Sigmund Freud (e.g., 1917, 1923/1962, 1940) at the turn of the century and later. Arnold Gesell (e.g., 1925, 1940, 1945) and his theory of the importance of maturation, and John Watson's (e.g., 1924, 1928) theory of behaviorism in the late 1920s and 1930s also helped shape the field. Also, the enormous contributions of Jean Piaget on cognitive development (e.g., 1929, 1951, 1952, 1954) and the work of Albert Bandura on social learning theory (e.g., 1969, 1977) are an integral part of current thinking and research about young children.

The concept of development is key to this chapter; *development* means the pattern of change that starts with conception, continues throughout life, and ends with death. Development is a complex concept that involves an interaction of biological and physical development, cognitive development and learning, and social emotional development. Further complicating the construct is the fact that development does not occur in a vacuum, but is an interactive process, occurring within a physical environment and a social context, with other individuals who are developing at the same time.

RESEARCH METHODOLOGY IN INFANT DEVELOPMENT

Beyond the theoretical formulations regarding infant and child development are the methods which have evolved for studying developmental phenomena. It is critical to understand research methodology, since much of what we know, understand, and accept in the infant and toddler developmental literature derives from experimental research. Research and experimental techniques have allowed developmentalists to move beyond observation to sophisticated methods for examining infants and their growth and development, to make assertions about developmental progress, and to develop and test theories (Miller, 1987).

As a field, infant development considers growth in terms of norms and expected ranges of development as well as individual differences. When physical growth and development is studied, for example, many infants are examined to establish the average rate of growth; then, within the determined range, individual differences among infants are considered. The range also establishes the parameters by which differences between groups of infants—for instance, those born to mothers who smoked during pregnancy and those born to mothers who did not—are examined. The concept of norms is an important one in the examination of infant development.

Research Designs

Research designs for studying infants for the most part have focused on group data and ranges of normal development. There are many research designs (e.g., Maccoby & Martin, 1983; Martin, 1981; Seitz, 1988), and infant developmental research tends to utilize one of five primary designs:

1. Longitudinal research
2. Cross-sectional research
3. Short-term longitudinal research
4. Cross-sectional/short-term longitudinal research
5. Single subject research

No one research design is the ideal methodological model; each has advantages and disadvantages, strengths and weaknesses. One design is chosen dependent on the developmental issue studied and various considerations such as the importance of discerning individual differences or focusing on group trends, and practical concerns such as availability of groups of children over time, researcher time commitment, availability, and cost issues.

Longitudinal research requires that a population be identified, each subject within the population be studied, and the study occurs over at least a 5-year span of time. This type of research provides rich data by identifying individual differences within populations and noting how they develop over time. A disadvantage of this research design is that it requires a relatively stable population, since attrition (loss of subjects over time) can seriously affect assertions that may be made about the data collected (Simons, Ritchie, Mullett, & Mingarelle, 1989). Classic developmental longitudinal studies include the Terman Gifted Child Study started in 1921, the Berkeley Growth Study in 1928, and, in 1929, the Berkeley Guidance Study, the Fels Research Institute Project, and the Harvard Longitudinal Study (Mednick & Mednick, 1984).

Cross-sectional research requires that several different groups of infants are studied, which are identified at specific developmental ages or stages, or chosen for other specific characteristics. For instance, Hubert (1989) studied parents of 6- and 24-month-old children to discern parental reactions to temperament behavior. She found high correlations between parent ratings of their own pleasure and infant temperament ratings, ratings which were not affected by other classification variables (i.e., age, birth order, and gender). By utilizing cross-sectional research, developmentalists collect data within a relatively short period of time, which allows them to make statements about developmental issues without waiting for a certain group of babies to mature. Because the analysis focuses on group change, however, individual developmental differences are lost.

A research design developed to capture individual differences in development without investing an enormous amount of time is the *short-term longitudinal research* method. In this method, one group of infants is identified and studied over a brief period of time, typically 1 to 5 years. Fox (1989), for example, examined emotional psychophysiological correlates by following a group of infants over their first year of life. By using this model, he found that there are individual differences in infant emotional reactivity to novel and mildly stressful events. The advantage of the research design is that individual differences may be studied over time without the subject attrition that can occur in longitudinal research. The distinct disadvantage is that some developmental issues may not be amenable to a short time span of study.

A combination approach, incorporating cross-sectional research with short-term longitudinal methods, attempts to capture many of the advantages of both. In the *cross-sectional/short-term longitudinal research* design, groups of individuals at different ages or developmental stages are identified and studied over 1 to 5 years. In this way, some assertions regarding individual differences may be made, as well as limited statements regarding developmental issues. Kline, Tschann, Johnston, and Wallerstein (1989), for example, considered children's adjustment in joint and sole custody families by considering children ages 3 to 14. They studied the group for one year after the parents filed for divorce, and then again one and two years later and found no difference in child postdivorce adjustment with sole and joint custody. Several problems occur with this approach, however. The different groups must have some measure of similarity in order to make assertions regarding long-term developmental issues, statements regarding individual differences are limited, and the logistics of studying several different groups of children simultaneously over a specified period of time is difficult.

A design relatively recently adopted for use with infants is the *single subject research* design in which one baby or a very small number of infants are studied extensively over a specified period of time. This type of design has been particularly amenable to behavioral examinations of children in which a specific behavior is identified, an intervention or treatment program developed and implemented, and an evaluation reported. Lamm and Greer (1988), for instance, used behavioral methods to induce and maintain swallowing with three infants who did not swallow food or liquid. Problems with this approach exist, in that only two or three infants are usually studied. This makes it difficult to make generalized assertions regarding infant and child growth and development.

Research Techniques

Within the various research designs, specific techniques have developed for the study of infants. The need for specific techniques, different from those used in studying older children, adolescents, and adults, is clear. Infants do not have the cognitive, language, motor, physical, or social-emotional maturity evidenced at other developmental levels and stages. Therefore, techniques which accommodate to their specific developmental functioning are necessary (Miller, 1987) (Table 2.1).

Early research techniques included the use of infant diaries, case studies, or journals. Darwin (Kessen, 1965), as well as others, wrote journals regarding specific infant development. This technique is still in use and provides a rich source of data on day to day individual infant and toddler developmental progress. However, it does not necessarily yield information that may be generalized to other children. Another technique which has been used successfully over time is systematic observation. Indeed, this tool was the primary technique employed by both Freud and Piaget in developing their landmark theories. Although their theories focus on different developmental issues, both theoreticians systematically observed children, made careful, documented statements regarding development, and advanced comprehensive theories on how infants and children grow and develop.

More recently, techniques such as habituation-dishabituation, visual preference, strange situation, questionnaire research, and standardized testing have been developed. *Habituation-dishabituation* refers to research that ex-

TABLE 2.1 Infant Study Research Techniques

	Research Technique	Description
1.	Diaries, case studies, and journals	One of the earliest forms of infant research in which individual infant development is recorded on an on-going basis
2.	Systematic observation	Systematic, careful, well documented observations of infants
3.	Habituation-dishabituation	The cessation of an infant's response to repeated stimuli, response recovery to the same stimuli
4.	Visual preference	The systematic study of what and how long an infant views stimulus material
5.	Visual search	Techniques developed to monitor infants' eye movements and complex visual behaviors
6.	Strange situation	A systematic set of situations designed to assess the infant's attachment to the parent
7.	Questionnaires and survey techniques	Paper and pencil assessment materials designed to study an array of infant development issues
8.	Standardized assessments	These materials are developed to have strong psychometric properties for studying infants in a standardized manner

amines how infants respond to and ignore various repeated stimuli such as objects or sounds (e.g., Bornstein & Benasich, 1986; Bornstein, Pecheux, & Lecuyer, 1988). Tamis-LeMonda and Bornstein (1989) considered infant attention as a predictor of toddler language, play, and representational competence. They drew infants' attention to a stimulus panel and, once the babies were oriented, a visual stimulus was projected. After the infant habituated and stopped looking at the stimulus, a new visual stimulus was presented. Continuous measurements were recorded of the infants' looking behavior. Using this technique, the results showed that infants who habituate to visual stimuli in a mature manner have more flexible language comprehension, more pretend play, and exhibit more advanced representational abilities as toddlers than infants who habituate in a less mature manner.

Visual preference and visual search are other techniques developed to study infant development. Fantz (1958) originated these techniques by developing a situation in which a trained observer systematically studies what an infant is viewing and the amount of time the infant spends observing a specific stimulus. Other researchers have developed more sophisticated techniques to monitor infants' eye movements, scanning patterns, and complex visual behaviors (Snow, 1989). For example, Di Catherwood and Freiberg (1989) examined infants' response to similar color and dissimilar shape stimuli. They placed infants in car seats on a low platform and screened all sides so that only a display screen was visible to the babies. One researcher monitored and timed infant visual attention to the display from behind the screen and over the top of the monitor, while a second controlled trial onset and offset. In addition, a video camera recorded infant responses. By examining babies' patterns of visual attention this study suggests that infants as young as 4 months respond on the basis of color to stimuli of uniform shape and also that they are capable of responding the same way with stimuli of dissimilar shape.

The Strange Situation technique is a tool developed specifically to study the issue of attachment; because it has been used almost to the exclusion of any other research technique in the issue of infant attachment, it has become a technique in its own right. In this technique, an infant is placed in a room with its mother and measures are taken with the mother, without the mother, and with and without a stranger being present (Lamb, Thompson, Gardner, and Charnov, 1985). Vaughn, Lefever, Seifer, and Barglow (1989) used this technique to study the relationship of attachment behavior, attachment security, and temperament during infancy. They assessed infants between 12 and 14 months of age and found that neither behavioral style nor temperament (e.g., "easy" vs. "difficult") are significantly associated with attachment classifications.

Questionnaire and survey techniques have also been developed to study infant growth and development. These techniques typically rely on the administration of written questionnaire and survey materials to the infant's primary caregiver. Widerstrom and Goodwin (1987) used this technique to discover the effects of an infant stimulation program on children and their families; they found families are receptive to such programs.

More recently, standardized assessment instruments have been used to study infant growth and development. Instruments and measures, such as the Bayley Scales of Infant Development afford researchers a standardized method for studying infant development. Redding, Morgan, and Harmon (1988) examined mastery motivation in infants and toddlers using, among their measures, the Bayley Scales of Mental Development and the McCarthy Scales of Children's Abilities. They discovered that both infant and toddlers show greater persistence at moderately challenging tasks compared to difficult tasks, and that the relationship between cognitive measures and persistence declines with age.

The study of prenatal development has employed different and diverse techniques, from the early use of direct observation of surgically exteriorized animal fetuses or aborted human fetuses, to the more recent indirect manipulation of the fetus and the use of inference from subsequent developmental consequences (Smotherman & Robinson, 1987). The latter methodology is common in teratological research, but Smotherman and Robinson (1987) caution that reliance on the postnatal approach influences the conduct of research, shapes the questions being asked, and brings possible bias to the field of infant study. More sophisticated methodologies have been developed recently, such as external fetal monitoring (Patrick, Campbell, Carmichael, & Probert, 1982) and real-time ultrasonography (Birnholz & Benacerraf, 1983)

ISSUES IN INFANT DEVELOPMENT

Historically the issue most frequently debated in the developmental literature is that of nature versus nurture (Miller, P.H., 1989). That is, what is the relative role of biological processes as opposed to environmental influences on development. Because infants are both biological as well as social beings, the issue is what is the relative influence of each, and does one predominate over the other. Extreme positions have been taken on this issue over time. Arnold Gesell (1925, 1940, 1945) held the view that maturational factors supersede all other considerations, while B.F. Skinner (1957, 1966, 1976) took the opposite position.

Another issue which has emerged in infant development is whether development is a collection of changes which occur over time or if development is qualitatively different at different points in development. This issue of quantitative versus qualitative changes (Miller, P.H., 1989) is more clearly seen when one views a variety of theoretical positions on infant development. Piaget (1929, 1951, 1952, 1954), for example, posits that development is qualitatively different at different stages. The infant is developmentally and qualitatively different from the preschooler, and the preschooler is qualitatively different from the elementary school–age child. For Skinner (1972, 1976), on the other hand, behavioral development occurs as a collection of learnings. That is, learning for the infant is essentially no different from learning for an adolescent or an adult.

A further issue with developing infants is whether they are active or passive in the developmental process (Sroufe, Cooper, & Marshall, 1988). In other words, do infants' actions and activities have an impact on their development, or are infants passive recipients of events or factors over which they have no control? Watson (1930) would maintain that an infant is passive in the developmental process, whereas Piaget (1952, 1954) maintains that the infant must be active in order to progress through the developmental stages.

The role of past experience in development has also been a major concern for infant developmentalists. What, for example, is the effect of an extremely deprived first three months of life? Does serious neglect early in an infant's life result in life-long developmental problems; can these developmental issues be overcome with time? Freud (1940) maintained that the effects of early experience are fundamental and affect all aspects of later development. Learning theorists, such as Bandura (1977), however, take a different point of view by demonstrating significant changes in behavior that can occur based on presentations of different models with various reinforcement histories.

Finally, the goal of development is a major issue for developmentalists. What are the expectations for developing infants? Is it anticipated, for example, that they successfully complete the stage of sensorimotor development and demonstrate object permanence (Piaget, 1970) or is there no particular expectation in terms of development; is each individual infant becoming a toddler, preschooler, child, adolescent, and then adult without any particular landmark in the developmental sequence?

GENETICS AND BIOLOGICAL DEVELOPMENT

Genetic Makeup

The study of infant development begins with a consideration of genetics and biological development. Essentially, an infant is a biological being whose development begins with conception, when a male gamete (sperm) unites with a female gamete (egg cell or ovum). After the ovum is fertilized, biochemical changes prevent other sperm from penetrating (Sutton, 1975). The single-celled zygote which is formed at conception contains the infant's entire complement of genes and chromosomes needed for development (Rosenblith & Sims-Knight, 1985).

Chromosomes are structures within human cells composed of DNA (deoxyribonucleic acid). Genes, in turn, are small bits of DNA (Nora & Fraser, 1989). Each of the 23 pairs of chromosomes found in every human body cell contains thousands of genes. Together, chromosomes and genes form the blueprint for development, specifying the structure of every individual human cell. (For a more complete discussion of the way genes and chromosomes affect development, see Chapter 3.) The actual combination of genetic material is referred to as the *genotype*; genotypes are never directly observed because they are the genetic material which resides within the human cell. *Phenotypes*, on the other hand, differ from genotypes because they are observed, measurable characteristics. Phenotypes include characteristics such as height, skin pigmentation, and weight. It is important to understand that not all developmental factors derive directly from specific individual genetic activity. *Polygenic inheritance* refers to the interaction of many different genes which, in turn, affect development.

Biological Development

Prenatal Growth and Development. From research, we know that after conception, the zygote undergoes extremely rapid growth and thus begins the germinal stage of prenatal development. The germinal stage lasts approximately 2 weeks, and during this time the zygote moves through the Fallopian tube to the uterus where it attaches itself to the uterine wall. By the end of this period, implantation has occurred and the cells have already begun to differentiate. The inner layer of cells, the *blastocyst*, will develop into the embryo, and the outer layer of cells, the *trophoblast*, will provide nutrition, protection, and support for the developing embryo.

The embryonic period begins approximately 2 weeks after conception and extends through the end of the eighth week. As this period starts, the embryo is firmly attached to the uterine lining and consists of two layers of cells, the endoderm and the ectoderm. The inner layer, the *endoderm*, will develop into the digestive tract, glandular system, liver, and respiratory system. The outer layer, the *ectoderm*, becomes the skin, hair, nails, sensory organs, and nervous system. Finally, approximately three weeks after conception, a third layer of cells develops between the endoderm and the ectoderm, called the *mesoderm*. The mesoderm will form the skeletal, muscular, circulatory, reproductive, and urinary systems.

During the embryonic period the supporting membranes, including the amnion, placenta, and umbilical cord, are also developing. The *amnion* is a protective wrapping of clear salty liquid in which the embryo floats. The *placenta* is a vital link between the embryo and the mother by providing passage of antibodies, nutrients, waste products, oxygen, and hormones. The mother's and embryo's bloodstreams do not actually mix because they are separated by thin membrane walls; however, oxygen, nutrients, and waste are easily exchanged through the placenta. From the placenta, a bluish red umbilical cord develops in which very small molecules, such as oxygen and food from the mother's blood, may pass between the infant and the mother.

Within a short period of time, by 4 weeks, the embryo and supporting membranes are approximately the size of a pea (Snow, 1989). A primitive heart is pumping blood, a rudimentary system for digesting and assimilating food is being formed, and parts of the brain are already in evidence. Limb buds are visible, eyes begin to appear, the spine has started to form, and the first of the kidneylike structures is present. The first bone cells appear at about 6 1/2 weeks (Musick & Householder, 1986); the skeleton is one of the first recognizable tissues to develop during the embryonic period (Ross, Mimouni, & Tsang, 1988). A technique known as ultrasound may be utilized by an obstetrician during this period of time to determine the developmental age, evaluate growth, detect twins, and find anatomical abnormalities (Nora & Fraser, 1989). Ultrasound imaging utilizes sound waves, which are passed through the amniotic fluid to the fetus. The waves produce images received as two-dimensional pictures on a screening monitor.

The first fetal movements can be observed at 7 1/2 weeks gestation (Ianniruberto & Tajani, 1981; DeVries, deVisser, & Prechtl, 1982), and the first sign of true responding appears about this time in the form of a head movement from the site of stimulation, from gentle brushing in the nose and lip regions (Bremner, 1988; Hooker, 1952). By 8 weeks, tremendous growth and differentiation has occurred. The head represents almost half of the body's length, facial features begin to form, and limbs become more evident. The brain has developed in size and complexity (Kolb & Fantie, 1989), all major body systems are present in some form of development, and the embryo is clearly recognizable as a developing human organism. By 8 to 9 weeks, quick startles and slow general movements are observed, followed quickly by hiccups and isolated arm and leg movements (Prechtl, 1987). Motion pictures show mouth opening and closing beginning at 8 1/2 weeks; swallowing, and lip and tongue movements between 10 1/2 and 12 1/2 weeks; squintlike and sneerlike expressions at 14 weeks; and strong gagging by 18 1/2 weeks (Chamberlain, 1988). By the end of the embryonic period, the embryo is approximately one inch in length and weighs about 1/30 of an ounce. Because growth is so rapid during the embryonic period, it is a time of extreme vulnerability. A new technique referred to as chorionic villus sampling allows cells to be suctioned from the placenta by a small tube passed through the vagina and cervix. This safe procedure, by which the fetus's genetic make-up is examined, can be performed within 8 to 12 weeks gestation (Chervenak, Isaacson, & Mahoney, 1986).

The fetal stage begins with the ninth week after conception and extends to birth. At the beginning of this period, the fetus continues dramatic growth and development. Prechtl (1987) finds that from 10 weeks onward rhythmical breathing movements can be observed, the head can be rotated, and by 10 1/2 weeks, jaw opening and complex stretch movements are added to the fetal repertoire. Yawns, rhythmical sucking, and swallowing follow closely at 11 and 12 weeks. From the beginning of this period to approximately 14 weeks is a time of spurting brain growth, when billions of cells develop into neurons (Strom, Bernard, & Strom, 1987). Taste buds function by 15 weeks (Bradley & Stern,

1967), and the fetus will experience the taste of a range of acids, proteins, salts, and other chemicals in the amniotic fluid for some time before birth (Mistretta & Bradley, 1977). From 10 to 18 weeks of gestation, as well as the last 3 months of pregnancy through the first 18 months of postnatal life, brain tissue can be damaged by toxic substances, nutritional deprivation, disruption of oxygen and carbon dioxide exchange, and combinations of these and other factors (Hunt, 1983).

As the third month of development after conception progresses, the fetus can kick its legs, turn its limbs and head, open its mouth, swallow, and make a fist. By the end of the third month, or 12 weeks, the external sex organs are observable and the fetus exhibits substantial movement. At this time the fetus is almost 3 inches long and weighs approximately one ounce.

During the fourth month of development, the mother begins to show her pregnancy and feels the fetus moving for the first time. Growth continues to be extremely rapid, with limbs, hands and feet, heart, and reflexes undergoing striking development. When the fetus is 16 to 20 weeks of age, an obstetrician may perform an amniocentesis. With amniocentesis, a hollow needle is inserted into the amniotic sac and fluid is withdrawn (Finegan, Quarrington, Hughes, & Doran, 1987). The amniotic fluid is analyzed to discern chromosomal abnormalities and a range of possible defects and disorders. Neural tube defects, including absence of part of the brain or skull or failure of the spine to close, may be found through amniocentesis because alpha-fetoprotein is leaked from the fetus into the amniotic sac (Brock, 1983); both a high or low level of alpha-fetoprotein has diagnostic implications (Lippman & Evans, 1987).

By the fifth month, the skin of the fetus is covered by a cheeselike substance called *vernix caseosa* (Snow, 1989), which protects the skin during the long immersion in the amniotic fluid. Extensive brain growth occurs, as well as formation of sweat glands, growth of eyebrows and eyelashes, and development of a soft, fine hair called *lanugo* which covers the body. At the end of the fifth month the fetus is approximately 12 inches long and weighs about one pound.

During the sixth month, the fetus engages in many reflexive activities such as sucking, swallowing, and grasping. The eyes and eyelids are completely formed, irregular breathing occurs, and the fetus moves and sleeps at regular periods of time. Fetal skin is still covered with vernix and there are few fatty deposits under the skin for insulation and protection. If the fetus is expelled from the womb at this point, the chances of survival are slim. The respiratory and digestive systems, in particular, are simply not mature enough to support the fetus as a neonate. Six months after conception the fetus is usually about 14 inches long and weighs almost 2 pounds.

By the end of the second or early in the third gestation trimester, the fetus is capable of auditory perception (Birnholz & Benacerraf, 1983). At 7 months of age, or 28 weeks, the fetus may survive if expelled from the womb. This period is called the "age of viability" and means that the respiratory system, brain functions, digestive and circulatory systems, and other developmental aspects of the fetus are mature enough to exist, with special care and attention, if birth occurs. By the end of the seventh month the fetus is usually 16 inches long and weighs about 2 pounds.

From 8 to 9 months after conception, the fetus gains weight, the functioning of biological systems is refined, and the fetus becomes increasingly sensitive to light, sound, and touch. The placenta facilitates transfer of the mother's antibodies to the fetus but begins to break down and becomes progressively less efficient in meeting the needs of the fetus. The fetus becomes ready for birth and at birth weighs approximately 7 pounds and is about 20 inches in length.

There are a number of scales developed for screening and predicting perinatal risk. Molfese (1989) discusses the University of Colorado Neonatal Morbidity Risk Scale, the High-Risk Pregnancy Screening System, Obstetrical Complications Scale, and Maternal-Child Health Care Index, as well as many other scales and systems. All of these scales include measurements of the mother's age, marital status, parity (number of previous births), income and education level of the mother and father, prenatal care, maternal physical factors, maternal nutrition, placental factors, and fetal factors. Molfese (1989) stresses the importance of perinatal risk scale development, since approximately 85% of perinatal mortality and morbidity cases can be identified as coming from the approximately 25% of pregnancies that have antepartum or intrapartum complications.

Birth and the Effects of the Birth Process. Birth moves the fetus from the protective environment of the womb, where the temperature is controlled and consistent, sounds muted, and nutritional needs continuously met, to a world where the newborn must breath, eat, and cope with a large array of needs and stresses. *Childbirth* is the process which moves the fetus out of the uterus to the complex world awaiting it. While nearly 95% of all infants are born within 2 weeks of their expected delivery date (40 weeks gestation), scientists are not clear about what actually causes labor to begin (Snow, 1989).

The birth process includes three stages, with the first being the longest. During the first stage, labor begins with the muscles of the uterus contracting. The contractions are involuntary and they cause the cervix to stretch, open, and prepare to expel the fetus. As labor progresses, the contractions come closer together, from initially being 15 to 30 minutes apart to every 2 to 5 minutes; they also increase in intensity. At the end of this stage, the cervix has approximately a 4-inch opening that is large enough for the infant to move through the birth canal.

The second stage of labor is the birth of the child. The contractions, with the help of the mother's abdominal muscle pushing, continue to move the infant out of the womb. Typically, the baby is in the head-first position; after the head appears, the rest of the body is eased out of the birth canal. In the third stage of labor, the placenta is delivered. This stage is the shortest and involves the uterine muscles expelling the fetal membranes, placenta, and umbilical cord.

Difficulties can occur during the birth process, including a baby being in a problematic birth position, a prolonged and complicated delivery, detachment of the placenta during the birth process, and anoxia or the lack of oxygen for the baby. These and other birth-related issues are covered in greater detail in Chapters 3, 4, and 5.

CASE STUDY: TYPICAL LABOR AND BIRTH
Ann and Joseph had prepared for their first child by attending Lamaze child birth classes. In the classes, they learned to prepare for their child's birth by practicing exercises that would help the delivery and birth. They also discovered that labor for a first-born child was about 8 hours duration, with the range being approximately 3 to 24 hours.

With this in mind, on the morning Ann's water broke (indicating that their baby would soon be born), the soon-to-be parents took their time getting to the hospital. Thinking that labor would be at least the typical 8 hours in length, Joseph had breakfast and Ann picked up a few things around the house. However, within a short period of time it was clear that the contractions were coming more frequently and that if they didn't get to the hospital soon, their baby would be born at home.

After rushing to the hospital, they went through the obligatory check-in procedures, including Ann being taken to the delivery area in a wheelchair. Once in the labor room (a dismal area painted in dark green with a single light bulb housed in wire mesh) the nurses took over preparation for delivery. They encouraged the use of the Lamaze exercises and integrated Joseph into their preparations while explaining the fetal monitors and other paraphernalia in the room. Shortly, however, the contractions were in close proximity to one another and Ann was brought into the delivery room. Within minutes, baby Melissa was born and was given her first Apgar score, a perfect 10.

The Neonate. The newly born infant typically has grown in the womb for 37 to 40 weeks and weighs about 7 pounds. The average gestation is 38 weeks, with 70% of neonates delivered at 36 to 40 weeks, and roughly 98% between 34 and 42 weeks (Meredith, 1978). The average 38-week-old neonate weighs 7.3 pounds and is 19.9 inches in length.

After birth, neonates must adjust to their new complex circumstances quickly. They breathe on their own, ingest and digest food for the first time, and eliminate waste. Their body temperature adjusts to their environment. There appears to be much variability in the relative coordination of sucking, swallowing, and breathing at birth (Woolridge & Baum, 1988).

Newborns exhibit many reflexive behaviors; a *reflex* is an automatic reaction or a built-in response to a stimuli (Sroufe, Cooper, & Marshall, 1988). Table

TABLE 2.2   **Examples of Infant Reflexes**

Reflex	Description	Developmental Pattern
Blink	To a flash of light or a puff of air, an infant closes both eyes.	Permanent
Babinski	When the side of an infant's foot is stroked from the heel toward the toes, the toes fan out and the foot twists inward.	Disappears around 1 year
Babkin	When an infant is lying on his back, pressure applied to the palms of both hands causes the head to turn straight ahead, the mouth to open, and the eyes to close.	Disappears around 3 months
Grasping	Pressure on an infant's palms produced by an object like a parent's finger causes the fingers to curl with a strong enough grasp to support the infant's own weight.	Weakens after 3 months and disappears by 1 year
Moro	This reflex pattern, which involves extending the arms and then bringing them rapidly toward the midline while closing the fingers in a grasping action, can be triggered by several kinds of startling stimuli, such as a sudden loud noise or holding the infant horizontally face-up and then rapidly lowering the baby about six inches.	Disappears around 5 months
Rooting	When an infant's cheek is stroked lightly, he turns his head in the direction of the stroked cheek and opens his mouth to suck the object that stroked the cheek.	Disappears around 4 months
Stepping	When an infant is held above a surface and then lowered until the feet touch the surface, the infant will make stepping movements like walking.	Disappears around 3 months
Sucking	When an object such as a nipple or a finger is inserted into an infant's mouth, rhythmic sucking occurs.	Changes into voluntary sucking by 2 months
Tonic Neck	An infant placed on his back tends to turn his head to one side and to extend the arm and leg on that side while flexing the limbs on the other side (like a fencing position).	Disappears around 4 months

Note: *From Child Development: Its Nature and Course* by L. A. Stroufe, R. G. Cooper, and M. Marshall, 1988. New York: Alfred A. Knopf. Copyright 1988, by Knopf. Reprinted by permission.

2.2 gives examples of infant reflexes. Some reflexes serve critical life survival functions, such as breathing, and others help the infant deal with threats to the developing body.

All senses are functional at birth, though they are immature and capable of signficant refinement and development. The infant can see at birth, but visual acuity for two-dimensions is poor for several months after birth and only gradually increases during the first year (Banks & Salapatek, 1983). Very young infants will attend to something moving across their line of vision and will show little interest in static objects and scenes (Gibson, 1988). Infants' acuity improves with time, nearly achieving adult levels by 6 months to one year of age (Acredolo & Hake, 1982; Rose & Ruff, 1987). Studies of newborns' eye scanning movements suggest that they are preprogrammed to search with their eyes and that their eye actions are spontaneous rather than reflexive in nature (Haith, 1980).

Hearing is also present at birth, though it takes a few days for the neonate's auditory canals to clear of amniotic fluid and for hearing to become fully functional. Infants selectively respond to human sounds, particularly the female human voice (Freedman, 1971) and especially the mother's voice (DeCasper & Fifer, 1980). In fact, research shows that newborns will increase their rate of nonnutritive sucking in order to gain access to tape recordings of their mothers' voices. They appear to prefer their own mother's voice to that of unfamiliar females (DeCasper & Fifer, 1980). Further, newborns show preference for the sound of the maternal heartbeat (DeCasper & Sigafoos, 1983), and they can discriminate between their father's voice and unfamiliar male voices (DeCasper & Prescott, 1984). Recent research also suggests that prenatal experiences with the mother's voice influence early postnatal auditory perceptions in terms of infant reaction and orientation (Spence & DeCasper, 1987).

Hearing and looking systems appear coordinated from birth and unite in the infant's attention to an auditory/visual stimulus (Gibson, 1988). Babies also feel, smell, and taste at birth. Infants respond to touch by reflexive action. Newborns can discriminate between strong odors at birth (Rieser, Yonas, & Wilkner, 1976; Steiner, 1977) and breast-feeding infants are adept at responding preferentially to their mother's breast or axillary odors (Cernoch & Porter, 1985). Newborns exhibit a clear preference for sweet liquids as opposed to salty or tasteless ones (Lipsitt, 1977) and readily learn a discrimination task when offered a sweet reward as one of the stimulus choices (Reardon & Bushnell, 1988).

INFANT PHYSICAL GROWTH AND MOTOR DEVELOPMENT

Infants are born with little physical control over their bodies. Reflexive behaviors predominate at birth. Two patterns govern infant physical growth and development (Sroufe, Cooper, & Marshall, 1988). The first is the *cephalocaudal pattern* in which the greatest growth occurs at the top of the body and proceeds downward; thus, the head develops first, then the neck, trunk, and so on. The second pattern is that growth occurs in a *proximodistal direction:* growth and control begins at the center of the body and moves toward the proximities. This is clearly exhibited in the muscle control of the trunk and arms compared with the hands and feet.

As the infant develops muscle coordination, it is important to recognize that there are gross motor skills and fine motor skills which evolve. *Gross motor*

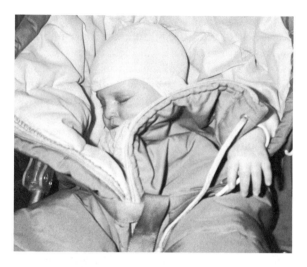

Growth is rapid during the first year life, and infants spend
a good deal of time sleeping.

skills include large muscle activities such as crawling, sitting up, and walking.
Fine motor skills refer to the dexterity infants develop, for example, in learning
to pick up objects with their hands. When infants are born they have little coordination of the arms, chest, or legs, their gross motor and fine motor skills are
extremely limited.

Growth is rapid within the first year of development and in a short period
of time, typically within 2 to 3 months after birth, the infant begins to smile
in response to external stimuli, usually an adult's face. Within 3 to 4 months,
the infant can lift shoulders and chest, arms extended, in a prone position. There
is evidence that infants point as early as 3 months of age (Hannan, 1987) and
can grasp at objects in their line of vision. By 6 months of age an infant usually
sits up with some aid and support (Cratty, 1986). When infants reach 8 to 10
months of age, they stand on their feet with adult help. At one year of age most
infants stand on their own and shortly thereafter walk unaided. By this time,
some baby teeth have appeared.

Growth slows somewhat in the second year of life. Additional teeth appear, gross motor skills become more refined (such as grasping, running, and
walking), and fine motor skills develop (Cratty, 1986). There is a great deal
of variation in maturation patterns; some infants develop very quickly, reaching
expected motor milestones early, while others develop more slowly or uneven-
ly, with some abilities developing early and others later than expected. Specific
maturation rates or patterns are little related to later growth and development;
therefore, children's early, late, or uneven maturation pattern are not particularly
predictive of later growth, skills, or abilities.

LANGUAGE DEVELOPMENT

The infant's cry is the baby's first use of language. The cry begins as a reflex and emerges as a major means of communicating discomfort and distress. Cooing, a response to comfort, occurs at approximately 2 months of age, followed closely by babbling, between 3 and 6 months. *Cooing* consists primarily of vocal sounds, while *babbling* includes consonant sounds and consonant-vowel combinations (Grieser & Kuhl, 1989).

Around 9 months infants display an understanding of some words spoken to them. From early in development, language comprehension consistently precedes language production (Lamb & Bornstein, 1987), and a baby's first words typically occur at about one year of age. From this point language development is rapid, and infants increasingly use words to communicate as well as understand more of what is said to them. By 18 months they typically comprehend body parts and respond to simple questions. Their expressive vocabulary ranges from 3 to 50 words, and they use one-word sentences like "Up!" (Baby wants to get up), "More" (I want some more milk), and "All gone" (My dinner is all gone).

By 24 months toddlers produce approximately 250 to 300 words and can speak intelligibly in two- and three-word phrases. They understand much of what adults communicate to them as well.

Language development is rapid and not well explained by traditional learning theories. Sophisticated theories of language development have emerged to explain the rapid, universal development of this remarkable human skill. Skinner (1957) was an early language theorist, with the view that language developed as any other learned behavior. He maintained that language could be explained as a conditioned set of responses; infants make sounds similar to words, adults respond enthusiastically, and sounds that approximate words are therefore selectively reinforced. In this way language develops as a response to parental reinforcement. He went further to propose that infants, toddlers, and young children learn language frames, such as "I want _____ ," then learn new words to utilize in the frame. This view of language has been criticized for generally not explaining the rapidity with which language occurs, the universality of language, and the production and comprehension of novel utterances.

Another early attempt to explain language development was made by Noam Chomsky, who proposed that language was a biological phenomena; humans were born with an innate disposition for language learning called the *language acquisition device* (LAD). Related to Chomsky's theory is that of Lenneberg (1967), who proposed a critical period for the development of language. He maintained that language learning is a universal human activity, illustrated by the fact that children the world over learn language in a similar manner, achieving language milestones in an unvarying order.

More recently researchers have argued that children learn language in a social context and have stressed the communication aspect of language (Bruner, 1983; Pinker, 1984; Shatz, 1987). This viewpoint suggests that some innate language learning ability, combined with environmental stimulation in the form of adult-child interactions, are responsible for children's language development.

Language development is an area of intense research interest. Researchers in this area seem in general agreement that there are universals for language acquisition, and that it includes the complex interaction of phonology, syntax, semantics, and pragmatics. Currently researchers are considering a variety of issues, including whether language is indeed species specific, the relationship between language and cognition, and the acquisition of language comprehension and production skills. For example, Bloom, Beckwith, and Capatides (1988) find a pattern of results that suggests an interactive, mutual influence between developments in language learning and affect expression.

Very recently, Pye, Ingram, and List (1987) proposed that children learn the phonology of a language in a uniform manner, but children acquiring different languages develop different phonological systems. They find that children quickly develop a highly predictable phonological organization within their own given language.

Pinker (1984) proposes a *continuity assumption,* by which children have innate cognitive and language acquisition mechanisms similar to adults. Nelson (1987) has developed the theory of the *rare event,* which states that the crux of language growth lies in rarely occurring language instances. Challenging and useful adult input strings are seized by the child's system and put into storage and compared with previously stored similar forms. To support his assertions, Nelson notes that only about 10% of adult utterances to children are selected and used in their language learning. That 10% represents adult language that expands on children's previous utterances and are at children's current level of language learning. Thus, adult utterances that are useful and challenging are incorporated in child language learning.

Snow, Perlman, and Nathan (1987) proposed the notion of *scaffolding,* in which children can imitate and incorporate adult model utterances or phrases into their own lexicon. Children imitate adult words that they do not fully understand, and this process provides a boost to the child in learning new words and phrases. Thus, scaffolded utterances are less demanding to produce than spontaneous utterances.

Bootstrapping is the idea that children construct their own knowledge of language by using what they already know in order to learn more advanced forms (Shatz, 1987). The early use of the bootstrapping concept applied to syntax to explain a child's grasp of abstract forms of syntax or grammar was based on a more basic semantic or pragmatic level of learning. More recently, Pinker (1984) and Shatz (1987) expanded the idea of bootstrapping to include the child's use of communication in general. Thus, children use whatever knowledge of language they have to gain an understanding of new forms, content, and uses.

For example, they use gestures, smiles, and vocalizations to elicit language from those around them which, in turn, facilitates language learning. They also use strategies for maintaining discourse and storing and analyzing language information in their own active role in language learning (Shatz, 1987).

Currently there are a number of attempts to explore the relationship between the mother and infant in the infant's language development (Ginsburg & Kilborne, 1988; Vibbert & Bornstein, 1989). For instance, Yoder and Kaiser (1989) propose alternative explanations for the relationship between maternal interaction style and the infant's language development. They find that early attempts to explain the relation between a mother's speech and later language development assumed a direct maternal influence model; more recent attempts have considered pragmatic and discourse aspects of maternal speech (e.g., Hoff-Ginsberg, 1986). Indeed, Olsen-Fulero (1982) provides a model of maternal pragmatic and discourse features that may positively and negatively influence child language development.

Finally, there are recent attempts to tie language learning to the research in infant cognition and learning. Gopnik and Meltzoff (1987) are linking language development with Piaget's stages of cognitive development. For instance, they note that around 18 months of age, toddlers will start to name many objects around them. The "naming explosion" seems to be linked to the development of categorization.

LEARNING AND COGNITION IN INFANCY

The field of infant learning is dominated by a number of theoretical perspectives. An early learning theory was classical conditioning. The key concepts involve an unconditioned stimulus (US), which automatically elicits an unconditioned response (UR); an example of an US is a puff of air directed toward the eye, and the UR is an eye blink. Additional concepts include the conditioned stimulus (CS), a previously neutral stimulus that becomes conditioned after being paired with the US over time. The CS takes on the properties of the US and itself elicits a conditioned response (CR); for example, a light which is turned on prior to a puff of air hitting the eye will elicit, itself, over time, the eye blink response (Houston, 1986). In regard to infant learning, the mother, initially a neutral stimulus, becomes paired over time with meeting the infant's various needs for affection, food, and warmth. The mother soon comes to signal to the infant that pleasant experiences, such as feeding, will occur (Miller, 1989; Sluckin & Herbert, 1986).

A view of learning related to classical conditioning is operant conditioning. Operant conditioning theorists maintain that individuals are active in the learning process, and their activity results in consequences. The consequences may be positive reinforcements, negative reinforcements, punishments, or no response. Reinforcements increase the likelihood that the behavior will occur again, and punishment causes a behavior to cease. No response to a behavior will eventually, but not immediately, cause the behavior to diminish (extinction).

The main proponent of operant conditioning is B.F. Skinner, who maintains that most behaviors are learned. This view of learning is called *behaviorism*. When it is used as a teaching method, it is called *applied behavior analysis*.

Another theory related to classical and operant conditioning is *social learning theory*. This behavioral theory extends the view of learning to include individual development and the social context in which learning occurs. Albert Bandura (1977) proposed a social learning theory in which he expanded operant conditioning to include learning without reinforcement. That is, individuals learn without receiving direct individual reinforcement simply by observing others. The concepts of vicarious reinforcement, vicarious punishment, and modeling explain much about how individuals learn by observing others. Infants, for example, early in their development, attempt to imitate those around them. The mimicking of an older child's behavior by the 9- or 10-month-old infant is an example of social learning theory. In later years individuals learn new behaviors by observing others perform and by viewing the consequences of those behaviors. The vicarious consequences, in turn, influence the likelihood of the observer performing the same behaviors.

Currently, learning theorists are focusing on cognitive development and how children process information. There are a variety of points of view on this matter, employing artificial intelligence paradigms, mathematical processing models, and cognitive architecture (e.g., Langley, 1983; Rabinowitz, Grant, & Dingley, 1987; Wilkenson & Haines, 1987). Some of the information processing models view human learning as analogous to information being processed by a computer.

Jean Piaget studied learning as it occurs within the developing individual. He and the neo-Piagetians were among the first to consider learning in a developmental and social context. Two fundamental, invariant human characteristics describe Piaget's theory: organization and adaptation (Shulman, 1985). *Organization* refers to Piaget's belief that human cognitive development is a highly coordinated activity rather than chaotic or without form. *Adaptation* refers to the continual adjustments which infants make to their environment.

Piaget maintained that infants are active in their cognitive development; in fact, this is a cornerstone of his work. Infants are born with reflexive actions; the reflexive actions are the infant's first activities. As the infant develops, the reflexes give way to voluntary actions. These sensorimotor activities form the basic components for the construction of knowledge. What the infant is trying to do, indeed what impels all cognitive development from Piaget's perspective, is to construct his or her own view of reality.

Piaget theorizes that there are four primary developmental stages through which individuals pass. Two of these are pertinent to this discussion. The neonate begins in the *sensorimotor stage* of development, in which information is received through the infant's sensory apparatus and motor activities. This stage begins at birth and extends to approximately 18 to 24 months of age. Piaget declined to tie specific age expectations to his developmental stages, maintaining that development was to a great extent dependent on internal, individual characteristics such as maturation rate. However, much detailed observation of children during the first two years has led other researchers to attach age approximations to Piaget's stages.

During the sensorimotor stage the typical infant moves from basic reflex activities to complex actions. The infant develops significant abilities to store, remember, organize, and utilize sensory and motor experiences and information. The sensorimotor stage is divided into six substages, beginning with the *reflexive* stage; it occurs from birth to approximately 1 month of age and involves primarily the reflex actions of sucking and looking. The next substage, *primary circular reactions*, begins at approximately 1 month of age and extends through 4 months. During this period the infant attempts to make the body do things, such as trying to get the thumb to the mouth and attempting to reach objects with their arms. The third substage is termed *secondary circular reactions*, beginning at approximately 4 months and lasting to 10 months of age. The infant begins to perform coordinated actions with objects to achieve a result, such as attempting to make a toy move by hitting it.

The fourth substage begins at 10 months and extends through 12 months of age and is known as the *coordination of secondary schemes*. In this substage, the infant increasingly combines activities to reach an end result. For example, he or she might crawl to an object, reach for it, move it to his or her mouth, and begin to suck. The fifth substage, *tertiary circular reactions*, begins at 1 year of age and extends to approximately 18 months. This substage is characterized by increased motor development and the ability to use improved motor abilities in new ways through trial and error. The final substage is termed *mental combinations* and starts at approximately 18 months. The toddler has some language and basic motor skills; mental representation is clear in his or her use of objects and words to stand for people and objects not present.

The typical toddler then moves to the second major developmental stage, *preoperational thought*. Characteristic of this stage is the child's egocentrism and basic unawareness of the thoughts and feelings of others. In this stage, the toddler tends to focus on one perceptible aspect of a situation or activity at a time; for example, he or she can attend to "short" or "fat," but not "short and fat" simultaneously.

Infant learning and cognitive development is a major interest area for developmentalists. The field has moved from a strict consideration of observable infant developmental characteristics to a fuller, richer view of how infants learn and organize their cognitive understanding of the world. Attention is currently focused on such issues as attention and verbal expression (Heinicke & Lampl, 1988), stability of infant measures of intelligence (Ramey, Lee, & Burchinal, 1989; Rose, 1989), the role of genetics in learning (Plomin, 1989), and development of new theories of intelligence (e.g., Feldman, 1982, 1986; Gardner, 1983, 1984; Sternberg, 1984, 1986).

INFANT SOCIAL-EMOTIONAL DEVELOPMENT

Attachment

Infants become attached to their parents and parents bond to their infants. This attachment-bonding activity forms the beginning of the infant's social-emotional development. Attachment is critical and is the basis for the infant's social-emotional well-being and the foundation for all other infant attachments and later relationships.

The issue of attachment has received significant interest by developmentalists over time. The early study by Skeels and Dye (1938) in which orphaned, institutionalized children were examined for the effects of a lack of human interaction, is frequently considered the beginning of this field of endeavor. More recently, the work of Mary Ainsworth (1973, 1982) and her students (e.g., Main & Cassidy, 1988) and John Bowlby (1969, 1973, 1980) form current thinking on the issue of attachment.

Attachment is usually described as an emotional tie or bond of affection between the infant and parent. Attachment includes many behaviors such as

An important development during the first year is mother-infant attachment.

calling out for contact, clinging, crying, eye contact, smiling, and touching. It is not the particular behavior itself or the frequency of one or many of the behaviors which describes attachment, but rather the pattern of attachment behaviors that indicates the quality and strength of the attachment between infants and their parents.

Ainsworth (1972, 1982) and her associates (Ainsworth, Blehar, Waters & Wall, 1978) identified stages of attachment. Phase 1 is the *initial preattachment* (baby shows orientation and signals without discrimination of figure) and this stage occurs during the first 1 to 2 months of life. The infant behaves in a way which elicits the proximity of adults; behaviors include crying, cuddling, and smiling, all of which tend to promote parent-infant contact. In the next phase, *attachment-in-the-making* (baby shows orientation and signals directed towards one or more discriminated figures) the infant begins to discriminate familiar from unfamiliar faces at approximately 2 to 7 months of age. In phase 3, *clear-cut attachment* (baby maintains proximity to a discriminated figure by means of locomotion as well as signals), from approximately 7 to 24 months of age, infants tend to have one person to whom attachment behaviors are directed. Not only does the infant direct the attachment figure to approach, but the infant will also making crawling and creeping attempts toward the attachment figure. In phase 4 (formation of a goal-corrected partnership) infants tend to develop *multiple attachments* (Lamb, Thompson, Gardner, & Charnov, 1985).

Research on attachment is usually conducted using the *Strange Situation paradigm* (Ainsworth et al., 1978). This laboratory procedure was designed to study the quality of the mother-infant attachment during separation and reunion (Table 2.3). The procedure (Ainsworth et al., 1978) involves eight, approximately 3-minute episodes in which the mother and child are observed. The episodes are arranged to create increased levels of stress for the 12- to 24-month-old infant so that researchers can determine how babies organize their behavior around attachment figures (Lamb et al., 1985) The parent and stranger are specifically instructed to avoid initiating behavior with the infant, but to respond appropriately to the baby.

The scoring of attachment behavior is based on the infant's proximity and contact seeking behavior, contact maintaining behavior, resistance, avoidance, and searching for the parent. Infants are classified as secure (type B) if they greet the parent positively upon reunion, are soothed if distressed, and exhibit little or no avoidance or resistance toward the parent; the insecure-avoidant (type A) infants actively avoid and resist the parent upon reunion; and, insecure-ambivalent infants (type C) show high levels of distress throughout the strange situation and show weak to strong proximity-seeking with a mild to obvious resistance and inability to be settled by the parent (Main & Solomon, 1986). The proposal of a type D attachment classification (Main & Solomon, 1986) comes from researchers' difficulty in classifying a small portion of infant-

TABLE 2.3   The Strange Situation Procedure

SEQUENCE	PARTICIPANTS	SITUATION
1.	Mother, baby, and observer	An introductory session during which the mother and infant become familiar with the room, which is usually a carpeted playroom laboratory with children's toys and available chairs.
2.	Mother and baby	The mother and baby are alone together in the research room.
3.	Stranger, mother, and baby	A female stranger enters the research room with the instruction to sit quietly for about one minute and then to converse with the parent for approximately one minute and finally to engage the infant in play so that the parent can leave the room; the parent leaves unobtrusively after 3 minutes.
4.	Stranger and baby	First separation episode. The stranger and the baby are alone; the parent is instructed to speak loudly before reentering the room so as to attract the infant's attention; as she returns to the research room she is asked to pause for the infant to respond to her presence. The parent is to make the baby comfortable and reinterest the child in toys; the stranger leaves.
5.	Mother and baby	First reunion episode. The mother and infant are alone together when the parent is instructed to leave the playroom.
6.	Baby alone	Second separation episode. The infant is left alone for approximately 3 minutes unless particularly distressed; the stranger returns to the playroom.
7.	Stranger and baby	The stranger and the baby are together in the playroom; when the mother returns to the playroom the stranger leaves.
8.	Mother and baby	Second reunion episode. The mother and child are alone together in the playroom.

Note: *From* "Patterns of Attachment" (p. 37) by M. D. S. Ainsworth, M. C. Blehar, E. Waters, and S. Wall, 1978. Hillsdale, NJ: Lawrence Erlbaum Associates. Copyright 1978 by Lawrence Erlbaum Associates. Adapted by permission.

attachment relationships; in almost all of these cases the infants were disorganized in the presence of only one parent. The type D, or insecure-disorganized/disoriented infant typically displays contradictory behaviors:

- Disordering of expected temporal sequences (e.g., the infant initially greets the parent with bids for contact and then turns away and looks blankly ahead)
- Simultaneous display of contradictory behavior patterns (e.g., approaching the parent, but from a sideways position or even backwards rather than face-to-face)
- Incomplete or undirected movements and expressions, including stereotypies (e.g., striking out at the parent's face, but with weak nearly undirected movements)
- Direct indices of confusion and apprehension (e.g., upon the approach of the parent, the infant may express confusion and apprehension)
- Behavioral stilling: "dazed" behavior and indices of depressed affect (e.g., an unfocused, "dead" stare with mouth and chin limp)

Babies are assigned to attachment categories by means of interactive rating scales, which measure contact-seeking, resisting, avoiding, and other behaviors (Table 2.4).

Ainsworth, Bell, and Stayton (1971) conducted classic, or foundational, research on mothers' responsiveness to their infants. They categorized mothers according to four aspects of the mothers' sensitivity and responsiveness toward their babies: *sensitivity-insensitivity*, the extent to which mothers are aware of their infant's needs and respond to them; *acceptance-rejection*, the mother's general acceptance of the problems, limitations, and responsibilities of having a baby; *cooperation-interference*, the degree to which mothers allow their infants autonomy or impose control; and *accessibility-ignoring*, a measure of mothers' attention to their babies' cues and signals.

Clarke-Stewart (1973) finds that when mothers are rated on responsiveness, expression of positive emotion, and social stimulation that high-scoring mothers have more securely attached infants than low-scoring mothers. Additional research (e.g., Cohn & Tronick, 1983; Osofsk, 1976) demonstrates that the numerous interactions between the mother and infant early in the child's development affect each member of the pair and confirm that attachment is a critical concept in understanding mother-infant interactions (Rosenblith & Sims-Knight, 1985). The relationship between attachment as measured in the laboratory setting and the sensitivity of care in the home (as documented by home observations in the first year of an infant's life) is well established (Bates, Maslin, & Frankel, 1985; Egeland & Farber, 1984; Grossman, Grossman, Spangler, Suess, & Unzer, 1985; Sroufe, 1989).

Research has been conducted on attachment behaviors and stranger sociability (Lutkenhaus, Grossman, & Grossman, 1985; Plunkett, Klein &

TABLE 2.4 The Interactive Rating Scales

SCALE	ABBREVIATED DESCRIPTION OF SELECTED ANCHOR POINTS*
Proximity and Contact Seeking	7. Very active effort and initiative in achieving physical contact (e.g., fully approaches the adult and achieves contact through its own efforts) 5. Some active effort to achieve physical contact (e.g., approaches but is picked up without any clear bid for contact) 3. Weak effort to achieve physical contact or moderately strong effort to gain proximity (e.g., approaches, does not request pick up, and is not held) 1. No effort to achieve physical contact or proximity
Contact Maintaining	7. Very active and persistent effort to maintain physical contact (e.g., while held more than 2 minutes, infant at least twice actively resists release) 5. Some active effort to maintain physical contact (e.g., while held for less than 1 minute, the infant actively resists release once) 3. Some apparent desire to maintain physical contact but relatively little active effort to do so (e.g., infant initiates contact at least twice in an episode, but on each occasion the hold is brief, and its cessation is not protested) 1. Either no physical contact or no effort to maintain it
Resistance	7. Very intense *and* persistent resistance (e.g., two or more instances of: repeatedly hitting the adult, strong squirming against hold, temper tantrum, repeated angry rejection of the adult or toys) 5. Some resistance—either less intense or more isolated and less persistent (e.g., at least 3 instances of the above, without as great a degree of anger) 3. Slight resistance (e.g., two rather modest instances of resistance) 1. No resistance
Avoidance	7. Very marked and persistent avoidance (e.g., no attention to adult despite repeated attempts by her/him to attract attention) 5. Clear-cut avoidance but less persistent (e.g., 30 seconds of ignoring in the absence of attempts by the adult to gain attention) 3. Slight isolated avoidance behavior (e.g., brief delay in responding) 1. No avoidance
Search†	7. Very active and persistent search behavior (e.g., approaches door promptly and actively bangs or attempts to open it) 5. Some active search (e.g., approaches door after delay or fails to make active effort to open it or bang) 3. Some apparent desire to regain the attachment figure, but the search behavior is weak (e.g., infant looks toward door for at least 30 seconds) 1. No search

TABLE 2.4   (*Continued*)

SCALE	ABBREVIATED DESCRIPTION OF SELECTED ANCHOR POINTS*
Distance Interaction	7. Very active and persistent distance interaction (e.g., reciprocal interaction for more than 45 seconds)
	5. Active distance interaction (e.g., smiles and vocalizes to parent at least 4 times)
	3. Little distance interaction (e.g., looks frequently at adult, and orients for at least 15 seconds)
	1. No distance interaction (e.g., just occasional glances)

*Full details regarding the rating scales are provided by Ainsworth at al. (1978). Patterns of Attachment (Appendix III). Hillsdale, N.J.: Lawrence Erlbaum Associates.

†Rated only in separation episodes

Note: From "Infant-Mother Attachment" by M. G. Lamb, R. A. Thompson, W. Gardner, and E. L. Charnov, 1985. Hillsdale, NJ: Lawrence Erlbaum Associates. Copyright 1985 by Lawrence Erlbaum Associates. Reprinted by permission.

Meisels, 1988), attachment and temperament (Bradshaw, Goldsmith & Campos, 1987; Belsky, Rovine, & Taylor, 1984), and attachment and social play (Connell & Thompson, 1986; Roggman, Langlois, & Hubbs-Tait, 1987). Attachment is further discussed as it relates to social/emotional disorders (Chapter 4) and as it relates to family dynamics (Chapter 6).

Theories of Infant Emotional Development

The earliest and one of the most well developed theories of emotional development is that of Sigmund Freud (1923/1962). Freud based development on early experience. He proposed that the human mind is divided into three systems, the id, the ego, and the superego. The *id* strives for immediate gratification by any possible avenue and is the source of all motivation. For Freud, the id is present at birth, while the other two structures, ego and superego, develop over time. The *ego* continually tries to control the id by being responsive to social conventions and expectations; therefore, the ego is responsible for the appropriate expression of emotions, delay of gratification, and perception and thought. The *superego* is the guide of morals and ethics. Together the three structures mediate need-gratification with social and environmental constraints.

Freud's importance lies in the comprehensiveness of his theory and his landmark influence on psychology. Despite his historical importance in the field of social-emotional development. His theory has lost prominence with theorists who take into account the influences of social and environmental factors and, more recently, cognitive factors on emotional life.

Another prominent theory of social-emotional development is that of Erik Erikson (1950). Erikson is considered a neo-Freudian because he accepted many of Freud's essential tenets. Erikson departed from Freud, however, in his consideration of the social context in which development occurs. Freud stated that development occurred primarily as a result of factors within the individual, but Erikson felt that development was far more dependent on the social issues which the developing individual faces. His theory of social-emotional development focuses on primary developmental issues, or "crises," which the individual encounters over the developmental life span.

For the infant, Erikson felt the primary issue was the development of basic trust or mistrust. By meeting the infant's needs in a reliable manner, the caregiver instills in the infant a basic sense of trust in the world. If needs are not met, or met in an unsatisfactory manner, the infant tends to develop a sense of mistrust. At about age 2, the toddler enters the stage of autonomy versus guilt. During this time, the toddler moves about in the environment and, if the exploratory behavior of the child is fostered, a sense of autonomy is developed. Erikson's other stages trace emotional development into adulthood and old age.

CASE STUDY: INFANT TEMPERAMENT

When Meredith was born, her parents were concerned about her. Born 3 weeks before her due date and just above 5 pounds weight at birth, she seemed to sleep through her first 2 weeks of development. After that initial period of time, however, Meredith exhibited a combination of traits. She responded to her parents whenever her name was said by turning her head in response. In addition, she molded to her mother's arms by moving and snuggling into a comfortable position, and shortly she began to smile.

Her distress cues were very clear to her parents and almost exclusively were for hunger, wetness, and need to sleep. Her needs were promptly met and the easy-going nature of her temperament extended through her first year of life. By the end of the first year, she approached most all people with a ready smile and was actively exploring her environment. She continued to enjoy the physical proximity and touch of her mother, and this remained a consistently effective way to sooth Meredith on the rare occasions when she was distressed.

The same combination of personality traits—easy social interaction, continual smile, and pleasant temperament—continued right through to her preschool years, where the teacher consistently notes a self-reliance and independence and overall comfort with self. Meredith is sought out by other preschoolers for play, actively explores and seeks out novel situations, and continues to display a joyful outlook on her world.

Temperament and Emotions

In considering infant social-emotional development, an important issue is infant temperament. Is social-emotional development more heavily dependent on social factors and environmental context or on the infant's temperament and personality traits? Two primary issues have dominated work in this area: the dimensions or characteristics of temperament and the stability of temperament over time and place (Lamb, 1988). Although we know personality factors are associated with temperament, the expression of these characteristics is dependent on the child's environment, including changing expectations and relationships. Current research in social-emotional development tends to take a longitudinal approach, focusing on interpersonal exchanges and the links between temperament and social factors like parental sensitivity and environmental context.

Worobey and Lewis (1989) studied infant response to stress and found that individual differences do exist and may reflect important temperamental differences. The consistencies that they identified in infants over time suggest that the relationship among newborn temperament, early environment, and later growth and development should be explored. Worobey and Blajda (1989) found that temperament may be studied in infants as young as 2 weeks by obtaining ratings from the mothers (Table 2.4). Levels of activity and emotionality are stable over the first 2 neonatal months. Distress-related responses which characterize early irritability may predict difficult temperament, other aspects of emotionality, and maternal behavior in caregiving. Importantly, however, Bohlin, Hagekull, Germer, Andersson, and Lindberg (1989) did not find that early temperamental characteristics influenced later attachment behaviors.

Another aspect of social-emotional development is emotions. The most recent approach to defining emotions and their measurement and regulation is an interactional one. Campos, Campos, and Barrett (1989) define emotions as not mere feelings, but rather, "processes of establishing, maintaining, or disrupting the relations between the person and the . . . environment" (p. 395). Their view stresses how emotions are formed, the function of emotions in adapting to the social world, and emotions as a basis for personality development. According to this viewpoint, person-environment interactions form the center for studying emotion regulation.

The common thread among current conceptualizations of emotional development is the attempt to understand how children respond to aversive environmental stimuli (Dodge, 1989) such as child abuse (Rieder & Cicchetti, 1989) and marital discord (Gottman & Katz, 1989). Kopp (1989) suggests that an interaction between reflex responses and cognitive development makes possible the control of negative emotions early in life. Gottman and Katz (1989) posit that regulatory behaviors are learned through interactions with parents, and that when the interactions are disrupted through marital discord, this learning is interrupted. Rieder and Cicchetti (1989) propose that children exposed to abusive situations lose their ability to use cognitive controls over aversive stimuli.

Recent Research

Further research on social-emotional development has taken several different directions. For example, Stifter, Fox, and Porges (1989) found that the infant's facial expressions give her or him a method to communicate with caregivers.

A more expressive infant may be more competent in eliciting caregiving behaviors than less expressive infants. Sroufe (1985) also suggests that sensitive caregivers adjust to the infant's characteristics.

In their studies of mother-infant interaction based on mutual gazing, Messer and Vietze (1988) found that previous analyses may have overestimated the influence of the partner in initiating gazing and may have underestimated the role of physiological responses. Fox (1989) has also uncovered psychophysiological correlates of emotional reactivity in infancy. And Stifter, Fox, and Porges (1989) have demonstrated that the infant's level of emotional expressivity at 5 months is related to physiological responses such as heart rate. These studies appear to lead to the conclusion that emotions have a biological basis, but are mediated by environmental factors.

By contrast, Emde (1980; 1983; 1988), taking a more psychodynamic view, stresses the relationships in which the infant is developing and the effect relationships have on social-emotional development. It is thus evident that the subject of infant emotional development remains a rich area for future research.

SUMMARY

Infant growth and development is a large and comprehensive field including infant physical, cognitive, behavioral, and social-emotional development. In a brief period of time, normal infants move from a position of total dependence on their adult caregivers to functional children who, by age 2, can express themselves to some extent with language, regulate motor activity, communicate and express emotions, feed themselves, and interact successfully with their environment. The field of infant development is heavily research-oriented, with the focus on exploring how infants grow and develop within their environment.

Suggestions for Further Reading

EMDE, R. N., & HARMON, R. J. (Eds.) (1982). *The development of attachment and affiliative systems.* New York: Plenum.

MAHLER, M., PINE, F., & BERGMAN, A. (1975). *Psychological birth of the human infant.* New York: Basic Books.

MCCALL, R. B. (1979). *Infants.* Cambridge, MA: Harvard University Press.

OSOFSKY, J. D. (Ed.) (1987). *Handbook of infant development* (2nd ed.). New York: Wiley.

Chapter 3

Determinants of Risk
in Infancy

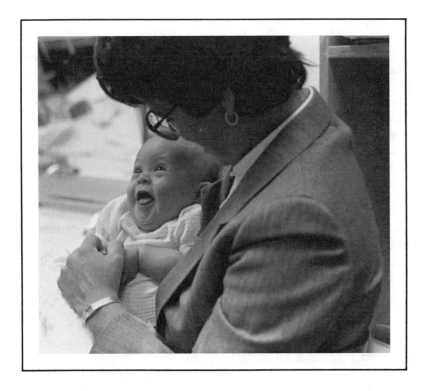

The at-risk or high-risk infant has become a great concern to professionals in medicine, developmental psychology, special education, and related fields during the past 15 years (Rossetti, 1986), and each field gives a somewhat different meaning to the term. For the present discussion we use the following definition adapted from Rossetti (1986):

> An infant who because of low birthweight (<2500 grams), prematurity (<37 weeks gestation), the presence of serious medical complications, or adverse environmental conditions, has a greater than average chance of displaying developmental delay or later cognitive or motor deficits or a combination of these in the neonatal or postnatal period (p. 3).

The definition of the risk must necessarily be broad, since we have increasing evidence that the quality of familial, medical, therapeutic, and educational care that are provided to the child immediately following birth has great influence on the ultimate quality of that child's life (Snyder-McLean, 1986). Inadequacies in any of these areas place the infant at risk for developmental delay.

This chapter examines the various risk factors that can occur in the prenatal, perinatal, and postnatal periods (Table 3.1) and includes biologic and environmental factors associated with each period.

PRENATAL PERIOD

The infant's environment in utero is critical to future well-being. That is why many prenatal risk factors have to do with the mother's health and behavior. However, genetic factors existing before conception also have an influence on the infant's development. It is estimated that 1 in 30 babies is born with a birth defect. Of those, 20% to 30% of defects are due to genetic influences and 10% are due to prenatal environmental influences. The remaining 60% to 70% of birth defects are of unknown origin (Thomson, 1989). In order to better understand genetic and chromosomal disorders, it is necessary to understand certain basic principles of human genetics.

TABLE 3.1   The Periods Surrounding Birth

TERM	DESCRIPTION
Prenatal	The period extending from conception to birth
Perinatal	The period from the 12th week of gestation through the fourth week after birth
Neonatal	The first 20 days after birth
Postnatal	The period from 28 days following birth to 11 months

Genetic Influences

Genes are the basic unit of inheritance. They are made up of molecules consisting of deoxyribonucleic acid (DNA), which are responsible for replication during cell division, coding for the production of proteins and enzymes, and regulating the rate of synthesis of these proteins and enzymes. Genes are arranged linearly along chromosomes, and each has a particular location on the chromosome. Like chromosomes, genes come in pairs, so that each pair of genes has its particular location on its chromosomes. One member of each pair is inherited from each parent. (Figure 3.1).

Each human cell contains 23 pairs of chromosomes, one of each pair from the mother and one from the father. Twenty-two pairs are identical in males and females; these chromosomes are called *autosomes*. The 23rd pair, known as the sex chromosomes, determine the child's sex. This pair consists of two X chromosomes in the female and an X and a Y chromosome in the male. The X chromosome is about three times as large as the Y (Figure 3.1). If the father's chromosomal contribution includes an X chromosome, the infant will be female; if he donates a Y chromosome, the infant will be male. Since the mother can only contribute an X chromosome, the child's sex is determined by the father. Every cell in the body contains these 46 chromosomes. Because both sexes have

FIGURE 3.1   Normal chromosome complements: male (A) and female (B). (*From "A Genetics Primer" by E. J. Thomson. Reprinted from *Infants and Young Children*, Vol. 2, No. 1, pp. 38–45, with permission of Aspen Publishers, Inc. © 1989.)

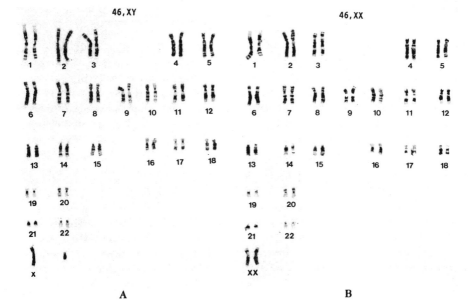

an X chromosome, disorders due to abnormal sex chromosomes are sometimes said to be X-linked.

Each chromosome contains thousands of genes which are responsible for the infant's physical characteristics and biochemical make-up, including the hormones and enzymes which regulate bodily function (Batshaw & Perret, 1986). Genes which govern these characteristics and functions are either dominant or recessive. Those governed by dominant genes tend to be inherited rather than recessive ones.

Estimates of the number of gene pairs in each human being range from 30,000 to 50,000. Scientists working in the field of genetics have identified the specific location on the chromosome of about 2,300 of them and suspect, but have not proven, the location of another 2,200.

Genetic disorders occur when a defective gene causes abnormal functioning of one or another of the body's systems. Scientists have identified approximately 500 disorders to date in which the location of the mutating gene is known (Thomson, 1989). For these disorders it is possible to develop more effective means for diagnosis and treatment. For example, scientists recently located the gene responsible for cystic fibrosis on the seventh chromosome, paving the way for early detection and ultimately prevention of the disease (Keren & Rommens, 1990).

The process by which human beings grow and develop is cell division, or *mitosis*, in all cells except those responsible for reproduction. Cell division in the production of egg and sperm cells is known as *meiosis*.

In mitosis, the 46 chromosomes contained in the parent cell duplicate themselves within the cell, separate, and then migrate to opposite ends, or poles, of the cell. The cell then splits in half, forming two new cells identical to the parent cell. Mitosis takes place thousands of times daily in adults as well as in growing children, since old and damaged cells are constantly being replaced. The exception to this general statement are the nerve cells (neurons) which make up the central nervous system; they do not reproduce themselves.

The process of meiosis differs from mitosis in that division of the parent cell—either sperm or egg (ova)—forms four new cells rather than two, and each of the four contains only half the genetic material of the parent cell. In order to reach the full complement of 46 chromosomes again, the sperm cell must join with the egg cell and each contributes 23 chromosomes to the union. (Figure 3.2). The resulting fertilized ova is called a *zygote*, ready to undergo mitosis and initiate embryonic and subsequently fetal development (Thomson, 1989).

Abnormalities in the genetic material of the mother or father may predispose the infant to any one of 500 genetic disorders. Some are well known such as tuberous sclerosis, cystic fibrosis, or Hurler's syndrome. Others are extremely rare and relatively unknown to service providers. Conversely, chromosome abnormalities occur that are not due to alterations in genetic material and therefore are not inherited. The best known example of a

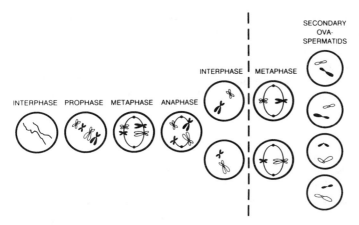

FIGURE 3.2 *Meiosis. (From "A Genetics Primer" by E. J. Thomson.
Reprinted from Infants and Young Children, Vol. 2, No.
1, pp. 38–45, with permission of Aspen Publishers, Inc.
© 1989.)*

chromosome abnormality is Down syndrome, first discovered in 1959 (Thompson & Thompson, 1986).

Gene Disorders. Gene disorders are caused by an alteration (mutation) in the chemical make-up of a single gene or gene pair. There are four types of gene disorders, depending on whether the gene is located on an autosome or on the sex chromosome, and whether the gene is dominant or recessive. The four types are known as autosomal dominant, autosomal recessive, X-linked dominant and X-linked recessive (Figure 3.3). Autosomal disorders affect males and females in equal numbers, since the genetic material on the chromosomes is identical. However, X-linked disorders occur with differing frequencies in males and females. Fewer X-linked disorders have been identified than autosomal disorders; only 139 are known, and another 171 are suspected (McKusick, 1988).

X-linked recessive disorders occur much more frequently in males. This is because they have only one X chromosome (the other is Y, inherited from the father), which will manifest the disorder if it is passed to them by their mother. Females have a second X chromosome and must therefore receive the disorder in a double dose from both father and mother, which is less likely to occur. If females receive a single altered X chromosome from one parent, the other (normal) X chromosome will dominate and they will simply carry but not manifest the disorder. The most common X-linked recessive disorders include Duchenne and Becker's muscular dystrophies, hemophilia, Hunter's syndrome, and Lesch-Nyhan syndrome. Color blindness is also caused by an X-linked recessive gene.

X-linked dominant disorders occur more frequently in females; however, such disorders are extremely rare. In an affected family they will occur twice as often in females as males, since females have two X chromosomes. A male will pass the affected gene to all of his daughters (to whom he passes his X chromosome) and none of his sons (to whom he passes his Y chromosome), whereas a female will pass the gene to half of her offspring, whether daughters or sons.

FIGURE 3.3   Types of single-gene disorders. *(From "A Genetics Primer" by E. J. Thomson. Reprinted from Infants and Young Children, Vol. 2, No. 1, pp. 38–45, with permission of Aspen Publishers, Inc. © 1989.)*

Inheritance Pattern	Characteristics	Examples
affected father parents / gametes / children X X X Y mother affected father X X X Y X X X Y X X X Y carrier daughter normal son carrier daughter normal son	Since males have only one X-chromosome, they need only a single altered gene to be affected. (There are no male carriers.) If a man is affected, all of his daughters will be carriers and not affected. All of his sons will be normal.	
X-linked dominant (rare) **affected mother** parents / gametes / children X X X Y affected mother father X X X Y X X X Y X X X Y affected daughter affected son normal daughter normal son	Either parent may be affected due to an altered gene on their X-chromosome. If a mother is affected, she has a 50 percent risk of having an affected son or daughter with each pregnancy.	Hypophosphatemia (Vitamin D-resistant rickets)
affected father parents / gametes / children X X X Y mother affected father X X X Y X X X Y X X X Y affected daughter normal son affected daughter normal son	If a father is affected, all of his daughters will be affected, and all of his sons will be normal.	

FIGURE 3.3 *(Continued)*

Inheritance Pattern	Characteristics	Examples

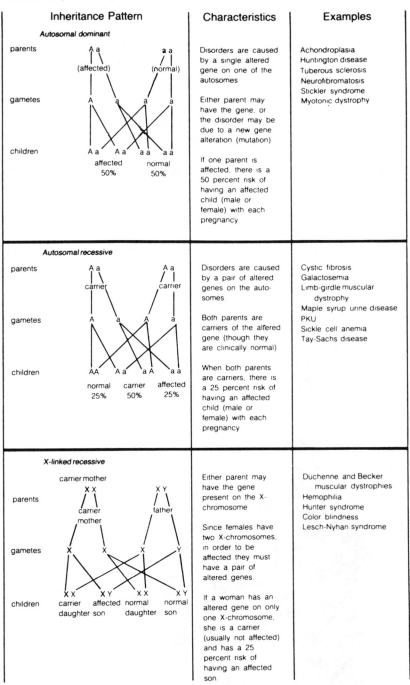

Autosomal dominant

parents — A a (affected)   a a (normal)

gametes — A a   a a

children — A a   A a   a a   a a
affected 50%   normal 50%

Disorders are caused by a single altered gene on one of the autosomes

Either parent may have the gene, or the disorder may be due to a new gene alteration (mutation)

If one parent is affected, there is a 50 percent risk of having an affected child (male or female) with each pregnancy

Achondroplasia
Huntington disease
Tuberous sclerosis
Neurofibromatosis
Stickler syndrome
Myotonic dystrophy

Autosomal recessive

parents — A a (carrier)   A a (carrier)

gametes — A a   A a

children — AA   A a   a A   a a
normal 25%   carrier 50%   affected 25%

Disorders are caused by a pair of altered genes on the autosomes

Both parents are carriers of the altered gene (though they are clinically normal)

When both parents are carriers, there is a 25 percent risk of having an affected child (male or female) with each pregnancy

Cystic fibrosis
Galactosemia
Limb-girdle muscular dystrophy
Maple syrup urine disease
PKU
Sickle cell anemia
Tay-Sachs disease

X-linked recessive

carrier mother
X X   X Y
parents — carrier mother   father

gametes — X   X   X   Y

children — X X   X Y   X X   X Y
carrier daughter   affected son   normal daughter   normal son

Either parent may have the gene present on the X-chromosome

Since females have two X-chromosomes, in order to be affected they must have a pair of altered genes

If a woman has an altered gene on only one X-chromosome, she is a carrier (usually not affected) and has a 25 percent risk of having an affected son.

Duchenne and Becker muscular dystrophies
Hemophilia
Hunter syndrome
Color blindness
Lesch-Nyhan syndrome

Autosomal dominant disorders are caused by a single altered gene along one of the autosomes. If only one parent carries the gene, there is a 50% risk that it will be passed to the affected person's offspring. If both parents are affected, the risk to offspring is 75%. However, if the gene is not inherited, there is no risk of passing the disorder to offspring. Approximately 2,500 autosomal dominant disorders have been identified or suspected (McKusick, 1988). Some commonly known examples are Huntington's disease, achondroplasia, tuberous sclerosis, and neurofibromatosis.

Autosomal recessive disorders occur when both parents pass the affected gene to their offspring. When both parents are carriers, the risk is 25% of passing the disorder to each offspring. At the present time there are approximately 1,500 known or suspected autosomal recessive disorders (McKusick, 1988), including cystic fibrosis, galactosemia, phenylketonuria, maple syrup urine disease, sickle cell anemia, and Tay-Sachs disease. Because the gene is recessive it is less likely to manifest the associated disorder than a dominant gene.

Chromosome Abnormalities. Certain chromosome anomalies or disorders are not inherited, rather, they occur if certain conditions are present. The best known of these is Down syndrome or trisomy 21, which occurs when an extra chromosome translocates and attaches itself to the 21st pair, causing the infant to display the characteristics associated with the syndrome.

Chromosome abnormalities may occur as a result of an abnormal number or an abnormal structure of the chromosomes. Problems of chromosome number include monosomies, trisomies, and mosaicisms. Problems of structure include deletions, additions, inversions, and translocations. Like genetic disorders, chromosome disorders can further be categorized according to whether they

Chromosome anomalies like Down syndrome involve the gain, loss or rearrangement of genetic material.

occur on the autosomes or the sex chromosomes. All of these problems are caused by an error in meiotic cell division and result in either too much or too little genetic material on the affected chromosome (Thomson, 1989). Most often, chromosome abnormalities are due to nondisjunction (lack of separation) of the paired chromosomes during meiosis. When nondisjunction occurs, both members of a chromosome pair go to an individual egg or sperm cell. The result is a cell with either a missing chromosome or one too many. When fertilization occurs, the zygote will have either a trisomy (47) or a monosomy (45). If the nondisjunction occurs after fertilization during mitotic cell division, the abnormality is labeled mosaicism, and only certain cells are affected.

Structural chromosome abnormalities involve the gain, loss, or rearrangement of some of the genetic material. When a chromosome acquires extra genetic material it is usually called a duplication, addition, or a partial trisomy. The loss of genetic material is usually referred to as a deletion or partial monosomy. Additions and deletions occur when a portion of one chromosome breaks off and is lost or becomes attached to another chromosome. An inversion occurs when there are two breaks in a single chromosome followed by reattachment, and the section of the chromosome between the breaks becomes inverted. The exchange of chromosome material between two chromosomes is called a translocation, and may result in either a balanced or unbalanced structural rearrangement (Thomson, 1989).

The most common chromosome anomaly is Down syndrome (Figure 3.4), which may occur as either nondisjunction trisomy 21 (95% of cases), translocation (4% of cases), or mosaicism (1% of cases). Other autosomal chromosome disorders are cri du chat syndrome, and trisomies 18 and 13. In the trisomies, children are born with multiple organ malformations that nearly always result in death during the first year. The survivors (20%) suffer severe mental retardation and failure to thrive (Thompson & Thompson, 1986). Sex chromosome anomalies include Klinefelter's syndrome and Turner's syndrome.

Certain maternal and paternal characteristics are statistically linked to chromosome abnormalities, namely, mother's or father's age over 35, previous birth of a child with a chromosomal disease, and identification of the mother as a translocation carrier (Legum, 1985).

Antenatal Screening and Genetic Counseling. Genetic counseling for parents who may be at risk of having a disabled infant is a major step forward in the early intervention field. The current procedures for antenatal screening are amniocentesis, chronic villus biopsy, fetoscopy, ultrasonography, and maternal serum alpha fetoprotein (ms-AFP). All are increasingly accurate, although some risk continues of false-negatives and false-positives, for detecting the primary disorders of Down syndrome, Tay-Sachs disease, Duchenne muscular dystrophy, and neural tube defects (spina bifida) as well as many of the low-incidence conditions (Legum, 1985). These screening procedures are described in Chapter 6.

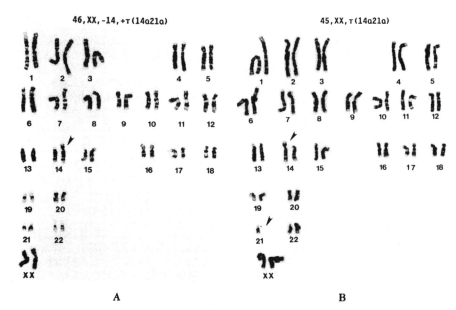

46,XX,-14,+т(14q21q)   45,XX,т(14q21q)

A   B

FIGURE 3.4   A. Karyotype of translocation trisomy 21 (Down syndrome). An extra
number 21 chromosome is attached to the number 14 (arrowhead)
chromosome. B. Karyotype of normal female with balanced translocation.
One of the number 21 (arrowhead) chromosomes is attached to the number 14
(arrowhead) chromosome. (From "A Genetics Primer" by E. J. Thomson.
Reprinted from Infants and Young Children, Vol. 2, No. 1, pp. 38–45, with
permission of Aspen Publishers, Inc. © 1989.)

Genetic counseling can assist prospective parents to avoid the risk of
genetic disorders, but chromosome abnormalities are much more difficult to
predict before conception. Antenatal screening techniques can play a role in
alerting parents of potential problems. Genetic counseling has evolved from
a purely informational service regarding reproductive risk to a diagnostic consultation and case-management approach for providing information, support,
and followup to families affected by birth defects and genetic disorders (Thomson, 1989).

Mother's Health and Behavior

In recent years much research has been conducted to determine what factors
related to the mother's behavior during pregnancy place the fetus at risk. It is
now well known that smoking and the use of alcohol may adversely affect fetal
development. Evidence is accumulating in regard to the deleterious effects of
other drugs such as methadone, heroin, amphetamines, and cocaine. In addition, the mother's age and general state of health and nutrition obviously have

an impact on the development of the fetus. Research also has shown that one very important maternal risk factor is the quality of prenatal care available.

Use of Drugs During Pregnancy

Alcohol. Because the effects of excess alcohol consumption during pregnancy are so harmful to the fetus and so predictable, causing low birthweight, mental and physical retardation, heart defects, and facial disfigurement, infants born with these characteristics are said to have *fetal alcohol syndrome*. This syndrome was first identified in the 1970s (Jones, Smith, Ulleland, & Streissguth, 1973; Shaywitz, Cohen, & Shaywitz, 1978). More recent studies have established that the central nervous system is particularly vulnerable to the effects of alcohol, with the most serious deficits occurring during the third trimester of pregnancy (Coles, Smith, Lancaster, & Falek, 1987). Infants born with fetal alcohol syndrome have been found to be slower to habituate as newborns (Streissguth, Martin, Barr, & Sandman, 1984) and to have poorer ratings on the Neonatal Behavioral Assessment Scale (NBAS) (Brazelton, 1984) as evidenced by less settled states and more abnormal reflexes (Coles, Smith, Fernhoff, & Falek, 1985).

Even when the mother stops drinking during the second trimester of pregnancy the infant is at risk for developmental delays. In a study of three groups of pregnant women, those who never drank, those who stopped during the second trimester, and those who drank throughout pregnancy, Coles et al. (1987) found differences in the infants' motor performance, autonomic regulation, and reflex behavior one month after birth. The third group of infants demonstrated the greatest impairments, and their performance was increasingly delayed from 3 to 30 days following birth. The second group, whose mothers stopped drinking midway through their pregnancies, also exhibited considerable delays. Only the babies whose mothers never drank had average or better performance ratings on the NBAS. Coles et al. (1987) reported real and persistent central nervous system damage to infants due to alcohol consumption during pregnancy.

Excess alcohol consumption sometimes causes the fetus to become dependent on alcohol in utero, resulting in withdrawal following birth. This condition is the *neonatal withdrawal syndrome* (NWS) (Coles, Smith & Falek, in press).

Studies of pregnant women who consume alcohol have revealed that they are also three times more likely to smoke cigarettes (but not marijuana) during the pregnancy than nondrinkers (Coles et al., 1987; Lancaster, Coles, Platzman, Smith, & Falek, in press). This increases the risk to the fetus. For example, Streissguth et al. (1984) found that children whose mothers smoked and consumed alcohol during pregnancy still exhibited impaired attention and reaction times at age 4.

Nicotine. Numerous studies over the past three decades have shown that infants born to mothers who smoke are small for gestational age, generally weighing about 200 g less than infants of nonsmokers. Between 20% and 40% of the incidence of low birthweight can be explained by smoking (Finnegan, 1985). The decrease in weight is directly related to the number of cigarettes smoked daily. The reduction in birthweight does not appear to be directly related to the smoker's lower weight gain (Finnegan, 1985).

In addition to greater fetal risk, maternal smoking is associated with higher rates of spontaneous abortion and perinatal mortality. According to information presented by Finnegan (1985) the rate for both is approximately double for smokers.

Caffeine. Although considered to be a less serious risk factor than either alcohol or nicotine, caffeine use during pregnancy has been found to be correlated with lower infant ratings in neuromuscular activity (hypotonia) and state (more irritable, less easily aroused and consoled) (Hronsky & Emory, 1987). Indeed, neuromuscular maturity in neonates is inversely related to the mother's caffeine consumption during pregnancy (Jacobson, Fein, Jacobson, Schwartz, & Dowler, 1984). This is particularly significant because 95% of American women drink coffee, and most do not stop during pregnancy (Hronsky & Emory, 1987). Caffeine crosses the placenta and reduces the blood flow to it. It also appears to elevate maternal serum epinephrine levels (Kirkinen et al., 1983). According to Lancaster et al. (in press), maternal use of alcohol, caffeine, and cigarettes has differential effects on prenatal growth and neonatal neurologic status, with alcohol causing the most damage and caffeine the least.

Heroin and Cocaine. Heroin and cocaine have recently come under scrutiny as their use among pregnant women appears to be increasing (Weston, Ivins, Zuckerman, Jones & Lopez, 1989). In a recent survey of hospitals nationwide conducted by the House Select Committee on Children, Youth, and Families, the number of drug-exposed newborns increased from 4% to 5% of total newborns in 1985 to 15% to 18% in 1988. In some hospitals one in six newborns is born addicted (Miller, G., 1989a). Half of the hospitals reporting stated that their figures underrepresented the prevalence of substance-abusing mothers. Infants born addicted must suffer withdrawal the same as infants born to alcoholics, and many experience neonatal withdrawal syndrome. Since some drugs are addictive, some toxic, and others teratogenic, drug-exposed infants may also suffer long-term injury or developmental delay (Jones & Lopez, 1988). Studies suggest that these infants have a higher chance of experiencing global developmental delay and physical handicaps and have striking deficits in representational play, manifested in a lack of self-organization, self-initiation and follow-through (Howard, 1989; Howard, Beckwith, Rodning, & Kropenske, 1989). In addition, these infants exhibit deviant attachment patterns, characterized by disorganization (Main & Solomon, 1986). Howard (1989) states that prenatal drug exposure increases the initial risk evident at birth by extending the organic, physiologic effects into emotional development (affect regulation), cognitive development (representation and symbolic play), and social development (organization of relationships). Those with a stable home environment following hospital release have a better developmental outcome at one year than those who do not, but few appear to have above average developmental potential (Howard, 1989).

Cocaine and methamphetamine taken during pregnancy appear to have similar effects on newborns, according to a study conducted at the University of California Medical Center, San Diego (Dixon, 1989). Neonatal outcomes included intrauterine growth retardation, decreased head circumference, preterm delivery with fetal distress, and anemia. The mothers in this study were in their mid-20s; most had received little or no prenatal care.

Drug-exposed infants are also at indirect risk from the mother's behavior. The types of drug-induced organic mental disorders that may affect mothers include maternal seizures following large drug doses; paranoid and suicidal ideation; violent or aggressive behavior; and delusions. In addition, mothers may have increased motor impairment which makes them accident prone, or respiratory depression following high doses that may be fatal. The need to find safer environments for these babies has led to a national shortage of foster care placements. In some regions drug-exposed babies account for 60% to 75% of foster care case loads, a situation that threatens to overload an already overtaxed system (Miller, G., 1989a).

Human Immunodeficiency Virus. Human immunodeficiency virus (HIV) infection in infants is tied to the mother's intravenous drug use. Currently 80% of HIV-infected children have a parent with acquired immune deficiency syndrome (AIDS) or AIDS-Related Complex (ARC), or who is at risk for AIDS (Falloon, Eddy, Warner, & Pizzo, 1989a).

Although the HIV virus appears to be nondiscriminatory, certain high-risk groups are more likely to become infected and to pass on the virus to their offspring. For example, a demographic breakdown from the Centers for Disease Control (CDC, 1988) reveals that 53% of pediatric AIDS patients are Black, 23% Hispanic, 24% Caucasian or other; 55% are males and 84% are under age 5. They are found primarily in New York (30.7%), New Jersey (13.4%), Florida (11.6%), and California (7.0%). In three quarters of the cases the source of the infection can be traced to perinatal transmission. This means that the mother was infected, either from intravenous (IV) drug use or from engaging in sex with an IV drug user. The most frequent high-risk behavior involved in the transmission of HIV virus is the sharing of contaminated needles in the course of IV drug use (Dokecki et al., 1989). In the remaining one quarter of cases the cause is due to either a coagulation disorder, hemophilia, or contaminated blood transfusions, or to an unknown cause (CDC, 1988).

The current crisis in health care is trying to provide adequate health, mental health, and social services to substance-exposed and HIV-infected infants and families in a time of shrinking federal commitment to such policies as drug abuse prevention and rehabilitation, and early intervention (Weston et al., 1989a). The Select Committee found, for example, that two thirds of the hospitals queried had no place to refer substance-abusing pregnant women for treatment (Miller, G., 1989a).

History of Poor Health. Several adverse health conditions of the mother are known to put the fetus at risk. Preexisting conditions such as diabetes, heart disease, or hypothyroidism, for example, place stress on the mother's body that may be passed on to the developing fetus. Exposure to infection such as rubella, cytomegalovirus (CMV), or influenza during the first trimester place the fetus at serious risk (Rossetti, 1986). Maternal rubella has been associated with multiple congenital malformations of the heart, eye, and ear; congenital heart disease; cataracts; and deafness (Holmes, Reich & Pasternak, 1984). CMV is associated with microcephaly, psychomotor retardation, and a high mortality rate (Bale et al., 1986).

A history of pregnancy problems such as repeated miscarriages, premature births, stillbirths, cervical incompetence, placental abnormalities, or intrauterine growth retardation increase the risk for the current pregnancy. Toxemia of pregnancy, in which toxic substances accumulate in the mother's bloodstream and are thus passed across the placenta to the fetus, obviously places the fetus at risk. Several risk conditions seen during pregnancy are unexplained, such as spontaneous abortion, abnormal bleeding, or premature rupture of membranes (Rossetti, 1986).

Socioeconomic Status. Socioeconomic status is an important factor in determining the infant's risk status. Mothers from low income environments may have difficulty maintaining optimal levels of nutrition and regular health care. Poor nutrition and lack of prenatal care are significant contributors to infant risk (Siegel, 1985) and are most common at lower income levels. In the United States mothers from minority backgrounds are more likely than not to belong to low income groups.

In the study by Cole et al. (1987) of alcohol consumption during pregnancy, it was found that all of those who continued drinking throughout pregnancy were single mothers who had significantly lower monthly incomes than nondrinking mothers. These women were at risk not only for their alcoholism but also for poor nutrition and lack of prenatal care, all associated with low socioeconomic status. Thus there appears to be an element of risk to the infant, statistically speaking, of being born to an unmarried mother.

Mother's Age. High rates of medical problems are found among the newborns of older mothers (over 36) and younger mothers (under 16) (Rossetti, 1986); some authors extend the risk to mothers under 20 (Holmes et al., 1984). For very young mothers, problems are especially likely if the woman is unmarried and has had previous pregnancies before age 20 (Peterson, 1987). The most common correlation between mother's age and infant status is birthweight, with low birthweight more commonly seen in these two age groups than in women ages 20 to 35 (Holmes et al., 1984). Additionally, the rate of teenage pregnancy is higher among nonwhite than white mothers. In a comparison of adolescent and older mothers, Culp, Appelbaum, Osofsky, and Levy (1988) found significant differences between the two groups in maternal psychosocial characteristics: adolescent mothers reported being less happy about their pregnancies, had less social support, and less support from the infant's father. Many of these mothers were unmarried, which added to their sense of isolation. All of these factors placed their infants at greater risk.

Availability of Prenatal Care. The United States is unique among developed countries of the world in not providing routine prenatal health care to all pregnant women. This fact, together with a general unavailability of maternal and paternal leave following the infant's birth, places a greater burden on low-income parents.

The risk to young infants from low-income families inherent in this lack of free prenatal care is illustrated by the development of Siegel's risk index (Siegel, 1985). The index, developed in Canada, includes risk factors for newborns in

Good prenatal care is the best prevention of birth defects.

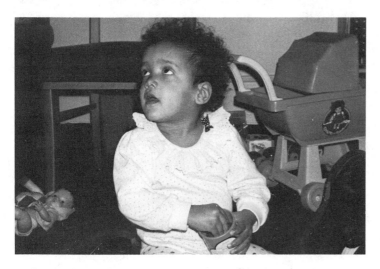

TABLE 3.2   **Siegel Newborn Risk Index Variables**

Reproductive Variables
  Gravidity (birth order)
  Amount of maternal smoking during pregnancy
  Number of previous spontaneous abortions

Perinatal Variables
  Birthweight
  Apgar scores (1-minute and 5-minute)
  Gestational age (if preterm)
  Severity of respiratory distress (if preterm)
  Severity of birth asphyxia (if preterm)
  Severity of apnea (if preterm)

Demographic Variables
  Socioeconomic status
  Sex
  Mother's educational level
  Father's educational level

Adapted from "Biological and Environmental Variables as Predictors of Intellectual Functioning at 6 Years of Age" by L. Siegel, 1985. In S. Havel and N.J. Anastasiow (Eds.), *The At-Risk Infant: Psycho/socio/medical Aspects,* Baltimore: Brookes.

three categories: reproductive, perinatal, and demographic (Table 3.2). When the index was exported to the United States for use with preterm and low birthweight infants born in American hospitals, a new factor had to be added, namely, lack of prenatal care. This fact illustrates the importance of adequate prenatal care in preventing later developmental delays.

In summary, the at-risk infant is likely to be sick, small, inactive, male, and nonwhite. He is also likely to have a mother who is poor, under age 20, unmarried, and living in an urban environment (Holmes et al., 1984). It is also likely that the mother did not receive adequate prenatal care during her pregnancy, and that she used drugs of some sort at the time.

CASE STUDY: ALICE

Alice had her first baby when she was 16 years old. "Believe it or not, I got pregnant my first time having intercourse, when I was 15 years old. When I found out, I was very angry at myself for being so stupid. I kept thinking, this is not happening to me, but it was. I was scared to tell my parents, and I was worried to death about what my boyfriend would say."

As it turned out, her boyfriend, too, was scared when he found out, and stopped seeing Alice, saying he was too young to get married. "He wanted me to have an abortion," Alice said. "But I didn't know where to go or who to talk to about it, and I just couldn't face it alone. By the time my parents found out about the pregnancy, it was too late to think about an abortion. And my mom said she'd help me through having the baby, and taking care of it after it was born. And she did. I love my baby and I'm really glad now that I didn't have an abortion."

Alice's baby was born four weeks before term, and weighed only 4 pounds at birth. "He was kept at the hospital in a special nursery for the first three weeks after he was born, until he weighed enough for us to bring him home. He didn't have any serious medical problems, thank goodness. I guess I was lucky. But it was hard to breast-feed him. I had to use a breast pump and take the milk to the hospital for him. They let me visit him every day, though. My dad would drive me over."

Alice is still living at home with her mother and father. She dropped out of school to have the baby, and didn't return after the birth. Now she works nights at a fast food restaurant to help support herself and her 2-year-old son, and takes care of him during the day. Her mother has a full-time job during the day, but takes care of the child in the evening and helps Alice on weekends. "I don't know where I'd be if it weren't for mom and dad. They've been wonderful to both of us."

CASE STUDY: CYNTHIA

Cynthia had a different experience. "I'd been fighting with my mother as long as I could remember. One of my girlfriends had a baby and it seemed like fun. I did drugs by the time I was 10. I started having sex at 11. School was a drag. When you have a baby, you're an adult. Nobody tells you what to do or when to do it. That kid was going to be my road to freedom and ticket to independence. So I quit school and had the kid. But being a mother is hard work. I sure didn't think it would be like this."

Cynthia had her first baby at 14, her second a year later. Neither of the fathers was a good candidate for marriage, being very young, unemployed, and still in school. During the second pregnancy she was using drugs again, mainly amphetamines and alcohol. She smoked quite heavily during both pregnancies and had no prenatal care. Her second child was born preterm with low birthweight and with serious problems. These included respiratory distress, anemia, hyperbilirubinemia, mild mental retardation, and cerebral palsy. "Jamie had to stay in the hospital intensive care nursery for two months. It meant I couldn't breast-feed him, which I wanted to do. I couldn't get up to see him very often because I don't have a car, and the buses are practically nonexistent in this town. Besides, I had to take care of Melissa. There's really no one to help me out. My mother and I barely speak to each other any more."

Cynthia manages to support herself and her two children with Aid to Families with Dependent Children (AFDC). Melissa is in kindergarten this year. Jamie now is 3 and attends a special education preschool for children with developmental delays. A bus picks him up three mornings a week and brings him home again. Every other week Cynthia goes with him and spends the morning helping out in the preschool. She enjoys these visits and is thinking about finishing school so she could get a full-time job in a school like Jamie's. "But *it's hard to go back to school when you're nearly 19-years-old and the oldest person in the class. Besides, what would I do with Melissa and Jamie? I'd sure like to have a job, though."*

After Jamie was born Cynthia attended a program at her neighborhood church to try to get off drugs, saying she didn't want to ruin her children's lives. She has managed to quit taking amphetamines, and has cut down on her drinking. She has also learned about birth control. "I know it's kinda late, but I've gone on the Pill. I wish I'd known about it earlier. But then I guess I wouldn't have these two darling children. And I do love them, you know, even though it's hard raising them on my own."

PERINATAL PERIOD

Risk factors associated with the perinatal period include medical factors during delivery and those associated with prematurity or low birthweight.

Perinatal Anoxia and Other Birth Complications

Perinatal asphyxia, anoxia, and hypoxia all refer to an inadequate supply of oxygen to the brain of the developing fetus or infant sometime during the perinatal period. Various causes may be identified including, for example, umbilical cord injury during delivery, respiratory distress due to underdeveloped lungs, or a fall in arterial blood pressure, which reduces cerebral blood flow in the developing fetus (Lou, 1985).

Perinatal anoxia affects both full-term and preterm infants. Brann (1985) reported a group of full-term infants with a history of perinatal asphyxia whose death rate was 7% and whose incidence of neurologic handicaps was 28%. Cerebral palsy is the most common disorder resulting from oxygen deprivation in the brain (Brann, 1985).

Prematurity

Infants born before 37 weeks gestation are classified as preterm, according to the recommendation of the World Health Organization (Rossetti, 1986). Several methods may be used for calculating gestational age. The most common method remains the obstetric history, based on the mother's self-report and the obstetric examination. Recent technological developments have made possible the use of ultrasound and amniocentesis for determining gestational age, as well as for screening for potential birth complications and infant disabilities.

Several risk factors are associated with prematurity. Primary among them are jaundice, intraventricular hemorrhage, hyalin membrane disease, and cardiovascular disorder. The most prevalent illnesses experienced by preterm infants are those associated with the respiratory system. Because the lungs are among the last organs to develop in the fetus, they are often underdeveloped at young gestational ages and place the infant at grave risk for death, disability, or developmental delay.

Low Birthweight. Infants born weighing less than 2,500 g are considered to be at risk. The greatest risk category is small for gestational age (SGA), since it implies that a serious developmental complication occurred during pregnancy which hindered the fetus from attaining normal size and weight for its age. Medical and physical characteristics of preterm and low birthweight infants are discussed in Chapter 4.

Perinatal AIDS. Perinatal AIDS (caused by HIV transmission in utero or during the birth process) is rapidly becoming a major problem in the United States. The rate of newly identified cases of full-blown pediatric AIDS (AIDS contracted by children under age 13) has virtually doubled every year since 1981 (Dokecki, Baumeister & Kupstas, 1989). This figure does not include infants and children who are HIV-infected but not symptomatic. Of the total number who had been diagnosed with full-blown AIDS, more than half died by 1988 (Dokecki et al., 1989).

Contamination of the fetus occurs in utero through transplacental passage of maternal blood or during delivery through neonatal contact with maternal blood or vaginal fluids (Dokecki et al., 1989). Rubinstein and Bernstein (1986) have presented evidence to suggest that fetal infection takes place as early as the first trimester.

The prognosis for perinatal and pediatric AIDS is poor. When compared with adults, progression from HIV infection to ARC to full-blown AIDS is much more rapid in young children (Rubenstein & Bernstein, 1986). The list of symptomatic infections associated with pediatric AIDS is a long one, including recurrent bacterial infections, hepatitis, renal disease, encephalopathy, gastrointestinal disorders, and pneumonia. Children appear to manifest more severe cognitive and motor delays, frequently accompanied by diminished brain growth (Dokecki et al., 1989). Although research continues to search for a vaccine for AIDS, success is not expected for 5 to 10 years. Meantime, the emphasis must be placed on prevention.

POSTNATAL PERIOD

Factors that can affect the infant's risk status following birth include the mother's and infant's quality of nutrition (especially if the mother is nursing), availability of well baby or hospital-based health care, and the socioeconomic status of the family, including whether the father is living with the family and available to the mother for support. But foremost is the infant's general state of health. Inherited genetic conditions which place the infant at risk to begin with, such as Down syndrome or cystic fibrosis, are only complicated by health problems such as respiratory disorders or food allergies. Similarly, a child born before term and below average size and weight is more susceptible to infections.

Evidence exists that children with developmental delays are more at risk for child abuse and neglect than normally developing children (Anastasiow, 1988). A common form of abuse found in newborns and infants, usually unintentional on the parent's part, is shaking by the shoulders. This is usually done to attempt to stop the infant from crying and may cause intraventricular hemorrhaging resulting in brain damage. Fragile infants are obviously at greater risk of injury from such treatment.

DETERMINING DEGREE OF RISK

The concept of multiple-variable risk is a relatively new one in the field of early intervention. With the introduction of the terms *reproductive risk* and *caretaking casualty* by Sameroff and Chandler (1975), professionals in psychology and education began looking at nonmedical factors that might place a child at risk for developmental delay. Sameroff and Chandler (1975) proposed a continuum of caretaking casualty to illustrate the fact that the degree of risk in infancy cannot accurately predict later developmental outcomes, because socioeconomic and familial factors may outweigh or overshadow biological factors. Since that time, greater attention has been given to the entire range of risk variables, including genetic factors, socioeconomic factors, health factors, and child abuse (e.g., Cicchetti & Toth, 1987; Sameroff, 1989).

Screening Techniques

One of the most important areas of study in the prevention of physical and mental handicaps in young children is the development of screening techniques which can accurately identify those who are at risk for later difficulties. Of particular interest are the high-incidence, low-severity problems such as learning disabilities, behavior difficulties, and mild delays in intellectual functioning that are economically and psychologically costly but that may be ameliorated if remediation is provided early in development.

Several authors have attempted to develop risk indices for use with infants which accurately predict achievement in later childhood (Broman, Nichols & Kennedy, 1975; Ramey, Stedman, Borders-Patterson & Mengel, 1978; Littman & Parmelee, 1978). More recently, Siegel (1985) has developed such an index containing 13 variables in three categories (see Table 3.2) which has been relatively successful in predicting cognitive and language delays at ages 2, 3, 5, and 6. The index appears to be a better predictor of later IQ scores than various infant IQ tests (Siegel, 1985).

Siegel's index is based on the concept of *cumulative* or *multiple risk factors*. Like other authors (e.g., Keogh & Kopp, 1978; Bee, Barnard, Eyres, Gray, Hammond, Spietz, Snyder, & Clark, 1982), Siegel argues that risk is not due to a single factor but to a variety of biological and environmental factors.

Incidence of High-Risk Infants

The most commonly used indicators of risk are birthweight and gestational age. The following statistics are based on that definition. The advent of the NICU has greatly modified the concept of risk, since many more infants now survive due to the environment it provides immediately following birth.

Before the advent of the NICU the risk of neonatal death was 30 times greater for low birthweight infants (Rossetti, 1986). Between 1958 and 1968 the neonatal mortality rate was 23 deaths per 1,000 births; by 1973 it had dropped to 15 per 1,000, and the current infant mortality rate in the United States is 10 per 1,000. It should be noted that the infant mortality rate is considerably lower than the neonatal rate because it includes infants up to age 12 months. There are three times more deaths in the neonatal period than in the postneonatal period (28 days to 11 months), with the highest number occurring on the first day, followed by the first week after birth (Rossetti, 1986).

The effect of the NICU has been to reduce the neonatal mortality rate but, at the same time, to increase the number of surviving infants who are at risk for developmental delays. Saving very small and very sick infants results in a greater incidence of handicapping conditions. Table 3.3 shows the proportion of low birthweight infants who survived due to NICU treatment.

Estimates of the incidence of high-risk infants range from 5% to 15% of all newborns (Rosetti, 1986), depending on classification criteria. The inclusion of congenital anomalies in the description helps to differentiate between earlier and later babies, with the incidence of anomalies at 2.3% for babies born at 40 or 41 weeks, and 30% for babies born before 28 weeks (Rossetti, 1986).

Infants at risk for delay also tend to come from nonwhite families, and this fact is in turn related to socioeconomic status. For example, low birthweight occurred in about 6% of white babies born in the United States in 1977 and in about 13% of black babies. Black infant and neonatal mortality rates are also twice those of white rates (Holmes et al., 1984). These statistics reflect the lack of prenatal care available to low-income families in the United States, as well as the risk factors related to mother's age and behavior during pregnancy.

TABLE 3.3   Infant Mortality Rates by Birthweight Categories

BIRTH WEIGHT	MORTALITY RATE
600–700 g	70%
700–800 g	63%
800–900 g	64%
900–1000 g	32%

Note: *From Infants at Risk for Developmental Dysfunction* (p. 78) by D. Parson and L. Eisenberg (Eds.), 1982, Washington, D.C.: National Academy Press. Copyright 1982 by National Academy Press. Reprinted by permission.

Survival by Birthweight (BW) Categories for Three Time Periods

BW/YEARS	BORN	SURVIVED	% SURVIVED
<750g			
1965–69	8	0	0
1970–75	12	1	8.3
1976–81	27	6	22.2
750–1000 g			
1965–69	26	7	26.9
1970–75	24	6	25.0
1976–81	77	46	59.7
1001–1250 g			
1965–69	31	17	54.8
1970–75	41	29	70.7
1976–81	81	70	86.4
1251–1500 g			
1965–69	35	21	60.0
1970–75	51	41	80.4
1976–81	104	97	93.3

Note: *From* "Learning Disabilities in Children with Birth Weights Less Than 1500 Grams" by Jo Hunt, W. Tooley, and D. Harvin, 1982, *Seminars in Perinatology, 6,* p. 280. Copyright 1982 by Grune & Stratton, Inc. Reprinted by permission.

According to a recently conducted national natality survey (Miller, G., 1989b), the number of women receiving prenatal care in this country declined between 1980 and 1982, despite slight increases in the number of births. The decline was greatest among pregnant women who were least educated, unmarried, younger than 18 years, and black. This finding is troubling in the light of evidence that good prenatal care could reverse these statistics. It is especially troubling given the U.S. Surgeon General's call for an increase in services by 1990 to ensure that 90% of women of all ages, ethnic, and income groups receive appropriate prenatal care beginning in the first trimester (Miller, G., 1989b).

Suggestions for Further Reading

GREENSPAN, S. I., et al. (Eds.). (1987). *Infants in multirisk families: Case studies in preventive intervention.* Clinical Infant Report No. 3 of the National Center for Clinical Infant Programs. Madison, CN: International Universities Press.

HAREL, S., and ANASTASIOW, N. (Eds.). (1985). *The at-risk infant: Psycho/socio/medical aspects.* Baltimore: Paul H. Brookes.

OSOFSKY, J. D. (Ed.) (1987). *Handbook of infant development* (2nd ed.). New York: John Wiley & Sons.

Chapter 4

Developmental Disorders in Infancy

Infants who are environmentally, genetically, or medically at risk for developmental disorders may encounter problems in any of several areas. First, there may be problems associated with the birth process itself, such as respiratory distress or jaundice. Infants born at higher altitudes may have lower than expected birthweights. Other medical problems may occur such as craniosynostosis, metabolic problems, gastrointestinal problems, infections, or intraventricular hemorrhage. Developmental disorders may affect the neuromotor system, as in cerebral palsy, seizure disorder, or spina bifida. Congenital disorders may result in Down syndrome, galactosemia, Tay-Sachs disease, or other syndromes and disorders. Other problems may affect the young child's cognitive, communicative, or social/emotional development. Although these problems are seen in full-term as well as preterm and low birthweight infants, this chapter focuses on the concerns and issues in treating at-risk or handicapped infants.

The information contained in this chapter represents important background knowledge for all members of the multidisciplinary team. Although some of it may seem to be specifically the concern of health professionals, psychologists or phypsical therapists, it is important that the infant's developmental problems are understood by all team members who provide intervention, and that these problems are taken into account when planning the IFSP. Sharing developmental and health-related information freely among team members can facilitate the creation of meaningful transdisciplinary team interactions, from which team members and clients alike can benefit.

HEALTH-RELATED PROBLEMS

Many of the health problems of preterm infants may be related to developmental disorders during infancy and early childhood. These include respiratory distress syndrome or bronchopulmonary dysplasia, cardiovascular dysfunction, metabolic disorders, and anoxia. If a shortage of oxygen to the brain occurs, mental retardation may result. In addition, respiratory or cardiovascular difficulties often accompany other handicapping conditions such as Down syndrome, fetal alcohol syndrome, or cystic fibrosis (see Chapter 5 and the sections on congenital and cognitive disorders in this chapter).

Failure to Thrive

Failure to Thrive describes infants who, for a number of possible reasons, fail to gain weight within the normally expected range. Some infants actually lose weight after they leave the hospital; others fail to gain at a fast enough rate. Babies who are confined to the hospital for long periods following birth due to other health-related problems may have feeding problems that put them at risk for failure to thrive due to poor weight gain. The poor weight gain may be due to one of several factors, but often is related to the mother's inability to provide sufficient nourishment in her breast milk. In that case the infant may simply need a formula supplement. Alternatively, the infant may have digestive problems that account for poor weight gain. Table 4.1 presents a summary of both life-threatening and general symptoms for failure to thrive syndrome, which can indeed lead to the infant's death if left undiagnosed and untreated.

Infections

Infants who are considered to be medically fragile are more prone to infection than other infants; this is also true of low birthweight and SGA infants. In the United States the greatest risk of infection is from staphylococcus and streptococcus bacteria, while throughout developing countries there still exists a high risk from tuberculosis.

TABLE 4.1   **Failure to Thrive Syndrome Symptoms**

Life-threatening symptoms
Severe dehydration
Low body temperature
Slow heart rate
Low blood sugar
Greater than 15% weight loss from birth
Seizures
Listlessness

General failure-to-thrive symptoms
Dehydration
Urate crystals appearing as "brick dust" on the diaper after 3 days
Infrequent bowel movements (fewer than four per day by 5–7 days of age)
Unexplained jaundice after several days of phototherapy treatment
Inappropriate weight and height gain; inadequate subcutaneous fat layer
Colic symptoms
Chewing on hands
Fussy after eating
Overly placid
High sucking need, frequent use of pacifier
Described by mother as having "finished nursing; baby can't be hungry"
Quits being hungry
Does not nurse from both breasts

Risk indicators in mothers
Abnormal appearing breasts or nipples
Previous breast surgery
Extremely sore nipples
Flat or inverted nipples
Previous infant(s) with insufficient weight gain
Milk that has not "come in" by four days after birth
Systemic illness (e.g., diabetes, hypertension)
Feeling that breast-feeding is not going well at the time of discharge
Requiring more assistance from nursing staff than time permits

Note: From Lactation Program, St. Luke's Hospital, Denver, CO. Reprinted by permission.

Cytomegalovirus (CMV) belongs to the herpes virus group, which also includes herpes simplex virus, varicella-zoster virus (the chicken pox–shingles virus), and the Epstein-Barr virus (the virus that causes infectious mononucleosis). These viruses are grouped together because of their common structure and similar biologic behavior. They result from contact with another infected human being.

Like other viral infections, CMV is found throughout the world. In the United States approximately 1% to 2% of newborns excrete CMV in their urine. Thereafter, CMV is steadily acquired throughout life, and nearly all adults have been infected with CMV by the time they are age 50 (Bale, Blackman, Murph, & Andersen, 1986).

Although infected, few infants with CMV exhibit symptoms at birth, although 10% to 15% will later develop some degree of hearing loss, and another 10% to 15% will develop *cytomegalic inclusion disease (CID)*, a serious congenital illness occurring in approximately one of every 1,000 newborns (Bale et al., 1986). Symptoms of CID include damaged heart, lungs, liver, spleen, or other organs, damage to the developing nervous system including the brain, and sensory impairment leading to blindness or deafness.

Although nearly everyone eventually acquires CMV infection, usually in a mild form, pregnant women who have not previously been exposed to the virus are in particular danger. The fetus in such cases is at risk for CID and its serious consequences. It should be remembered, however, that since the virus is so commonly found, particularly in day-care and preschool settings, isolating an infected infant is not warranted (Bale et al., 1986).

Neonatal herpes simplex virus (HSV) is related to the CMV virus, and is transmitted from mother to fetus in a similar manner. HSV causes very serious problems in the neonate, and may cause death. Mortality rates have declined in recent years with antiviral drug therapy; however, infants who survive usually suffer severe complications such as cerebral palsy, sensory impairment, or mental retardation (Blackman, Andersen, Healy, & Zehrbach, 1985).

In the newborn the effects of HSV can range from simple skin disease to more serious neurologic damage. Type 2 infection, sexually transmitted and causing genital lesions, is usually the kind found in newborns. It is contracted at birth as the neonate passes through a lower genital tract colonized with the virus. Birth by cesarian section is therefore prescribed for mothers known to be infected. Type 1 infection causes oral lesions and is seen in some infants in the form of primary gingivostomatitis of infancy (Blackman et al., 1985).

The greatest risk for infants from HSV infections is during the first postnatal month. Beyond one month of age, the risk of serious disease is low.

Gastrointestinal (Feeding) Problems

Infants who are at risk or who have multiple handicapping conditions may have difficulty in maintaining adequate nutrition. Infants with developmental delays and related health problems are most often below average in weight and therefore have a greater need for successful feeding than other babies. Weight gain is an indicator of stable growth and is often a criterion for dismissal from the intensive care unit. Special feeding problems for these babies are associated with a poorly developed gastrointestinal tract, which makes weight gain especially difficult.

In addition to difficulty with sucking, chewing, and swallowing, they often have *gastroesophageal reflux (GER)*, a condition that can cause vomiting and aspiration of food into the lungs. Gastroesophageal reflux occurs when the muscle sphincter of the lower esophagus, which normally prevents food from backing up (reflux) from the stomach into the esophagus, is weak. The gagging and vomiting that result cause considerable discomfort and prevent the infant from obtaining adequate nutrition (Orenstein, Whittington & Orenstein, 1983). Risk of aspiration in these infants and inability of formula to reach the stomach may seriously interfere with feeding. In addition, neuromuscular involvement of the oral and pharyngeal musculature can hinder oral feeding and thus cause inadequate intake. Finally, structural anomalies or diseases of the bowel may lead to the need for nutrition provided directly into the bloodstream (Nelson & Hallgren, 1989).

For infants with these problems, nonoral nutrition is often implemented through surgical insertion of a gastrostomy tube or catheter into the infant's abdomen or stomach wall, through which feedings can be administered. The catheter is not sutured to the stomach or skin, so it can be removed and replaced easily, even between feedings if the opening in the stomach wall is a permanent one (Figure 4.1).

Several gavage methods may be used with the gastrostomy catheter, either hand-controlled syringe, gravity-controlled bag, or mechanical pump. In each instance the formula passes from the syringe or bag and flows through the

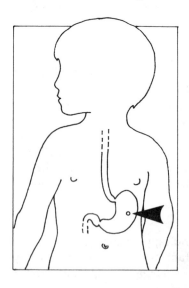

FIGURE 4.1.   The surgically created gastrostomy fistula is usually placed midway between the navel and the left nipple (arrowhead). (Note: *From* "Gastrostomies: Indications, Management, and Weaning" by C. L. Nelson and R. A. Hallgren. Reprinted from *Infants and Young Children*, Vol. 2, No. 1, pp. 68–69, with permission of Aspen Publishers, Inc. © 1989.)

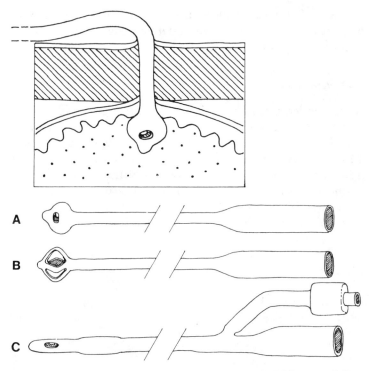

FIGURE 4.2.   Gastrostomy catheters: A, de Pezzer; B, Malecot; and C, Foley. (Note: *From* "Gastrostomies: Indications, Management, and Weaning" by C. L. Nelson and R. A. Hallgren. Reprinted from *Infants and Young Children,* Vol. 2, No. 1, pp. 68–69, with permission of Aspen Publishers, Inc. © 1989.)

gastrostomy tube into the stomach. Figure 4.2 illustrates three types of catheters and how the catheter is inserted into the stomach through the fistula. While feeding is a somewhat slower process with the gravity-controlled method, it is the most comfortable for the infant, since gagging and vomiting are avoided (Nelson & Hallgren, 1989).

Sometimes children with GER require antireflux surgery to improve the function of the lower esophageal sphincter. The operation is often performed at the same time as the gastrostomy surgery (Nelson & Hallgren, 1989).

Craniosynostosis

The infant born with craniosynostosis has a skull in which the opening to allow for normal growth is sealed. Since there is not enough room for the brain to expand as it grows, the infant is at risk for brain damage and retardation. Treatment consists of surgery to open the seam between the two halves of the brain to permit normal growth. This usually allows the infant to develop normally. The cause of craniosynostosis is unknown, but relatively high incidence rates in certain communities would suggest that the cause is environmental.

Infants Born at High Altitudes

There is accumulating evidence (Moore & Reeves, 1983; Liebson, Brown & Moore, 1986) that there are increased developmental risks for infants born at altitudes at or above 10,000 feet. Infant mortality is nearly two times greater at high altitudes (Moore & Regensteiner, 1983). Many of the problems exhibited by such infants are related to their lower than average birthweight. These include respiratory problems, susceptibility to infection, and gastrointestinal problems. In addition, elevated bilirubin levels (jaundice) are found in four times as many infants born at high altitudes than at sea level (Moore et al., 1984).

SENSORY DISORDERS

This category includes hearing and vision impairment as well as problems with vestibular and tactile development.

Hearing Impairment

Hearing impairment covers the entire range of auditory impairment, from mild hearing loss to deafness. *Deafness* is defined as the threshold below which human speech cannot be understood (Hallahan & Kaufman, 1982). Other levels of hearing impairment are defined in terms of decibels of hearing loss. Children are usually diagnosed as having a mild, moderate, severe, or profound loss according to the range of pitch (frequency, measured in Hertz or Hz) and loudness (intensity, measured in decibels or db) they can hear. The pitch of the human voice in normal speech falls within a range of 500 to 2,000 Hertz, and most hearing tests are conducted within that range. Levels of hearing loss within that Hertz range are determined according to the following criteria:

Normal hearing:	1–25 db
Mild hearing loss:	26–54 db
Moderate hearing loss:	55–69 db
Severe hearing loss:	70–89 db
Profound hearing loss:	90 db or more

A child with a mild hearing loss can understand speech when spoken to face to face but has some difficulty with normal conversations. The child with a moderate loss has difficuclty with normal conversations, especially if there is background noise, but can understand amplified speech. The child with a

Hearing loss can lead to language delay. Early prescrip-
tion of a hearing aid can often prevent serious language
delay.

severe loss will have difficulty even with amplified speech and will probably
require some type of augmented communication. If the hearing loss is profound,
there will be little if any ability to hear speech sounds, even if they are amplified
(Thurman & Widerstrom, 1990).

Whether a hearing loss is mild or severe is often related to the type of
loss experienced by the child. Hearing losses are categorized by their location
in the ear.

Conductive hearing loss is the result of damage or of a structural problem in the outer or middle ear, often caused by infections in the middle ear,
known as *otitis media.* The infection causes an excess of fluid to accumulate
in the eustachian tube that blocks sounds from traveling to the inner ear and
the auditory nerve. Conductive hearing losses are the easiest to treat, and both
medical and surgical procedures, including draining fluids from the eustachian
tubes, may be indicated. Usually the child with a conductive loss responds well
to hearing aids, and often hearing can be restored to nearly normal ranges.

Sensorineural hearing loss is a more serious problem. This type of loss
occurs in the inner ear or the auditory nerve leading to the brain. The function
of the inner ear is to transform sound waves received from the outer and middle ear into electrochemical impulses capable of being processed by the brain.
These are sent to the brain by way of the auditory nerve. Sensorineural damage
may be caused by illness, high fever, drugs, or congenital birth defects. Such
losses do not respond well to hearing aids, and damage is usually permanent
and difficult to treat.

Recently a surgical procedure has been developed that offers hope to children with sensorineural hearing losses. Cochlear implants are available to both children and adults who suffer damage to the cochlea, the part of the inner ear where sound waves are transformed to electrochemical impulses. An artificial cochlea is implanted in the inner ear, replacing the damaged one. Initial reports of the success of this procedure have been favorable.

Testing for hearing loss can be carried out with great accuracy today, both for infants and 2- to 3-year-olds. Hearing tests for infants are conducted by means of auditory-evoked responses (AER), in which changes in brain waves are recorded at the same time auditory stimulation is presented to the infant. This method does not depend on conscious response by the infant to auditory input and is therefore relatively accurate. Many NICUs currently test all children immediately prior to discharge (Hayes, 1986). For older children (ages 2 to 3) a combination of behavioral and physiological measures are used. To test behavioral audiometry, the audiologist observes responses to both noise signals and speech. Testing may be conducted in a play situation, and the child is rein-

FIGURE 4.3.   Pre- and post-treatment behavioral audiogram from a 6-year-old boy with recurrent otitis media with effusion. This audiogram was obtained by conditioned play audiometry. Pretreatment audiogram shows mild bilateral conductive hearing loss. Following treatment (insertion of pressure-equalizing tubes in the tympanic membrane) the pure tone audiogram is normal (ANSI-69: American National Standards Institute 1969 standard for audiometric normal hearing). (Note: From "Audiological Assessment" by D. Hayes. In D. L. Wodrich & J. E. Joy (Eds.), *Multidisciplinary Assessment of Children with Learning Disabilities and Mental Retardation* (p. 123). Copyright 1986 by Paul H. Brookes. Reprinted by permission.)

forced visually or with food for responding to test items. An audiogram is plotted for each ear (Figure 4.3).

The greater the child's hearing loss, the greater will be potential language deficits. Due to the inability to hear speech sounds, the child with a severe or profound hearing loss will have little or no intelligible speech. The child with a mild or moderate loss may have some articulation problems, also. But the greatest disability will be in the area of normal language development, that is, learning to employ correctly the form, content, and uses of language. Because learning oral language is so difficult for most hearing impaired children, many speech/language professionals advocate teaching the child sign language as part of a total communication program (Ling, 1984).

Visual Impairment

The eyes develop from outgrowths of the forebrain, differentiating prenatally into specialized sensory organs that are nearly fully developed in the typical infant at term. Because the eyes develop from the brain, their growth and development in early childhood parallel that of the brain, resulting in an enormous increase in size during the first 3 years of life (Thurman & Widerstrom, 1990). By age 15, the child's eyes have tripled in size, with three fourths of this growth occurring in the first 3 years.

Several conditions may cause visual problems for infants. Symptoms may include redness, swelling, or watering of the eyes, extreme sensitivity to light, or squinting or frowning. The infant may be inattentive to visual stimuli, neglect to make eye contact, or be unresponsive to interactions with adults.

Most infants are *hyperopic* or far-sighted, a condition that worsens to about age 3, remains constant to age 7, and then gradually improves. About 25% of infants are *myopic* or near-sighted; these infants must be monitored for possible fitting of glasses or contact lenses. The initial fitting of contact lenses is often done under general anesthesia, and parents must be prepared to cope with the stress of the child's adjustment period.

The other refractive error commonly seen in young children is *astigmatism*, which prevents the accurate focusing of the retinal image. Astigmatism may be either hyperopic or myopic.

Amblyopia, a reduction in visual acuity, is commonly referred to as a lazy eye, since it interferes with the eye's fusional reflexes, preventing it from focusing with the other eye. With amblyopia the infant's eyes appear to be crossed.

Strabismus is caused by the imbalance of the eye muscles, causing the eyes not to focus together. Forms of childhood strabismus include *pseudostrabismus*, an apparent crossing of the eyes in infancy that disappears with age, and *manifest strabismus*, a misalignment of the eyes that results in either *esotropia* (cross-eyed, or turning in of the eyes) or *exotropia* (wall-eyed, or turning out of the eyes). Exotropia, the most common type of childhood strabismus, should be identified by 6 months so that corrective lenses, or in some cases surgery, may be prescribed as early as possible. Sometimes strabismus is associated with conditions such as Down or Turner's syndrome. In such cases the eyes are often severely crossed, do not respond well to glasses, and require early surgery. Strabismus and amblyopia often occur together, and one often causes the other (Thurman & Widerstrom, 1990).

Leukokoria refers to the presence of a white pupil in the child's eye. It can have several causes, including cataracts and retrolental fibroplasia, or it can indicate the presence of a malignant retinal tumor known as *retinoblastoma.*

Retinoblastomas usually occur in only one eye. A small number are genetic in origin. Treatment consists of removal of the tumor, followed by radiation or chemotherapy. With early detection, the prognosis for unilateral cases is good.

Retinopathy of prematurity (ROP) or retrolental fibroplasia (RFP), results in visual impairment from a detached retina due to the administration of oxygen to premature infants. The incidence of ROP has greatly decreased as hospital staff have learned to carefully monitor the amounts of oxygen administered to high-risk infants. (For more information about ROP, see Chapter 5.)

Like strabismus, *glaucoma* occurs in many forms in young children. The most serious is congenital and causes blindness through excess accumulation of intraocular fluid, which causes pressure on the eyeball. Primary congenital glaucoma is usually diagnosed early in infancy. It responds well to treatment, which consists in draining excess fluid from the eye by means of a surgically created drainage channel.

A *cataract* is any opacity in the eye's lens. It may or may not lower visual acuity, depending on its size and location. Several types of cataracts are hereditary (usually autosomal dominant), and they may also be associated with medical problems such as maternal rubella, galactosemia, diabetes mellitus, and Down syndrome.

Cataracts in children may now be removed as early as 4 to 6 months of age, if there exists a visual disability. The infant is then fitted with contact lenses.

The primary educational need of infants with serious visual impairments is for gross motor training. Infants blind from birth generally experience significant developmental delays (Adelson & Fraiberg, 1975).

Tactile Defensiveness

Infants with developmental disorders may suffer from impairments in other sensory modalities. Tactile defensiveness, for example, is commonly seen in infants with cerebral palsy, resulting from the same brain lesion responsible for the motor disabilities. Damage to the sensory-motor strip of the brain may result in distortion of tactile input, causing the infant to resist tactile stimulation of any kind. If, indeed, such damage exists, infants with a variety of brain-damage-related conditions will exhibit tactile defensiveness to varying degrees. Some tactile input is generally better tolerated than others, namely firm as opposed to soft handling, warm rather than cold stimulation, and smooth rather than rough fabric. Many infants with physiologically based mental retardation have feeding problems compounded by tactile defensiveness of the oral area.

NEUROMOTOR DISORDERS

Disorders which affect the central nervous system and the child's motor functioning include cerebral palsy, spina bifida, muscular dystrophy, and seizure disorder. Although they vary in cause or etiology, they are alike in limiting the child's ability to achieve normal motor functioning.

Infants with neuromotor disorders may also suffer from problems in the vestibular system. This sensory system is based in the inner ear, and is responsible for balance and maintenance of upright posture. Damage to the vestibular system causes disorientation, dizziness, and sometimes the inability to process higher level sensory information. Infants with vestibular problems have difficulty in developing righting and equilibrium reactions and may exhibit delays in motor development generally.

Cerebral Palsy

Cerebral palsy is a general term given to nonprogressive brain lesions that cause motor impairments. The lesion or damage may occur in any of several areas of the brain and be due to a variety of causes. The lesion is nonprogressive because it does not directly increase in severity nor cause deterioration in the child's motor function. This is in contrast to muscular dystrophy, in which the child experiences increasingly more severe loss of function.

Etiology. The causes of cerebral palsy are numerous. They include prenatal insult from the mother's intake of drugs or alochol, perinatal apnea (cessation of breathing for greater than 20 seconds), birth complications resulting in oxygen deprivation (anoxia), neonatal seizures, intrauterine infections, and chromosomal abnormalities. Table 4.2 presents a summary of the primary causes of cerebral palsy.

An estimated 95% of cases of cerebral palsy are caused by problems during pregnancy, labor, delivery, and the neonatal period. Neonatal complications include sepsis, asphyxia, and prematurity. However, in only about 60% of cases is the cause actually known (Batshaw & Perret, 1986). Nevertheless, it is not surprising that premature and SGA babies have a higher incidence of cerebral palsy than term babies (Alberman, Besson & McDonald, 1982).

Characteristics. Infants with cerebral palsy may exhibit mild to severe motor problems. Depending on the type of cerebral palsy, characteristics include increased muscle tone (*hypertonia*), decreased muscle tone (*hypotonia*), and involuntary body movements associated with persistence of primative reflexes.

TABLE 4.2   **Primary Causes of Cerebral Palsy**

Anoxia (lack of oxygen) during prenatal development or birth

Birth trauma

Heavy use of alcohol by the mother during pregnancy

Hyperbilirubinemia (a condition involving excessive destruction of red blood cells or an interference with bile excretion)

Chromosomal abnormalities

Rh blood incompatibility

Complications of twin pregnancy delivery

Prenatal conditions, such as rubella

Complications of the placenta during pregnancy or delivery

Thyroid disease

Kidney infection or diabetes in the mother

Depending on where the damage to the brain occurs, different parts of the body are affected. In the premature infant, for example, the area surrounding the ventricles or cavities of the cerebral cortex is particularly fragile. Blood vessels in this part of the brain bleed easily, particularly when the infant is deprived of oxygen, as may occur with respiratory distress syndrome (Batshaw & Perret, 1986). Infants with ventricular hemorrhage may thus develop *spastic diplegia*, a type of cerebral palsy in which arms and especially legs have increased muscle tone.

Similarly, if the damage occurs in the basal ganglia, which lie beneath the cerebral cortex, the infant will have choreoathetoid cerebral palsy. The various types of cerebral palsy and their characteristics are summarized in Table 4.3.

Treatment. Traditional treatment methods have emphasized improving muscle tone and suppressing primitive reflexes, but therapists working with infants and young children with cerebral palsy during the past decade have adopted more global methods. This recent trend, reflecting multidisciplinary goals and intervention plans, views motor therapy as only one aspect of the child's development, together with cognitive, social, and communication development. At the same time, emphasis is placed on helping the child to achieve normal movement patterns to the greatest extent possible to facilitate learning in other developmental areas.

Neurodevelopmental treatment (NDT) (Bobath & Bobath, 1972) is an example of a therapy mode quite compatible with current multidisciplinary team methods of intervention. NDT emphasizes the child's active participation in therapy. The therapist acts as facilitator for movement the child chooses to make. It is a hands-on, individually administered treatment. Other team members, if properly trained and certified, can use NDT methods.

Conductive education (Cotton, 1975) is a method developed in Hungary

TABLE 4.3   Types of Cerebral Palsy, Characteristics and Symptoms

TYPE	AREA OF DAMAGE	CHARACTERISTICS
Pyramidal (Spastic)	Motor cortex or pyramidal tract of brain	Rigidity, spasticity
Diplegia		Lack of control of movement in legs and (less severely) arms
Paraplegia		Lack of motor control in legs
Hemiplegia		Lack of motor control of one side of body
Quadriplegia		Lack of control in both arms and both legs
Extrapyramidal	Basal ganglia	
Choreoathetoid		Abrupt, involuntary movements of arms and legs
Rigid		Rigidity of movements ("lead pipe")
Atonic		Low muscle tone (hypotonic)

following World War II and used extensively today in parts of Europe. In conductive education, rehabilitation and education are considered inseparable, and are carried out in a single set of activities and lessons in the child's classroom beginning at age 2, and in mother-infant groups from birth. Activities include motor tasks performed on special furniture to learn independent sitting and standing, movement to music and song, toilet training, pre-reading and prewriting lessons with emphasis on hand skills, practice with independent eating and drinking, lessons in listening and speaking, using numbers, swimming, and arts and crafts.

CASE STUDY: MARGARET

Margaret was born with cerebral palsy. Her doctor was unable to tell her parents why this happened, for nothing in her birth history predicted it. The doctor pointed out that in about 40% of cerebral palsy cases there is no known cause.

Margaret has spastic diplegia, which means that movement in both her legs is limited due to spasticity. With spasticity there is an increase in muscle tone with a characteristic clasped-knife quality. When Margaret moves her leg, there is an initial stiff resistance, but it gives way abruptly like a pocket knife closing. Not only is movement difficult under these circumstances, but Margaret's legs are weak, and cannot support her weight. Her arms are less affected than her legs, and so her form of cerebral palsy is called diplegia rather than quadriplegia, which would be the case if all four limbs were spastic.

Margaret wears leg braces and walks fairly well in them by now. She needs help sometimes, though, and tires easily. She used to use a wheelchair most of the day but would like to give it up altogether one day.

When she was 3 years old her parents enrolled her in a special program at the United Cerebral Palsy Center in her town. Her mother drove her to the program every day. Now she attends a public school class, with three other classmates who also previously attended the center. All four of the children are enrolled in a regular first grade class, which has three adults to supervise 27 children. Mr. Johnson, Margaret's teacher, has a degree in elementary education. Mrs. Bacon, his associate in the classroom, is a special education teacher who has had a great deal of experience working with children with motor handicaps. Together with Miss Mallory, a young teaching assistant, the three make a great team, in Margaret's opinion, and she never feels scared or neglected at school.

"I can write my name and almost read a book, and I'm learning to feed myself," she says. "Mother says school is very good for me."

Spina Bifida

Another source of motor difficulties in young children in spina bifida, the most common of the several possible neural tube defects. Spina bifida, sometimes called myelomeningocele, results when early during the gestational period the neural tube fails to close perfectly. As the fetus develops, the imperfect closure results in an opening or meningocele in the spinal cord. Neural impulses to the lower part of the body are interrupted by the meningocele, as is the flow of cerebrospinal fluid which circulates through the brain and along the spinal cord. Before techniques were available to surgically close the opening, serious motor disabilities resulted. In addition, because cerebrospinal fluid tended to accumulate in the brain due to poor circulation, mental retardation often resulted. If the opening was in the upper region of the spine, disabilities were more serious than if the opening was in the lower region, because more of the body's motor system was affected.

Current surgical techniques for closing the meningocele and shunting cerebrospinal fluid to another body cavity (usually the stomach) have lessened the disabling effects of spina bifida in recent years. Nevertheless, not all spinal openings can be closed, so the child with spina bifida still can experience difficulty in gross motor activities like walking and running and in bladder and bowel control.

The most recent surgical experiments have been to introduce a shunt into the fetal brain in utero, since spina bifida and other neural tube defects can be identified prenatally by means of amniocentesis (Batshaw & Perret, 1986). This prevents the accumulation of cerebrospinal fluid and greatly reduces the risk of mental retardation. It is a controversial procedure, however, and not widely practiced at this writing.

Infants with spina bifida may have average intelligence and nearly average motor ability. As they grow older, their treatment generally is limited to corrective braces and special adaptive equipment for sitting and standing. Some must depend on wheelchairs; others can walk. They can usually attend regular classrooms and need little special educational assistance.

Muscular Dystrophy

Duchenne muscular dystrophy is another condition of early childhood which, like cerebral palsy, is due to brain lesion. However, in muscular dystrophy the lesion is progressive, which means that the child's condition deteriorates over time, often resulting in death before the teen years. The cause of muscular dystrophy is unknown, but the disease is thought to be an inherited recessive metabolic disorder. It affects three times as many males as females.

Although muscular dystrophy can be diagnosed early in life, it is often not diagnosed until about age two, after the child begins walking. Early diagnosis is possible through identification of elevated levels in the bloodstream of the enzyme creatine phosphokinase (CPK), which is released by dying muscle cells. Alternatively, a muscle biopsy may be performed which will show weak muscle fibers containing too much fatty tissue (Thomson, 1989).

Characteristics. The most common form of muscular dystrophy is Duchenne juvenile muscular dystrophy, which is usually diagnosed at the time the child should normally begin to walk, about the second year. The disease gradually destroys the voluntary muscles of the body, replacing them with fat cells and fibrous tissue.

The characteristics of Duchenne's are related to the loss of muscle strength caused by dying cells: difficulty in walking, running, climbing, and other gross motor activities. That is why diagnosis is sometimes not made until the second year of life. The disease is progressive, meaning that gradual disintegration of the tissue of both voluntary and involuntary muscles (e.g., heart, diaphragm) continues as the child grows into adolescence, accompanied by pain in the legs and arms and respiratory problems. Many children with Duchenne muscular dystrophy die before reaching adulthood because there is at present no effective treatment.

Children with Duchenne muscular dystrophy may exhibit a swelling of the calf area as fat cells replace muscle cells, and they may display some or all of the following characteristics:

- Running with an awkward, flat-footed gait
- Tiptoeing as a result of muscle weakness
- Walking with a sway back (lordosis) due to weakness in the abdominal wall
- Difficulty getting up from a lying or sitting position on the floor (Cratty, 1986)

As the disease progresses the child loses the ability to walk, appears to gain weight, and becomes increasingly weak and immobilized. Confinement to bed is finally necessary, and death usually follows an infection.

Treatment. At present there is no cure for muscular dystrophy. Treatment consists of postural drainage, physical therapy for contracted muscles, and the administration of antibiotics to combat infection. The services of a specialist in motor development and physical therapy are necessary for effective treatment. Often this professional can improve the child's functioning and thus lengthen the time he can remain in the classroom.

Seizure Disorder

In a discussion of seizure activity in infants during the first two years of life, it is necessary to distinguish between febrile convulsions which may occur only once and are associated with high fever or head trauma, and seizure disorders, which may result in abnormal brain wave patterns on an electroencephalogram (EEG) and are characterized by repeated seizures. Although febrile convulsions are rare before 6 months of age, neonatal seizures may occur from birth.

Febrile Convulsions. Although they are seen in children from ages 6 months to 5 years, the peak age for febrile convulsions is 18 months. Common antecedents are upper respiratory illnesses, influenza, roseola, and immunization for diphtheria-pertussis-tetanus (DPT), polio or measles (Hirtz, Ellenberg, & Nelson, 1984). Although most children experience only one episode of febrile convulsions, the risk of having a second is 30% to 40% and 50% for a third or fourth. Only about 10% of children go on to have recurrent seizures, and often these are children with a family history of such disorders, suggesting a possible genetic factor (Nelson & Ellenberg, 1981).

The febrile convulsion is grand mal in type and generally lasts 5 minutes or less. Treatment is usually not necessary, although the physician may perform a spinal tap to rule out possible meningitis (Gerber & Berliner, 1981). Following a second convulsion an anticonvulsant is usually prescribed and continued until about age 3.

Neonatal Seizures. Because the cerebral cortex is not well developed at birth, seizures in newborns are more localized than those experienced by older children and adults. Seizures happen when an abnormal firing of neurons or brain cells occurs, causing an abnormal electrical discharge in the brain. The greater the number of brain cells involved, the more severe and general in scope the seizure, and the more damaging. In the newborn the network of neurons is not well developed (Figure 4.4), resulting in fewer cells available for abnormal firing activity. Seizures tend to be limited to abnormal spasms in a single arm or leg rather than involve the entire body, as in the grand mal or infantile spasm.

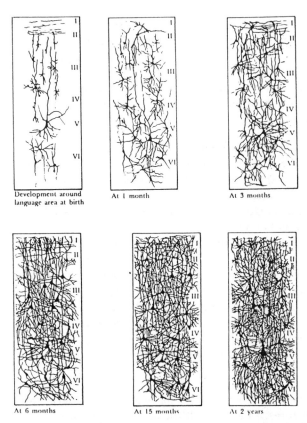

FIGURE 4.4.   Dendritic branching. Sections from the cerebral
cortex of children between the ages of birth and
2 years. (Note: *From Biological Foundations of
Language* by E. H. Lenneberg, 1976, copyright
by John Wiley & Sons. Reprinted with
permission.)

Neonatal seizures may be caused by a number of factors, and the prognosis for good recovery depends on the underlying cause. If the spasms are simply the result of depressed levels of calcium or glucose, the infant generally
recovers quickly following the administration of supplemental doses of the deficient element. Full-term infants are at greater risk for calcium deficiency;
premature and SGA babies appear to be more prone to hypoglycemia or glucose
deficiency (Freeman, 1983).

More serious and long-term effects may result from neonatal seizures
caused by anoxia, sepsis, or intraventricular hemorrhage. In the case of these
potentially serious conditions, the seizure is simply a manifestation of damage
occurring in the brain as a result of the condition. Thus, anoxia may lead to
brain damage resulting from oxygen deprivation; hemorrhaging may cause

damage to cells in the brain ventricles; and the high fever associated with sepsis may result in long-term damage to brain cells. Infant whose seizures result from these conditions usually require anticonvulsant treatment throughout childhood.

Seizures may accompany certain brain malformations associated with severe mental retardation or cerebral palsy (Freeman, 1983). In this instance, the long-term prognosis is poor and anticonvulsant treatment is usually required.

Grand Mal Seizures. Of the several different kinds of seizures that can occur in young children, only infantile spasms and grand mal seizures are seen before age 4; they may occur as young as 6 months. The grand mal is the most common of the generalized seizures, a category which includes petit mal, atonic, and infantile spasms. A second category, partial seizures, is not discussed here because it is not seen in infants below age 2.

A grand mal seizure usually lasts up to 5 minutes. It consists first of a *tonic phase,* during which the infant loses consciousness and becomes rigid. This is followed by a *clonic phase* characterized by jerking body movements, and then by a deep sleep. Grand mal seizures are usually very well controlled by anticonvulsant drugs such as phenobarbital or dilantin.

An infant with grand mal seizures is placed on anticonvulsants until he or she has been free of seizures for 2 or 3 years. At this time stopping the medication is successful in 80% of children, and no further long-term effects are seen (Batshaw & Perret, 1986).

Infantile Spasms. These generalized seizures have more serious long-term consequences than grand mal seizures. In about half the cases they are associated with Down syndrome, phenylketonuria, or Tay-Sachs disease (Lacy & Percy, 1976). Although infantile spasms usually last only until about 24 months, and can be controlled effectively by administration of steroids; 90 percent of affected infants have mental retardation (Snead, Benson & Meyers, 1983).

The infantile spasm lasts about 30 seconds and consists of a series of rapid spastic movements in which the body repeatedly jacknifes forward. These episodes may occur as often as every 10 minutes (Freeman, 1983).

In the past, infants and children with a history of repeated seizures have been labeled epileptic or said to have epilepsy. At the present time, as part of the general ongoing discussion among professionals on labeling handicapping conditions, some practitioners question the continued use of this term, preferring the more general term, *seizure disorder.*

CONGENITAL DISORDERS

In this category are found the syndromes, metabolic disorders, and other birth defects which result from abnormal genes or chromosomes. There are a great many of these problems that may potentially occur, but most are quite rare in actual occurrence. For this reason, the present discussion is limited to the most commonly seen congenital disorders.

In order to understand the differences between autosomal or X-linked, dominant or recessive, genetic or chromosomal disorders, the reader is referred to the discussion in Chapter 2 on genes and chromosomes and how they determine future development.

Genetic Disorders

In the following discussion the primary birth defects due to inherited factors are reviewed. These *metabolic disorders* include phenylketonuria, cystic fibrosis, galactosemia, congenital hypothyroidism, Tay-Sachs disease, and sickle cell anemia.

Phenylketonuria (PKU) is an autosomal recessive metabolic disorder resulting from a lack of the enzyme necessary to break down the amino acid phenylalamine. Without this enzyme, phenylalamine accumulates in the blood and brain shortly after birth, causing brain damage and severe mental retardation. Before birth the excess phenylalamine from the fetus passes across the placental membrane, where it is metabolized by the normal maternal enzyme. Thus, infants with PKU appear normal at birth, but they begin to deteriorate without treatment during the first year. This is also the case with other inborn metabolic errors: the infant appears normal at birth, but soon after toxins begin to accumulate and the infant deteriorates (Batshaw & Perret, 1986).

Treatment for PKU consists of a diet with restricted amounts of phenylalamine, and limits on high-protein foods such as meat, cheese, and poultry. This disease can be identified through blood and urine tests at birth. This neonatal screening procedure has been available for the past 30 years and is now required in every state. As a result, mental retardation from PKU is extremely rare (Thurman & Widerstrom, 1990).

Cystic fibrosis is an autosomal recessive condition that affects about one in 2,000 Caucasian children in the United States. The gene is carried by about one in every 20 North Americans, and currently some 30,000 children and young adults in this country have the illness (Kerens & Rommens, 1990). At present the disease is fatal, and most young adults die before their twenty-first birthday.

Infants with cystic fibrosis have a faulty protein, missing an important amino acid that interferes with normal transfer of salt and water between cells. Instead of the thin, wet mucus that typically allows lungs to resist infection, children with cystic fibrosis suffer from a buildup in the lungs of a sticky, thick, dry mucus that encourages bacterial infections and eventually leads to death of the child.

In 1986 scientists identified the seventh chromosome as the carrier for the cystic fibrosis gene; in 1989 the gene itself was identified. These advances make early detection, diagnosis, and eventually treatment possible. For example, scientists are now searching for new drugs that may be effective for the disease.

They are also in the process of developing more accurate prenatal screening tests that will identify adult carriers as well as affected fetuses (Kerens & Rommens, 1990).

Galactosemia is a autosomal recessive metabolic disorder which manifests in the newborn period in an enlarged liver and jaundice. Infants with galactosemia lack the enzyme necessary to metabolize galactose, a milk sugar, into glucose. They are susceptible to mental retardation, cataracts, and various infections. Currently newborns are routinely screened for galactosemia. Treatment consists of enzyme replacement therapy or provision of a galactose-free diet (Thurman & Widerstrom, 1990).

Congenital hypothyroidism is another autosomal recessive metabolic disorder. In this case there is a deficiency in the production of thyroid hormone which causes the infant to be small, floppy in tone, with severe mental retardation. Treatment consisting of a thyroid extract has been available for over a century. Hypothyroidism is one of the most common metabolic disorders seen in young children, occurring in approximately one of every 6,000. For the past 15 years newborn screening has made early detection possible, and early treatment results in a normally developing infant (Batshaw & Perret, 1986).

Tay-Sachs disease is an autosomal recessive disorder caused by the absence of an enzyme that converts a toxic nerve cell product into a nontoxic substance (Batshaw & Perret, 1986). Tay-Sachs is a progressive disease of the nervous system, with neurological damage resulting from the buildup of toxic substance in the brain. No cure is presently available, and the disease is always fatal.

The origin of the mutation leading to Tay-Sachs disease has been traced to Jewish families living in eastern Poland in the 1800s. Although the original mutation occurred by chance, subsequently the disorder was passed to succeeding generations on the recessive gene. It now affects about one in 3,000 Ashkenazic Jews and one in 360,000 non-Jews. Infants with Tay-Sachs can be identified prenatally through amniocentesis, and genetic counseling is available to parents who are carriers of the recessive gene.

Children with this disorder usually develop normally during the first 6 months. At this time they lose their ability to sit up, cease communicating, and lose their sight and hearing. They become severely debilitated and develop severe mental retardation. Death generally occurs by age 5.

Sickle cell anemia is another recessive disorder that is caused by mutation of genetic material, in this case the gene that controls the production of blood hemoglobin. Children born with sickle cell anemia have defective hemoglobin, which causes the blood cells to be sickle-shaped and to lose their ability to carry their normal supply of oxygen. When this oxygen deprivation occurs, the child is subject to extreme pain, dizziness, and weakness. Swelling of toes and fingers also occurs. These bouts of severe pain, known as sickle cell crises, usually begin before age 2 and are common during the preschool years. They decrease in frequency as the child approaches adulthood (Thurman & Widerstrom, 1990).

Sickle cell anemia is found almost exclusively among black children. Carriers of the disease can be detected through blood tests, and it can be identified prenatally through amniocentesis (Thurman & Widerstrom, 1990). No cure is currently available, and treatment consists of blood transfusions, pain relievers, and bed rest.

Chromosomal Disorders

In this section we review the most common chromosomal abnormalities due to accidents during cell division at conception. Included are the syndromes most commonly seen in infants with handicaps.

Down syndrome is also known as trisomy 21 because, of the three types of Down syndrome, nondisjunction trisomy 21 is by far the most common, occurring in approximately 95% of children with Down syndrome. The other two types, translocation Down syndrome and mosaicism, are seen in 5% of affected children (Thomson, 1989). Equal numbers of males and females have Down syndrome.

Characteristics of Down syndrome include mild to severe mental retardation, hypotonicity (low muscle tone) and certain physical features such as malformation of the ear, eye, and hand. These babies have cardiovascular problems and must often undergo heart surgery.

Whereas 20 years ago many children with Down syndrome were routinely institutionalized immediately following birth, most are now raised at home with the support of early intervention programs beginning at birth. Many programs report great success in promoting the development of Down children, and some are currently succeeding in integrating them with nondisabled children (Hanson, 1987; Hanson & Harris, 1986, Widerstrom & Goodwin, 1987).

Cri du chat syndrome is also known as 5p-syndrome because it is caused by deletion of one portion of the short arm (p) of chromosome 5. (The long arm of a chromosome is referred to as the q arm.) The severity of the disorder depends on the amount of chromosomal material that has been deleted.

Infants born with cri du chat syndrome are smaller than average at birth, with microcephaly, epicanthal folds of the eyes, poorly formed ears, and facial asymmetry. They usually have severe mental retardation. The syndrome is named for the high-pitched cry characteristic of these babies, which has been described as sounding like a mewing cat.

Prader-Willi syndrome, caused by partial deletion of chromosome 15, results in moderate mental retardation and serious problems with obesity. Infants are hypotonic, and males have small testes and penis. The cause of the deletion is unknown, but the condition can be passed to the next generation. Prenatal diagnosis of Prader-Willi syndrome can be made by chromosome analysis of fetal cells in families with chromosome 15 deletion.

Klinefelter's syndrome is a sex chromosome abnormality that affects one in 1,000 males. This syndrome is also known as 47,XXY because it is caused by an extra X chromosome from the mother or father during meiosis. Boys with Klinefelter's syndrome have normal intelligence and above average height, and are infertile.

Turner's syndrome affects one in 2,500 newborn girls and is caused by a sex chromosome abnormality known as 45,X (Smith, 1988 in Thomson). Girls with Turner's syndrome receive only a single X chromosome from their parents. Characteristics include puffiness of the hands and feet at birth, a low posterior hairline, and extra skin in the neck region. They are susceptible to cardiovascular problems and may have a heart murmur. Usually they have normal intelligence.

As adults, women with Turner's syndrome usually are shorter than average in height. They do not go through puberty unless given hormone treatment, and even so are usually infertile (Thomson, 1989).

Although these are the most commonly seen chromosome abnormalities, many others exist. Genetic research continues to increase our understanding of both genetic and chromosomal disorders, with new findings contributing to earlier diagnosis and, eventually, effective treatments.

COGNITIVE DISORDERS

Problems in cognitive development that are evident during the first years of life are usually more severe than those that appear later in life. This is because the serious problems that are identified in children at birth tend to be physiologically based and often are not medically treatable. For example, many types of severe mental retardation are caused by abnormalities in genes or chromosomes, by birth trauma, or by the effects of low birth weight or prematurity, as previously discussed.

Mental Retardation

Definition. During the past 30 years there has been much discussion concerning the most appropriate definition of mental retardation. Earlier definitions related to biological or genetic factors (Ireland, 1900; Tregold, 1908; Penrose, 1949). It was not until 1959 that the American Association on Mental Deficiency (AAMD) produced a definition, periodically revised, that included environmental factors (Heber, 1961). In 1973 the AAMD definition was revised for the sixth time to read as follows:

> Mental retardation refers to significantly subaverage general intellectual functioning existing concurrently with deficits in adaptive behavior, and manifested during the developmental period. (Grossman, 1973, p. 5)

The new definition was incorporated into the Education of All Handicapped Children Act of 1975 (PL 94–142) as the legal definition of mental retardation. Grossman's definition was reaffirmed with minor revisions in 1977.

The significance of the 1973 revision lies first in its limiting of mental retardation to those with "significantly subaverage" intellectual functioning; that is, an IQ of 70 or below, or two standard deviations below the mean. This is a much more conservative definition than Heber's, which included those individuals classified as borderline, with the result that fewer individuals could be identified as mentally retarded. Second, the 1973 revision clearly established the place of adaptive behavior deficits in defining mental retardation.

The eighth and most current revision of Grossman's definition was published in 1983 and reads as follows:

> Mental retardation refers to significantly subaverage intellectual functioning resulting in or associated with concurrent impairments in adaptive behavior and manifested during the developmental period. (Grossman, 1983, p. 11)

In this current definition the American Association on Mental Retardation (AAMR, formerly AAMD) has emphasized the importance of clinical judgment in determining whether to label a person mentally retarded (Patton et al., 1986). Instead of relying strictly on standard deviations, the concept of standard error of measurement is emphasized. The *standard error of measurement* is an estimate of the degree to which test scores would be expected to vary due to random error alone (Patton et al., 1986). If, for example, the standard error of measurement on an IQ test is 3 IQ points, the clinician should report an IQ score of 70 as within a range from 67 to 73. In addition, the clinician would need to look at the child's adaptive behavior before deciding whether to label the child mentally retarded. This may involve observation, informal interview, or the use of a standardized scale (Patton et al., 1986). Thus, the emphasis is placed on the clinician's judgment rather than on test scores.

This current definition and its interpretation by the AAMR represents the present thinking in the field of mental retardation about the labeling process. The emphasis is on the judgment of the professionals involved, with some flexibility provided, which earlier definitions lacked.

It is interesting to note that the authors of the 1983 definition collaborated with representatives of two other major classification systems as a first step in developing a worldwide classification system. The two organizations were the World Health Organization (*International Classification of Diseases*) and the American Psychiatric Association (*Diagnostic and Statistical Manual of Mental Disorders*) (Patton, 1986). Table 4.4 summarizes the provisions of the 1983 AAMD definition of mental retardation.

In addition to the definition discussed above, Grossman (1973) presented a classification scheme based on the medical etiology associated with various forms of mental retardation. It included the following ten conditions:

- Infections and intoxications
- Trauma or physical agents

TABLE 4.4   Mental Retardation as Defined by 1983 AAMR

General definition	Significantly subaverage general intellectual functioning resulting in or associated with concurrent impairments in adaptive behavior and manifested during the developmental period
Significantly subaverage	IQ of 70 or below on standardized measures of intelligence; could be extended upward through IQ 75 or more, depending on the reliability of the intelligence test used
Developmental period	Between conception and 18th birthday
Adaptive behavior	Significant limitations in an individual's effectiveness in meeting the standards of maturation, learning, personal independence, and/or social responsibility that are expected for his or her age level and cultural group
Levels of mental retardation	Mild retardation (50–55 to approximately 70), moderate retardation (35–40 to 50–55), severe retardation (20–25 to 35–40), and profound retardation (below 20 or 25) unspecified

Note: *From Manual on Terminology and Classification in Mental Retardation* by H. J. Grossman (Ed.), 1983, Washington, DC: American Association on Mental Retardation. Copyright 1983 by AAMR. Reprinted by permission of the American Association on Mental Retardation (formerly the American Association on Mental Deficiency).

- Metabolism and nutrition
- Gross brain disease
- Unknown prenatal influences
- Chromosomal abnormalities
- Gestational disorders
- Following psychiatric disorders
- Environmental influences
- Other conditions

The most widely used assessment instrument for measuring the intelligence of infants and toddlers is the Bayley Scales of Infant Development (Bayley, 1969), which contains scales for assessing both mental and motor functioning. However, in recent years many more screening and assessment tools have been developed for children from birth to age 3. These are discussed in Chapter 6.

Because these instruments by and large have been found to have poor predictive validity (Bayley, 1969; McCall, 1971) and because adaptive behavior is difficult to measure below age 2, the AAMR definition is not valid for children under age 2. The term *developmental delays* is usually used to describe infants and toddlers with below-average intellectual functioning.

Characteristics. Developmental delay is an accurate term for infants and toddlers with cognitive deficits, because in their daily activities they perform at a younger age level. In the perinatal period, for example, they are delayed in achieving head and trunk control, making eye contact and initiating social behaviors (e.g., smiling), and demonstrating early sensorimotor behaviors like sucking the nipple. During the first year infants with delays demonstrate more primitive reflex patterns and fewer righting and equilibrium responses than typical infants. They are slower in gaining independent skills in feeding, communication, and sensorimotor activities. During the second and third years they are slower in achieving object permanence, developing verbal communication, and learning independent feeding and dressing skills. They exhibit motor delays manifested in poor coordination, balance, and control of movement. Severely retarded children may be completely nonambulatory. Their social and play skills are generally delayed as well; they are less able to initiate social interactions with adults and peers, and they engage in simple parallel play activities typical of younger children.

SOCIAL/EMOTIONAL/COMMUNICATIVE DISORDERS

Attachment Disorders

Recent research has isolated factors that affect the quality of attachment between parent and infant (Belsky, Rovine, & Taylor, 1984). These include the infant's temperament, the mother's personality, and environmental influences such as the level of parenting skills, the family's social network, and the quality of the marriage. Noting that all marriages tend to deteriorate following the birth of a baby, Belsky, Rovine, and Taylor (1984) found that both secure and insecure mothers are rated about the same on marital quality at 3 months following birth (down from prenatal ratings), but by 9 months ratings of mothers of securely attached infants have stabilized whereas those of insecurely attached infants continue to decline.

In examining attachment as an aspect of developmental psychopathology, differences have been found in infants born with handicaps when compared with abused or maltreated infants (Cicchetti & Schneider-Rosen, 1984; Gersten, Coster, Schneider-Rosen, Carlson & Cicchetti, 1987). Babies with Down syndrome, for example, despite their low affect and passive temperament which make them difficult to rouse, are likely to be securely attached to their mothers. Cicchetti (1987) notes that as a result of this secure attachment Down syndrome babies tend to perform language and other symbolic tasks at developmentally appropriate levels. Many also develop mastery, self-esteem, and trust at appropriate mental age levels.

Abused or maltreated infants, on the other hand, are far less likely to develop secure attachments with their mothers. Cicchetti estimates that 70% of these infants are insecurely attached at 12, 18, and 24 months, and that there is a continuity of maladaptation that leads to increasingly delayed development. This is not surprising, since psychologically unavailable mothers produce infants who begin life with full mental capacities but who are retarded by 15 months. Cicchetti further notes that even when an infant is premature, a factor which places the infant at biological risk, the greater risk comes from the insecure attachment.

Tronick (1982) has pointed out the necessity for a synchronous interaction between mother and infant to achieve a successful attachment. If either fails to perform, that is, if the infant fails to engage the mother or she fails to respond, a lack of synchrony may lead to a mismatch. Although mismatches can be repaired, it is often difficult to do so because they are due to rather stable factors such as temperament or personality. If the infant fails to engage the mother, other noninteractive behaviors are substituted in the infant's repertoire: gaze aversion, focus on objects instead of on mother, and self-regulatory behaviors such as fist in mouth when distressed.

Depressed mothers, according to Tronick, do not look at or play with their infants as much as other mothers do. Their infants look at and play with objects less than other infants do, and look at their mothers less. The mismatched interaction causes the infant to withdraw from exploration of the external world; this in turn adversely affects the infant's development of cognitive, social, communicative, and motor skills.

Quality of Attachment as Predictor of Later Performance. Attachment quality has been found to be a good predictor of both cognitive and social competence. Attachment measured at 13 and 24 months, for example, predicted impulse inhibition, school performance, and social behaviors at age 6 (Olson, Bates & Bales, 1984). Attachment quality also predicted later problem-solving skills and social competence (Main & Cassidy, 1986).

The preceding examples illustrate the growing interest in attachment theory as an important factor in child development. It is part of a more general in-

Secure attachment promotes later cognitive and social competence.

terest in the interactions between child and parent that may facilitate or hinder optimal development. Study of the atypical or maltreated child has aided our understanding of the attachment process and has demonstrated that insecure attachments may have long-term consequences in behavior and performance.

Infantile Autism

Perhaps the most severe disorder affecting the young child's social and emotional development is early infantile autism, which manifests during the first year. The infant does not seek human contact and, in fact, may resist being held by the mother, failing to mold to her body or anticipate her contact (Kanner, 1943). The classic symptoms of infantile autism, according to Kanner (1943) and Rutter (1985), are found in Table 4.5. Related to autism is *pervasive developmental disorder (PDD)*, which results in severe delays of language, cognition, and social development. According to Rogers et al. (1986), there are currently between 5,000 and 10,000 children nationwide with the diagnosis of either autism or PDD.

Etiology. The etiology of autism is not precisely known, but most experts today agree that it is a form of organic brain dysfunction (Schopler & Mesibov, 1986; Rutter, 1984, 1986) probably involving a deficit in information processing (Rutter, 1985). According to Dawson (1983) it is associated with cerebral lateralization; in a study of autistic children, 7 of 10 were found to have right hemisphere dominance. Several authors have suggested a physiological cause. For example, the research of Fein, Skoff, and Mirsky (1981) found irregular patterns of auditory-evoked responses, and Ornitz and Ritvo (1977) found elevated levels of serotonin in the blood of autistic subjects. Unfortunately, the studies that have purported to define the causes of autism have been difficult to replicate, leaving the question of etiology essentially unanswered.

TABLE 4.5 **Symptoms of Infantile Autism**

Onset at birth or before age 2 after apparently normal development

Inappropriate social interactions with parents, other adults, and other children

Severely impaired communicative ability

Delayed cognitive development

Inability to make eye contact

Self-stimulating behaviors

Compulsive behaviors and inability to tolerate changes in routines and environments

Extreme distress for no discernible reason

Hyperactivity or hypoactivity often together with erratic sleep patterns

Difficulty in processing auditory stimuli, seeming not to hear certain sounds and overreacting to others by placing hands over ears

Apparent insensitivity to pain

According to Rutter (1985), it is necessary to differentiate between disorders arising during infancy involving a serious abnormality in the developmental process itself (autism and PDD) and psychoses arising in later childhood involving a loss of reality in individuals who previously functioned normally. The latter is known as *childhood schizophrenia.*

Rutter (1986) mentions five characteristics that differentiate autism from childhood schizophrenia:

1. Onset before 30 months
2. Deviant language development
3. Deviant social development
4. Stereotyped behavior
5. Absence of delusions, hallucinations, or thought disorders

In most cases of autism the developmental pattern is abnormal from birth, but in approximately one fifth of cases there is a period of normal development during the first 2 years.

Treatment. Effective intervention for autistic children has been limited. In the 1950s and 1960s psychodynamic approaches were tried, and in the 1970s there was a movement to operant conditioning. None of these proved entirely effective, and recent authors (Schopler & Mesibov, 1986; Rogers et al., 1986) have adopted more eclectic approaches incorporating developmental, behavioral, and psychoanalytic theories. These recent approaches to intervention emphasize the teaching of social and communication skills to the autistic child, since those are the primary deficits which characterize the disorder.

Suggestions for Further Reading

BATSHAW, M. L., and PERRET, Y. M. (1986). *Children with handicaps: A medical primer.* Baltimore: Paul H. Brookes.

BLACKMAN, J. (1990). *Medical aspects of developmental disabilities in children birth to three* (2nd ed.). Rockville, MD: Aspen

HANSON, M. (Ed.) (1984). *Atypical infant development.* Baltimore: University Park Press.

THURMAN, S. K., and WIDERSTROM, A. H. (1990). *Infants and young children with special needs: A developmental and ecological approach.* Baltimore: Paul H. Brookes.

Chapter 5

Preterm and
Low Birthweight Infants

Although many factors may place an infant at risk for developmental disabilities, those related to the birth process are most closely associated with later difficulties. Infants born too soon or too small, as Batshaw and Perret (1986) have stated, are at risk for a number of problems. First, they may have difficulty adapting to the postnatal environment due to their less mature body organs, especially their lungs. Second, they may have restricted growth potential. Third, they may exhibit certain biochemical or physiological disturbances that place them at risk for brain damage. Last, they may be born into environments in which certain socioeconomic factors combine with the physical factors of prematurity to place them doubly at risk (Guralnick & Bennett, 1987; Parker, Greer & Zuckerman, 1988).

It is not surprising that the risk of infant mortality increases as birthweight and gestational age decrease. Several factors may be associated with retarded fetal growth, among them the genetic, chromosomal, and congenital factors described in Chapters 1 and 3. Alternatively, any of the several maternal factors discussed in Chapter 1 may be responsible. Or thirdly, factors associated with the inadequate health of the placenta can result in low birthweight. For example, a decreased placental mass may provide insufficient nutrients for fetal growth and inadequate elimination of waste products (Ensher & Clark, 1986).

In this chapter the specific characteristics and etiologies associated with prematurity and low birthweight are examined, as well as the neonatal intensive care unit (NICU) in which these problems are treated.

DEFINITIONS

Term and *Birthweight* are defined using the criteria of the World Health Organization. The full-term infant is one born between 37 and 41 weeks gestation; the preterm is less than 37 weeks. Similarly, newborns weighing less than 2,500 g (about 5.5 lbs) are labeled low birthweight. Very low birthweight infants are those weighing less than 1,500 g (about 3.3 lbs).

Infants born before term are usually also low in birthweight. However, it is important to distinguish between those infants whose birthweight is close to what would be expected, given their early delivery date, and those whose weight is lower than would be expected. The latter group is labeled small for gestational age (SGA), and includes infants whose birthweight is below the 10th percentile, or two standard deviations below the mean for the gestational age (Bennett, 1987).

It is reasonable to separately define the two categories because the risk of delay is greater for SGA babies than for babies born early but appropriate in size. This point may be illustrated as follows. An infant born at 34 weeks gestation whose birthweight falls at the 40th percentile would be labeled preterm. A second infant born at the same gestational age but with a birthweight at the

10th percentile would be labeled SGA. It is logical to assume that some medical problem inhibited the growth of the SGA infant in utero, resulting in the lower birthweight. This same medical problem places the infant at greater risk in the postnatal period than the preterm infant. Obviously SGA babies from low-income families are at greatest risk. These babies have been labeled "doubly vulnerable" (Guralnick & Bennett, 1987).

It should be stated that full-term infants may also be SGA, and therefore at risk for postnatal difficulties. In addition, many babies born post-term (after 41 weeks gestation) are found to be at risk. These two categories occur less commonly, however, and are outside the scope of the present chapter.

Premature births are primarily due to maternal factors such as numerous previous pregnancies, weak cervical muscles, or third trimester infections. Women who carry twins are at greater risk for delivering early, as are women with chronic illnesses such as diabetes. Early rupture of membranes may also cause premature delivery (Batshaw & Perret, 1986). As noted in Chapter 1, adolescent pregnancies are particularly susceptible to prematurity.

Factors related to low birthweight include those maternal factors discussed earlier, namely, the use of drugs including alcohol, caffeine, nicotine, cocaine, and heroin; lack of prenatal care; and certain maternal illnesses.

Determining Gestational Age

Methods for accurately determining gestational age have been difficult to develop. Using maternal dates is not very accurate, given the irregularity of maternal menstrual periods, the possibility of first-trimester hemorrhaging, and of abnormal fetal size. Intrauterine assessment based on x-ray films or sonograms may also be inaccurate if the fetus is retarded in growth.

The most accurate methods thus far developed have been based on physical or neurologic examination (Ensher & Clark, 1986). Among the first to develop such methods in the 1960s were European neurologists (Amiel-Tison, 1968; Prechtl & Beintema, 1964), who based their examinations primarily on the development of the primitive reflexes and muscle tone. For example, the premature infant demonstrates low muscle tone and very flexible joints. He or she is likely to be found in an extended, floppy position, whereas the full-term infant rests in a flexed position. Certain primitive reflexes which do not appear until 30 to 32 weeks gestation will not be evident in the preterm infant (Batshaw & Perret, 1986).

Today in the United States the most commonly used assessment is the scoring system developed by Dubowitz and his colleagues (Dubowitz & Dubowitz, 1981; Dubowitz, Dubowitz, & Goldberg, 1970), which combines Amiel-Tison's neurologic measures with physical characteristics of the preterm infant, including lack of ear cartilage and skin creases, lack of breast buds, and reddish skin color. Several shortened versions of the scoring system are currently in use, requiring less handling of the fragile, premature infant (e.g., Narayanan et al., 1982).

CHARACTERISTICS OF THE PRETERM OR LOW BIRTHWEIGHT INFANT

Neurological Function

An examination of neurological function in the preterm infant may be divided into three parts: motor function, sensory function, and autonomic responses. Much that is presently known about neurological development in the fetal period has been learned through research conducted on preterm and low birthweight infants who are at risk for sensorimotor handicaps. (For a review of this research see Willis and Widerstrom, 1986).

Motor Function. Early students of neurological development based their understanding on abnormal adult or animal models, which resulted in at least two misconceptions (Prechtl, 1981). First, early neural function was considered to consist of a bundle of reflexes, which, with later development of the cortex, became incorporated into more complex mechanisms but which reappeared in the adult if brain damage occurred. Second, the development of neural function was seen to consist of the simple adding of more rostral (higher) structures to the earlier developed spinal cord and brain stem, resulting in a hierarchy of reflexes associated with increasingly rostral structures (i.e., cerebellum, hypothalamus, cerebrum). Systems analyses of the brain have refuted the latter of these premises, and recent studies of the neurological function of healthy infants that has provided evidence of the qualitatively different organization of the young nervous system from that of the adult have refuted the former premise (Prechtl, 1981). Nevertheless, despite Prechtl's view, shared by other neurologists (e.g., Touwen, 1978), that neurological development is too complex to accommodate the simplistic premise of primitive reflexes coming under increasingly voluntary control as the infant nervous system matures, many practitioners in the field of infant intervention still hold this view (e.g., Ayres, 1986; Fiorentino, 1973; Zelazo, 1976). The practice of occupational therapy has been particularly guided by principles of sensory integration, which are based on this view of reflex development (Ayres, 1986).

In her rationale for assessing the neurological organization of preterm infants, (Als, 1983; Als & Brazelton, 1981; Als, Lester, Tronick, & Brazelton, 1982), Als discusses four principles of development that relate to the present discussion. The first states the ethological view that the human newborn is a biologically social and active partner in interaction with its caregiver. The second states that the key characteristic of the central nervous system is to differentiate and develop through interactions with its environment. Third, development follows a pattern of increasing differentiation and hierarchic integration. This principle is illustrated by the fact that infants at first move their entire bodies in response to a stimulus and only gradually develop the ability to move one part at a time. A fourth principle asserts that organisms are motivated by two basic physiological responses: approach (exploration) and avoidance. Taken together, these principles tend to support both of the views discussed above, that development indeed consists of increasing hierarchical integration and differentiation of neuromotor function, and that the young nervous system is qualitatively different from the mature one.

In addition, Als and her colleagues propose that development requires interaction with the social and physical environment. In the Assessment of Preterm Infants' Behavior (APIB) developed by this group (see Chapter 7), the level of neurological integration is evaluated by placing increasing demands on the preterm infant's physiological, motor, attentional, and self-regulatory systems.

Since the preterm infant exhibits early developing reflexes but not later ones, it is possible to determine gestational age from reflex activity. While early research has shown that the human embryo is capable of movement from the fifth week of gestation (Hooker, 1939, 1969), the earliest reflexes appear to be evoked by oral stimulation beginning at the eighth week. By the 12th week the swallow reflex is in place, and by 24 weeks the sucking reflex can be elicited. The first spontaneous cry occurs at about the same time, around the 25th week.

Several extension reflexes which develop prenatally are present in the preterm infant. These reflexes, the positive support reflex, the Moro response, the crossed extension reflex, and the asymmetrical tonic neck reflex (ATNR), encourage the full-term newborn into extension patterns from the flexed position maintained in utero during the final weeks of gestation. The preterm infant, however, is usually prevented from attaining this state of flexion by early delivery, and exhibits extension and low muscle tone. Nevertheless, the ATNR is present in nearly all preterm and about half of all full-term infants at birth (Capute, Pasquale, Vining, Rubenstein & Harryman, 1978). Clinically, absence of the Moro response at birth may be diagnostic of central nervous system dysfunction in either the preterm or full-term neonate (Willis & Widerstrom, 1986).

Other reflexes present in the prenatal period and exhibited by the preterm infant are the Babinski reflex (Parmelee, 1963), the rooting reflex (Prechtl, 1958), and the grasp reflex. Like all of the primitive reflexes, they are evident in the healthy infant during the first six months of life, when they promote the development of feeding, reaching, extending, grasping, and head/trunk control. After that period, the healthy infant relies on automatic responses which facilitate the development of righting and equilibrium. If the primitive reflexes persist after six months postnatal age (corrected for prematurity), it may be an indication of neurological dysfunction (Willis & Widerstrom, 1986).

Sensory Function. The preterm infant's capabilities for sensory processing have been evaluated by measurements of *response latency* or *response decrement*, that is, determining how long it takes for the infant to respond to the stimulus initially, and how long it takes for him or her to habituate to it and cease responding. Shorter response latencies and quicker response decrements are associated with a more mature nervous sytem and thus more efficient learning and memory (Willis & Widerstrom, 1986). Studies comparing preterm with full-term infants have identified a developmental sequence in tactile, auditory, and visual processing that appears to be related to neurological development. These studies suggest that the tactile system is the first to develop and is functional by 17 weeks gestation, followed by the auditory system, which is established during the sixth, seventh, and eighth months (25–33 weeks) gestation, and finally the visual system which is not structurally established until the ninth month. It is not surprising, therefore, that the greatest differences are found in the visual performance of preterm and full-term infants. Active visual attention and visual recognition memory are not in evidence until 35 to 36 weeks gestation (Banks & Ginsburg, 1987). Many preterm infants are born before this age.

An interesting study has been reported by Parmelee and Sigman (1983) which examined the differences in auditory processing of preterm and full-term infants. Two groups were matched for conceptional age and tested for response to auditory stimulus. The preterm infants had spent their eighth and ninth gestational months in the noisy environment of the NICU, whereas the full-terms had remained in utero for that period. Nevertheless, no differences were found in their ability to respond to sounds, leading Parmelee and Sigman (1983) to conclude that the auditory system is not vulnerable to premature exposure to the extrauterine environment, because of the limited capacity of the immature auditory cortex to process auditory stimuli. Thus, the preterm infant is protected from some potentially destructive external influences. Since the visual system develops even later than the auditory, it may be presumed that this holds true for visual stimulation as well. Their study addressed widespread concern that NICUs were potentially harmful to the preterm infant's immaturely developed auditory and visual systems.

Research on sensory function in preterm infants suggests that neurological maturation rather than environmental experience is associated with increased efficiency in information processing.

Autonomic Responses. The nervous system coordinates the interplay of numerous physiological systems by means of complex homeostatic feedback mechanisms. It is therefore possible to analyze the functioning of the central nervous system by measuring certain autonomic activity, such as heart rate, respiration, or cry threshold. Various researchers have studied neonatal neurological function in this manner (Gardner & Karmel, 1983; Parmelee, 1981; Porges, 1983; Zeskind, 1983) in order to plot the maturation of the nervous system.

The *sympathetic nervous system* consists of those functions related to arousal of response; whereas, the *parasympathetic nervous system* governs the inhibition of response. An infant's cry is a sympathetic function, and self-quieting is a parasympathetic one. Although both are necessary for normal development of the organism, arousal is necessary for basic survival and develops first.

Sympathetic functions are present at birth, but since they develop during the third trimester, they may be poorly developed in the preterm infant. Anyone who has observed the weak cry and generally lethargic demeanor of the preterm infant will understand this. The parasympathetic nervous system, on the other hand, matures throughout infancy, resulting in poor inhibitory capacity for all infants at birth, and slower development of inhibition for preterm infants.

From this brief description it may be seen that preterm infants must first learn to respond to stimuli (arousal) and then to inhibit responses when appropriate. They generally exhibit difficulty in both of these areas.

CASE STUDY: JACKIE AND FRED

Jackie and Fred are the parents of a preterm infant who weighed only 3¼ lbs at birth. Donald was born at 29 weeks gestation, which means that he was 7 weeks early. He was born with several of the problems common to low birthweight infants, such as respiratory distress, apnea, jaundice, and a very weak suck. Jackie had a difficult labor and a pregnancy marked by infection during the third trimester. She had had excellent prenatal care from her family obstetrician, who decided to induce labor and deliver the baby by cesarean section. Despite labor difficulties, the delivery was uneventful, and the delivery room staff felt optimistic about Donald's chances.

Following delivery Donald was moved to an incubator in the intensive care unit where he was placed on a ventilator and treated with fluorescent lights for jaundice. He was fed through a tube inserted into his nasal cavity and then to his stomach. When attacks of apnea occurred, an NICU nurse would touch him to get him breathing again. Due to this treatment, Donald gradually gained strength, began to breathe without assistance, and to drink from a bottle.

During these weeks, Jackie and Fred traveled every weekend from their ranch in southern Wyoming to the hospital to visit Donald. Because the ranch was nearly a 4-hour drive from the hospital, daily visits were impossible. But because Donald was their first child, they did not have the needs of other children to consider, and this made weekly visits possible. After Donald's suck became strong enough to take nourishment from a nipple, Jackie brought her refrigerated breast milk with her each week to the hospital, so that she could continue breast-feeding when Donald came home. In the meantime, the nursing staff bottle-fed the breast milk to Donald during the week when Jackie could not be there.

The happy event—Donald's homecoming—occurred when he was 8 weeks old and weighed nearly 5 lbs. He was active, alert, eating, and sleeping well, and his respiratory problems seemed to be well under control. Fred and Jackie kept the crib in their own bedroom during the first months after Donald came home, and Jackie says that she hardly slept a wink at first. "I kept getting up to make sure he was breathing. The apnea attacks scared me so much." In fact, Donald did have two episodes of apnea at home, but Jackie and Fred had been instructed at the hospital how to rouse him to get him breathing again. When they realized they were capable of taking care of Donald's problems, both Fred and Jackie became more relaxed parents. "We know he's going to be slower developing than other babies," said Fred, "but we aren't in any hurry. He can take his time. He's already beginning to gain weight, and he's lost that ruddy color he had in the hospital. He's a great-looking little guy!"

Jackie says that she is grateful for Fred's close support during and after the ordeal of Donald's birth. "I don't think I could have gone through it alone. I don't know how some women do. And I had the support of my parents and Fred's parents, too. You need all that support when your baby is born with problems and spends two months in the hospital. I feel very lucky."

Medical Complications

Factors which place the infant at risk at birth include respiratory problems, asphyxia and hemorrhage, retinopathy, hyperbilirubinemia, hypothermia, infections, and certain biochemical or metabolic problems.

Respiratory Problems. Of the risk factors listed above, one of the most commonly seen in preterm infants is *respiratory distress syndrome (RDS)*, also known as *hyalin membrane disease*. Approximately 20% of preterms develop RDS during their first week of life, and the earlier the birth, the greater the incidence of RDS (Batshaw & Perret, 1986). Respiratory distress is caused by a lack of surfactant, a chemical that coats the air pockets (alveoli) of the lungs

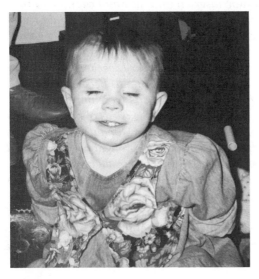

Preterm and low-birthweight infants are at risk for neurological and medical complications.

and prevents them from collapsing during normal breathing. Because the lungs are the last organ to develop during the gestational period, surfactant is not produced in sufficient quantities until close to term, at approximately 34 to 36 weeks gestation. Therefore, the more premature the infant, the less surfactant is produced and the greater likelihood of the lungs collapsing.

Treatment for RDS involves administering supplemental oxygen to the infant, and, if necessary, providing artificial ventilation. Artificial ventilation consists of applying a constant low pressure to the alveoli to keep them open at all times, allowing the ongoing exchange of oxygen and carbon dioxide. Research has shown that premature infants whose lungs are treated with surfactant before they take their first breath have less need for artificial ventilation (Enhorning, Shennan, Possmayer et al., 1985).

Most infants with RDS recover, achieving normal lung function several weeks following birth. However, infants who have had intense life-support therapy at birth may develop chronic lung disease as a result. Several forms may be seen in the neonate, and each implies a long-term dependence on supplemental oxygen. The most common are chronic pulmonary insufficiency of prematurity (CPIP) and bronchopulmonary dysplasia (BPD). The combination of supplemental oxygen, positive pressure from mechanical ventilation, and the resulting trauma usually causes retarded alveolar growth and increased mucus production. The infant often must remain on a respirator from 6 months to a year, until adequate alveolar development takes place. In most cases normal lung function is acquired by age 5 or 6 years (Enhorning et al., 1985).

As many as 50% of all preterm newborns experience irregular respiratory patterns, often characterized by 10- to 15-second pauses in the breathing cycle. If the pauses are longer than 20 seconds, or if they are accompanied by a slowing of the heart rate or lowered blood oxygen levels, they are termed apnea. Apnea results from an immature or damaged central nervous system. Damage may be due to hemorrhage, infection, or metabolic disorder. Treatment consists of correcting the damaging condition if the etiology is known, and if it is not, use of tactile stimulation or medication (Ensher & Clark, 1986). Often maturation of the central nervous system is the best solution to the problem of apnea.

Retinopathy of Prematurity. Physicians for many years have given oxygen to newborns who exhibit respiratory problems. However, many infants received oxygen in too high a concentration, which caused detachment of the retina of the eye and blindness. This condition is known as *retinopathy of prematurity (ROP)* or *retrolental fibroplasia (RLF)*. Although careful monitoring and reduced levels of oxygen intake are now more commonly practiced than formerly, reducing the incidence of ROP, it is still sometimes necessary to administer oxygen to VLBW babies and to thus put them at risk for ROP. When the physician must choose between losing an infant and risking development of ROP or RLF, it is obvious what the choice must be.

Birth Asphyxia and Hemorrhage. Asphyxia is defined as interference with the circulation and oxygenation of the blood, leading to loss of consciousness and possible brain damage (Batshaw & Perret, 1986). Because it results in an inadequate blood supply to the brain, asphyxia represents a major metabolic insult. In preterm infants the insult is manifested as *intraventricular hemorrhage (IVH)*, in which the infant shows decreased alertness and poor feeding, finally loses consciousness, and may enter a coma. Hypotonia, difficult respiration, and lowered heart rate are also symptoms. In premature infants, the blood vessels surrounding the ventricles of the brain are fragile and susceptible to damage from hypoxia and irregular blood pressure. Bleeding starts in the ventricles and may move into surrounding brain tissue. The infant's blood count may drop, and seizures may begin (Saylor, Levkoff & Elkenin, 1989).

Confirmation of IVH is made by means of ultrasound or computed tomography (CT) scan, which shows whether there is blood in the ventricles and surrounding tissue. Treatment consists of increasing blood pressure, blood oxygen level, and blood glucose. In addition, the infant is monitored for hypothermia and seizure activity (Horbar, Pasnick, McAuliffe, et al., 1983).

Besides IVH, the preterm infant may have other types of hemorrhage, ranging from minor extracranial bleeds called *cephalohematomas* to more serious intracranial hemorrhages which may be subarachnoid or subdural, depending on their location in the brain. Many infants, especially preterms, have a small amount of bleeding at birth but do not suffer any long-term consequences. These cephalohematomas are caused by trauma to the blood vessels in the scalp during delivery, and soon disappear. However, if delivery is prolonged, leading to hypoxia and poor blood circulation, more serious brain damage may occur, resulting in cerebral palsy or even death.

If the blood vessels inside the cranium are affected, either below the dura mater (outer) layer or the arachnoid mater (middle) layer of tissue surrounding the brain, intracranial hemorrhage results. Subdural and subarachnoid hemorrhages do not affect the brain ventricles and are thus treated more directly than IVH. Surgical drainage of the blood from the tissue layers is possible, and is often lifesaving (Batshaw & Perret, 1986). A summary of intracranial hemorrhages found in preterm infants is presented in Table 5-1.

The outcome for infants with birth asphyxia can be positive, but very small preterm infants are at risk for cerebral palsy. The prognosis depends on the size, location, and severity of the hemorrhage.

Hyperbilirubinemia. Jaundice is the most prevalent problem that pediatricians confront in full-term and preterm newborns (Peabody & Lewis, 1985). Nearly all babies are jaundiced, and this is due to elevated levels of the chemical bilirubin in their bloodstream. Bilirubin is a yellow pigment that results from the breakdown of red blood cells in the liver. Before birth, the fetus's blood supply contains a greater percentage of red blood cells to enable it to extract oxygen from the mother. Following birth this high percentage is no longer necessary, since the neonate obtains oxygen through normal respiration. The

TABLE 5.1   Intracranial Hemorrhages in Preterm Infants

TYPE	LOCATION	TREATMENT	PROGNOSIS
Subdural	Beneath first fibrous protective layer inside skull (*dura mater*)	Surgical drainage of accumulated blood to relieve pressure on brain	Moderate to good
Subarchoid	Beneath second protective layer inside skull (*arachnoid mater*)	Surgical drainage of accumulated blood to relieve pressure on brain	Moderate
Intraventricular (Intracerebral)	Brain ventricles	Repeated spinal taps to remove accumulated blood; administration of oxygen and glucose; monitoring of body temperature and seizures	Generally poor

result is a higher blood level of bilirubin while the red cell count in the blood supply is being lowered. Generally this occurs in the first three or four days after birth, and the result is a yellow cast to the baby's skin.

There is a risk to premature and low birthweight infants from elevated bilirubin levels. The condition is known as hyperbilirubinemia and it places the infant at risk for cerebral palsy and sensorineural hearing loss (Peabody & Lewis, 1985). Treatment consists of lowering the level of bilirubin in the bloodstream through exposure to fluorescent lights. This procedure, called phototherapy, includes protection of the infant from potentially harmful ultraviolet light, monitoring of body temperature to avoid overheating, and monitoring for dehydration. In severe cases blood exchange transfusions may be necessary. If brain damage occurs, the neurological disease is known as kernicterus or bilirubin encephalopathy.

Hypothermia. Infants who are preterm and low in birthweight generally have difficulty in maintaining an adequate body temperature. As a result they nearly always need an external source of warmth such as that provided by incubators, isolettes, radiant warmers, or other heat source. As they grow in size and weight, body temperature tends to stabilize.

Several studies have shown that infants transported from their birth hospital to an intensive care unit in another hospital may experience decreases in body temperature. The mortality rate of transported neonates who arrive at the NICU with rectal temperatures below 35.5 ° C is significantly greater than that of neonates whose rectal temperatures are greater than 35.5 ° C (Moffat & Hackel, 1985).

Infants born in developed countries have available to them various sources of external warmth in the NICU. In developing countries NICUs with incubators are scarce, and techniques must be developed to keep infants warm that rely less on modern technology. One such technique relies on the mother's own body warmth. The infant is held by the mother in the kangaroo position, inside the blouse or sweater and against the chest (Ebrahim, 1989). Mothers in developing countries are taught to monitor their babies' temperature by comparing it to their own and keeping the babies as warm as themselves. Hypothermia is recognized worldwide as a source of risk for newborns, especially those of low birthweight.

As hypothermia occurs, the impact is first noted in the lungs. Normal lung expansion is accompanied by reduced pulmonary vascular resistance. If hypothermia prevents a reduction in pulmonary vascular resistance, the flow of blood through the lungs is impeded, and hypoxia may result. This, in turn, means a decrease in the amount of oxygen delivered to body tissue (Moffat & Hackel, 1985).

Another result of hypothermia is a decrease in central nervous system function, leading to a gradual shutting down of the body's organ systems and a change in enzyme and hormonal balance. The sympathetic nervous system becomes rapidly more active, causing a pooling of the body's blood in the central part of the body in an effort to conserve heat (Moffat & Hackel, 1985).

Infections. According to the National Center for Health Statistics (1978) one of the greatest causes of neonatal mortality is infection, second only to severe congenital defects. In 1978 12% of neonatal deaths were due to infection. Preterm and low birthweight infants are more susceptible to infection than full-term infants. With the advent of antibiotics the risk to both groups has been greatly reduced. However, because more very low birthweight infants are surviving than previously, the incidence of infection among neonates has increased.

VLBW and SGA babies are susceptible to both viral and bacterial infections. The former are usually contracted from the mother during delivery; the most common is the herpes virus infection of the vagina. Infants born to mothers with untreated herpes may contract the infection, which then spreads throughout the body causing death in about 60% of cases.

A bacterial infection frequently seen in preterm and low birthweight infants is *sepsis*, a form of streptococcal infection spread by the blood throughout the body. It may also be called blood poisoning. In newborns, the bacteria causing sepsis are different from those causing sepsis in older children and adults. Since newborns lack a completely developed immune defense system, they are more susceptible to these infections and have more serious symptoms. Before antibiotics more than 90% of newborns with sepsis died (Krugman & Gershon, 1975). Fewer die currently, but the incidence of sepsis has risen significantly due to increased numbers of VLBW infants surviving who are more susceptible to infection.

Treatment for sepsis consists of blood cultures to confirm the diagnosis, followed by intravenous antibiotics. Unlike herpes, a viral infection that does not respond to antibiotics, sepsis does respond well, and the infant's condition usually improves in 2 or 3 days. However, if the infection reaches the covering of the brain, meningitis results and the mortality rate is much higher.

Since the newborn is deficient in so much of the body's immune system, it is understandable that infection in the neonate can be devastating. Infections can be contracted through the placenta (congenital rubella), the maternal vagina (herpes), or by contamination of the amniotic fluid (*beta streptococcus* or sepsis). The latter constitutes the major infection problem in today's neonatal nursery.

Metabolic disorders. Infants with low birthweights and early delivery dates are more susceptible to biochemical and metabolic problems than full-term infants. For example, they may experience a deficiency in glucose, which is essential to brain metabolism. The resulting *hypoglycemia* or low blood sugar may cause brain damage if left untreated. Other likely deficiencies include minerals such as calcium, potassium, sodium, phosphorus, iron, and magnesium. In the case of calcium, for example, it has been estimated that 50% of the calcium content of a full-term infant's bones is deposited during the last trimester (Ensher & Clark, 1986). This means that infants born prematurely have a greater risk of abnormal bone growth and are susceptible to *hypocalcemia* (calcium deficiency).

It is usual to provide supplemental glucose and minerals in the diet of the preterm, usually intravenously, in the intensive care unit. Additionally, early feedings immediately following birth have been found to reduce the risk of hypoglycemia (Batshaw & Perret, 1986).

Most developed countries now have screening programs for metabolic errors that can be corrected through diet or therapy. The most common are *phenylketonuria*, in which the protein phenylalanine is omitted from the diet; *galactosemia*, in which intake of lactose is restricted; and *hypothyroidism*, in which the hormone thyroxine is administered orally.

CARE OF THE PRETERM AND LOW BIRTHWEIGHT INFANT

As stated earlier, the best treatment for the preterm and low birthweight infant is prevention in the form of adequate prenatal care, including education about the effects of drug and alcohol use, good nutrition, and diet.

The Neonatal Intensive Care Unit

Once the at-risk infant is delivered, treatment consists of adequate medical care and, increasingly, attention to developmental needs. Once body temperature is stabilized, immediate placement in an isolette in the NICU is the practice in developed countries in order to prevent hypothermia.

If there is evidence of RDS, the infant is either given oxygen or is intubated and mechanically ventilated. Heart and respiratory rates are monitored, as are levels of glucose, calcium, bilirubin, blood pH, and electrolyte (blood minerals) by means of blood samples taken from the infant's heel. Intravenous fluids are given to compensate for any biochemical imbalances, and antibiotics are given to avert infection. If apnea is present, the infant receives medication to stimulate normal breathing. If the bilirubin level is elevated, the infant is placed under fluorescent lamps.

Once the baby achieves normal lung function, has a normal stabilized body temperature, and begins to gain weight, growth can begin. At that time, if the jaundice has abated and the biochemical levels are normal, a move to an intermediate care unit will probably be recommended. Here the infant will continue to be monitored, especially for adequate nutrition and ability to suck the nipple. When weight gain has reached 2,500 g, hospital discharge will usually soon follow.

Each year approximately 2% to 9% of all live births require intensive care, or between 200,000 and 250,000 infants. The average length of stay in special care for these infants is 15 to 20 days for those weighing 1,500 g to 2,500 g; for small infants weighing between 1,000 g and 1,500 g the stay averages 40 to 50 days (Gottfried, 1985).

Although the majority of special care infants have good outcomes, there is a concern among researchers and clinicians working in NICUs that very small premature babies suffer cognitive and sensory impairments that may be partially attributable to environmental conditions present in the intensive care unit. The concern is that deficits due to brain damage may be exacerbated by the NICU environment. Various authors have found fault with this environment for 1) causing sensory deprivation; 2) being overstimulating; or 3) providing disintegrated or inappropriate patterns of stimulation (Gottfried, 1985).

Gottfried (1985) concluded that infants in NICUs and newborn convalescent care units (NCCU) receive a considerable amount of stimulation, but this stimulation lacks rhythmicity. Furthermore, NICU and NCCU infants receive a negligible amount of social sensory experiences, with most human contact being devoted to medical-nursing care. Gottfried's overall finding was that the occurrence, regularity, quality, and organization of social contacts in special care units are not impressively high.

This emphasis on nonmedical aspects of the special care unit environment began to receive greater emphasis as professionals from various fields studied the development of babies who had left the NICU. They expressed concern at the great differences between that environment and the one the infants had left too soon, namely, the womb. The NICU is characterized by high levels of noise (70–80 db, with upper levels reaching to 120 db, well above the usual conversational speech range of 30–60 db), bright fluorescent lights unvaried day and night, and with people moving about at all hours (Gaiter, 1985). Isolettes provide no sheltering from this visual and auditory environment; recordings of light and sound have been found to be virtually identical both outside and inside the incubator.

An added concern is the adverse effects of phototherapy used in the treatment of hyperbilirubinemia. Biological side-effects may include numerous skin changes, changes in stool, moderate dehydration, depletion of vitamins and amino acids, and impairment of lactase activity (Peabody & Lewis, 1985).

In addition, studies have shown that newborns receive a great amount of handling during the daily routine, averaging 40 to 70 contacts per day, reaching as high as 132 contacts for some infants. Furthermore, these contacts are fairly evenly distributed throughout the day and night (Peabody & Lewis, 1985). Contacts tend to be with professional staff rather than with parents, despite open visiting policies of some NICUs, and are usually frequent and of short duration (Gaiter, 1985; Gottfried, Hodgman & Brown, 1984; Gottfried et al., 1981). This means that the contacts are nonsocial in nature, with the result that the infants may suffer a lack of social interaction. Gottfried and his colleagues found that medical staff in the nurseries were not inclined to approach infants for the purpose of socializing, nor to soothe their cries during contacts. In fact, caregivers in these units tended not to respond to infant cries.

These factors, together with the large amount of technological equipment required for life support, create an environment that is far removed from that of the dark, relatively peaceful womb. Absent also from the NICU is the soothing rocking motion experienced by the fetus as a result of the mother's normal movement and a form of physical stimulation. As Bennett (1987) has stated, "Despite the constant bombardment of visual, auditory, and tactile physical stimulations, the NICU appears to be a startling, nonsocial environment for newborns. Unfortunately, there is also frequently little or no organization, rhythmicity, or developmentally appropriate pattern of either physical or social stimulation incorporated into the treatment plan of newborn intensive care" (p. 89).

The high frequency of handling means that infants in the NICU are allowed little time for uninterrupted sleep. The 28- to 32-week-old fetus sleeps approximately 80% of the time in utero, much of it in REM sleep. It has been postulated by some physiologists that these uninterrupted sleep periods are necesary for neuronal maturation (Oswald, 1969). Infants in special care may experience sleep deprivation that affects their cognitive development.

In order to create a psychologically facilitating environment in the NICU without undermining the critical medical care that it provides, early interventionists have introduced some techniques and materials to improve the infants' level of comfort. For example, special small buntings are available in which the infants may be wrapped, adding coziness and comfort and an added means of maintaining body temperature. The bunting is more suitable for well babies, since it limits access (Moffat & Hackel, 1985). Small hammocks have also been developed, that will fit into the incubator and imitate the rocking motion of the womb (Als, 1984b). In some NICUs the lights are turned down low during those times of day and night when bright lights are unnecessary. Rocking waterbeds installed in some NICUs have been found to stimulate weight gain in preterms (Kramer & Pierpont, 1976) and to reduce apnea attacks (Korner et al., 1975; Korner, 1985), although they require careful temperature monitoring to avoid heat loss in the infant (Moffat & Hackel, 1985).

Because studies have shown that the heel stick, by which blood samples are obtained, is very painful and therefore a source of stress for the infant, some hospitals have developed alternative means of obtaining these samples (Field & Goldson, 1984). Finally, to help the NICU infant better cope with the high levels of stress resulting from the medical interventions, some NICUs provide special tiny nipples for non-nutritive sucking. Studies have shown this to be an effective means of reducing stress in newborns (Field & Goldson, 1984).

A review of 17 neonatal developmental intervention programs that were either infant-focused, parent-focused, or a combination of the two, revealed that, although all the studies reported significantly greater gains by the experimental compared to the control infants, results were mixed and often contradictory (Bennett, 1987). The infant-focused studies were primarily hospital-based and consisted of interventions that emphasized auditory, visual, vestibular, and tactile stimulation. The positive effects reported in these studies

Research on newborns at risk has shown that positive infant-parent interactions can ameliorate physiological and emotional factors contributing to the risk.

were generally very short-term, disappearing by one year of age. The most positive long-term effects were found in studies that continued the interventions at home following hospital discharge with considerable parent involvement. In fact, interventions that attempt to facilitate effective parenting by focusing on the parent-infant interaction and by incorporating a plan of extended home visitation appear to fit current child development models better than those that are exclusively infant-focused. Such models are more useful to families and have a greater likelihood of achieving meaningful results (Bennett, 1987).

Research on newborns at risk has shown that positive parent/caregiver interactions with the infant can ameliorate physiological and emotional factors contributing to the risk (Beckwith, 1979; Gorski, 1983a, 1983b). In fact, parent-infant interaction measures have been found to be better predictors of later development than Apgar scores, newborn neurologic examinations, or postnatal complications (Mahoney & Powell, 1986; Parmelee, 1979). Nevertheless, medically fragile preterm infants generally have a lower threshold for sensory overload than those who are full-term. This means that preterm infants may not be able to tolerate social interactions which overstimulate them.

In addition, the daily routine of the NICU may provide too much aversive stimulation for many of these babies, precipitating crises of apnea or other autonomic responses, such as greatly accelerated heart and respiratory rates, vomiting, diarrhea, or even cardiac arrest (Als, 1984b; Gorski, 1983a). Gorski described the "ear-piercing cacophony of daily medical team rounds" (p. 257) in the intensive care nursery and suggested that some infants may need care plans that take into account their susceptibility to external stimulation. He advocated changes in NICU routines that would take into account the infants' neurobehavioral as well as medical needs. These changes included training caregivers to be more sensitive to the infant's need for normal sleep periods, and teaching nurses, doctors, and parents to read infant signals such as gaze aversion, changes in skin color, pulse, or respiratory rate, or irritability that may indicate sensory overload and distress. Infant care plans included rest periods between caregiving procedures when necessary, and reductions in social interactions for certain babies (Gorksi, 1983a).

The role of parents in the NICU has changed in recent years, due to realization by professional staff that a secure parent-infant attachment is beneficial to infant recovery, and that parents' needs for interacting with their infant were not being taken into account in the NICU schedule (Gorski, 1983b; Gottwald & Thurman, 1990; Minde, Shosenberg, Thompson, & Marton, 1983). Parents in many NICUs are more involved in care and handling of their infant than previously, and support groups are more widely available, including peer-oriented self-help groups (Minde et al., 1983) and groups led by a social worker or other member of professional staff.

As a result of the studies summarized above, practical guidelines have emerged to ensure more positive outcomes for the graduates of intensive care nurseries. They include these measures:

- Recognize the unusual physiological stresses being endured by the premature infant.
- Modify the environment to decrease overstimulation (specifically screen out grossly bombarding and unnecessary sensory stimuli such as handling during periods of quiet sleep).
- Introduce diurnal rhythms to promote behavioral organization.
- Gradually facilitate reciprocal visual, auditory, tactile, vestibular-kinesthetic, and social feedback during alert periods.
- Immediately terminate or alter approaches that produce avoidance responses.
- Educate and assist parents in reading, anticipating, and appropriately responding to their own infant's cues and signals, thus fostering and reinforcing parents' feelings of competence (Bennett, 1987, p. 108).

These recent trends provide an interesting example of the extent of collaboration currently occurring in the care of infants at risk. The inclusion of educators, psychologists, and therapists on the infant team brings to the NICU a more global view of the infant's development, with concern for cognitive, communicative, physical, and social growth.

The Multidisciplinary Team

In developed countries the NICU and the special care unit represent the usual early environment for low birthweight and preterm infants considered at risk for developmental delays. The team that cares for these babies includes the pediatrician; neurologist; nurse; physical, occupational, or speech therapist; and more recently, the educator, psychologist, and social worker. It is the NICU nurse who has the day-to-day responsibility for the infant's well-being, in consultation with other professionals. Although the baby's medical situation is of primary concern, recent emphasis has been placed on the child's need for affection, parental interaction, and communication, especially if a long hospital stay is required (Gorski, 1983a, 1983b; Minde et al. 1983). These developmental areas fall within the realm of the psychologist, social worker, and early interventionist.

The infant's transition to home and community after leaving the hospital is also receiving attention; communication is established between hospital staff and community-based early intervention programs. Often these links are made by therapists who continue to work with the child in the new community setting, and by the social worker who continues to see the parents following hospital discharge.

Suggestions for Further Reading

Zero to Three, monthly newsletter of the National Center for Clinical Infant Programs, Washington, D.C.

BATSHAW, M.L., & PERRET, Y.M. (1986). Born too soon, born too small. *Children with handicaps: A medical primer.* Baltimore: Paul H. Brookes.

Chapter 6

Family Dynamics

Nothing influences the infant as does the family. Family interactions, relationships, and the environment it provides affect infants' bonds of affection and development of abilities, interests, language, and skills (Emde & Sameroff, 1989). Families vary in a multitude of ways, including beliefs, education, ethnic background, friends and extended family, geographic location, religion, and values; the complexity of family variables affecting children is further complicated by changes that occur in the family life cycle over time (Terkelson, 1980). Given the possible combinations of characteristics and changes, every family is to some extent unique (Turnbull & Turnbull, 1986).

Early parent-infant family interactions set the stage for each infant's growth and development. The view of the family as the critical element in child development is the foundation for PL 99-457 and for the provision of services to at-risk and handicapped infants and toddlers. The assumptions underlying the legislation which guide professional practice in this area hold that families are the primary factor in facilitating children's growth and development. Guralnick (1989) succinctly presents the argument:

> By enhancing natural parenting skills and providing the conditions for families to become more competent and confident in their unique relationship with their children, conditions for optimal child development may well be created. A common element appears to be the child-oriented nature of the relationship, which allows a harmonious, sensitive, and stimulating interactive match to develop. It is important to emphasize that these principles are likely to apply across children's risk or disability status (p. 12).

Parents have not always been viewed as essential, integral, and primary in facilitating children's development. Turnbull and Turnbull (1986) remind us that parents, over time, have assumed or been expected by professionals to assume a variety of major roles, including the source of the child's problem, organization member, service developer, recipient of professionals' decisions, learner and teacher, political advocate, educational decision-maker, and family member. Responding to all roles and expectations has been difficult if not impossible for parents. Regardless of specific roles or expectations, however, researchers agree that parents play a tremendous role in infants', toddlers', and children's development.

For the purposes of this chapter, a *family* is defined as two or more individuals, at least one of whom is an adult and the other a child, who are legally bound to each other through birth, adoption, or legal guardianship. The family represents a complex set of bonds, dynamics, relationships, systems, and subsystems, in which each individual is developing and at the same time interacting with and adjusting to the family. Family dynamics are a particularly important factor when the child in the family is at-risk or has a handicapping condition: the family can play a key role in how the handicapping condition ultimately affects the child and the child's functioning. This chapter is organized to address family dynamics and infant exceptionality and includes early factors in infant-parent interaction, attachment and bonding, gender differences in family dynamics, family dynamics and family systems, family interactions with at-risk and handicapped infants, parenting dynamics and child characteristics, abuse and neglect, and future issues in family dynamics.

PARENT-INFANT INTERACTION

Early Factors

From research we know that spontaneous infant behavior is transformed into interactive behavior by a parent who responds to the infant (Hetherington, 1983). The contingent, interactive parent-infant behavior becomes socialized behavior in the context of the family. The family provides the infant's introduction to cognitive development, social and emotional bonds, language, a sense of security in the world, and skill development. Family interactions lead to relationships which evolve over time and are, at their simplest level, regularities in patterns of interaction (Sroufe, 1989b). Relationships characterized by parental attentiveness, responsivity, sensitivity, stimulation, and warmth promote infant, toddler, and child intellectual and social competence (Belsky, Lerner, & Spanier, 1985; Bornstein, 1986; Lamb, 1980; Lamb & Bornstein, 1987).

The early family interactive process, which evolves and develops over time, incorporates three major elements: personality characteristics of the parent, situational influences on the parent, and infant behavioral characteristics (Lamb & Bornstein, 1987). For example, major parental personality traits which contribute to the developing parent-child relationship include adaptability, self-centeredness, sensitivity, and a sense of self as a competent parent (Ainsworth et al., 1978; Lamb & Bornstein, 1987). Situational influences involve parental factors such as parental stress, social support systems, and cross-generational familial expectations. Individual infant characteristics affecting the parent-child relationship include characteristics such as soothability, irritability, and predictability. Together, these three major factors interact and contribute to each individual family's developing interaction patterns.

Family interactions involving a baby typically lead to a strong relationship between parent and child that is unique in its initial asymmetry (Hetherington, 1983); although the relationship is mutual and interactive, the infant must depend totally on the parent for survival. Parents provide affection, food, clothing, shelter, and warmth to the baby. In addition, parents respond to continuous environmental demands, such as meeting financial obligations, maintaining the home, and meeting family and household needs. Hetherington finds that although parent characteristics are influenced by the infant's arrival, to a great extent they remain constant. In contrast, the infant makes vast adjustments to the parent and the parent's milieu.

According to many researchers, the parent-infant relationship bond is not present at birth, but develops over time. There is considerable research on the specific relationship bond that develops between the infant and the parent. Two separate literatures have evolved regarding the bond—one from the side of the parent, known as *bonding,* and the other from the side of the child, which is referred to as *attachment* (Emde, 1989). Essentially, normally developing newborns and infants give cues such as cooing, crying, cuddling, and smiling, which are signals for parents to respond. As parents respond to their baby's signals and the infant anticipates needs being met, interactions occur that lead to the relationship bond, a bond which is critical to the development of a healthy child.

For parental bonding to occur, Klaus and Kennell (1981; Kennell, Voos, & Klaus, 1979) make the controversial assertion that there is a "sensitive period" immediately after birth. Affectionate attachments or bonds between the parent and infant must be formed at this time; if the bonding is interfered with, aberrant parenting may occur which, in turn, could affect infant development. de Chateau (1980), too, maintains that fostering early physical contact between the mother and neonate is important and that the effect of early close body contact with infants can be observed in closeness between the two one year after the baby's delivery. However, the importance of close early physical contact is controversial (Lamb & Bornstein, 1987); research evidence fails to support the importance of early contact (Goldberg, 1983; Lamb, 1982b; Myers, 1987) and there is little evidence that early contact has significant effects on maternal behavior (Lamb & Hwang, 1982).

Regardless of the merits of a specific sensitive period for bonding, the early close physical contact creates a situation of mutual contingency in which the parent and the newborn continuously adapt to one another's behavior. Behaviors involved in the early interactive process include eye contact, smiling, and vocalizations, which all contribute to the parent-child relationship. Trevarthen (1977) points out how these behaviors affect the turn-taking nature of mother-infant interactions, and Thoman (1981) views the interactive process as an early form of communication between parent and infant. Gazing, looking, and mutual visual regard, in particular, appear to contribute substantially to the interaction (Stern, 1974; Stern, Beebe, Jaffe, & Bennett, 1977).

The relationship that evolves depends not only on what occurs, but how the interaction pattern develops. It is the patterning of relationships that is closely related to the quality of the interaction, according to Sroufe (1989):

> *Patterning* refers to timing, sequences, and combinational features of the ongoing interaction. *When* does the caregiver pick up the infant: Is the pickup in response to a gesture by the infant? Is there an ongoing tuning or synchronizing of the behavior of each to the other? Does the infant mold to the caregiver or mix molding with stiffening, squirming, and pushing away?
>
>   In one case, an infant's distress may be terminated efficiently and smoothly. The caregiver responds promptly to the infant's cry, bending to

pick up the infant and conferring meaning to the cry. Reciprocally, the infant leans or reaches toward the caregiver, yields her body to the pickup, and then actively snuggles into the caregiver's shoulder, both arms wrapped around her neck. The caregiver rocks the infant with a swaying motion, gently pats the infant's back, and whispers in soothing tones. The infant settles, relaxes, and returns to play.

By contrast, in response to the baby's wail, a second caregiver bristles, then after some delay picks him up with a jerky motion. The infant's body stiffens and the crying seems to intensify. The infant shifts from side to side and alternates leaning in with pushing away from his mother, whose own irritation and tension show through pats that are too rough and movements that are stiff. The distress persists for several minutes (p. 99).

During the first year of a baby's life, both the infant and the parents undergo developmental changes. Parents adjust to the infant and the infant's characteristics, interests, and needs, in the context of their own personal characteristics and circumstances. Infants develop increasing competence in motor and physical skills, communication abilities, and cognitive growth and development as they respond and interact within the family environment. By approximately 12 months of age, the nature of the infant's attachment to the parent can be assessed. Bowlby (1980) asserts, "Intimate attachments to other human beings are the hub around which a person's life revolves, not only when he or she is an infant or a toddler, but throughout adolescence and the years of maturity as well and on into old age" (p. 442).

Attachment

Attachment is the child's side of the relationship bond that is formed and develops after birth. By the time an infant is one year of age, attachment may be reliably measured. Based on parent-infant interactions, through the Strange Situation research method (see Chapter 2), infants are categorized as insecure-avoidant, securely attached, insecure-resistant, or insecure-disorganized/disoriented (Main & Solomon, 1986).

The measurement of attachment, to a great extent, is an indication of how the emerging individual is organizing attitudes, expectations, and feelings. The organization is based on the history and pattern of affective and behavioral regulation that has occurred within the caregiving system (Sroufe, 1989b) and has significant implications for the child's future adjustment. For example, infants identified as securely attached are found to be more enthusiastic, affectively positive, and confident in solving problems than infants with histories of avoidant attachment (Arend, 1984; Matas, Arend, & Sroufe, 1978; Sroufe & Rosenberg, 1980; Sroufe, 1989b). In addition, securely attached children have greater ego strength at age 3½ (Waters, Wippman, & Sroufe, 1979), and are more resilient at ages 4 and 5 (Arend, Gove, & Sroufe, 1979; Sroufe, 1983). "Thus, young children with histories of secure attachment are seen to be independent, resourceful, curious, and confident in their approach to the environment" (Sroufe, 1989b, p. 87).

Avoidant attachment relationships, on the other hand, mirror a history of insensitive care and rejection. This pattern of attachment reflects the infant's internalized working model of the caregiver as unavailable and unresponsive to the infant's needs (Sroufe, 1989b). Later, these children are characterized as hostile, with displays of unprovoked aggression and generally negative peer interactions (LaFreniere & Sroufe, 1985); in school, they disrupt the classroom routine and engage in devious or antisocial behavior (Sroufe, 1983). In addition, these children behave in ways which recreate their early relationships and they often influence their environment to confirm their models of self and others (Sroufe & Fleeson, 1986).

Gender Differences

Most research on family dynamics examining parent-infant interaction focuses on the relationship between the mother and the child. However, within the last decade, researchers have become increasingly interested in the father's role in the socialization process. The interest stems from two major issues: an increasing consideration of infant sex role development and both parents' influences on such development, and the changing role of women and the impact of that change on child development. The latter issue has been particularly striking as women have moved from care of children and upkeep of the home, to a co-equal (or sole) participant in the economic well-being of the family. Mothers' pursuits of economic and vocational interests have changed dynamics in that the mother is no longer necessarily the sole or primary caregiver (Zigler, 1990). The potential change in the female's role in the family has raised the question of the relative influence of each parent in the infants' development (see Case Study: Bill and Sally).

Some of the changes in roles have occurred with the birth process itself. It has only been within the past two decades that fathers have been involved in the birth process. Now, the expectation for many fathers is that they are present at birth and play an active role in facilitating the birth process. Fathers may even be the first individuals to hold and cuddle the infant while the mother is still in the final stage of labor, the delivery of the placenta. Research in maternity wards shows that fathers are competent and interested in their newborns and display interaction involvement with their infants (Parke & Tinsley, 1981).

Researchers discern that both males and females play a significant role in infant development, although the specific roles may differ somewhat (Hetherington, 1983; Kotelchuk, 1976). Studies of early father-infant interaction document the affectionate and nurturant involvement between the father and the neonate (Parke & O'Leary, 1976). Pedersen (1975) also studied early parent-infant interactions and discovered that fathers play both a direct and indirect role in the early parent-child relationship. The direct role involves holding and caring for the infant, whereas the indirect role, in supporting the mother, allows the mother to more effectively interact with the infant.

The relative roles of the mother and father still vary, however. Fathers spend less time with their infants, on the average, than mothers and engage in fewer caretaker activities (e.g., changing diapers, feeding) (Kotelchuck, 1976; Lamb and Bornstein, 1987). However, fathers engage in affectionate behavior and are sensitive and responsive to their infants. Parke and O'Leary (1976), as well as Yogman (1982), found that fathers are active with their infants, but in ways that differ from mothers. Mothers engage in more caretaking activities while fathers are involved in relatively more play activities.

CASE STUDY: BILL AND SALLY

Bill and Sally married when he was in graduate and she in medical school. They rejected a traditional marriage, in which the husband works and the wife maintains the home and raises children. Based on the premise of shared commitments and responsibilities, their marriage was up-tempo with the promise of two professional careers ready to unfold.

During her medical residency program, Sally became pregnant with their child, Ann. Sally stayed home with Ann for 4 months, and then resumed her residency program. Sally was the only resident intern with an infant, one of very few women in the training program, and she worked under the skeptical eye of senior colleagues who silently questioned her commitment to medicine. Working a 60- to 70-hour-per-week schedule and being on call every third night left little time for her participation in child rearing and child-care activities.

What started as a co-equal partnership in marriage quickly became a lopsided arrangement of child-care responsibilities, in which Bill, with the more flexible college professor schedule, became the primary parent. His responsibilities included arranging child care during the day, supervising the day-care, rearranging his schedule when the day-care provider was ill or unavailable, being with Ann in the evenings and on weekends, securing diapers, baby food, clothing, and seeing to all of her other needs. Bill began to feel as if were in a traditional marriage but with the roles reversed; the traditional child-care and home responsibilities were falling on the husband instead of the wife.

As Sally's schedule maintained its excessive time demands and remained inflexible in terms of adaptability to child-care, parenting, and marital concerns, a strong relationship formed between Bill and Ann. As Bill supervised day-care during the week, cared for Ann at all other times, and included her in all social activities, their relationship became the dominant subsystem in the family. During the times when Sally was home, tensions arose over the unequal distribution of child-care responsibilities, questions regarding parental authority, and career demands and frustrations. Over time, the day-care issues subsided, but the residual family dynamic concerns awaited resolution.

The type and relative frequency of activity does not appear to affect infants' attachment to their fathers (Rosenblith & Sims-Knight, 1985). Schaffer & Emerson (1964), for instance, demonstrated that babies cry when their fathers leave and Pedersen and Robson (1969) found that babies display positive greeting behaviors when their fathers appear. Research on father-infant, as well as mother-infant, interaction has been conducted primarily on parents of typical infants. There is a distinct need for researchers to consider father-infant and mother-infant interaction with at-risk and handicapped newborns and infants.

Role of Day-Care

Changing roles within the family and mothers' increasing involvement in the work force make day-care a primary issue of concern. Fishbein (1984) makes the point that child care by nonfamily members is not unique in human history; for 99% of human existence humans lived as hunters and gatherers in close-knit groups in which child rearing was the responsibility of both family and nonfamily group members. For North American and Western industrialized societies, however, child rearing has consistently involved the mother being available to the infant.

With the increasing pattern of mothers working, less availability of extended family members for day-care, and the increasing reliance on day-care facilities, research is beginning to compare home-reared and day-care infants. In the main, these studies (e.g., Blanchard & Main, 1979; Brookhart & Hock, 1976; Vaughn, Gove, & Egeland, 1980) show that there are no persistent or systematic ill effects of day-care on infants' attachment behavior.

Zigler (1990) places tremendous importance on the issue of day-care availability and quality. He sees this as the most significant issue regarding children and families today and as an issue which will only become more important in the future, as even more women enter the work force and require child-care support. He is dismayed over the lack of standards for day-care provision, in the light of overwhelming consistency in professional judgment for quality day-care. Further, he finds troublesome the lack of effort politically in terms of social policy; if children are the primary social resource, we must expend more resources to maintain and enhance that resource.

Family Systems

During the first two years of life, if the relationship is going well, parents/caregivers become increasingly sensitive to the individual characteristics of their babies, and a strong, consistent, positive relationship bond becomes established. Infants give signals which elicit parent behavior, parents respond, and a complex set of interactions begin. By the end of the first year, a clear sense of attachment is discerned, and by the end of the second year, the relationship becomes further refined and the infant and parent have developed a highly complex set of interactions forming the basis for the infant's cognitive, emotional, and social development.

Salvador Minuchin and his colleagues (Minuchin, 1974, 1980; Minuchin & Fishman, 1981; Minuchin, Montalvo, Guerney, Rosman, & Schumer, 1967; Minuchin, Rosman, Baker, & Liebman, 1978) and Murray Bowen (1978) introduced the ideas and practice of structural family theory and therapy some time ago to help describe the family dynamic relationship patterns that evolve as a consequence of parent-child interactions. From this general point of view, individuals are shaped by their own individual characteristics as well as all the various contexts to which the individual is exposed (e.g., peers, school, etc.). The most significant factor in individual development from a family systems perspective is the family. The family is made up of dynamics, structures, functions, change mechanisms, and dysfunctions, all of which contribute to the development of the individual (Liebman & Ziffer, 1985).

Minuchin (1974) sees the family structure as, "the invisible set of functional demands that organizes the ways in which family members interact. A family is a system that operates through transactional patterns. Repeated transactions establish patterns of how, when, and to whom to relate, and these patterns underpin the system" (p. 51). Within families, subsystems develop which are formed by interest, generation, sex, or function; they include one, two (a dyad), or more members in roles which may be temporary and changeable (Minuchin et al., 1978).

Typical subsystems include the *spouse dyad* (husband and wife bonds), *parent dyad* (those in parenting roles), and the *sibling subsystem*. The subsystems must have sufficient freedom to function without interference from other subsystems in order to facilitate individual growth and development; for example, children will not learn to resolve their own differences if parents consistently intervene and solve problems for them (Liebman & Ziffer, 1985). There are communication patterns within and between subsystems. Goldstein (1988) has examined communication deviance in families, and others have considered generational boundaries between parents and children (Kreppner, Paulse, & Schuetze, 1982) and the links between abusive parental histories and child maltreatment (Main, Kaplan, & Cassidy, 1985; Ricks, 1985).

Marital harmony, disharmony, or a dysfunctional relationship can all have significant effects on the baby. Even the lack of an adult relationship can affect the level of stress within the family. Beckman (1983), for example, examined the influence of selected child characteristics on stress in families with handicapped infants. She reports that the only demographic variable associated with the amount of stress in the home was the number of parents in the home. Single mothers report more stress than do mothers in intact homes.

The family system also may involve siblings in terms of sibling-sibling interaction as well as sibling interactions with parents. Stevenson, Leavitt, Thompson, and Roach (1988) introduce a Social Relations Model for understanding interactions between parent-child and sibling play and suggest that

Siblings are an important part of the family system.

adjustments that family members make with one another outweigh family members' general tendencies to act in certain ways. Vandell and Wilson (1987) also explore the issue of sibling interaction and find that infants' turn-taking experiences with their mothers were related to the infants' subsequent interactions with their siblings and peers.

Gibbs, Teti, and Bond (1987) find that infants are more responsive to siblings widely spaced in age than those closely spaced. In addition, widely spaced siblings direct more social behavior to one another and are involved in more interactive engagements than closely spaced siblings. Older siblings often act as subsidiary attachment figures, caregivers, and teachers (Stewart, 1983; Stewart & Marvin, 1984).

From the family systems literature, *functional* families are defined as those in which communication, boundaries, hierarchies, and subsystems meet the needs of family members' developmental stages. *Dysfunctional* families suffer when one or more of these factors contribute to the family's failure to meet an individual's developmental needs. Liebman and Ziffer (1985) describe five general dysfunctional patterns:

1. *Overprotectiveness:* The tendency of parents to literally hover over the child, perhaps to the point of rarely letting him or her leave the house, except to attend school.
2. *Enmeshment:* An overinvolvement between two or more people resulting in a lack of age-appropriate autonomy, independence, privacy, and peer group relationships for both parties.
3. *Rigidity:* The family's tendency to rely on accustomed usual patterns of transactions when circumstances call for flexibility and change.

4. *Detouring:* A way of avoiding conflict between two people by invoking a third person or situation as the focus of the disagreement.

5. *Disengagement:* The lack of affective bonds, limits, or nurturance between two or more family members (pp. 185–186).

As a result of dysfunctional family patterns, boundaries may be too permeable, not permeable enough, or have failed altogether. The lack of resolution results in submerged stress, which potentially can create one of five crystallized problematic family types (Liebman & Ziffer, 1985):

1. *Triangulated family system:* Characterized by shifting subsystem coalitions and splitting of the spouse dyad. In this situation children feel trapped because they cannot agree with one parent without at the same time being perceived as disagreeing with the other.

2. *Detouring protective family system:* Parents superficially present an appropriate nurturant-supportive response to their child; however, there is typically overprotectiveness and enmeshment in these families.

3. *Detouring attacking family system:* Characterized by strength in the spouse dyad, with the parents focusing blame on the child for causing family problems.

4. *Stable coalition family system:* Found with close and constricting relationships between the identified child and one parent. This dyad usually excludes or attacks the other parent.

5. *Disengaged child family system:* The child or adolescent explicitly states their disinterest in being involved with the problems of the family.

In sum, parent-child interactions develop over time, as relationship bonds form and patterns of behavior within the family are established. The behavior patterns become family dynamics involving dyads and subsystems. When working well, the family dynamics accommodate the individual, subsystem, and family system developmental changes and needs. When not functioning well, family dynamics lead to patterns of behavior which fail to facilitate the growth and development of one or more family members.

FAMILY INTERACTIONS WITH AT-RISK AND HANDICAPPED INFANTS

With the addition of any infant to the family, adjustments are made; parents sleep less and are available to their baby at all times of the day and night to provide food, warmth, and shelter. With the birth of an at-risk or handicapped baby, however, the adjustment is more striking and typically involves more accommodations within the family and the home (Emde & Brown, 1978). For example, there may be additional feeding and caregiving tasks and responsibilities, additional modifications of schedules and activities to meet the medical or related infant needs, adjustments to separation if the infant's medical needs are great and require hospitalization, additional and unforeseen financial obligations, and readjustment of the marital relationship.

Parents with infants in at-risk nurseries are often described as angry, emotionally distraught, or shocked (e.g., Klaus & Kennell, 1976; Kopf & McFadden, 1974; Slade, Redl, & Manguten, 1977). Drotar and colleagues (1975) describe five stages which parents pass through in adapting and attaching to their handicapped infant. Initially, parents experience shock and dismay, which gives way to a period of denial. In the third stage, parents express anger, anxiety, and sadness about their baby; fourth, there is a gradual adjustment as the parent gains confidence in caring for their infant. Finally, parents accept responsibility for their child and begin to plan for the baby's care and future. This particular set of stages has been questioned in the literature, but it is clear that the birth of an at-risk or handicapped baby does require a period of parental and familial adjustment (see Case Study: Mary Kay and Joe).

Feeding disturbances are common with at-risk or handicapped infants (Klaus & Fanaroff, 1979), which place greater demands on their caregivers than with normal babies. Some babies (e.g., premature infants) are alert less and are more difficult to keep alert (Goldberg, 1978). More severely affected infants may require complex medical procedures at specific times during the day or night. The sounds and cries of at-risk and handicapped babies are even different from those of normal infants; Frodi and Lamb (1978), for example, found that the cries of premature infants are judged to be more aversive to parents than cries of full-term babies.

CASE STUDY: MARY KAY AND JOE

Mary Kay and Joe prepared for the birth of their child by attending child birth classes. In the classes, the instructor posed thought-provoking questions such as what would you do if your baby had difficulties at delivery. Because they had thought and discussed such an occurrence, they knew what to do when their daughter was born with problems and after delivery was taken immediately to the intensive care unit. Joe went with baby Katherine to intensive care and was with her during the critical time she was receiving oxygen and being examined by pediatric specialists. Mary Kay feels that there is a special bond between Joe and Katherine because of that initial period of time they spent with one another.

Although she was born at 38 weeks gestation, Katherine was a low birthweight baby. She weighed 4 lbs, 13 oz at birth, exhibited low muscle tone, a soft palate cleft, and a heart murmur. The physicians did not offer a specific diagnosis of Katherine's difficulties, and as time went on, a significant hearing loss also was found. Probably the most striking physical issue for Mary Kay and Joe is feeding Katherine. Their strongest feelings of frustration revolve

around not being able to help her eat. With much patience and help from pro-
fessional therapists, they have tried to work with her on sucking and feeding.
After much frustration, repeated failures, and a sense that Katherine was los-
ing ground developmentally, they decided to accept physicians' recommenda-
tions that a feeding tube be inserted surgically.

As Mary Kay and Joe have adjusted to being new parents and parents
of a child with birth difficulties, many issues have emerged. First, they have
worked hard on agreeing what to do with Katherine and coordinating their ideas
on Katherine's needs and her future. This has required that Joe be very sup-
portive of Mary Kay and that their level of communication stay high. Second,
issues have emerged regarding grandparents and their expectations for Katherine
and, more particularly, for Mary Kay as the mother. The struggle to have the
grandparents understand Katherine's needs and be supportive of Joe and Mary
Kay as parents has been significant.

Third, many issues have emerged regarding professionals involved in help-
ing Joe, Mary Kay, and Katherine. The speech therapist wanted to come to
the home three times during the week. Frequently Katherine would not be awake
when the therapist arrived and the therapist scheduled meetings during the day
when Joe could not participate. In addition, coordinating surgery and medical
issues have proven to be a major concern; during one month, Katherine had
surgery to repair the cleft palate and the next month surgery to insert the feeding
tube. It was hard for Mary Kay and Joe to get anyone to coordinate the two
surgeries, which was absolutely necessary because the proposed nose tube which
was part of the feeding surgery would interfere with the cleft palate repair, which
had just been done a month before. Because of the hierarchy in the medical
setting and the inability of physicians to respond to any professional other than
another physician, Mary Kay and Joe find it hard to see how anyone other than
a doctor can serve as a coordinator for a child's needs when significant medical
issues are involved.

Two other issues which are significant for Mary Kay and Joe are the ex-
haustion they face and their inability to leave Katherine with anyone who is
not specifically trained to care for her needs. Fortunately, Mary Kay's sister
lives in their town and is available for child care when Mary Kay and Joe want
some relief.

For Joe, there are father-child issues. He feels a strong bond with Katherine
and spends a good deal of time holding, cuddling, and talking with her. But,
as Katherine has received services, it has been hard for him to keep up with
her development. At times, he feels out of the information flow and this is the
down side of not being at home during the day more consistently. For him,
if therapy schedules could be more flexible, with at least some evening hours,
he could feel more involved in her care and development.

Mary Kay, a school psychologist, and Joe, a businessmen, feel that it would
be extremely hard to be a single parent or have an uninvolved spouse and still
function effectively for a baby with special needs. The need to coordinate ac-

tivities for the infant is a real priority for intervention to be successful. Both parents feel that parents must be advocates for their children; in their situation, services for Katherine would not be as well coordinated as they are if Mary Kay and Joe were not consistently involved in planning, implementing, and evaluating the service activities.

At-risk and handicapped infants may also be less adept at responding to parental cues than normal, full-term babies. Jones (1977), for example, finds that Down syndrome infants engage in less eye contact with their mothers, use fewer "referential" looks, and have poorer vocal turn-taking compared with normal infants. Indeed, preterm infants contribute less to the parent interactive flow than do full-term babies (Brown & Bakeman, 1980). It would be inappropriate, however, to assume that parent-child relationships are necessarily disordered or that at-risk or handicapped infants have a distorted understanding of themselves, others, or of their relationships (Adams & Weaver, 1986; Drotar & Bush, 1985; Drotar, Crawford, & Bush, 1984; Parmelee, 1989). One of the major problems for these relationships may be the difficulties that parents have in gaining confidence in themselves as effective parents and caregivers (Cadman, Boyle, Szatmari, & Offord, 1987).

At-risk infant factors and infantile impairments can affect the parent-child interaction in two basic ways: by the baby's own behavior in stimulating and reacting to the parent or failing to do so, or by parental perceptions and assumptions about what the baby is capable or incapable of perceiving or doing (Hetherington, 1983). In either case, the parent-child interaction and attachment basic to healthy infant development may be at risk. With at-risk or handicapped babies, the signals or cues which normal infants give may not be clear or may be distorted (Yoder, 1987); consequently, parents may respond inadequately or not at all to their baby's needs.

The birth of an at-risk or handicapped infant also appears to affect parents' perceptions of the infant's competence and development. As a whole, Goldberg's (1978) analysis demonstrates that mothers of preterm infants speak with them less, engage in less gazing and looking behavior, vocalize less, and smile and touch less than parents of full-term infants. However, the results reported by Goldberg are not universal. Yoder and Feagans (1988) report that some mothers of severely handicapped babies identify as many cues as mothers of mildly handicapped infants. Some mothers seem to adapt to their infant's handicaps by becoming adept at interpreting their baby's behavior.

The obvious question is what is the effect of a potentially different pattern of parent-infant interaction on the development of attachment. Beckwith (1984) reports that neonatal medical problems do not adversely affect mother-infant interaction. This issue was considered in a comparison of attachment in nonhandicapped and physically handicapped infants when nonretarded infants with facial or orthopedic anomalies were compared to typical infants in a variant of the Strange Situation procedure; high-risk and low-risk subjects did not differ in attachment. Responsivity, availability, and positive affect all contributed to measured attachment, but risk and the risk interaction factors did not (Wasserman, Lennon, Allen, & Shilansky, 1987). Wills (1979) also found that, except in the most extreme circumstances, parents adjust and attach to their handicapped infant.

Although further research is necessary on the interaction between parents and at-risk and handicapped infants, it seems clear that attachments can and are formed. However, there is a risk that parents may not be sensitive to their infant's cues and that infants with early developmental difficulties may be at risk for developing normal attachment behaviors. For example, in recent research on the development of affective expression in normal and physically handicapped infants, Wasserman (1986) found that developmentally, over time, handicapped infants are increasingly unwilling to engage a stranger in a positive affective exchange. In addition, they show a delay, compared with normal infants, in their ability to control distress during maternal separation. This gives some indication of possible early diminishment in sociability among physically handicapped infants and potential eventual difficulties.

PARENTING STYLES AND THEIR INFLUENCE ON THE CHILD

Regardless of whether or not an infant or toddler has a handicapping condition, parenting functions must be carried out. Radke-Yarrow and Kuczynski (1983) present the range of parenting functions:

- Providing physical care, physical protection, and psychological support
- Controling, motivating, and regulating children's behavior
- Teaching and providing knowledge and skills
- Providing an affective environment
- "Investing" in and identifying with their children
- Facilitating their children's interaction with their physical and interpersonal environments

Parenting functions and the way they are carried out affect infants and toddlers and how they develop. Martin (1981), for example, distinguishes between mothers in terms of their involvement, employing the concepts of involvement with the infant versus being autonomous and focused on self.

Much of the parenting dynamics literature has focused on parents' control and regulation of their children's behavior. In the early studies of parenting dynamics, techniques of discipline tended to be categorized under two major classifications: *power-assertive discipline*, including forceful commands, punishment, shouting, threats, and yelling, and *love-oriented discipline*, including contingent giving of affection, isolation, reasoning, showing disappointment, and withdrawal of love (Heatherington, 1983).

Baumrind and her colleagues (Baumrind, 1966, 1967, 1968, 1970, 1971) are significant researchers in this area. They have considered parenting in terms of parental demandingness and parental responsiveness. Baumrind and her colleagues identify clusters of parenting behaviors:

- *Authoritarian parenting* is characterized by attempting to control and shape child attitudes and behaviors according to an absolute set of standards; valuing obedience, the preservation of order, and the respect for authority; and discouraging mutual verbal interaction between parent and child. Their research shows that socially withdrawn and unhappy preschool children tend to have parents who fit this parenting pattern.

- *Indulgent-permissive parenting* is characterized by parents who have an accepting attitude, are tolerant, and use little punishment. These parents tend to make few behavioral demands and let children regulate their own behavior. Children raised in this parenting manner, as preschoolers, tend to lack impulse control, self-reliance, social responsibility, and independence.

- *Authoritative parenting* style includes the following characteristics: expectations for mature behavior, clear standard setting, firm enforcement of rules and standards, encouragement of independence, open communication between children and parents, and a recognition of children's and parents' rights. Preschool children raised in this parenting style tend to act cooperatively, behave in a socially responsible manner, and are independent.

- *Indifferent-uninvolved parenting* style is characterized as an indifference to the developing child. This parenting style refers to parents who are to a great extent uninvolved and uninterested in their children. The children who receive this type of parenting have various problems, ranging from severe behavioral difficulties to withdrawn social behavior.

Research in the area of parenting dynamics and consequent child characteristics has been dominated by work with parents of nonhandicapped children and, thus, generalizations regarding the research are necessarily limited.

Additional parenting dynamics have also been explored, including multicultural issues and the effects of socioeconomic factors. Multicultural issues influence parenting in a number of ways. Sameroff (1989) discusses differing cultural codes, including customs, beliefs, and patterns of control and support,

Differing customs, beliefs, values, and patterns of child-rearing affect the way parents feel about early intervention.

which influence parent-child interactions. For example, parents who do not participate in school activities do not necessarily care any less about their children than those who do. They may simply be reflecting cultural norms regarding interactions with school officials (Turnbull & Turnbull, 1986).

Parenting has also been explored in the context of socioeconomic (SES) factors, including level of education, parent occupation, and income level. Researchers have found that higher SES families have more resources available to cope with handicapping conditions and a higher level of education and, thus, more knowledge about impairments; however, a higher SES does not necessarily lead to better coping skills or parenting behaviors (Turnbull & Turnbull, 1986). It is clear that a child born to a family which is poor, from a nondominant culture and language, and with few social support systems will experience an environment very different from that of the baby born to an upper middle class family, from the dominant culture, with many, extensive social support systems.

Optimum parenting dynamics include the competent performance of parenting activities and responsibilities, combined with parent-child interactions which are sensitive, responsive, and warm. However, many children experience less than optimum parenting behaviors. In some cases, the parenting dynamics are so problematic that they result in child abuse and neglect.

CHILD ABUSE AND NEGLECT

When parenting dynamics become so dysfunctional, the situation may lead to abuse and neglect. Estimates of abuse and neglect vary, but Harrison and Edwards (1983) estimate that approximately 20% of all children may be neglected or emotionally, physically, or sexually abused by their parents. Abuse occurs in all cultural groups, across all socioeconomic levels, typically with younger parents, and with parents who have few friends and sources of social support (Embry, 1980). Table 6.1 lists some of the characteristics of abused and neglected children.

Child abuse appears to be more frequent with handicapped children. Estimates range from 8% to 55% of abused children exhibiting intellectual or physical impairment (Frodi, 1981). Turnbull and Turnbull (1986) are quick to point out that just because a large percentage of abused children have excep-

---

TABLE 6.1   **Characteristics of Abused and Neglected Children**

Abused or neglected children are likely to share some of the following characteristics:

1. They appear to be different from other children in physical and emotional make-up, or their parents describe them as being different or bad.
2. They seem afraid of their parents.
3. They may bear bruises, welts, sores, or other skin injuries which seem to be untreated.
4. They are given inappropriate food, drink, or medication.
5. They are left alone with inadequate supervision.
6. They are chronically unclean.
7. They exhibit extremes in behavior: cry often or cry very little and show no real expectation of being comforted; they are excessively fearful or seem fearless of adult authority; they are unusually aggressive or extremely passive or withdrawn.
8. They are wary of physical contact, especially with an adult. They may be hungry for affection yet have difficulty relating to children and adults. Based on their experiences, they feel they cannot risk getting close to others.
9. They exhibit a sudden change in behavior, exhibit regressive behavior, such as wetting their pants or bed, thumb-sucking, whining, or becoming uncommonly shy or passive.
10. They have learning problems that cannot be diagnosed. Their attention wanders and they easily become self-absorbed.
11. They are habitually truant or late to school. Frequent or prolonged absences from school may result from the parents' keeping an injured child at home until the evidence of abuse disappears. Or they may arrive at school early and remain after classes instead of going home.
12. They are tired and often sleep in class.
13. They are not dressed appropriately for the weather. Children who wear long sleeves on hot days may be dressed to hide bruises or burns or other marks of abuse, or they may be dressed inadequately and suffer frostbite or illness from exposure to the weather.

Note: *From Child Abuse* (p. 65) by R. Harrison and J. Edwards, 1983, Portland OR: Ednick Publications. Copyright 1983 by Ednick Communications. Reprinted by permission.

tionalities does not mean that a large number of children with handicapping conditions are abused. Indeed, the majority of parents with handicapped children do not abuse their children (Embry, 1980).

The incidence of child abuse can be explained by the work of Sroufe and Fleeson (1986), who maintain that relationships have four primary characteristics: relationships are wholes; relationships have continuity and coherence; individuals internalize whole relationships, not simply roles; and early relationship patterns are incorporated into later close relationships. The abusing parent has internalized an abusing role from his/her own parents and carried it forward to a present parent-child relationship (Egeland, Jacobvitz, & Sroufe, 1988). From this point of view, the insecurely attached infant internalizes a relationship model which sets the stage for subsequent maltreatment of his or her own child (Lamb & Bornstein, 1987). From a social learning perspective, the relationship the child learned at home through modeling and imitation, enhanced through direct and vicarious reinforcement, leads to the transmittal of abusive behavior to the next generation (Patterson, 1982).

FAMILY ASSESSMENT AND INTERVENTION

Assessment

Bailey and Simeonsson (1988a, 1988b) developed a rationale and model for family assessment in early intervention. To a great extent their rationale rests on the imperatives from PL 99–457, in which parents of infants and toddlers are directed to develop an individualized family service plan with a multidisciplinary team. Their model rests on a goodness-of-fit concept in which goals and services are appropriate only if they match with parents' perception of the need for such services.

Bailey and Simeonsson's (1988a, 1988b) assessment model is driven by their model for a family-focused intervention. In this model, family needs are assessed, a focused interview conducted, followup assessments made, an IFSP meeting held, services implemented, and an evaluation plan carried out. They suggest assessing child characteristics, parent-child interaction, family stress and needs, critical events in the family's life, family roles and support systems, and family environments. With the assessment data, interventions are planned, implemented, and evaluated. (See also Chapter 7.)

A hidden factor in the assessment process may be stress in families of children at risk. Hutliner (1988) finds that the effects of stress in families with very young handicapped or at-risk children are often pervasive, multiple, and sometimes unsuspected. She suggests the implementation of stress reduction strategies which build on family strengths. In addition, medical stabilization should be pursued and the families provided with social and economic stability.

Often, stress is related to the amount of support available to the family. Beckman and others (Beckman, 1983; Beckman & Pokorni, 1988) found that stress in families with 3-month-old babies was significantly negatively related to the amount of formal family support.

Intervention

Many intervention programs involving families have been developed (see also Chapters 9 and 10). For example, Rosenberg and Robinson (1985) considered the impact of training on mothers' interactional skills with their handicapped infants or toddlers. The results indicate that training focusing on interaction strategies enhances maternal abilities to interact with their handicapped babies. Other researchers, too, find that mother-child interaction patterns differ in families with at-risk and developmentally delayed children (Holaday, 1987; Kysela & Marfo, 1983), and that parents' interaction skills are enhanced with professional support (Crnic, Greenberg, & Slough, 1986).

Mahoney and Powell (1988) describe a transactional intervention program designed to modify the interaction patterns between parents and their handicapped children, from birth to age 3. This home-based intervention program results in decreased parent interactional dominance and frequency of directives, increased parent responsiveness, and relative developmental gains for the handicapped infants and toddlers.

Beyond the interaction issue, parents can be taught skills in handling their handicapped babies (Scatterfield & Yasumura, 1987). Professional and social support stand out as important resources in fostering positive family dynamics (Crnic, Greenberg, Robinson, & Ragozin, 1984; Crockenberg, 1985). Beyond professional support, Weinraub and Wolf (1983) find that optimum interaction within two-parent families is associated with fewer stressful life events, satisfaction with emotional support, and the availability of household help.

In the future, family systems theory may be taught to parents in parent education programs (Getz & Gunn, 1988) or to counselors for use in training teachers to work more effectively with handicapped children's parents (Berry, 1987). Minuchin (1985) recommends the use of systems theory to study parent-child interactions. Wendt and Zake (1984) make the case for a family systems perspective in school psychological services, and a family systems approach has also been stressed by many in the provision of psychological services for children and families (e.g., Anderson, 1983; Pfeiffer & Tittler, 1983). Most programmatic developments for at-risk and handicapped infants focus on the family.

The professional literature on family dynamics and research with at-risk and handicapped infants, toddlers, and their families make it clear that services need to be developed and delivered within the family context. Families must be encouraged to make crucial decisions for their children.

FAMILY-PROFESSIONAL RELATIONSHIPS

Historically, the family-professional relationship is an uneven one whenever an at-risk or handicapped infant or toddler is involved. In some relationships, family decision-making and empowerment have been valued, facilitated, and fostered, but in others, families have been made to feel the root of their child's difficulties and even as impediments to their child's growth and development. Fortunately, the implementation of PL 99–457 has strengthened the assumption that parents are the primary decision-makers in their child's developmental assessment and intervention.

To some extent, establishing parents as the primary decision-makers is difficult for both parents and professionals. Parents are socialized to seek, respect, and follow professional advice; professionals are trained to deliver, advise, and anticipate adherence to their perscriptions. Therefore, it will take time, training, and practice for parents and professionals to learn to work together as effective partners in efforts to facilitate infants' and toddlers' growth and development.

Chapter 7

Screening and Assessment

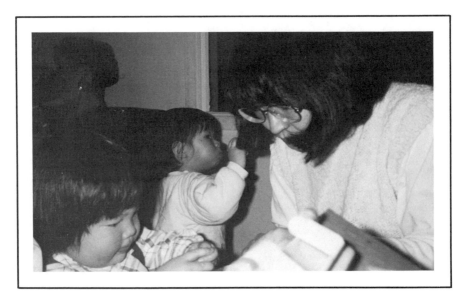

When designing and implementing assessment procedures for identification and intervention with high-risk and handicapped infants, the team will need to consider a number of variables. Team members must identify the purpose of the assessment and select assessment tools and strategies that will help meet that purpose. The assessment should yield information about the infant's strengths as well as weaknesses. For many high-risk and handicapped infants this means that the assessment should allow for adaptive responses. Further, the assessment should provide information that will lead directly to the specification of intervention targets and activities. The assessment tools and procedures should be compatible with the philosophy of the program and the theoretic orientation of the curriculum.

Parents are joint participants in the planning process. In addition to sharing their priorities and concerns, parents can also help decide where and when the assessment will be held, and who should be involved. They can also decide upon their role in the assessments.

The assessment of infants is different from the assessment of older children and adults. Accurate assessments require that the examiner be patient, creative, observant, and energetic. Infant behavior is highly variable. Such factors as temperament, state, physical comfort, and health will influence the assessment. In addition, between the developmental ages of about 7 and 18 months, infants and toddlers may demonstrate anxious or wary behavior towards strangers, including examiners.

Rogers (1982) described five important characteristics of an effective examiner of infants:

- Enjoys young children
- Has a strong knowledge of child development
- Has experience with young children
- Is able to read the young child's signals and match the child's interactive style
- Reads the parent's signals and is able to ease their anxiety

ASSESSMENT TOOLS AND TECHNIQUES

Hospitals, health-care settings, and early intervention programs use a variety of assessment tools and techniques. Table 7.1 introduces some of the terminology that is helpful to understanding these procedures.

The Apgar Scoring System

The Apgar Scoring System (Apgar, 1953) was designed to measure a newborn infant's physical responsivity, development, and overall state of health. It is typically administered by medical personnel in the delivery room, within minutes

TABLE 7.1   Test and Measurement Terminology

Validity: The extent to which the measure fulfills the purpose for which it is intended

> Content validity: The extent to which the measure covers a representative sample of the behaviors it supposedly samples
>
> Criterion-related validity: The correspondence between test scores and present (concurrent) or future (predictive) performance as measured in another way
>
> Construct validity: An indicator of how well the test actually measures the theoretic construct such as cognition, creativity, or intelligence

Reliability: The consistency with which a test measures what it is supposed to measure

> Test-retest reliability: The correlation between two administrations of the same test to the same individual on two occasions
>
> Alternative-form reliability: The correlation between scores from two forms of a test given at essentially the same time
>
> Interrater reliability: The extent to which two or more scorers are consistent in their judgments

Standardized test: A measure with fixed procedures of administration and scoring; standard materials, stimulus items and instructions; empirical testing of the items; and norms

Norm-referenced test: A test in which an individual child's performance is compared with a normative group, usually of others of the same age

Criterion-referenced test: A test in which an individual child's performance is compared to a standard of mastery or sequence of skills

Note: Adapted from *Psychological Testing* (5th ed.) by A. Anastasi, 1982, New York: MacMillan, Copyright 1982 by MacMillan; and *Handbook for Measurement and Evaluation in Early Childhood Education* by W.L. Goodwin and L.A. Driscoll, 1980, San Francisco; Jossey Bass, copyright 1980 by Jossey-Bass Inc., Publishers.

after birth (at 60 sec., 5 min., and 10 min. following birth). The Apgar score helps to identify newborns in immediate need of special care and treatment.

The optimal Apgar score is 10. Each of five characteristics—activity (muscle tone), pulse (heart rate), grimace (reflex to stimulation), appearance (color), and respiration (respiratory effort)—are scored 0, 1, or 2. A score of 0 indicates that the sign is not present, a score of 2 is the best possible condition, and a score of 1 is given for intermediate conditions. Infants who earn a score of 6 points or less are considered to be at-risk.

The Apgar scoring system is widely used in western countries. There seems to be a general relationship between the score and such variables as maternal health and emotional status, perinatal conditions, and infant mortality during the neonatal period, but the specific relationship between the Apgar score and later development is not clear (Self & Horowitz, 1979). When such variables as socioeconomic status and race are controlled, the Apgar score is not substantiated as a predictor of later development (Broman, Nichols, & Kennedy, 1975; Shipe, Vandenburg, & Williams, 1968).

Many states mandate newborn screening tests other than the Apgar score to determine the absence or presence of disorders that result in handicapping conditions. The screening test for phenylketonuria (PKU), which consists of blood and urine analyses to detect the presence of the enzyme phenylalanine, is one of the most common of these tests. This enzyme defect can be managed effectively through diet if identified early. Newborn screening tests are also available for galactosemia, congenital hypothyroidism, cystic fibrosis, and other disorders. Such screening tests are not yet routine in all locations, however. Whereas all but two states required PKU screening in 1975, only eight states routinely screened for the other disorders (Thurman & Widerstrom, 1990).

Neonatal Behavioral Assessment Scale

The Neonatal Behavioral Assessment Scale (NBAS) (Brazelton, 1984) was designed as an interactive assessment of the newborn's behavioral repertoire and neurological responses. The assessment is appropriate for infants (over 37 weeks gestation) from the first day of life through the end of the first month. In its revised form, the NBAS consists of 28 behavioral items such as orientation to visual, auditory, and social stimuli, alertness, self-quieting, and activity level. Behavioral items are scored on a 9-point scale. The NBAS also includes 18 reflex items (e.g., plantar grasp, Moro, rooting, sucking) that are scored on a four-point scale. The examination takes 20 to 30 minutes and should be administered by a skilled, observant examiner. The NBAS conceptualizes the infant as active, competent, and social. The aim is to identify the infant's best performance. The examiner assesses the infant's ability to modulate its own systems in response to external manipulation.

The NBAS has been used in numerous research studies. Reviews of this literature are provided by Horowitz and Linn (1984), Lydic and Nugent (1982), and Sostek (1978). Reliability and validity information are provided in the test manual. Training is necessary to achieve adequate interrater reliability estimates.

An interesting clinical application of the NBAS is its use as a teaching tool with parents. The examiner assesses the infant in the parents' presence so that the infant's skills and capabilities are demonstrated. Through observing methods to comfortably handle and position the baby, strategies to facilitate behaviors, and other responsive techniques, parents are alerted to their infant's own particular signals. This relatively simple treatment may help parents learn that their babies are skillful and may also promote significant changes in parenting skills and knowledge of child development (Nugent, 1985; Szajnberg, Ward, Krauss, & Kessler, 1987; Widmayer & Field, 1981).

Assessment of Preterm Infants' Behavior

The Assessment of Preterm Infants' Behavior (APIB) (Als et al., 1982) was designed as a refinement and extension of the NBAS for preterm and high-risk infants. It includes many of the NBAS items and presents them in gradated fashion in order to observe the infant's current level of functioning or organization in the presence of varying demands. Five subsystems are observed:

physiological, motor, state, interactive and attentional, and self-regulation. These evolving subsystems make up the model of preterm development, or the synactive model (Als, 1986). Particular attention is given to the observation of the infant's communicative signals. For preterm infants these signals may be visceral (e.g., color changes, burping), motor (e.g., postural changes, movements), state-related (e.g., drowsy, hyperalert), or neurological (e.g., tremors, startles).

Assessment of preterm and very-high-risk infants requires special knowledge as well as flexible procedures. Handling, movement, and various positions can negatively affect some babies. Data are derived from observing the infant at rest and during necessary treatments. When the infant is handled, the examiner carefully watches the infant's responses. When stress is detected, support and recovery time are given. For the very ill preterm infant, a naturalistic observation system such as that provided by Als (1984a) may be more appropriate than a method that requires handling.

A trained examiner may utilize the APIB to assess the infant's current status and to identify the amount of support needed to optimize the infant's development and organization. With training, good interrater reliabilities can be achieved. The APIB has been used to discriminate the organizational abilities of preterm infants (Als, 1985). This assessment has been used successfully to identify intervention targets for infants in the NICU (Als et al., 1986). The following example illustrates the use of the APIB:

> Kelly is a 4-month-old infant in the NICU. She was born at 27 weeks gestation and weighed 905 g. She has bronchopulmonary dysplasia and is on a ventilator. Using the APIB, Kelly was observed during rest, taking of vital signs, diaper change, and return to rest. Based on these observations, recommendations were made:
>
> - Side-lying is a good position for Kelly. Make sure she is in total flexion without occluding airways. Use rolled blanket or sandbag behind head and neck to help her maintain this position.
> - Kelly likes to suck on her fingers. In side-lying make sure that her arms are positioned forward so that she can easily "find" her fingers. When holding her, also position her shoulders and arms forward, so that her fingers are easily available to her.
> - During caregiving, slowly uncover Kelly. Watch for signs of stress (color change, arching, grimace). Use your hands to contain her limbs and keep her in flexion. Give Kelly something to suck on during and after handling.

Other screening tests

In addition to the NBAS and the APIB, several other instruments are available for the assessment of the neurological status and integrity of infants. A few of the most widely used instruments are described in Table 7.2.

Vision Tests

Heredity is a major cause of visual impairment as are infectious diseases, poisoning, tumors, and prenatal factors. Preterm infants are at risk for retinopathy of prematurity, which in its most severe form may result in blindness. Three approaches have been used to assess visual acuity in infants: checking the optokinetic response, measuring visual evoked responses, and forced preferential looking.

To check the optokinetic response, a black and white striped cylinder is twirled in front of the infant (London, 1982). The eyes should jiggle as they rapidly focus on one stripe and then the other. Lack of this response may mean that the infant has a serious visual problem. However, lack of response may also mean that the infant has not attended to or focused on the stripes and, thus, this test is not very reliable.

The visual evoked responses technique (Tyler, 1982) determines the electrical reaction of the occipital cortex to a visual stimulus. Electrodes are attached to the back of the infant's head, and a light is flashed. The electrode that rests on the occipital lobe should record an electrical impulse within a split second. If this does not occur, there may be an abnormality in vision somewhere between the eye and the occipital cortex (Harley, 1983).

Forced preferential looking is based on the premise that an infant shown a blank target and a patterned target will prefer to look at the patterned target (Fantz, 1958). During testing, the infant sits or is held in front of a screen containing a black-and-white grating and a blank gray target. The infant is shown a number of presentations of gratings of varying spatial frequencies (stripe widths), with the left-right placement of the grating varied from one presentation to the next. The examiner uses the infant's eye and head movements to make a forced-choice judgment on each trial as to the infant's preference. Thus, the infant's visual acuity is determined. The procedure has been used in research, and adaptations are available for wider use (Teller, McDonald, Preston, Sebris, & Dobson, 1986).

In addition to the assessment of visual acuity, an infant's functional vision should be assessed. Functional vision refers to the individual's use of vision with everyday activities. Descriptions of methods and materials are provided by Langley (1980) and Baird and Hemming (1982).

Hearing Tests

Among the major causes of deafness are heredity, rubella, prematurity, and meningitis. Fortunately, hearing can be assessed in newborns and infants through behavioral responses, brain-stem auditory evoked response, and visual reinforcement audiometry. One may observe the infant's response (e.g., eye blink, startle, arm or leg movements) to different sounds (e.g., bell, buzzer, rattle). This behavioral approach is the least accurate of the three procedures for infants, in part due to the possibility of observer bias. A more sophisticated device,

TABLE 7.2 Selected Infant Neuromotor Assessment Instruments

NAME	AGE RANGE	DESCRIPTION	CONTENT	PSYCHOMETRIC PROPERTIES
Neurological Examination of the Full-Term Newborn (Prechtl, 1977)	Newborns at 38–42 weeks post-conception	Measure of CNS integrity; to identify those infants in need of followup	Postures, movements, reflexes, reactions; structural/physical signs; behavioral state	Interrater reliability, .70 to 1.00
Primitive Reflex Profile (Capute et al., 1978)	Very young infant and older retarded child	Developed as a standard means of measuring reflex activity, used for screening early motor problems	Nine primitive postural reflexes	Interrater reliability, described in manual but no indices reported; predictive validity continues to be studied.
Movement Assessment of Infants (Chandler, Andrews & Swanson, 1980)	Birth–12 months	To identify motor problems; serve as basis for early intervention; monitor effects of physical therapy; aid in research; teach skillful observation and handling	65 items covering muscle tone, primitive reflexes, automatic reactions, volitional movement	Interrater reliability, ≥90%; test-retest reliability, $r = .76$; modest predictive validity
Neurological Assessment of the Preterm and Full-Term Newborn Infant (Dubowitz & Dubowitz, 1981)	Newborns	To document abnormal development of neurological behavior; to compare full-term and preterm infants; also includes measure of gestational age.	Habituation, movement and tone, reflexes, neurobehavioral items	Interrater reliability described in manual but no indices reported; prospective data are being collected.

Test	Population	Purpose	Content	Reliability
Assessment of Preterm Infants Behavior (APIB)	Preterm infants, full-term neonates	To identify infant's current level of functioning in the face of varying developmental demands	Observations of physiological responses, motor behaviors, behavior state, interaction/attention, and self-regulation	Satisfactory interrater reliability with training; test discriminates infants with difficulties.
Neurologic Examination of the Newborn and the Infant (Amiel-Tison & Grenier, 1983)	Birth–12 months	To systematically assess neuromotor abilities of infants; to identify abnormalities; to monitor course of development	Structural features, posture and spontaneous motor behavior, muscle tone, reflexes	Limited reliability data; some prospective studies have been reported.
Neonatal Behavioral Assessment Scale (Brazelton, 1984)	Full-term neonates, preterms over 37 weeks	To measure the infant's abilities on a variety of behavioral parameters	28 behavioral items, 18 elicited responses (neurological items), behavior state	Interrater reliability $\geq 90\%$; low to moderate test-retest reliability; moderate predictive reliability
Infant Neurological International Battery (Infanib) (Ellison, Horn, & Browning, 1985)	Infants 1–18 months	To assess the neurological integrity of infants	20-item scale with 5 factors: spasticity, vestibular function, head and trunk control, resting tone, and description of legs	High internal consistency; discriminates normal-abnormal; additional studies in progress

the Crib-O-Gram (Simmons, 1977), which includes a motion-sensitive transducer and an automatic recording device, may alleviate this problem.

In the brain-stem auditory evoked response (BAER) or auditory brain-stem response (ABR) approach, electrodes are pasted to the base of the head. A clicking sound is presented to the infant through earphones and a burst of neural activity results. A computer averages the intensity of the responses, which are presented on a viewing screen in the form of waves. An absence of one or more of the waves suggests an abnormality in the hearing pathway leading from the inner ear to the brain stem. The rapidity of the conduction of the nerve impulse is also measured. This type of testing does not require active participation by the infant. However, some infants may resist the placement of the earphones.

Infants over 6 months of age may be tested successfully using visual reinforcement audiometry (VRA) (Thompson & Wilson, 1984). Depending on developmental skills, the infant sits in an infant seat, on the parent's lap, or in a high chair in a soundproof room. The infant is taught to look at a lighted display when a sound is presented. Then, sounds of varying frequencies are presented; if the infant turns, the display lights up. This technique can be very successful until the child outgrows interest in the reinforcer. Play audiometry may then be used. In this technique, the child is conditioned to indicate that he or she hears a sound by responding to a repetitive game, such as putting a block in a container or a ring on a stick (Garrity & Mengle, 1983).

THE EARLY INTERVENTION ASSESSMENT PROCESS

The early intervention assessment process is a series of recurring steps and decisions. There are six major steps: case finding, screening, in-depth assessment (or diagnosis), assessment for planning intervention, monitoring change (described in Chapter 8), and program evaluation (Table 7.3).

Assessment refers to the process of gathering information regarding a child's developmental status for the purpose of making a decision. By gathering and integrating information from direct testing, interview, records review, and observation, decisions can be made regarding diagnosis, referral, and appropriate services. Further information gathering may be necessary to make decisions about specific intervention strategies and the effectiveness of those interventions. Assessment is an ongoing process and should involve multiple measures and multiple sources of information (Table 7.4).

Case Finding

Case finding is the process of locating those infants and toddlers and their families who might be eligible for early intervention. Case finding involves a variety

A good infant assessment procedure includes parents as participant/observers.

of activities related to defining the target population, increasing public awareness of services, encouraging referrals, and canvassing the community for children in need of services. Case finding or Child Find activities are required by PL 94-142 and PL 99-457.

TABLE 7.3   The Early Intervention Assessment Process

STEP	DESCRIPTION
Case-finding	The process of locating those infants and toddlers and their families who might be eligible for early intervention
Screening	The process of identifying those infants and toddlers in need of further in-depth assessment
In-depth assessment	The process of conducting in-depth assessments to verify a developmental problem, to determine the nature of the problem, and to determine the types of appropriate services
Assessment for planning intervention	The process of gathering information to determine the child's current level of functioning, to identify strengths and weaknesses, to determine intervention outcomes and objectives, and to identify useful intervention strategies
Monitoring change	The process of tracking the infant or toddler's rate of progress and determining the effectiveness of intervention strategies and activities
Program evaluation	The process of gathering information to determine the effectiveness of the program on infants, toddlers, and their families

TABLE 7.4   Assessment Procedures

PROCEDURE	DESCRIPTION
Direct testing	Objective measures of how the infant, toddler, or other individual responds to requests, instructions, standard stimulus, or set of materials
Naturalistic observations	Direct observation by professional or parent of the infant, toddler, or other individual in natural situations. The observer records various behaviors and dimensions of behaviors.
Records review	Review of medical records, records from previous assessments, and developmental records from early intervention programs. This review provides additional perspective.
Interviews	Parent(s) and caregiver(s) provide their perceptions of the child's abilities and history and their concerns about the child.

Assessment for Screening

Screening is the process of identifying those children in need of further in-depth assessment. By means of procedures that are quickly and easily administered, those children who do not fall within the normal ranges of development are identified. Screening does not specify the nature of the problem, nor the reasons for its existence. Screening informs us of the suspected presence of developmental problems. Further assessment is then done to confirm (or disconfirm) the presence of a developmental delay or handicapping condition.

The scope of screening programs varies. For example, a school district may offer screening to all infants and toddlers in the community two or three times a year. These screenings might be conducted by volunteers trained to administer the Denver Developmental Screening Test. As another example, the National Program for Early and Periodic Screening, Diagnosis, and Treatment (EPSDT) (for Medicaid-eligible families) typically includes a pediatric examination, a developmental history provided by the parents or primary caregiver, parental (caregiver) report of special problems or concerns, and an assessment of the child's developmental status using a screening instrument. A number of instruments have been developed for the purpose of screening very young children (Table 7.5).

As with all assessment activities, several sources of information should be used at the screening step. In particular, parent (or caregiver) input is crucial. Parents have a rich history of observations and experiences with their infant and can provide professionals with a more complete picture of the infant. To increase the accuracy of parental input, it is important that parents know in advance the purpose and limitations of screening, and that professionals be skilled in interview techniques (Table 7.6).

The results of the screening should be shared with parents as soon as possible, and information should focus on the child's present level of functioning. Results of a screening are not used to label a child. In sharing results, the professional may make recommendations and suggest referrals for additional assessment, service, or assistance. If screening results indicate the possibility of a developmental problem, families may then elect to act on these recommendations and referrals. A family might also decide not to proceed in this process. In this situation, the professionals need to determine if the family has been provided with the opportunity to make an informed choice, including an understanding of the implications of their choice. In addition, the professionals should ask the parents if they are willing to be contacted in the future.

In-Depth Assessments

Through screening, an infant's behavior or development may be determined to be questionable or significantly different from the norm. The next step is an in-depth assessment to verify or deny a developmental problem. The assessment will also provide a more complete description of the infant's developmental status including capabilities and weaknesses. This step in the assessment process is sometimes called *diagnosis*. The term diagnosis as used by the medical profession refers to the determination of the cause of a disease or physical disorder in order to prescribe treatment leading to a cure. In early intervention, however, it is important to remember that the cause of a developmental problem may be unknown or difficult to determine. Diagnosis in early intervention is the process whereby the nature of the problem is determined so that intervention services and plans can be implemented.

As in the previous step, the results of the in-depth assessment should be shared with the parents as soon as possible. Their participation throughout this step will help to verify and clarify the behaviors observed by the assessment team. Advanced preparation will aid in the delivery of potentially sensitive results. As part of the planning process, parents should be told of the purpose and limitations of the in-depth assessment methods. In sharing results, the goal is to give direct, honest, accurate, yet hopeful information. Because a great deal of emotion-laden information may be presented, it is important to schedule a followup meeting or telephone call.

Numerous assessment instruments are available for use in an in-depth assessment. For purposes of organization, we will first describe standardized measures, followed by Piagetian measures, and information-processing techniques. The in-depth assessment step should not be limited to formal, direct testing. Important information will also be provided by observations, reviews of the infant's records, and interviews with the parents and caregivers.

Standardized Measures. Standardization refers to uniformity of procedure in administering and scoring the test (Anastasi, 1982). Many of the commonly used screening and assessment instruments are standardized. Uniformity in administration requires that the test include specific instructions that may include exact test materials, verbal directions, procedures for demonstrations, numbers

TABLE 7.5 Selected Screening Tests for Infants

NAME	AGE RANGE	DESCRIPTION	CONTENT	COMMENTS
Denver Developmental Screening Test (DDST) (Frankenburg, Dodds, & Fandal, 1975)	2 weeks–6 years	An individually administered test to aid in the identification of children with development problems	105 items in four areas: personal-social, fine motor-adaptive, language, gross motor; results are categorized as normal, abnormal, questionable.	Interrater amd test-retest reliability .66–.93; correlations with Stanford-Binet and Bayley .74–.97; test currently being revised and restandardized.
Developmental Activities Screening Inventory-II (DASI-II) (Fewell & Langley, 1984)	1–60 months	To provide early detection of developmental disabilities in young children	15 skill categories ranging from sensory intactness, means-ends, memory, etc.; instructions given verbally or visually.	Flexibility allows use with nonverbal children; evidence of concurrent validity .97 with Preschool Attainment Record, .95 with DDST.
Developmental Profile II (Alpern, Boll & Shearer, 1980)	0–12 years	Quick inventory of skills to assess the child's development	Multiple items scored through parent interview or observation by teacher; items in 5 areas: physical social, self-help, academic, communication	Moderate interrater reliability, significant concurrent validity with Standford-Binet; 1972 standardization sample provides norms.

Measure	Age Range	Purpose	Description	Psychometric Notes
Developmental Screening Inventory (Knobloch, Stevens, & Malone, 1980)	4 weeks–36 months	Screens for abnormalities requiring more detailed examination	Five areas: adaptive, gross motor, fine motor, language, personal-social; yes/no questions answered by parent	Screening inventory drawn from Gesell Developmental Schedules
Early Language Milestone Scale (Coplan, 1982)	Birth–36 months	Very quick screening test of early speech/language development	42 items in 3 areas: auditory expressive, auditory receptive, visual; most items scored by parent report	Norm-referenced; yields percentile values; evidence of validity in manual
Kent Infant Development Scale (Kid Scale) (Reuter & Bickett, 1985)	Birth–12 months	To assess the developmental age of infants and young handicapped children	252-item inventory of 5 areas: cognitive, motor, language, self-help, social; parent/caregiver responds to multiple choice inventory.	Test-retest and interrater reliabilities > .85; concurrent validity .84 for 38 subjects with Bayley; Standardization sample of 357 infants

TABLE 7.6 Interview Techniques

Create a warm atmosphere.

Explain the purpose of the interview.

Confirm the time allotted. Parents should not feel rushed.

If the child is present, provide toys and tell the parents that it is okay for the child to play while the adults talk.

Identify in advance the broad topics to be covered.

Use both open- and close-ended questions.

Listen.

Use clear, jargon-free, respectful, and honest language.

Express appreciation for the parents' participation in the interview and make additional plans.

Note: Adapted from *Psychological Assessment of Handicapped Infants and Young Children* by G. Ulrey and S. J. Rogers, 1982, New York: Thieme-Stratton. Copyright 1982 by Thieme-Stratton; and "The Family Focused Interview: A Collaborative Mechanism for Family Assessment and Goal-Setting" by P. J. Winton and D. B. Bailey, 1988, *Journal of the Division for Early Childhood, 12*(3), pp. 195–207.

of trials, and time limits. Detailed instructions for scoring of individual items as well as the overall test must also be included.

In addition, the establishment of norms is another step in the standardization of a test (Anastasi, 1982). A *norm* is the normal or average performance. To establish norms, the test is given to a large, representative sample of individuals for whom the test is designed. Norms permit the comparison of an individual's position relative to the normative or standardization sample.

In evaluating the usefulness of such a test, reliability and validity are also considered. *Reliability* refers to the consistency of the test in repeated administration. *Validity* refers to the degree to which the test actually measures what it was designed to measure (see Table 7.1).

A particular psychometric issue concerning tests of infant development is the lack of *predictive validity*. It is frequently noted that tests in infancy do not predict performance at a later time (e.g., McCall, 1979). Traditional tests of infant development typically rely on motor and sensory abilities to assess intelligence. Thus, immaturity or inability to perform a test item may not truly reflect a deficiency in problem-solving, memory, attention, or other cognitive ability. In addition, the child-rearing environment exerts a strong influence on subsequent development, and traditional tests do not capture this variable. However, traditional tests do have greater predictive validity with infants who perform at a significantly below-average level (DuBose, 1977; McCall, 1982). Standardized tests may be useful and necessary for such purposes as diagnosis, determination of program eligibility, and research.

The Bayley Scales of Infant Development (Bayley, 1969) were developed to assess "a child's developmental status in the first two and one-half years of life" (p. 3). These scales are probably the most widely used standardized measure of infant development. There are three scales: the Mental Scale, the Motor Scale, and the Infant Behavior Record. Items from the mental scale are designed to measure such cognitive abilities as memory, perception, problem-solving, and learning, as well as vocalization and early verbal communication. The motor scale includes gross motor items such as head control, rolling, sitting, standing, walking, and stair climbing, in addition to fine motor items that measure prehension, reaching, and midline skills. After the mental and motor scales are administered, the examiner completes the Infant Behavior Record. This is a rating scale designed to assess such characteristics as persistence, attention, social behavior, and goal directedness. The mental and motor scales yield standard scores expressed as developmental indices. Developmental ages can also be determined.

The Bayley is considered outstanding among infant tests in terms of the technical quality of the test construction procedures (Anastasi, 1982). However, a recent study (Campbell, Siegel, Parr, & Ramey, 1986) suggests that the 1969 norms are outdated. In addition, many items require motor or sensory responses. For example, a memory item (mental scale item 86, uncover a toy) credits the child if "the child removes the tissue (covering the toy) for the evident purpose of viewing or securing the toy" (Bayley, 1969, p. 59). A child with a physical disability involving the upper extremities might not be able to lift the tissue, but might be able to indicate memory of the covered toy by smiling, vocalizing, or eye-pointing to the covered toy on a choice task. Alternatives for children with disabilities have been described (e.g., Hoffman, 1982). Use of such modifications, however, alters the standardization procedures. Nevertheless, because of its good realiability and concurrent validity, the Bayley remains a useful tool for infant assessment. This and other examples of commonly used standardized measures are described in Table 7.7.

Piagetian Measures. Piagetian measures of sensorimotor development are based on the assumption that development proceeds in an ordinal manner. Ordinal scales differ from other psychometric measures in several ways. They are constructed hierarchically, that is, they contain items arranged in the order in which they emerge developmentally. By contrast, other types of standardized scales contain groups of items that emerge at specific developmental ages, but the group of items at each age level are not arranged in developmental order.

In addition, ordinal scales yield only ceiling or optimal performance scores rather than the intelligence or developmental quotient of more traditional scales. General administration procedures are more flexible, too, allowing for the use of varied materials and eliciting situations. This flexibility allows young children with physical and sensory impairments more opportunities to demonstrate their capabilities. Ordinal or Piagetian measures, like more traditional standardized measures, are used to determine an individual's current developmental status. Both also help to identify an individual child's devleopmental strengths and weaknesses.

At least three scales have been designed to look at Piaget's stage I or sen-

TABLE 7.7 Selected Diagnostic Measures for Infants

NAME	AGE RANGE	DESCRIPTION	CONTENT	PSYCHOMETRIC PROPERTIES
Battelle Developmental Inventory (Newborg, Stock, Wnek, Guidubaldi, & Svinicki, 1984)	Birth–8 years	Comprehensive assessment to identify child's strengths and weaknesses and then plan for intervention	341 items in 5 areas: personal-social, adaptive, motor, communication, cognitive; scored by direct testing, observation, or interview; modifications for handicapping conditions provided	Interrater reliability .77–1.0; test-retest reliability .71–1.0; evidence of criterion-related validity; nationally standardized on 800 children
Bayley Scales of Infant Development (Bayley, 1969)	2–30 months	Provides a basis for early diagnosis of developmental delay	Consists of 3 scales: mental (163 items) measures perception, memory, learning, problem-solving, language; motor (81 items) measures gross and fine motor; infant behavior record for rating of infant's observed behavior	Used in multiple studies with multiple samples; test-retest reliability .76; test is often used as the criterion in other validity studies; national standardization of 1262 children

Test	Age Range	Purpose	Items	Reliability/Validity
Cattell Infant Intelligence Scale (Cattell, 1940/1960)	3–30 months	Measure of infant's developmental progress; downward extension of Stanford-Binet	Multiple items for direct testing of mental development	Low predictive validity to Stanford-Binet; standardization on 274 children (1940 norms)
Gesell Developmental Schedules (Gesell & Amatrada, 1947; Knobloch & Pasamanick, 1974)	4 weeks–6 years	Designed to provide an adequate developmental diagnosis	Multiple items in 4 areas—adaptive, motor, language, personal-social, testing supplemented with parent information	Interrater reliability .98; concurrent validity; original norms based on 107 children, but clinical observation of hundreds
Griffiths Mental Developmental Scales (Griffiths, 1978)	0–8 Years	Used to assess progress of cognitive/intellectual development in infants and children	Items in social, fine motor, gross motor, hearing, eye-hand coordination, speech; Scale I for birth–2 years (27 items)	Moderate interrater reliability; test used in Great Britain and Canada
Minnesota Child Development Inventory (Ireton & Thwing, 1979)	6 months–6 years	Measures development of child based on mother's observations	320 yes/no items grouped into to general development, gross motor, fine motor, expressive language, comprehension, conceptual, situation comprehension, self-help, personal-social	Adequate reliability and validity reported; norms based on sample of 796 white suburban children; Minnesota Infant Development Inventory (1–16 months) also available

sorimotor period of development. These are the Albert Einstein Scales of Sensorimotor Development (Escalona & Corman, 1966), the Casati-Lezine Scale (Casati & Lezine, 1968), and the Ordinal Scales of Psychological Development (Uzgiris & Hunt, 1975). Of these the Uzgiris and Hung Ordinal Scales of Psychological Development are the most commonly used in early intervention programs. The other two scales are no longer generally available.

The Uzgiris and Hunt Scales consist of six parts: visual pursuit and permanence of objects, means for obtaining desired environmental events, imitation (vocal and gestural), operational causality, object relations in space, and schemes for relating to objects. Each of these subscales includes developmentally arranged sets of items. Using these scales the child's performance can be described according to the level of organization demonstrated in each of the branches of psychological development. An example of assessment results using the Uzgiris and Hunt Scales is provided in Table 7.8.

These scales have been demonstrated to be reliable over time and across testers (Kaplan, 1976; Uzgiris & Hunt, 1987). Dunst (1980) offers a guide for the use of the scales in clinic or school programs. He provides procedures that yield both quantitative and qualitative information, including a system for estimating developmental age, and strategies for the design of intervention.

Information Processing Approaches. Another alternative to traditional infant tests is the use of information processing techniques. Vietze and Coates (1986) describe information processing techniques as those to which the infant must analyze some aspect of the situation presented and make a specific

TABLE 7.8 Sample Uzgiris and Hunt Results

SCALE	HIGHEST DEVELOPMENTAL ATTAINMENT	SCALE STEP	STAGE PLACEMENT
Object permanence	Secures object hidden under one of three screens, hidden alternatively	7	V
Means-ends	Uses string vertically; pulls object up from floor	10	V
Vocal imitation	Shows positive response to familiar babbling sounds	2b	II
Gestural imitation	Imitates simple familiar gestures	2	III
Causality	Uses procedure as causal action in response to behavior created by an agent using a toy	3d	III
Space	Places objects in cup; dumps out contents	8	V
Schemes	Drops or throws objects; visual monitoring of results of action/terminal location of object	7	IV

Note: Adapted from *A Clinical and Educational Manual for Use with the Uzgiris and Hunt Scales of Infant Psychological Development* by C. J. Dunst, 1980, Austin: Pro-ed. Copyright 1980 by Pro-ed.

behavioral response. The early behaviors most often studied include measures of attention, discrimination, and memory. The infant's behavioral responses can provide important information.

Traditional infant tests provide scores on skill attainment. As noted previously such tests have poor predictive validity. Information processing techniques provide measures of the process underlying the test and offer information on how long it takes an infant to learn a task or to solve a particular problem. These techniques appear promising in that they may better predict later intellectual functioning (Fagan, 1982; Fagan & McGrath, 1981; Miranda, Hack, Fantz, Fanaroff, & Klaus, 1977). Further, these techniques may be particularly useful for children with motor impairments that may restrict their performance on traditional tests (Zelazo, 1979).

A prime example of the usefulness of information processing techniques for infant assessment is offered by Fagan and associates. This work utilizes the preference for novelty paradigm to study infant visual memory. Infants spend more time attending to a novel stimulus (a picture) than to a familiar one. If an infant is shown a stimulus for a period of time and a novel stimulus is then paired with it, the infant will look longer at the novel stimulus. By varying the stimuli, we can learn about the infant's ability to discriminate. Further information on memory is obtained by varying the time between familiar stimuli and novel stimuli. These features are incorporated into an infant visual recognition and memory test (Fagan, 1984). This test is used as a screening device for the early identification of later cognitive delay. Studies of predictive validity suggest that this provides better results than traditional tests such as the Bayley (Fagan, 1988). Although still experimental, this test and other information processing techniques appear promising for high-risk infants.

Assessment for Planning Intervention

In this assessment step information is gathered to plan the intervention targets and activities. The purpose of assessment at this step is to determine the infant's current level of functioning, to determine strengths and needs, and to identify intervention techniques that can be incorporated into the intervention plan. Some of the assessment tools and procedures described in previous sections may well provide the starting point for intervention. Assessment at the intervention phase should be considered an on-going process; that is, the process recurs as intervention targets are achieved.

The intervention team attempts to answer several questions. One question is, what can the infant do? Does he or she respond to sounds, babble, grasp, or play pat-a-cake? The intervention team is not only interested in what the baby does, but also how the baby performs these activities. For example, a baby may bang toys together by holding them securely in each hand and bringing them together at midline, or he or she may brace one toy against the table and bang another against it. The baby may perform the behavior purposefully, and display apparent pleasure in the performance, or she or he may knock the toys together with seeming lack of interest. Interventionists are interested not only in the simple performance of a behavior, but also the quality of the performance.

In addition to determining what the infant does and how, another question is, what does the infant need to learn next? Is the infant demonstrating solid patterns of development and learning? Does the baby demonstrate clusters of similar skills? Or, is he or she displaying isolated or scattered skills? For example, a child may be able to tower blocks but is unable to demonstrate other activities requiring eye-hand coordination, such as stacking other objects or dropping pop beads into a bottle.

Interventionists also ask, what is the baby unable to do and why not? For example, a young child with cerebral palsy may not be able to pull a string to get the attached object. Is the child failing to perform the task because he or she lacks cognitive requisites, or because she or he cannot perform the necessary physical movements? Unsuccessful attempts may signal the need for practice or intervention, or may signal the need for alternative testing or teaching strategies for that child. Physical, sensory, or neurological disabilities may limit performance. Disabilities may also account for uneven performance across developmental domains.

A further question is, how does this infant learn best? A sensory, neurological, or motor impairment may affect the child's method of learning. Some infants may not yet demonstrate coordinated use of senses, such as looking and hearing, looking and grasping, and so forth. There are also important environmental factors. The infant may do best when interacting with a particular person (often mom or dad), or in a particular position or setting, or with favorite toys and materials. These factors need to be considered both for assessment and intervention. A variety of assessment tools and procedures have been developed for the purpose of identifying intervention targets and strategies.

Criterion-Referenced Developmental Measures. Earlier in the chapter several norm-referenced measures were described. Norm-referenced measures provide a comparison of the infant's skills and characteristics to an appropriate referent group. In contrast, criterion-referenced measures compare an infant's score or performance with a specified level or standard of achievement. Curriculum-based measures are a form of criterion-referenced assessment. Curriculum-based measures assess an infant's achievements along a continuum of objectives especially within a developmentally sequenced curriculum (Neisworth & Bagnato, 1988). Some examples of commonly used criterion- and curriculum-referenced measures are described in Table 7.9.

Domain-Specific Measures. To this point, most of the tests and assessment tools that have been described have taken a comprehensive look at development. Numerous others exist that examine one domain of development. Often these tests, by concentrating on just one developmental area, provide much more detailed information of an infant's strengths and weaknesses within that domain. Examples of domain-specific measures of infant development are described in Table 7.10. Information on monitoring change is provided in Chapter 9.

Play

Play offers an excellent medium for the assessment of the young child's social, cognitive, communication, and motor skills. In addition, a child's play behavior can in itself be assessed and the information used to facilitate play skills.

Bailey and Wolery (1989) identify four rationales for assessing and facilitating the play skills of young children with handicaps: play is an enjoyable activity; play may facilitate the development of other behaviors; play normalizes children's interactions with the environment; and play has practical value.

Play skills are typically assessed by direct observation of play sessions. Important variables include types of toys, access to toys, space, and social partners who may be parent(s), caregivers, or peers. Changes in these variables may alter the information obtained. Thus, the team must specify the purpose of the play assessment and plan the session accordingly. Guidelines for using naturalistic observations are provided in Table 7.11.

The Play Assessment Scale (Fewell, 1986) is a useful instrument for assessing the young child's play with toys or objects. The scales consist of 45 behaviors representing typical play behaviors of children from birth to three years. An example of a scale item is found in Table 7.12. Readily available toys and objects are the assessment stimuli and are grouped into sets. Assessment is conducted in two conditions. In the first condition, *spontaneous play*, the child's behavior is observed, and occurrences of the scale items are recorded. In the second condition, *facilitated play*, the play partner uses verbal prompts and modeling in an attempt to elicit more advanced skills. The current version of the scales provides instructions for determining play ages based on preliminary field test data. The scales are perhaps more useful for describing a child's approach to and use of toys, identifying intervention targets, and understanding the effectiveness and need for assistance or prompting.

Westby's (1980) play scale focuses on symbolic play and early language skills. Symbolic play is divided into 10 stages of the child's development, from 9 months to 5 years. Through parent or teacher interview and direct observation, the child's behaviors are assigned to the corresponding play and language stage. This scale is also useful for pinpointing intervention targets across domains. Another system for assessing symbolic play was developed by McCune-Niccolich (1980). This system covers the 8- to 30-month age range. The five play levels are related to the Piagetian stages of development. Again, the focus is the relationship between symbolic play and language.

Others have explored the opportunities for assessing a variety of developmental skills during play sessions. Assessment of other skills (e.g., fine motor coordination, social interaction) may occur while the child plays. Linder (1989) developed a system for a comprehensive developmental assessment within the context of play. This approach provides a format for the play session as

TABLE 7.9   Selected Criterion-Referenced Measures for Infants

NAME	AGE RANGE	DESCRIPTION	CONTENT	COMMENTS
Callier-Azusa Scale (Stillman, 1978)	Birth– 9 years	Developmental scale designed for assessment of deaf-blind and severely handicapped children	18 subscales in 5 areas: motor, perceptual abilities, daily living, language, social; scored based on classroom/home observations	Each subscale consists of sequential steps; may be appropriate intervention targets; no specific curriculum
Carolina Curriculum for Handicapped Infants and Infants at Risk (Johnson, Martin, Jens & Attermeier, 1986)	Birth– 24 months	To assess child's developmental abilities for entry into the curriculum	24 areas of development, traditional domains (e.g., cognition) broken down into finer sequences; scored by direct testing and observation	Assessment linked to the curriculum; focuses on infancy rather than whole early childhood period; theoretical base provided
Diagnostic Inventory of Early Development (Brigance, 1978)	Birth– 6 years	Assessment of development status and progress	Multiple items in psychomotor, self-help, communication, general knowledge, comprehension; scored by direct testing, observation, parent report	Useful for developing intervention targets; no specific curriculum

Early Intervention Developmental Profile (Schafer & Moersch, 1981)	Birth–36 months (Vols. 1, 2, 3); 36–72 months (Vols. 4, 5)	Provides for comprehensive developmental assessment and program planning	Multiple items in perceptual/fine motor, cognition, language, social/emotional, self-help, gross motor; direct testing, observation, team assessment	Linked to curriculum; evidence from field testing provided; theoretical base provided
Hawaii Early Learning Profile (HELP) (Furuno et al., 1979)	Birth–36 months	To assess child's strengths and weaknesses	HELP charts have assessment items in cognition, language, gross motor, social-emotional, self-help.	Linked to curriculum; developmental milestones model
Learning Accomplishment Profile for Infants, Revised (Early LAP) (Sanford, 1981)	Birth–36 months	Provides a simple profile of overall development of young child	Multiple items in 6 areas: gross motor, fine motor, cognitive, language, self-help, social-emotional	Linked with activity cards and other resources; developmental milestones model
Vulpe Assessment Battery (Vulpe, Pollins, & Wilson, 1979)	Birth–6 years	Comprehensive developmental assessment for program planning	Items and activities in areas of motor, sensory, environment, cognition and learning behaviors, language, daily living; scoring accounts for performance and style	Items useful for developing intervention targets; no specific curriculum

TABLE 7.10 Selected Domain-Specific Tests for Infants

NAME	AGE	DESCRIPTION	CONTENT	COMMENTS
Communication				
Assessing Linguistic Behaviors (Olswang, Stoel-Gammon, Coggins & Carpenter, 1987)	9–24 months	Informal assessment procedures of early language learning and linguistic skills	5 scales: cognitive antecedents to word meaning, play, communication intention, language comprehension, language production; observational scales	Materials include theoretical background, field testing data; training video available.
Birth to Three Developmental Scale (Bangs & Dodson, 1979)	Birth–3 years	Assessment of developmental delay and program planning	Multiple items in basic skills/perceptual motor, social/emotional, auditory, receptive and expressive language; direct testing and parent interview	Norm-referenced screening test; criterion-referenced checklist; includes an intervention guide
Early Social Communication Scales (Seibert, Hogan & Mundy, 1987)	Birth–30 months	To assess early social and communicative behaviors up to use of word combinations	Social interaction, joint attention, behavior regulation; structured assessment with social partner	Based on cognitive-developmental approach (i.e., Piagetian); test-retest reliability with same tester
Receptive-Expressive Emergent Language Scale (REEL) (Bzoch & League, 1971)	Birth–3 years	To identify young children with specific language handicaps	Parent interview regarding early and expressive skills	Does not include pragmatic skills; norm-referenced; may be more useful for screening
Sequenced Inventory of Communication Development-revised (Hendrick, Prather, & Tobin, 1984)	4–48 months	Diagnostic test of early communication abilities	Receptive and expressive scales completed by direct testing and parent interview	Adequate reliability and validity; standardization sample of 242 children

160

Social

	Age range	Purpose	Description	Comments
Carolina Record of Individual Behavior (CRIB) (Simeonsson, Huntington, Short & Ware, 1982)	Birth–24 months	To assess basic areas of development of individuals functioning at sensory motor level	Assessment of state, social orientation, participation, fearfulness, endurance, communication, consolability, reactivity, goal-directedness, responsiveness	Qualitative measure; moderate reliability; useful for describing behavioral characteristics of infants and handicapped children
Infant Temperament Questionnaire (Carey & McDevitt, 1978)	4–8 months	Assesses the general pattern of an infant's reaction to the environment	95-item questionnaire completed by caregiver measures activity, rhythmicity, approach, adaptability, intensity, mood, persistence, distractibility threshold	Provides description of infant's behavioral characteristics; norms based on 203 infants
Toddler Temperament Questionnaire (Fullard, McDevitt & Carey, 1984)	12–36 months	Assesses the behavior pattern of the toddler's reaction to the environment	97-item questionnaire completed by caregiver measures toddler's responses as in Infant Temperament Questionnaire	Provides description of toddler's behavioral characteristics

Motor

	Age range	Purpose	Description	Comments
Peabody Developmental Motor Scales (Folio & Fewell, 1984)	Birth–83 months	To assess young child's gross and fine motor development	Gross motor scale includes 170 items; fine motor includes 112 items; scored by direct testing and observation	Standardized on 617 children; evidence of reliability and validity; includes teaching activities

TABLE 7.11 Naturalistic Observations

Decide what to observe. Carefully define and describe the focus of observation.

Decide how to observe.

> Event recording: Continuous, narrative record of ongoing behaviors, or detailed account of single event
>
> Time sampling: Record of frequency of occurrence of selected behavior
>
> Checklists or rating scales: Record of presence or absence of selected behaviors or the quality of the behaviors
>
> Coded Observations: Record of multiple or complex behaviors or sets of behaviors

Decide when and where to observe.

Check the accuracy of the data.

Use the data for the intended purpose.

Note: Adapted from *Early Intervention* by M. J. Hanson and E. W. Lynch, 1989, Austin: Pro-ed. Copyright 1989 by Pro-ed; and *Assessing Infants and Preschoolers with Handicaps* by D.B. Bailey and M. Woley, 1989, Columbus, OH: Charles Merrill. Copyright 1989 by Charles Merrill.

well as detailed observation guidelines for assessing a young child's cognitive, communication, sensorimotor, and social-emotional development. Descriptions of other assessment and intervention procedures can be found in Fewell and Kaminski (1988); Johnson, Christie, and Yawkey (1987); and Musselwhite (1986).

Arena Assessment

Arena assessment may provide a workable, efficient alternative to traditional multidisciplinary assessments (Wolery & Dyk, 1984). In an arena assessment, there are both participants and active spectators. Typically one of the professionals or the parent interacts with the infant and guides the infant through prescribed activities or tasks. Meanwhile, the other team members record observations and score portions of assessment tools relevant to their discipline. The play assessment designed by Linder (1989) follows this approach. Periodically, team members may suggest specific tasks or administer test items directly. Parents are present throughout to provide information and to validate the infant's performance.

This assessment procedure increases efficiency, reduces the number of professionals who must handle the infant, provides team members with observations of the infant across developmental domains, and should result in more team consensus for intervention planning. The case study of Molly illustrates the use of arena assessment (see Case Study: Molly).

TABLE 7.12 Play Assessment Scale

Item #23	Appropriate serial acts involving doll or adult
Representative behaviors	Loads block on truck, pushes truck to adult, gives block to adult
	Stirs in cup with spoon, feeds doll with spoon

From *Play Assessment Scale* by R. R. Fewell. Copyright 1986 by Author, Tulane University, New Orleans, LA.

CASE STUDY: MOLLY

Molly is a 15-month-old girl with spina bifida. She is enrolled in a center-based early intervention program which she attends twice a week (one individual session and one small play group time). Her babysitter brings Molly to the center where they are joined by Molly's mother, Mrs. Benson.

Molly is being reassessed to evaluate her progress, to update her Individualized Family Service Plan (IFSP), and to identify new intervention targets. The program uses a transdisciplinary model and arena assessment. The team consists of Molly's parents, teacher, physical therapist, speech therapist, and social worker. The physical therapist is the case manager. She and Mrs. Benson talked the week before about priorities and concerns for this reassessment. These included Molly's progress toward assisted walking, encouraging Molly to talk, and finding alternative child care. The early intervention program typically uses the Early Intervention Developmental Profile (EIDP) (Rogers, D'Eugenio, Brown, Donovan, & Lynch, 1981) for reassessments. It was decided that the EIDP, along with a clinical evaluation by the physical therapist, observation of play and eating, and a focused interview with the social worker would fulfill the purposes identified by Mrs. Benson and the other members of the team. It was also decided that the assessment could be accomplished during Molly's usual individual session.

The session was structured as follows: 20 minutes free play with mother; 20 minutes with the physical therapist to check reflexes, reactions, and quality of movement; snack with mother; and mother's interview with the social worker while Molly plays with toys and other team members. When the team set up this schedule they noted that since language was a priority, the speech therapist should interject suggestions as needed to elicit specific communicative behaviors.

Since Molly was familiar with the playroom and was used to adults being present, very little warm-up time was needed. During the play time, the physical therapist sat near Mrs. Benson. The other team members sat away from the play area. Each team member had a copy of the EIDP. Their primary responsibility was to complete "their" section (e.g., the teacher completed the cognitive section). In addition, team members recorded their observations across domains. The speech therapist also collected a communication sample. She wrote down Molly's communicative intents as they occurred and also noted whether these were verbal or gestural. She used sections from Assessing Linguistic Behaviors (Olswang, Stoel-Gammon, Coggins, & Carpenter, 1987) to guide her observations.

The social worker used Mrs. Benson's priority concerns as topics during the interview. She also asked Mrs. Benson if she would like to look at or complete the Family Support Scale (Dunst, Jenkins, & Trivette, 1984). She suggested that this might help their discussion of child-care possibilities. Mrs. Benson willingly completed the scale.

As the interview drew to a close, the other team members joined Mrs. Benson and the social worker. The team took this time to discuss their observations and initial results. They also made plans for a meeting to revise the IFSP.

FAMILY ASSESSMENT

Identification of Family Strengths and Needs

Public Law 99–457 states that the Individualized Family Service Plan (IFSP) must include a statement of the family's strengths and needs relative to the child's development. The child grows and develops within the family. The birth of any child adds stress and change to the family system. The birth or identification of a child with developmental problems may further stress the system. Therefore, it is important to work with family members to help them identify their own resources and strengths as well as their needs as they strive to optimize the development of the child with special needs and to optimize the development of the entire family.

As with any assessment procedure, when we look at family assessment we need to consider the purpose. In most situations it will be to simply work with the family to help them pinpoint their strengths and resources as well as their needs and concerns. This can be accomplished through a conversational, but focused, interview (Winton & Bailey, 1988). In the focused interview, the interviewer provides a moderate degree of structure by specifying topics to be covered and by using an interview guide. The interviewer has flexibility in the order and manner in which topics are discussed. A format that allows parents to tell their own story sets the stage for an exchange of concerns, questions, and information. The effective interviewer uses this information to delineate areas of concern (Boone & Sandall, 1989).

The purpose of family assessment is simply to help the family pinpoint their strengths and resources as well as their needs and concerns.

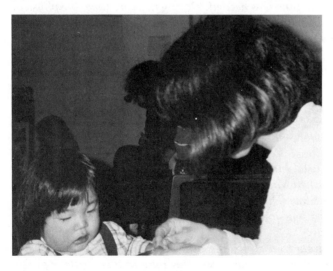

Sometimes a written needs inventory or specialized assessment scale will help to structure the interview. If the interview is too open-ended a family member may not focus on areas of true concern. Or, without the support of suggestions provided by a scale or skilled interviewer, families may not think of their rich support system of family, friends, and coworkers in relation to their special needs child.

A growing number of specialized scales are available to early intervention teams. These scales, if used at all, should be used judiciously. Some of the available scales are designed to measure such variables as marital relationships, depression, and family dynamics and therefore should be used only by professionals specifically trained in these areas. Some scales were developed from a deficit or pathological perspective. The use of such scales is questionable for early intervention purposes. It must be remembered that the purpose of assessment is to identify infant and family needs, to identify and locate formal and informal sources of support, and to enable families to obtain the resources needed to maximize infant and family functioning. Scales which emphasize family deficits or focus on negative aspects of family functioning do not yield information useful for these purposes.

Measures of Social Support

Social support can be defined as "the emotional, psychological, physical, informational, instrumental, or material assistance that is provided to others to either maintain well-being or promote adaptions to different life events" (Dunst & Trivette, 1985, p. 3) Social support networks nurture us through day-to-day activities. Social support networks may serve as buffers at times of crisis and stressful events. Measures of social support may provide the early intervention team (including family members) with useful assessment information as to how to use social support as an intervention (Bailey & Simeonsson, 1988b; Dunst & Trivette, 1985; and Fewell, 1986). Scales of social support and other family variables that have been used in early intervention programs are described in Table 7.13. As with other scales designed to assess family functioning, caution should be exercised in choosing and administering these scales.

Measures of Parent-Child Interaction

Interactions between a parent and young child can be experiences of joy. These interactions set the stage for social, cognitive, and language development. When the child is at-risk for developmental problems these interactions may be jeopardized. The promotion of productive and pleasurable interactions between parent and child are a likely goal of early intervention specialists.

Available measures of parent-child interaction include rating scales that provide somewhat broad categories such as responsivity and warmth; more narrowly defined coding systems of targeted behaviors; and observational checklists

TABLE 7.13   Selected Measures of Social Support and Family Variables

NAME	FORMAT	DESCRIPTION	COMMENTS
Family Environment Scale (Moos, 1974)	Rating scale	Measures intrafamilial supports, emotional well-being, coping, family integrity	Evidence of reliability and validity
Family Inventory of Resources for Management (McCubbin, Comeau, & Hankins, 1981)	Rating scale	Measures intrafamilial supports, well-being, management	Evidence of reliability and validity
Family Needs Survey (Bailey & Simeonsson, 1985)	Rating Scale	Measures needs for information, support, explaining to others, community services, financial family functioning	Designed for early intervention services; useful for developing family goals
Family Support Scale (Dunst, Jenkins & Trivette, 1984)	Rating scale	Measures familial supports (intra-, extra-, kinships)	Evidence of reliability and validity; designed for early intervention assessment and goal planning
Prioritizing Family Needs Scale (Finn & Vadasy, n.d.)	Rating scale	Measures basic needs, health and safety, social needs, personal needs	Designed for early intervention services and for goal planning
Questionnaire on Resources and Stress-F (Friedrich, Greenberg & Crnic, 1983)	Rating scale	Measures intrafamilial and kinship supports, emotional well-being, family integrity, attitudes	Evidence of reliability and validity

(Table 7.14). Rosenberg, Robinson, and Beckman (1986) suggest that measures of parent-child interaction should allow for reliable assessments even if a member of the dyad displays ambiguous behavior; should be easily incorporated within an intervention program; and should identify effective intervention strategies.

A frequent comment from interventionists as well as from parents is that measures of parent-child interaction can be intrusive. Since many rely on videotape, the procedure may produce anxiety if not used carefully. It is suggested that such measures be used following a period of trust- and rapport-building among parents, infants, and professional team members. Further, observation and taping should take place in a comfortable setting; often this is the family home. Professionals should always maintain appropriate standards to ensure the family's privacy. Videotape can be an extremely useful medium for both parents and professionals. Parents will often identify both effective and ineffective interaction strategies upon viewing segments of interaction. If used periodically, videotape also provides an ongoing record of infant progress.

THE ASSESSMENT TEAM

Public Law 99–457 provides for multidisciplinary team evaluation. There are at least three team models common to early intervention: multidisciplinary, interdisciplinary, and transdisciplinary (Table 7.15). Regardless of the model used in a particular setting, several characteristics of the transdisciplinary team are necessary for effective assessment: trust, role release, and easy and open information sharing.

The team can work together to plan an assessment process that will provide an accurate picture of the infant and family. The family and the other team members can plan an assessment process that addresses family priorities and concerns. This requires a positive, collaborative relationship. From their first contacts with the family, the professionals on the team can help to establish a positive relationship, which leads to shared planning and decision-making. An effective team works together to identify the purposes of the assessment, the methods to be used for gathering information, the setting or settings for assessments, and the individuals to be directly involved. Respect for the family also means that the family can choose the level and intensity of their involvement in this process.

A national task force (Johnson, McGonigel & Kaufman, 1989) proposed a set of principles to guide the assessment process. These are:

- Assessment is a continuing, evolving process rather than a discrete activity that can be initiated and completed at a single point in time.
- Child assessment should be shaped by family priorities and information needs, as well as by child characteristics and diagnostic concerns.
- Informed consent must be obtained from a family for any and all assessment activities.
- The identification of family strengths and needs must be based on an individual family's determination of which aspects of family life are relevant to the child's development.
- The assessment process must reflect a respect for family values and styles of decision-making.

TABLE 7.14 Selected Measures of Parent-Infant Interaction

NAME	AGE RANGE	FOCUS	FORMAT	RELIABILITY/VALIDITY
Home Observation for Measurement of the Environment (HOME) (Caldwell & Bradley, 1984)	Birth–36 months	Quality of care infants receive at home, e.g., responsivity, acceptance, organization, play materials, involvement, stimulation	Observation and interview with parent; binary checklist	Interrater reliability ≥ .90, internal consistency .80; relationship between HOME and cognitive development
Maternal Behavior Rating Scale (Mahoney, Powell, & Finger, 1986)	Birth–36 months	Parent variables, e.g., sensitivity, responsiveness, physical handling, warmth (short form has 7 items)	Likert-type rating scale scored following observation of videotaped free play	Interrator reliability ≥ .76; based on review of child development literature and study of interactional behavior
Nursing Child Assessment Teaching and Feeding Scale (Barnard & Bee, 1982)	Birth–36 months	Parent variables and infant variables, e.g., verbalizations, clarity of cues, responsiveness	Checklist based on observation of short teaching session, feeding session	Interrater reliability .79–.83, internal consistency .76–.89; moderate relationships with cognitive/language measures; used to identify training needs (extensive training required)

Instrument	Age Range	Description	Reliability/Notes
Parent Behavior Progression (Bromwich, 1981)	Birth–36 months	Binary checklist based on observations and conversations	Reliability data not found; used in increasing understanding of interactive behavior reported by case studies
Parent/Caregiver Involvement Scale (Farran et al., 1987)	Birth–36 months	Rating scale scored following live or taped free play	Interrater reliability .77–.87 live, .54–93 taped; moderate to high correlations with behavior counts (videotape available for training)
Parent variables, e.g., responsiveness, control, verbalizations			
Social Interaction Assessment/Intervention (McCollum & Stayton, 1985)	Birth–36 months	Behavioral count scored from videotaped play interaction	Interrater reliability .80; used to demonstrate changes in parent/infant behavior following intervention
Parent variables and infant variables, e.g., turn-taking, imitation, vocalizations			
Teaching Skills Inventory (Rosenberg, Robinson, & Beckman, 1984)	Birth–36 months	Rating scale scored following observation of videotaped interaction	Interrater reliability .64–.83; internal consistency .96; shows changes following intervention
Parent variables, e.g., clarity of instructions, effectiveness of prompts, task modification			

TABLE 7.15   **Early Intervention Teams**

MODEL	DESCRIPTION	CONDUCTING ASSESSMENTS
Multi-disciplinary	Professionals from a variety of disciplines work independently. Families generally meet with team members separately by discipline.	Team members conduct separate assessments by discipline.
Inter-disciplinary	Professionals from a variety of disciplines may work independently but come together for planning and sharing. Families generally meet with team or a team representative. Families' role on the team varies.	Team members conduct separate assessments by discipline and share results.
Trans-disciplinary	Professionals from a variety of disciplines work together actively planning, sharing, problem-solving, and teaching/learning across disciplines. Families are full team members with decision-making authority.	Staff and family participate in an arena-style assessment, observing and recording across disciplines.

Note: Adapted from "The Individual Family Service Plan and the Early Intervention Team" by M. J. McGonigel and C. W. Garland, 1988, *Infants and Young Children, 1*(1), 10–21.

- A team process for assessment means that all information should be shared in a give-and-take fashion. Family members of the team should have the opportunity to be present for all discussion.
- Language associated with the assessment process should reflect family preferences as much as possible (p. 32).

Suggestions for Further Reading

Assessment of Infants and Toddlers

BAGNATO, S.J., NEISWORTH, J.T., & MUNSON, S.M. (1989). Linking developmental assessment and early intervention: Curriculum-based prescriptions. Rockville, MD: Aspen.

BAILEY, D.B., & WOLERY. M. (1989). Assessing infants and preschoolers with handicaps. Columbus, OH: Charles Merrill.

SIMEONSSON, R.J. (1986). Psychological and developmental assessment of special children. Boston: Allyn & Bacon.

ULREY, G., & ROGERS, S.J. (1982). Psychological assessment of handicapped infants and young children. New York: Thieme-Stratton.

WACHS, T.D., & SHEEHAN, R. (Eds.) (1988). Assessment of young developmentally disabled children. New York: Plenum Press.

WOODRICH, D.L., & KUSH, S.A. (1990). Children's psychological testing: A guide for nonpsychologists. (2nd ed.). Baltimore: Paul Brookes.

Family Assessment

BAILEY, D.B., & SIMEONSSON, R.J. (1988). Family assessment in early intervention. Columbus, OH: Charles Merrill.
DUNST, C.J., & TRIVETTE, C.M. (1985). Measures of social support, parental stress, well-being and coping, and other family-level behavior. Chapel Hill, NC: TADS.

Chapter 8

The Individualized
Family Service Plan

Public Law 99-457 alters the focus of early intervention from a child-centered to a family-centered approach. Further, the law states that early intervention services for families should be coordinated and comprehensive. In this chapter, two provisions of the law which were designed to bring about family-centered, coordinated, and comprehensive services are discussed: the Individualized Family Service Plan (IFSP) and case management.

BACKGROUND TO A FAMILY-CENTERED APPROACH

The importance of the family in programs for infants and young children with special needs has been acknowledged at least from the time of the first demonstration models funded by the Handicapped Children's Early Education Program (United States Department of Health, Education, and Welfare, 1968). Such programs were required to design and implement a parent involvement component as part of their eligibility for federal funding. The history of early childhood education includes many examples of parent organized and operated cooperative preschools, in which parents assumed roles of leadership and decision-making in their children's early education (Evans, 1975).

From parent participation in Head Start and other specialized programs 20 years ago to the present legal requirements for family service plans, the concept of involving families has changed. At first parents were invited to observe in their child's classroom, to attend parent meetings, or to serve on the program advisory board. They were usually not consulted on a formal basis in regard to the educational program their child was experiencing. Later the emphasis shifted to training parents to help carry out their child's intervention program at school or home. Parents were recipients of information and plans. Many professionals expected parents to defer decision-making to them. Parents still had little formal control over their child's educational and therapeutic program. While parents and professionals continued to struggle with changing notions of parent participation and involvement, the definition of *parent* widened from meaning just mother to both mother and father as well as other primary caregivers. More recently, professionals have been encouraged to think of the *family* as being the context of early intervention. In practice, this involves recognition and respect for the family, however an individual family might define itself.

During the early 1970s parents, advocates, and policy makers worked together to ensure passage of PL 94-142. They came together again to work for passage of PL 99-457 in 1986. These are examples of empowerment that resulted in change at the legislative level. Today the concept of family empowerment implies maintenance or acquisition of a sense of control over their lives

The authors wish to thank Lou Landry, Colorado Department of Education, for his valuable contribution to this chapter in the case management section.

by family members. This concept is being tested today as parents and children face increasingly complex service delivery systems which, while in many cases provide needed services and support, also make increasing demands upon their time and energies (Dunst, Trivette, & Deal, 1988). It is important to note as we explore the term empowerment that parents are not without power. Traditionally and legally, parents' rights are valued in this country. However, when a child is born with a handicap or at significant risk for a developmental problem, parents may develop a sense of helplessness or powerlessness. As parents and families then contact professionals or enter service systems, they may relinquish control (Table 8.1).

In their book on enabling and empowering families, Dunst, Trivette, and Deal (1988) ask us to rethink the ways in which we view families and the helping relationships we have with them. They suggest that we view family empowerment as the major goal of intervention practices, and that these practices emphasize building upon capabilities and the existing social networks of families as a means of strengthening families as they seek to optimize the development of their young child with special needs. To accomplish this, a shift is necessary in the role professionals play in interacting with families, from paternalistic approaches that view differences as deficits in need of "treatment" to partnerships in which families are viewed as capable decision-makers (Dunst, 1985b; Solomon, 1985). This perspective presents real challenges for early interventionists who wish to follow the spirit as well as the letter of PL 99-457, for it is clear that the legislation intends the IFSP to document strengths and needs, to detail interventions, and to assign case managers. In such a process, it is not so easy to maintain the partnership and forego the paternalism.

In order to develop a meaningful and useful IFSP, the IFSP process itself must be one that encourages and respects families and responds to their strengths and needs. The atmosphere surrounding this process will determine whether it empowers parents or encourages their dependence. At least five potential barriers to a family-centered approach to the IFSP process can be identified:

TABLE 8.1   **Important Terms**

Enabling families:	Creating opportunities and means for families to apply their present abilities and competencies and to acquire new ones as necessary to meet their needs and the needs of their children.
Empowering families:	Interacting with families in such a way that they maintain or acquire a sense of control over their family life and attribute positive changes that result from early intervention to their own strengths, abilities, and actions.

Note: *From Enabling and Empowering Families: Principles and Guidelines for Practice* by C. J. Dunst, C. M. Trivette, and A. Deal, 1988, Cambridge, MA: Brookline Books. Copyright 1988 by Brookline Books. Reprinted by permission.

1. The assessment and intervention process is potentially intrusive into family life.
2. In determining family needs, goals, and services, professionals may disagree with the family's perception.
3. The formality of IFSP meetings may not allow the parents the opportunity to assume a position of leadership in the development of goals and plans for their child.
4. Professionals may be at different stages in their ability to let go of authority.
5. Assigning case managers to families may represent a continuation of paternalistic practices.

Each of these issues requires brief examination. The assessment/intervention process can be made less intrusive if early interventionists are trained to be sensitive to family concerns and to use nonintrusive assessment methods and instruments. Further, it is important that identification of family strengths and needs is undertaken with the family's concurrence and participation. Whereas invasion of privacy is a risk, the participation of families at all steps of the IFSP process—from planning through implementation—should temper this risk. Professionals must recognize that families change and that their level of participation in assessment and intervention may change as well.

According to Dunst, Trivette, and Deal (1988), disagreements between professionals and the families they work with often result from the professional's tendency to view things as black or white, right or wrong, either/or. These authors point out that this attitude inevitably leads to the professional seeing himself or herself as right and the family as wrong, and trying to convince or coerce the family into doing what the professional thinks is right. The answer to this dilemma, turning such encounters from oppositional to supportive, lies in starting from the family's position, basing intervention on family strengths, and reaching compromises in planning intervention programs that satisfy both family and professional.

Those strategies may also work to increase the role of the family in decision-making during IFSP development. Professionals who demonstrate that they are genuinely interested in the family's viewpoint, are cognizant of each family's perceived needs and aspirations, and show respect for the various family members and their points of view, will create a democratic atmosphere for the IFSP process, allowing family members the opportunity for participation.

All professional members of the multidisciplinary team face the challenge created by PL 99-457 to become introspective in their professional development. Each team member associated with the IFSP process must assess his or her own commitment to empowering families by giving them more control over their child's education and therapy. The concept of role release has been employed to describe the process of professionals working together and sharing expertise; now this concept takes on new meaning, that of the professionals sharing information, communicating openly, and sharing decision-making with parents and other family members.

The law states that one case manager be assigned to each family. This is the individual who ensures that the child and family receive the services and supports to which they are entitled. A case manager must fulfill a variety of functions and activities, and in doing so must display the same sensitivity described above. In addition, the case manager must be able to form a close working relationship with the family while linking them with other resources.

THE INDIVIDUALIZED FAMILY SERVICE PLAN

A major requirement and a guiding feature of early intervention services, as outlined in PL 99-457, is the IFSP. The IFSP includes specific expected outcomes and serves as the plan of action for achieving those outcomes. The IFSP venture involves family and early intervention professionals working together to develop a plan that includes services and supports that will enhance the development of the child and the capacity of the family to meet the special needs of the child (Federal Register, 1989, Vol. 54, p. 26320).

More specifically, the law states that the IFSP shall include seven components.

1. A statement of the infant's or toddler's present levels of physical development, cognitive development, language and speech development, psychosocial development, and self-help skills, based on acceptable objective criteria.

2. A statement of the family's strengths and needs relating to enhancing the development of the family's handicapped infant or toddler.

3. A statement of the major outcomes expected to be achieved for the infant and toddler and family, and the criteria, procedures, and timelines used to determine the degree to which progress toward achieving the outcomes is being made and whether modifications or revisions of the outcomes or services are necessary.

4. A statement of specific early intervention services necessary to meet the unique needs of the infant or toddler and the family, including the frequency, intensity, and the method of delivering services.

5. The projected dates for initiation of services and the anticipated duration of such services.

6. The name of the case manager from the profession most immediately relevant to the identified needs of the family who will be responsible for the implementation of the plan and for coordination with other agencies and persons.

7. The steps to be taken to support the transition of the handicapped toddler to services provided by school districts.

Theoretical Framework

Family systems theory provides a theoretical framework for the development and implementation of the IFSP. Family systems theory proposes that families are composed of interdependent parts, and that interactions between and among parts create properties not contained in the separate components (Minuchin, 1974). Using the family systems literature, Turnbull, Summers, and Brotherson (1984) developed a family systems conceptual framework that consists of four components: family resources, family interaction, family functions, and the family life cycle.

A change in any of the components necessarily affects other components of the family system. For example, the birth of a child may alter the responsibilities of other family members, as well as the allocation of resources to meet new or different family functions. If the child is born with or develops a disability, this may further stress the family system. The family may be introduced to an early intervention program or to a set of providers to assist with the new baby. The ramifications of particular treatments or interventions will likely extend beyond the effects upon the baby. For example, the mother may devote her time and physical and emotional energy to specialized feeding procedures and therapeutic exercises several times a day. This takes time away from her husband, the other children, and herself. Some specialized treatments may strain the family's financial resources. Others may require numerous appointments and creative solutions to child care. Even relatively simple interventions (from the professional team's perspective) may have ripple effects on other family members.

It is not just changes in time, energy, or resource allocation that will affect the family system. The family's values and beliefs will also influence their level and type of involvement with external agencies or individuals. Further, the interaction style of a family or of individual family members will also influence the flow of information and the decision-making process. An effective IFSP process must recognize the diversity of families, respect that diversity, and collaborate with families to help them meet their needs.

Implementation of the IFSP Process

The rules and regulations for the infant and toddler portion of PL 99-457, along with best practices, provide guidance for implementation of the IFSP process.

The concept of family-centered plans and family-centered early intervention means increased family involvement. The IFSP process presumes family involvement. It is incumbent on those who implement this process to recognize that involvement may come at many levels of time, energy, and intensity. Families must be allowed the opportunity of making informed choices at all of the decision points in the process. Parents want to know what their options are in terms of services, providers, and financial resources so that they can select

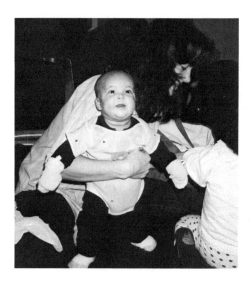

Family-centered assessment and family-centered early intervention mean increased family involvement in programs.

from those options or create new options (Boone, Sandall, Loughry, & Frederick, 1990).

Components of the IFSP

The content of the IFSP is specified in the law. It must contain information on the child's present levels of functioning based on professionally acceptable objective criteria and may include information gathered by direct testing, parent report, or observation. Methods and tools for determining a child's present levels of physical, cognitive, language and speech, psychosocial, and self-help skills were described in the previous chapter. A multidisciplinary assessment must be provided; that is, two or more disciplines must be involved in the provision of integrated and coordinated assessment activities. Figure 8.1 is a completed IFSP for Molly Benson, a 15-month-old girl with spina bifida.

The IFSP must also include a statement of the family's strengths and needs related to enhancing the child's development. As clarified in the regulations accompanying PL 99-457 (Federal Register, 1989, p. 26320), this activity is undertaken with the concurrence of the family. Some families may choose to actively participate in this activity from their first contacts with early intervention personnel. But for others, there will necessarily be a period of trust and rapport building before they feel comfortable to reveal information about their family. If the IFSP is viewed as a dynamic, working plan that can be changed as needed, then the early intervention team can easily add family goals or modify intervention strategies as a family becomes more comfortable in communicating with other team members.

CASE STUDY: THE BENSON FAMILY

Molly is a 15-month-old girl with myelomeningocele (spina bifida). She lives at home with her mother, father, and two older brothers (Tyler, 6, and Mark, 5).

Molly was born by planned cesarean section following prenatal diagnosis of spina bifida. The lesion (located in the lumbar area) was sugically closed shortly after birth. After 5 days in the hospital, Molly joined her family at home.

Molly wore a hip splint during the neonatal period. She had a shunt inserted at 6 months of age to prevent hydrocephalus. At 8 months of age, she had surgery on her feet and ankles and was in casts for about 6 weeks. She now wears plastic ankle/foot orthoses.

The Bensons live in a neighborhood of single family homes in a large city. Molly's health care is provided by a team at a local medical center. During her first 3 months of life, Molly received outpatient physical therapy at the medical center. For a variety of reasons, the Bensons then enrolled Molly in a center-based early intervention program. At the center, Molly receives services from a teacher, physical therapist, and speech therapist. There is also a social worker on the team. Over the past year, the frequency and intensity of services has changed depending on Molly's needs, family needs, and scheduling constraints. At present, Molly attends the center twice a week. During one session, she is seen individually by the teacher and physical therapist. The second session is conducted as a play group with three other children. The speech therapist and teacher facilitate this session. In addition, the teacher makes a home visit about once a month, usually in the early evening

Both Mr. and Mrs. Benson work full-time outside the home. Finding suitable child care has always been a problem. Currently the boys go to an after-school child-care center. A woman in the neighborhood cares for Molly and transports her to the early intervention center. This will soon end, however, as the woman plans to return to other work.

Mrs. Benson is able to attend Molly's sessions by scheduling her lunch break accordingly. Mr. Benson's work schedule doesn't allow this on a regular basis, although he has attended a few times. Evening home visits do allow Molly's father and brothers to participate.

This is Molly and her family's second formal IFSP. In planning the IFSP meeting, Mrs. Benson indicated that it needed to be at a time when her husband could attend. The team also discussed inclusion of the clinical nurse specialist who serves as the family's liaison with the medical center staff, and is familiar with Molly's medical history. Then the therapist/case manager called the Bensons a couple of days later and they confirmed a date, time, and place of 5:30 p.m. at the center. She also talked with Mr. Benson about some of his concerns and described the goals for the meeting. The nurse could not attend but prepared a written update on Molly's health status. Mrs. Benson picked it up at the medical center. Molly, Tyler, and Mark also attended the IFSP meeting. A place was made for them at the conference table, but they spent most of their time playing in another part of the room.

INDIVIDUAL FAMILY SERVICE PLAN

Section 1. Identifying Information

Child's Name: _Molly Benson_   Date of Birth: _7-30-88_

Address: _121 S Woodland_   Phone: _222-5327_

                County/School District: _Farmington_

Medicaid/Insurance Company and Number: _Blue Cross / Blue Shield_

Parent(s) or Legal Guardian(s):

(1)   Name: _Denise Benson_   Phone: _222-5327_

      Address: _121 S. Woodland_

(2)   Name: _Paul Benson_   Phone: _222-5327_

      Address: _121 S. Woodland_

Section 2. Case Management and Plan Reviews:

Name of Case Manager: _Patty Lee_   Phone: _242-1977_

Case Manager Agency: _TOTS Program_

IFSP Date	Initiation Date	Review Date
_11-2-89_	_11-2-89_	_May 1990_

Section 3. Staffing

INTERVENTION PLANNING TEAM

Team Members	Title	Date
Denise & Paul Benson	Parents	10-30-89, 11-1-89
Patty Lee	Physical Therapist	10-30-89
Sarah Shanklin	Teacher	10-30-89
Lucy Klein	Speech Therapist	10-30-89
Carolyn Mason	Social Worker	10-30-89

FIGURE 8.1 Sample IFSP of a 15-month-old girl with spina bifida.

180

FIGURE 8-1 (continued)

Section 4. Child Family Strengths and Concerns

Name: ___Benson family___

INDIVIDUAL FAMILY SERVICE PLAN

Present Levels of Functioning	Strengths	Needs
CHILD Assessments used: Early Intervention Developmental Profile Behavioral observations Clinical evaluation by PT	Molly is a healthy, happy little girl. She crawls on hands & knees, moves in & out of sitting. She plays with variety of toys w.n good hand and finger function. Uses gestures + vocalizations to communicate. Understands some instructions. Demonstrated object permanence, means-ends. Attempts to self-fed. Normal hearing.	Needs to learn to pull-to-stand. When placed feet point out, hips abducted. No protective extension to rear. Doesn't use words yet, nor point to body parts, toys, etc. No awareness of soiled/wet diapers.
FAMILY Family Support Scale	Intact family. Both parents employed and pleased with jobs. Many friends, family to help. Family is delighted with Molly's progress	Mr. & Mrs. Benson identified 3 needs: 1) information or helping Molly's motor and language development, 2) help in finding attractive child care, 3) help in scheduling early intervention and medical appointments.

(continued)

FIGURE 8-1 (continued)

Section 5. Early Intervention Services

Type of Service	Begin Service	End Service	Frequency	Intensity	Location	Method	Payor	Provider & Discipline
Phys. Therapy	Continuing 11-2-89		1x/week	45 min.	TOTS program	1:1 Direct therapy	State	Patty Lee Phys. Therapy
Speech Therapy	Continuing 11-2-89		1x/week	1 hr.	TOTS program	Small group consult	State	Lucy Klein Speech Therapy
Education	Continuing 11-2-89		2x/week	approx. 1 hr/session	TOTS program	1:1 Small group	State	Sarah Shanklin Education
Education - home visits	Continuing 11-2-89		2x/month	1 hr.	Benson's home	home visit	State	"
Social work	11-2-89		as needed		center or home as requested	problem-solving	State	Carolyn Mason Social work

SUMMARY OF CURRENT STATUS:

Molly is doing well in her current program. The Bensons and the rest of the team agreed to increase home visits to 2x/month. Schedule of services may change following family meeting with Carolyn.

182

FIGURE 8-1 (continued)

Section 6. Child and Family Outcomes

Child's Name: Molly Benson

CHILD

Date of Plan: 11-2-89

MAJOR OUTCOMES	STEPS TOWARD MAJOR OUTCOMES	PROCEDURES	Timelines Status	COMMENTS/ STATUS
① Molly will improve strength + control in preparation for assisted walking.	1. Molly will pull herself to kneel standing at a 12-inch step from hands + knees position, maintain position for 30 sec. or move.	Physical therapy with Patty.	Achieved Modified Made Progress Initiated ½	
	2. Molly will pull herself to half-kneeling position at step or chair + maintain position for 30 sec. or move.	Practice at home + i. during play group.		
	3. Molly will pull herself to standing at chair or shelf + maintain position for 1 min. or move.	Let Molly play with toys when she gets in position.		
	4. Meeting will be held to discuss use of crutches or walker with Molly, by Feb. 1.	Parents, physician + pt will meet to discuss walking.		

(continued)

183

FIGURE 8-1 (continued)

Section 6. Child and Family Outcomes

CHILD

Child's Name: Molly Benson

Date of Plan: 11-2-89

MAJOR OUTCOMES	STEPS TOWARD MAJOR OUTCOMES	PROCEDURES	Timelines Status	COMMENTS/STATUS
② Molly will use words to communicate with others.	1. Molly will use 2 or more words to indicate wants at least 5 times during day. 2. Molly will use 1 or more exclamations (e.g. "uh-oh") consistently during appropriate situation. 3. Molly will use 3 or more word labels when seeing object/person.	Consultation by speech therapist. Use conversational strategies (ECO) Use activities from HELP, Developmental Programming at home + play group.	Achieved Modified Made Progress Initiated 1. 1/2 2. 1/2	

184

FIGURE 8-1 *(continued)*

Section 6. Child and Family Outcomes

CHILD

Child's Name: Molly Benson

Date of Plan: 11-2-89

MAJOR OUTCOMES	STEPS TOWARD MAJOR OUTCOMES	PROCEDURES	Timelines Status	COMMENTS/ STATUS
③ Molly will improve her comprehension skills.	1. Molly will point to 3 or more objects or people consistently when named.	Consultation by speech therapist, teacher.		
	2. Molly will point to or look at most common objects consistently when they are named.	Use activities from HELP, Small Wonder, Developmental Programming at home + play group.		
	3. Molly will point to 3 or more body parts consistently when named.	Incorporate comprehension activities into PT.		

Status: Achieved / Modified / Made Progress / Initiated 1. ½

(continued)

185

FIGURE 8-1 (continued)

Section 6. Child and Family Outcomes

FAMILY

Child's Name: _Molly Benson_

Page _7_ of _11_

Date of Plan: _11-2-89_

MAJOR OUTCOMES	STEPS TOWARD MAJOR OUTCOMES	PROCEDURES	Timelines Status	COMMENTS/ STATUS
			Achieved	
			Modified	
			Made Progress	
			Initiated	
① Family will find alternative child care for Molly.	1. Identify child care options in neighborhood by end of January.	1. Mrs. Benson will talk to friends, neighbors, co-workers. Sarah will provide list of names.	1/16	
	2. Contact/visit prospective centers or day care homes by end of February.	Carolyn will call child care referral.		
	3. Select child care arrangement by end of March.	2. Mr. + Mrs. Benson will visit.		
		3. Mr. + Mrs. Benson will make decision.		

(continued)

186

FIGURE 8-1 (continued)

Section 6. Child and Family Outcomes   FAMILY

Child's Name: Molly Benson

MAJOR OUTCOMES	STEPS TOWARD MAJOR OUTCOMES	PROCEDURES	Timelines Status	COMMENTS/ STATUS
② Family needs more information on motor + language development to help Molly.	1. Teacher will make regular home visits.	Home visits by Sarah.		Information to be provided by end of January
	2. PT will locate + lend videotape on motor development.	Contact Spina Bifida Association for materials (Patty).	Initiated 11/9	
	3. ST will locate + lend videotape on language development.	Use program resource file + public library.		
	4. Team will provide list of books to The Bensons.			

Timelines Status: Achieved / Modified / Made Progress / Initiated

(continued)

FIGURE 8-1 (continued)

Section 6. Child and Family Outcomes

FAMILY

Child's Name: _Molly Benson_

Date of Plan: _11-2-89_

MAJOR OUTCOMES	STEPS TOWARD MAJOR OUTCOMES	PROCEDURES	Timelines Status	COMMENTS/STATUS
③ Family needs assistance in scheduling early intervention and medical appointments so that Mrs. Benson doesn't miss work.	1. Mrs. Benson will make list of regular appointments.	Mrs. Benson will make lists.	Initiated 1/2 Made Progress Modified Achieved	
	2. Mrs. Benson will make list of other upcoming appointments (e.g. vision exam).	Carolyn will assist with brainstorming.		
	3. In 2 weeks, Mr. + Mrs. Benson + Carolyn will meet to work out a better schedule though the end of March.			
	4. After new child care is selected, a new meeting will be held.			

188

(continued)

FIGURE 8–1 (*continued*)

Section 7. Transition Plan

Child: _Molly Benson_   Expected transition Date: _Summer, 1991_

Case Manager: _Patty Lee_   Target receiving site: _____

Reason for transition: _Molly will turn 3 during Summer
of 1991. Start planning for transition to preschool
Services during Summer of 1990._

Transition Event	Person Responsible	Dates Achieved
1. Parents informed of possible options	Case Manager	
2. Receiving agencies contacted	Parents Case Manager	
3. Parents visit agencies	Parents Case Manager	
4. Transition conference to determine appropriate placement	Parents/Case Manager Receiving Agency/ Intervention Team	
5. Transfer of records	Receiving and Sending Agencies	
6. Written transition plan developed	Parents/Case Manager Receiving Agency	
7. Placement	Parents/Child/ Receiving Agency	
8. Follow-up	Sending Agency/ Case Manager	

(*continued*)

FIGURE 8-1 *(continued)*

Section 8. IFSP Team

Family:

I had the opportunity to participate in the development of this IFSP. I understand the plan, and I give permission to the ___TOTS Program___ to carry out the plan with me, leading toward the agreed upon outcomes.

Paul Benson   Denise Benson _____   11-2-89
Parent(s)/Legal Guardian(s)   Date

I had the opportunity to participate in the development of this IFSP. I do not agree with this plan and I do not give my permission to the _____ to carry out the plan.

_____   _____
Parent(s)/Legal Guardian(s)   Date

Other IFSP Meeting Participants:

The following individuals participated in the development of the IFSP. Each person understands and agrees to carry out the plan as it applies to their role in the provision of services.

Patty Lee   RPT   _Fred Shallin_ MEd

Amy Allen MA-CCC-SP   _____

Carolyn Mason MSW   _____

The IFSP was developed with telephone consultation from the following people:

Mary Jo Peterson, RN, Farmington Medical Center provided written report.

The IFSP must also include the early intervention services that are necessary to meet the needs of the child and family. It will specify the number of days and sessions that a service will be provided, the length of time of each session, and whether the service is individual or group. In addition, the plan will give the location of the service. This may be at home, or in an early intervention center, hospital, clinic, child care center, or other setting. Further, the plan will specify other needed services including medical services that the child needs but which are not required by the law and, if necessary, the steps to be taken to help the family acquire the services.

The projected dates for initiation of services and the anticipated duration of early intervention services are also to be included. For children approaching age 3, the IFSP must also include the steps to facilitate the child's transition out of infant/toddler services. Dependent on a number of variables including child characteristics, family needs and wishes, and community options, this transition may be to preschool services under Part B of PL 99-457, community preschools, or child care, or no specialized services.

The name of the case manager must also be included on the written IFSP. This individual will be from the profession most immediately relevant to the child's and family's needs. According to the law, this individual will be responsible for implementation of the ISFP and coordination with other agencies. Deal, Dunst, and Trivette (1989) suggest that this wording places families in a dependent role. Rather, it is suggested that the case manager will help families achieve and use skills and knowledge to mobilize the various resources to meet their needs. That is, case management should be based on a capacity-building model. Families may react negatively to the term "case manager" (Boone et al., 1990) because they may not view themselves as "cases." Such terms as "family consultant" or "family services coordinator" may be more suitable. The case management component of the IFSP is examined in greater detail later in this chapter.

The law specifies a number of "IFSP meetings." Participants at the initial and periodic review meetings include the parent or parents of the child, other family members, advocates or friends at the parent's request, the case manager, the person or persons directly involved in the assessments, and, as appropriate, any service providers. From this list it is easy to see that over 10 people might be invited to such a meeting. The parent's perspective must be considered. This is another point of shared planning and decision-making; some families may be comfortable sharing and working on a family plan with 8 or 10 other people, but others may prefer to work just with those individuals they have come to know well. The federal regulations provide alternatives to physical presence at a meeting. These include making telephone conference calls, using a knowledgeable authorized representative, or making pertinent records available.

The meetings themselves must take place at times and places that are convenient for the family. The meeting might be held at a school or clinic, but might also be in the family home or at a neutral location such as the community center or even a coffee shop. Again, families can be involved in the planning for these meetings. Families can help select a location where all will feel comfortable in sharing information, disagreeing, negotiating, and creating a plan that makes sense. An additional provision is that meetings must be in the families' native language or mode of communication unless it is not feasible to do so.

PL 99-457 allows for the provision of early intervention services for eligible children prior to the completion of the multidisciplinary assessment and development of the IFSP. This allows for rapid initiation of services upon diagnosis or identification of need. For example, a physician may refer a youngster with cerebral palsy for physical therapy at the early intervention center. In many instances, the therapist will initiate the evaluation and therapy concurrently. As another example, a family with an infant newly diagnosed with Down syndrome may decide to enroll in the early intervention program and parent support group immediately. The regulations support this with the following conditions: that parental consent is obtained and an interim IFSP is developed with the name of the case manager and a list of the needed early intervention services. This interim IFSP serves as the initial building block for the multidisciplinary assessment and development of the IFSP within 45 days.

To this point, IFSP development may appear to be a highly formalized process. Regulations which are designed to ensure accountability may unfortunately reduce the friendliness and openness of the process. It is suggested that a guiding principle be that the IFSP is a dynamic process. The plan should always be considered a working plan. This means that it could be modified with parents and team members working together. It must be reviewed every 6 months, but it should always be part of the early intervention sessions. So if on a home visit, the parent and teacher through conversation find that a goal has been achieved (e.g., parents have completed all their applications for respite care and identified two providers), this should be indicated on the plan; then the opportunity is taken to discuss additional outcomes or projects that have become important. Likewise, the child may demonstrate a new skill (e.g., Jenny has learned to crawl) and it is time to modify and expand the plan. The changes are then shared with other team members. This means that it is important for team members to communicate honestly.

Selecting Outcomes

A major activity of the IFSP process is selecting child and family outcomes. An IFSP outcome is a statement of the changes family members want to see for their child or themselves (Johnson, McGonigel, & Kaufman, 1989). An outcome must be stated in functional terms that specify what is to occur and what is expected as a result of these actions. Further, outcomes should be written in easily understood language. Deal and colleagues (1989) extend the notion of outcomes to include needs, goals, aspirations, or projects. Two examples of outcome statements are provided in Table 8.2.

TABLE 8.2   Sample IFSP Outcomes

Jason will develop strength and control of his muscles in order to sit by himself.

Kim's grandparents, aunts, uncles, and cousins will learn about supplemental oxygen so that they won't be afraid of playing with her.

Most early intervention personnel are skilled at developing child-level goals and objectives based on a multidisciplinary assessment. However, the IFSP requires that outcomes directed to enhancing the child's development be developed with the family. Outcomes may be directed at the child, the family, and sometimes, at the program. For each outcome, the resources and sources of support for the child, family, or program are identified. Next, the strategies and activities that will lead to achievement of each outcome are specified. These action steps should flow out of the preceding discussion. The next step is agreement on timelines and criteria. The family will help define what they mean by success or achievement for each of their outcomes. An example of an IFSP is found in the story of Molly and her family. Additional examples are provided by Johnson, McGonigel, and Kaufman (1989).

To optimize the growth and development of children, it is necessary to look at their social and physical environments. Sometimes it will be important to change and modify those environments through both new and existing resources, supports, and strategies. Although families can help identify what works or does not work for them, professionals can share their information and knowledge of resources, supports, and strategies that families might not know about, or might not have had any reason to use in the past. By working together, families and professionals can develop both creative and effective action plans.

Look again at Table 8.2 and the example of Kim's family. As Kim's parents and other team members discussed her IFSP outcome they identified several sources of support, including a videotape on oxygen therapy, written information, and demonstrations to family members by early interventionists. Then Kim's father said that it would be more helpful if another child's relative would just talk to the extended family and show them that there was no need to be afraid of Kim's oxygen tank and tubes. After this comment, Kim's teacher suggested that another child in the program was on oxygen and that the grandfather often came to his early intervention sessions. It was decided to approach this man to see if he would talk to Kim's family.

Research informs us that family-identified needs have a higher probability of being acted upon than those needs identified by the professional (Dunst, Leet & Trivette, 1988). Therefore, it seems not only reasonable but imperative that families participate in the identification of outcomes and in the development of the plans to meet those outcomes. This requires mutual respect, honesty, and cooperation. These are some of the elements of collaboration.

Review and Evaluation of the IFSP

The IFSP must be reviewed every six months. Young children grow and change rapidly and their needs may change rapidly. Further, families of young children are undergoing major changes and their needs may also change. Thus, the law specifies 6-month periodic reviews, but the law also specifies more frequent review if conditions warrant. Within the IFSP itself, the timelines and criteria provide the opportunity for regular review of this working plan.

A review meeting should lend itself to an open discussion of some basic issues. These can be formulated as questions such as, How are we doing? Is the child/family achieving their outcomes? Do we need to make changes, and if so, what should we change? In the past, teams have sometimes been caught in the snare of specific but non-useful criteria for measuring progress toward accomplishment of goals and objectives. Alternatives that are respectful of families and useful to all team members need to be explored. Simeonsson, Huntington, and Short (1982) have adapted goal-attainment scaling for early intervention. Dunst, Leet, and Trivette (1988) provide a rating scale for evaluating the effectiveness of implementation efforts. Each outcome is evaluated against this scale:

1. Situation changed or worsened; no longer a need, goal, or project
2. Situation unchanged; still a need, goal, or project
3. Implementation begun; still a need, goal, or project
4. Outcome partially attained or accomplished
5. Outcome accomplished or attained, but not to the family's satisfaction
6. Outcome mostly accomplished or attained to the family's satisfaction
7. Outcome completely accomplished or attained to the family's satisfaction

CASE MANAGEMENT

As a result of the IFSP process, each family will have a written plan that lists the early intervention services and the names of the individuals who will work with the family. Some plans will be relatively simple in that the services and individuals are available in a single program. However, many plans will be more complicated and will specify services and individuals available through various agencies and programs. Case management can be viewed as the glue that holds together the services, supports, organizations, and individuals represented on the family's service plan. Acknowledgment of the importance of coordinated services is explicit in PL 99-457 in the requirement that each eligible family be assigned a case manager. Yet, case management may be difficult to provide in a family-centered manner.

Definitions

Case management has been variously defined:

- Provision of an individual who is responsible for helping coordinate the client's care and treatment within a complex human service system (Schwartz, Goldman, & Churgin, 1982)
- A set of logical steps and a process of interaction within a service network which assures that a client receives needed services in a supportive, effective, efficient, and cost-effective manner (Weil & Karls, 1985)
- Services designed to help families locate, access, and coordinate a network of supports and services that will allow them to live a full life in the community (Vohs, 1988)

The task force assigned to define case management under PL 99-457 agreed that it meant gaining access to early intervention services, ensuring timely delivery of services, and coordinating the provision of early intervention services with other services such as health or nutrition (Garland, Woodruff, & Buck, 1988). According to the law, case management consists of the following activities:

- Coordinating the performance of evaluations and assessments
- Facilitating and participating in the development, review, and evaluation of individualized family service plans
- Assisting families in identifying available service providers
- Coordinating and monitoring the delivery of available services
- Informing families of the availability of advocacy services
- Coordinating with medical and health care providers
- Facilitating the development of a transition plan to preschool services, if appropriate

It is interesting to note that case managers, according to this list, must facilitate, assist, coordinate, and inform on behalf of families. This role-focused approach could place the case manager in a controlling, directive capacity vis-a-vis the family. By contrast, case management is defined in the regulations accompanying PL 99-457 as "activities carried out . . . to assist and enable a child and the child's family to receive the rights, procedural safeguards and services that are authorized to be provided under the State's early intervention program" (Federal Register, 54, p. 26311). These contrasting views of "doing for" the client vs. enabling the client to "do for him/herself" occur repeatedly in the case management literature.

Historical Antecedents

According to Dunst and Trivette (1989), three historical approaches to case management may be identified: *role-focused approaches* such as the list above; *resource procurement approaches,* which emphasize the case manager's role in helping clients obtain what they need to function successfully; and *client empowerment approaches,* in which the case manager focuses on enhancing the clients' abilities to procure their own resources and services. The first two of these approaches originated early in the century as responses in the field of social work to the need for service coordination, accountability, and nonduplication of services. With the growing urbanization of American society and the proliferation of programs to address economic, social, and health-care problems, coordination among diverse service providers became a necessity. At the same time program accountability became important. Gradually, these two functions were placed under the rubric of case management. Finally, as client advocacy emerged as an issue, it was added to the case manager's responsibilities (Weil & Karls, 1985). The deinstitutionalization movement for both persons with mental retardation and persons with mental illness in the 1960s led to an increased need for case managers and a review of then-existing case management practices.

Much of the historical development of case management is rooted in service systems focused on individuals who, for various reasons (e.g., mental illness or limited intellectual capacity), have required considerable assistance in obtaining needed services. Deficit models of case management have emphasized the dependence and dysfunction of these clients and have utilized role-focused or resource procurement approaches. Such approaches place the case manager in the position of primary decision-maker regarding services. This has often resulted in case management practices which do not empower the individuals receiving services, but rather foster dependence and perceptions of inadequacy and dysfunction (Bailey, 1989; Dunst, 1989). In contrast, the empowerment approach assumes that clients have the potential ability to manage their own affairs, participate in the process, and make their own decisions.

The early intervention field has generally embraced this more recent empowerment approach to case management, reflecting the family-centered spirit of PL 99-457. Let us examine the implications of this approach for the IFSP process and for the various professionals who work with families in early intervention settings. As Bailey (1989) puts it, "Although infants with handicaps generally exhibit developmental delays, the assumption that their families are incompetent would undermine both the intent and the effect of the legislation" (p. 121).

The Family Empowerment Model of Case Management

This model of case management supports families in maintaining or building upon their own capabilities (see Table 8.1). It is a model that fosters active participation and views the family as basically competent. The birth or identification of a child with special needs does not alter the family's basic capacity to make and implement decisions. However, the birth or identification of a child with special needs may necessitate the acquisition of new knowledge and skills. The empowerment model of case management is dedicated to supporting families as they acquire skills in accessing and mobilizing resources, services, and supports in a confident and competent manner. Case management services are themselves individually tailored, in recognition of the changing capacities of families.

Dunst and Trivette (1989) further define the empowerment model of case management as effective helping. It is the act of enabling families to become better able to solve their own problems, meet their own needs, or achieve their aspirations by promoting the acquisition of competencies that develop a greater sense of control over the intervention process. In this model, effective helping consists of providing contingent helping, enabling experiences, and fostering a sense of empowerment.

The notion of *contingent helping* is that help must be provided to clients contingent on their behavior. That is, people get resources when they are actively involved in solving their own problems. If people perceive that help will be given no matter what they do, a sense of helplessness and dependence results. If, however, families perceive that the help is contingent on their own behavior, and they have control over whether they receive that help or not, they feel a greater sense of control over the process. For example, a young mother who is dependent on drugs is offered the opportunity to place her handicapped infant in an extended day-care and intervention program contingent upon her entry into a drug treatment program. She is offered the services of a home health visitor on a regular basis if she will take the initiative to schedule the visits far enough in advance and not cancel appointments at the last minute. This is just one example. Contingent helping is an individualized process.

Enabling experiences are those that afford individuals opportunities to learn new competencies that strengthen their functioning as parents and independent citizens. They are experiences that allow active participation on the part of families in decisions that affect them. They increase the family's sense of control over future events. For example, parents of an infant with multiple handicaps may set goals for their child and other family members, decide which professionals they wish to work with and for how long, the evaluate the effectiveness of their early intervention program. They may participate in a parent support group in which they learn to share ideas with other parents less experienced than they are.

Empowerment implies that the family already has many competencies that may have previously gone unrecognized by either themselves or the professionals, that what is seen as poor functioning is really the result of the existing social structure or a lack of resources, and that new competencies are best learned in the context of daily living.

Effective case management can assure that each family member has a sense of participatory competence, a belief in their own ability to make things happen.

Desired family outcomes for the case management process include an enhanced sense of personal control, an increased belief in each family member's own ability to make things happen, and a sense of participatory competence on the part of the family. Participatory competence means that family members see themselves as able to take effective action on their own behalf. Empowered families take the initiative, find meaningful services and supports, reject or change those that are not helpful, decide how to allocate their resources, choose where to live, and with whom to associate. Such families take an active role in the management of their service plan.

IMPLICATIONS FOR THE MULTIDISCIPLINARY TEAM

The IFSP and case management provisions of PL 99-457 mean changes for the professional members of the multidisciplinary team. Professionals require skills in consulting in addition to the provision of "hands on" service; they will need to consult with parents and other team members including providers at other agencies. This necessitates improved interpersonal and communication skills such as relaying information, asking good questions, listening, and setting the stage for sharing.

Team members will be asked to serve multiple roles. For example, sometimes a professional will be both direct service provider and case manager. Professionals must be flexible in their thinking, be able to define their changing role, and be able to consider the consequences of their actions. Flexibility has always been necessary in early intervention programs. This requirement is expanded in a family-centered approach that is truly responsive to the family's changing needs, resources, and goals.

A family-centered approach demands that professionals view families as basically strong and capable. This view must be expressed not only in words but also in such actions as seeking other's opinions, taking the family's perspective on an issue or problem, and jointly solving problems.

Although the provisions and requirements of PL 99-457 lead to certain changes in the role and function of professionals in early intervention, some things do not change. Professionals will retain their commitment to children and their families, and to the provision of high-quality early intervention services.

The message of PL 99-457 is that early intervention for children with special needs must respect the family. It is up to the states to determine their own specific procedures for implementation of the various components of PL 99-457 including the IFSP and case management provisions. However, it is up to the implementers—families and early intervention professionals—to put a family-centered approach into action. It takes time to form good relationships and establish effective procedures, but a foundation of caring and respect is crucial to the success of our endeavors.

Chapter 9

Intervention for At-Risk and Handicapped Infants and Their Families

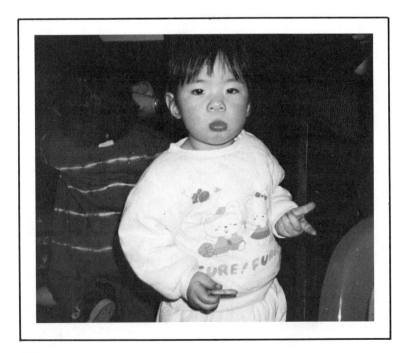

Early intervention takes many different forms and involves several professional disciplines. Successful early intervention services address the special needs of the young child while supporting and enhancing the family. This chapter will address two primary questions, what do handicapped and at-risk infants need to learn, and what strategies will be most helpful and effective. In educational parlance, these are issues of curriculum design and implementation.

Family systems theory, research, and PL 99-457 support a family-centered approach to early intervention services (Bailey & Simeonsson, 1988b; Dunst & Trivette, 1989; Shelton, Jeppson, & Johnson, 1987). A family-centered approach appreciates and understands the infant's dependence on the family for survival and nurturance. In subsequent sections of this chapter, attention is focused on intervention objectives and methods for infants. However, the reader needs to place the suggested objectives and methods within the context of the family. Intervention planning and implementation are accomplished through teamwork, with parents as members of the team. Parent and family priorities and needs, as well as their values and beliefs, will continually influence the content and style of intervention.

SETTING INTERVENTION OBJECTIVES

Child Outcomes

In Chapter 7 the assessment process and several assessment tools and procedures were discussed. The various assessment activities lead to the identification of important outcomes. *Outcomes,* or statements of desired changes, are a basic component of the IFSP. Some outcomes will focus on the child; some will address other family concerns.

In selecting *child outcomes,* team members apply their knowledge of typical child development as well as knowledge of handicapping conditions and risk factors and the implications they carry. This information, together with assessment data and the family's concerns, lead to individual child outcomes.

Several steps are necessary to translate these child outcomes into effective activities and experiences that promote learning and enhance development. In analyzing assessment information, the team has identified the relative priority given to these outcomes. Further, by looking at the whole child and the environments in which the child interacts, the team gains a greater understanding about the variables that may promote or constrain intervention efforts.

Outcomes typically represent goals or projects that may take several weeks or months to accomplish. Within the IFSP process, discussion with parents and other team members should ensure that outcomes are both important and socially appropriate.

Intervention Objectives

The next step is to restate the outcome as one or more intervention objectives. *Intervention objectives* are specific statements about a change in one of a child's repertoire of skills which is expected to occur soon. Objectives should also be important and socially appropriate. This means that by learning, acquiring, and using the particular skill or behavior, the child becomes more independent and more capable of solving problems. Intervention objectives have three major components: the behavior, the conditions under which the behavior will occur, and the criterion for evaluation. Examples of intervention objectives are given in Table 9.1

Enabling Steps. Objectives can then be broken down into smaller components or enabling steps. This can be accomplished by *task analysis;* that is, doing the task oneself or watching someone else perform the task, and writing down the process step by step. Another method involves a logical analysis of the behavior drawing upon normal developmental sequences. For example, an analysis of the behavior, "Says approximation of the word bottle upon seeing the bottle," might be broken down to (1) shows excitement upon seeing bottle, (2) vocalizes upon seeing the bottle, and (3) says "ba-ba" upon seeing the bottle. In addition to breaking down objectives into smaller parts, a task or logical analysis involves sequencing the parts or steps for intervention, making adaptations for individual children, and identifying prerequisites.

The use of existing curricula offers one means of translating child outcomes to objectives and learning experiences. Many curricula provide very useful objectives, sequences, and activities. Several of these curricula will be referred to in subsequent sections. However, not every young child will fit neatly into a curriculum. Individual children may require smaller steps or alternative responses. Many curricula, for example, do not provide adaptations for youngsters with sensory or motor impairments (Fewell & Sandall, 1983). Skills in task analysis, logical analysis of behaviors, modification, and adaptation of curricula are valuable to early interventionists.

The process of breaking down the outcomes and objectives is not meant to imply that instruction or therapy is implemented in lock-step fashion. Rather, these smaller steps may be incorporated within daily routines and play. Interventionists can use problem-solving skills to arrive at potentially effective activities.

TABLE 9.1   Intervention Objectives

Jason will sit without support and use his hands to play with toys for 3 to 5 minutes at a time.

Annie will point to desired object when asked a question, with the object in view, at least five times during a 10-minute play session.

When adult places cup to his lips, Brian will drink from cup, keeping his lips closed and losing only small amounts of liquid, with jaw support from side.

TABLE 9.2 Sample Activity Plan

Child: Annie

Domain: Communication

Outcome: Annie will increase her use of gestures in order to communicate.

Objective: Annie will point at desired object when asked a question with the object in view at least
five times during a 10-minute play session.

Steps: 1. Looks at desired object.

2. Reaches for desired object.

3. Points to desired object.

Activity:

Implement during Annie's scheduled free play time in the mat area. Use high interest
toys such as ball, wind-up toys, slinky. Incorporate questions naturally into play, "What do
you want?," "Where's the _____ ?" Pause following the question.

If Annie points at the object, give her the toy, name it for her. If she looks at or
reaches for the object, demonstrate pointing before giving her the object. If she shows no interest in the object, wait for the next opportunity.

Alternate Activity:

Try activity during snack time as well.

The intervention objective or steps are the "problems." The team can brainstorm
to generate many activities, experiences, toys, materials, and situations. The
team uses existing curriculum materials, research findings, child and family
preferences, and their own experiences to generate potentially useful "solutions."
Then, the team selects those activities which would seem to be most effective
and suitable. The team plans the details of intervention, implements, and
evaluates the effectiveness of the intervention.

There should be a clear link between asessment and intervention (Bagnato,
Neisworth, & Munson, 1989; Bricker & Gumerlock, 1988). Assessment and intervention can be considered a series of recycling events. As intervention activities proceed, new objectives are targeted for intervention based on the child's
performance. The example in Table 9.2 illustrates the steps from child outcome,
based on assessment results, to a lesson or activity plan.

DESIGNING A CURRICULUM

A *curriculum* may be defined as a set of activities or experiences designed to
achieve stated developmental or learning objectives (Hanson & Lynch, 1989).
Curricula may vary along several dimensions, including number of content
areas, number of objectives, and amount of structure provided or imposed on
the activities or experiences. Infant curricula have a recent history, corresponding with the growth of early intervention services for handicapped and at-risk
infants. A variety of infant curricula are readily available (Table 9.3). Such curricula may be used singly; however, early intervention teams often use several

TABLE 9.3 Selected Infant Curricula

NAME	AGE RANGE	TARGET POPULATION	CONTENT	COMMENTS
Carolina Curriculum for Handicapped Infants and Infants at Risk (Johnson, Martin, Jens, & Attermeier, 1986).	Birth–24 months	Children with handicaps and their families	Covers traditional domains of development (fine motor, gross motor, cognition, communication, social, self-help) expanded to 24 areas; includes teaching procedures, individual assessment logs, and developmental progress charts	Based on normal developmental sequences but does not assume even development across domains. Based on logical teaching sequences. Format clear and easy to follow. Adaptations and suggestions are provided for children with motor or sensory impairments.
Developmental Programming for Infants and Young Children (Schafer & Moersch, 1981)	Birth–36 months	Children with handicaps and their families	Covers perceptual/fine motor, cognition, language, social/emotional, self-care, gross motor; provides suggested teaching activities; includes assessment tool: Early Intervention Development Profile.	Based on normal developmental sequences. Activities can be incorporated into play and routines. Adaptations for children with motor and sensory impairments.
Early Learning Accomplishment Profile and Activities (Glover, Preminger, & Sanford, 1978)	Birth–36 months	Infants, young children, multi-handicapped children	Covers fine motor, gross motor, language, self-help, social, cognition. Includes learning activity cards. Profile can be used for summative evaluation.	Based on normal developmental sequences. Widely used program. Does not include adaptation.

204

Program	Age	Population	Coverage	Basis
Evaluation and Programming System for Infants and Young Children (Bricker, Bailey, Gummerlock, Buhl, & Slentz, 1986)	1–36 months	Children at risk or handicapped	Covers fine motor, gross motor, self-care, cognitive, social-communication, social; includes sequences and teaching procedures; includes format for daily/weekly, quarterly assessment and program evaluation.	Based on normal development and research/experience with children with handicaps. Uses an activity-based intervention format. Comprehensive program.
Hawaii Early Learning Profile (HELP) and Activities (Furuno, O'Reilly, Hosaka, Inatsuka, Allman, & Zeisloft, 1979)	Birth–36 months	Children with handicaps	Covers gross motor, fine motor, cognition, expressive language, social/emotional, and self-help. Includes activities, assessment checklists, and HELP charts.	Based on normal developmental sequences. Activities can be incorporated into play and routines. Adaptations for children with sensory and motor impairments, and the older delayed child.
Hicomp Curriculum (Willoughby-Herb & Neisworth, 1983)	Birth–5 years	Children with handicaps	Covers communication, own care, motor development, and problem-solving; includes strategies to promote learning; includes system for monitoring progress.	Based on normal development. Activities can be incorporated into play and routines.
Infant Learning (Dunst, 1981)	Birth–24 months	Children functioning at sensorimotor level	Covers cognition, social, linguistic development; includes suggested activities and intervention strategies; can be used with Uzgiris-Hunt Scales.	Based on normal development and research on social, cognitive, linguistic development. Activities are designed for daily routines and play. Requires careful reading.

(continued)

TABLE 9.3 (Continued)

NAME	AGE RANGE	TARGET POPULATION	CONTENT	COMMENTS
Learning through Play (Fewell & Vadasy, 1983)	Birth–36 months	Children with and without handicaps, and their families	Covers sensory, perception/fine motor, movement in space, cognition, language, social; provides suggested activities; includes screening checklist	Based on normal development. Activities incorporated into play and routines, designed for parents and children. Adaptations for children with sensory and motor impairments.
Peabody Developmental Motor Scales and Activity Cards (Folio & Fewell, 1984)	Birth–83 months	Children with handicaps	Covers gross motor, fine motor; includes activity cards; linked to the motor scales	Based on normal development and experience with children with handicaps. Activities easy to understand, can be done at home or center. Assessment tool has been standardized. Adaptations for children with handicaps.
Portage Guide to Early Education (Bluma, Shearer, Frohman, & Hilliard, 1976)	Birth–5 years	Children with handicaps	Covers infant stimulation, socialization, language, self-help, cognitive, motor; file of activities; includes frequency charts, and checklist.	Based on normal development. Activity cards are easy to use.

Small Wonder (Karnes, 1981)	Birth–36 months	Children with developmental delays and normally developing children and their families	Covers balance and motion, body awareness, cognition, fine motor, language, listening, self-help, socialization, visual; includes suggested activities; includes diary and progress chart	Based on normal development. Activities designed for parents to incorporate within daily routines and play.
Teaching the Infant with Down Syndrome (Hanson, 1987)	Birth–36 months	Children with Down Syndrome and their families	Covers gross motor, cognition, fine motor, communication, social, self-help. Includes teaching procedures and suggested activities. Includes baby record and format for formative record-keeping.	Based on normal development and research with children with Down Syndrome. New edition includes suggestions for activities within daily routine and play. Intended for use by parents at home.
Teaching the Young Child with Motor Delays (Hanson & Harris, 1986)	Birth–24 months	Children with motor delays and their families	Covers gross motor, fine motor, and oral motor. Includes teaching procedures and suggested activities. Includes baby record and format for formative record keeping.	Based on normal development and research/experience with children with motor delays. Also includes suggestions for social, cognitive, and communication development. Designed for parents and professionals.

curricula and other resources to meet the multiple needs of individual children. In doing so, it is important to establish and use a consistent program philosophy.

Infant curricula differ on the basis of theoretical approach. Although almost all infant curricula share the goal of enhancing the infant's development, the underlying theoretical approach, whether explicit or implicit, causes the content, organization, and methods to vary. We will discuss four different approaches.

The developmental approach draws from observation and description of normal development. This maturational perspective views development as proceeding in a genetically predetermined manner. The work of Gesell (1925) is often associated with this approach. Many infant curricula (e.g., Hawaii Early Learning Profile, Portage Guide to Early Education) draw content from this work. Developmental milestones are the curriculum objectives.

More recently, *the transactional model* of development articulated by Sameroff and Chandler (1975) has greatly influenced intervention practices. This model recognizes the importance of the caregiving context and the transactions or interplay between the infant and the environment (Thurman & Widerstrom, 1990). Building on this model, greater attention has been given in recent years to developing and maintaining environments that are nurturing and supportive.

The cognitive approach is typically associated with the work of Piaget (1952, 1970). Important elements of this approach include hierarchical stages, active interaction of the child with the environment, and intrinsic motivation. Piaget's work has exerted a strong influence on the specific content of infant curricula, most notably in the cognitive, social, and communicative domains. *Infant Learning* (Dunst, 1981) is one example of a curriculum based on Piagetian theory.

The behavioral approach influences instructional strategies (the how of curriculum) rather than content. Associated with the work of Skinner (1972), the behavioral approach incorporates the importance of planned environmental events and extrinsic motivation of the child. Typically, instructional objectives are specified and systematic instruction is provided through a predetermined series of steps to change or teach new behaviors to reach that targeted objective. Teaching the Infant with Down Syndrome (Hanson, 1987) incorporates a behavioral approach.

Curricula may also differ on the issue of functionality. The intent of functional curricula is to identify goals and objectives that are critical for daily living, and provide instruction to reach those goals (Guess et al., 1978). Sometimes viewed as a developmental-functional dichotomy, the two perspectives are not mutually exclusive during infancy. Many functional behaviors (e.g., shaking a toy, eating with a spoon) are also appropriate to the infant's developmental level. Adopting a functional perspective when making intervention decisions may be particularly important for young children with severe handicaps.

Organized, written curricula specify the goals and content of the intervention, provide direction to what is done within a program, and define the role of the child and the adults in the learning process. Rigid adherence to a curricula may be a hindrance. It may unfortunately lead some to limit goals, objectives, and sequences to what is found in the curriculum. This may reduce individualization, opportunities for social interaction, and a variety of experiences provided for the child. Thus, early interventionists must intelligently adopt and use curricula. Wolery (1983) and DuBose and Kelly (1981) provide useful frameworks for evaluating curricula. Important considerations include applicability to the children and program, useability, and effectiveness. Infant curricula do offer helpful guidance to an early intervention program.

IMPLEMENTATION

Developmental Domains

For purposes of organization, the following discussion of infant-level interventions is organized by developmental domain. The reader is reminded that while this provides a useful format, it artifically separates early development. Early skills are interrelated and interdependent (Lewis, 1984). The interrelatedness of early development has implications for both assessment and intervention and provides further support for a transdisciplinary team approach in which all team members are mutually concerned with all developmental areas.

In the following sections, the developmental domains are examined and intervention strategies designed to facilitate development and learning are described.

Psychosocial. State, temperament, and attachment are important variables for assessment and intervention. Even in very young children, these variables may influence others in the infant's environment and influence development and learning.

State. State, or level of arousal, reflects central nervous system integrity and maturation. Central nervous system dysfunction is a characteristic of many of the children in early intervention programs. An infant responds to stimulation by changing states. Behavior states also influence responsiveness to stimulation. In an alert state, the child is available for social interaction and learning. Other states common to newborns range from deep sleep to crying (Brazelton, 1984).

It is important for early interventionists and parents to understand behavioral states, the influence of states upon behaviors, changes over time, and the interaction of environmental and biological status on the child's ability to self-regulate state. Expected developmental changes include reduction in response variability and increased state constancy and organization. Thus, as infants develop they experience increasingly longer, more stable periods of sleep and alertness.

State is often assessed in newborns for research or intervention purposes (e.g., Brazelton, 1984). This research examines the range, quality, and stability of the infant's states. Simeonsson, Huntington, and Parse (1980) suggest that assessment and understanding of state are important in understanding handicapped and at-risk children beyond the neonatal period.

State difficulties include rapid or unusual change or fluctuation between states, unclear states, and extended periods of deep sleep or agitation. For example, cocaine-exposed babies are observed to move immediately from deep sleep to excessive agitation with screaming (Griffith, 1988). Extreme agitation means not only is the child not available for interaction, but caregivers may reduce their attempts at engaging the infant since the infant's response is so unpleasant.

Researchers and interventionists are examining ways to deal with state difficulties. First, the careful interventionist rules out other reasons for state difficulties (e.g., irritability may be triggered by gastrointestinal upset; poor alerting may be related to a sensory impairment). Then the interventionist searches for ways to improve the stability, clarity, and pattern of the infant's state.

Interventions with preterm infants (Als, Lawhorn, Brown, et al., 1986; Hedlund, 1989; Katz, Pokorni, & Long, 1989; VandenBerg, 1985), and drug-exposed infants (Schneider, Griffith, & Chasnoff, 1989) provide us with potentially effective intervention strategies. Interventions may involve changing the environment or using particular caregiving techniques. Environmental changes include reducing excess stimulation from noise, light, or activity. Relatively simple changes such as moving or covering the infant's crib may be effective. Other infants may need boundaries within their crib. Positioning with blanket rolls or swaddling are sometimes used. Nonnutritive sucking or finger rolls may increase alertness and self-regulation. By timing and sequencing caregiving according to the infant's sleep-wake cycle and stress responses, the caregiver may also promote state regulation. Intervention also includes the gradual introduction of greater environmental demands.

Temperament. Temperament refers to behavioral style. Temperament characteristics appear in infancy, are relatively constant, and have a constitutional base but may be influenced by the environment (McDevitt, 1988). The concept of temperament is greatly influenced by the work of Thomas, Chess, and Birch (1968). Using their system of assessment, temperament should be studied for activity, rhythmicity, adaptability, approach-withdrawl, threshold,

Temperament plays an important role in toddlers establishing peer friendships.

intensity, mood, distractibility, and persistence. Recent evidence suggests that there is both stability and change of behavioral style during the early years, with individual differences in temperament becoming more stable after age 3 (McDevitt, 1986). This suggests that temperament is affected by the environment, and that intervention during infancy may result in changes.

Thomas and Chess (1977) describe three clusters of temperament characteristics: difficult, slow-to-warm-up, and easy. "Goodness of fit" between the infant and the environment is the critical point rather than assignment of a particular label. Poor fit may lead to behavioral problems, especially when temperament patterns do not meet parental expectations. A difficult infant in a supportive environment may be well adjusted. In another environment, this infant may do poorly. Intervention is warranted when there is a mismatch. The goal of intervention is to reduce the pattern of mismatch between child and environment (i.e., parents, other caregivers, elements of the physical environment) by making changes in the environment.

Carey (1979) described three levels of clinical intervention: increase awareness of individual differences of temperament, discuss an individual child's temperament characteristics and implications (i.e., interpretation of a child's behavior), and provide suggestions or guidance for more specific environmental changes. *Anticipatory guidance* is an intervention strategy proposed by Cameron and Rice (1986) as a preventive measure. Guidance materials describe the temperament issue (e.g., mealtime control, sleep problems) in positive nonjudgmental terms, outline why the issue might occur, validate parental feelings that are likely to occur, and suggest ways to handle or manage the issue.

Attachment. A major task of infancy is the establishment of a positive and satisfying relationship with at least one primary caregiver. This relationship, called attachment, shows developmental changes. It begins to form around 3 to 4 months; the social smile to maintain proximity to the attachment figure is a behavioral sign. The relationship solidifies around 12 to 18 months, when the child displays such signs as using locomotion for maintaining proximity, reacting negatively to strangers, and reacting negatively to separation. By the end of infancy, the child displays apparent cognitive understanding of separation. During the preschool years, the child is able to recognize the attachment figure's goals and cooperates in achieving them.

Many young children with handicaps successfully establish positive attachments with one or two significant caregivers. There is some indication, however, that attachment may be delayed or expressed differently (Berry, Gunn, & Andrews, 1980; Blacher & Meyers, 1983; Sigman & Ungerer, 1984). Certain infant characteristics may interfere with the expression of attachment. For example, young children with handicaps may smile, vocalize, gaze, or respond to being held differently or more slowly than other children. Temperament characteristics such as irritability or inconsolability may also interfere with attachment. Parent or caregiver behaviors also play a part. The parent must respond to the infant, play with the infant, and discriminate the infant's signals. Psychological (e.g., personality disorders) and sociological (e.g., inadequate social networks) factors affecting the parent may jeopardize attachment (see Chapter 4).

Members of the early intervention team need to understand the importance of a secure attachment and its positive implications for social and cognitive development. Conversely, insecure attachments may have negative outcome (Ainsworth, Blehar, Waters, & Wall, 1978). Providing support for a satisfying relationship is an important goal of early intervention.

Intervention with infants and families around attachment issues may focus on parent-infant interaction or may be more broadly based, particularly with multi-risk families. Cicchetti and Toth (1987) describe a comprehensive intervention program for families with a history of maltreatment. Intervention includes concrete assistance as well as therapeutic interventions aimed at individuals, dyads, and larger family constellations. Greenspan, Wieder, Lieberman, Nover, Lourie, and Robertson (1987) also describe intervention practices with multi-risk families.

For children with very insecure or ambivalent attachments, and multi-risk, multi-problem families, mental health specialists are important members of the early intervention team. The mental health specialist, in addition to participating in the assessment process, brings special skills in parent guidance, parent training, parent-infant psychotherapy, and family therapy, which may be critical to effective intervention with very high-risk families. Further, as a collaborating member of the team, the mental health specialist assists in identifying and mobilizing community resources for these families.

Parent-Infant Interaction. Interactions between parents and their young child may provide in part the basis for social, language, and cognitive development (Bruner, 1975; Schaffer, 1977; Stern, Beebe, Jaffe, & Bennett, 1977). When the infant is handicapped or at-risk for developmental problems, these interactions may be jeopardized.

Early interaction is a complex process in which the infant influences the adult's behavior and the adult influences the infant's behavior. From birth, development proceeds in conjunction with the ability to interact with other humans in a reciprocal manner. During the earliest days and months, environmental effects are mediated through the interactive social relationship between the infant and caregiver. For example, the infant cries and is picked up and soothed. Or, the infant smiles and coos and the caregiver returns the smile and maintains contact with the infant. The establishment and support for a satisfying relationship between infant and parent/caregiver are primary goals of infancy and early intervention programs.

When one or both partners in a social interaction does not behave in a predictable or readable manner, the exchange may be disrupted (Goldberg, 1977). Infants with handicaps or at-risk for developmental problems may produce behaviors that are infrequent, difficult to interpret, or poorly timed. For example, the infant with a visual impairment may not gaze at the caregiver to initiate or sustain an interaction. The infant with cerebral palsy may not mold into the caregiver's arms in response to the caregiver's attempt to cuddle the infant. Some infants seem to produce few vocalizations or gestures. The parent or caregiver may also disrupt the interaction. Studies of mothers of young children with handicaps reveal a tendency to be more directive and dominant than mothers of children without handicaps (Buium, Rynders, & Turnure, 1974; Cunningham, Reuler, Blackwell, & Deck, 1981; Eheart, 1982; Guttman & Rondal, 1979; Jones, 1977; Mahoney & Robenalt, 1986; Marshall, Hegrenes, & Goldstein, 1973). Debate continues as to the effects of such parental adaptations (Crawley & Spiker, 1983; Mahoney & Powell, 1988).

Researchers and early interventionists are designing and examining strategies to promote positive interactions. Before describing some of these strategies, we should note that some parents and infants successfully establish productive interaction patterns. Their interactions are fun and balanced, and the parent is able to gradually extend the infant's communicative abilities. When this is observed, the role of the interventionist is to support these patterns and to learn from them.

Other dyads may need assistance. Interventions that focus on parent-infant interaction are known by a variety of names including turn-taking, guided interactions, interactive coaching, social reciprocity interventions, and relationship-focused interventions. A shared goal is the facilitation of more playful and productive interactions. Some shared intervention techniques include getting into position (usually face-to-face), reading and responding to the infant's cues, following the infant's lead, taking turns, and learning the infant's

TABLE 9.4   **Strategies to Enhance Interaction**

STRATEGY	COMMENTS
Get into position.	Interacting with babies usually means getting face-to-face with the baby. With mobile children this means being available and being willing to follow the child's lead and topic of interest.
Read the infant's cues.	Observe and try to understand the infant's cues—sounds, facial gestures, body movements. Sometimes this requires redefining the "meaning" of a reflex or physiological response.
Respond to the infant's cues.	Treat sounds, gestures, and body movements as meaningful. Over time, respond more quickly to more conventional cues.
Follow the infant's lead.	Provide a response that is linked to the infant's cue. Respond to infant's current interest, activity.
Imitate the infant.	Copy the infant's action or sound. This is one way of following the infant's lead. It also serves to slow down the adult and allow for turns.
Take turns.	Allow the infant the opportunity to behave. Respond to the behavior as meaningful. Use intonation and body language to show that you expect the baby to take another turn.
Learn the infant's pace.	Adjust your timing to the infant's. Whether fast or slow, aim for episodes of balanced turns.

Note: Adapted from *Eco: A Partnership Program* (Kit) by J.D. MacDonald and Y. Gillette, 1989, San Antonio, TX: Special Press, copyright 1989 by Special Press; and *Transactional Intervention Program: A Child-Centered Approach to Developmental Intervention with Young Handicapped Children.* (Monograph No. 1) by G. Mahoney and A. Powell, 1986, Farmington, CT: University of Connecticut School of Medicine.

pace (Table 9.4). Table 9.5 provides descriptive information on intervention approaches that focus on parent-infant interaction.

Motor. Movement allows a child to explore the world. Through movement, the child interacts with and acts upon the social and physical environment. The infant accomplishes some remarkable feats in terms of motor development during the first year. The newborn is dependent on others, with movement generally dominated by reflexes. By the end of the first year, however, the infant is upright and beginning to walk, and by the end of infancy, the child is mobile, independent, and capable of a variety of controlled actions.

Many handicapped and at-risk infants demonstrate problems in the motor domain. Motor impairments may limit a child's interaction and exploration and restrict learning opportunities. Moreover, they may leave them at risk for becoming passively dependent on others.

Children with motor impairments may have limited or poorly controlled movement. They often have difficulty assuming and maintaining postures against gravity (e.g., sitting, standing). In addition, attainment of motor milestones is delayed. While abnormal muscle tone or tension may account for some motor difficulties, other factors include retention of primitive reflexes, delayed development of postural responses, skeletal deformities, abnormal muscle strength, or problems related to speed, accuracy, or timing of movements.

The major goals of intervention in the motor domain are to help the child move as normally as possible, to teach the child to use movement to initiate interactions with and to control aspects of the environment, and to provide opportunities that allow the child to grow and gain independence. Careful identification of individual intervention objectives is particularly important, since the purpose of intervention for infants with neurological impairments is different from intervention for infants with delayed motor development. For the infant with neurologic impairment, intervention may be aimed at preventing abnormal patterns while facilitating independent and functional movement.

For many children, the physical or occupational therapist will be actively involved in the child's program. This individual may assess the child, help write outcomes and objectives, and provide direct therapy. This individual will also provide information, demonstration, and feedback to parents and other team members so that facilitative handling, positioning, and exercises will be incorporated into the child's day whether at home, clinic, or child care.

The therapist may subscribe to a particular method of treatment such as neurodevelopmental treatment, sensorimotor, or sensory integration (see Harris & Tada, 1983, for a description). Perhaps the most widely used treatment for individuals with cerebral palsy is the neurodevelopmental treatment (NDT) approach (Bobath & Bobath, 1972). This approach has also been used for children with Down syndrome (Harris, 1981), severe mental retardation (Ellis, 1967), and sensory impairments (Bobath & Bobath, 1964). NDT incorporates handling techniques designed to facilitate normal muscle tone, inhibit abnormal reflex patterns, and facilitate automatic reactions in order to allow the child to move actively and experience normal movement. Four guidelines for positioning and handling the child with motor impairments are useful. These are to use key points of control (head and neck, shoulder girdle, and hips), to work toward symmetry, that is, equally effective movement of both sides of the body, to work toward midline positioning, and to use only minimal support, thus encouraging maximum independent movement (Hanson & Harris, 1986).

Smith (1989) and Harris (1988) suggest that in selecting and using this or any other treatment approach one must consider the child's various environments and ensure that the functional skills that help improve the child's performance in all those environments are included in the treatment plan. Parents and other team members with their knowledge of the child's daily environments and needs have critical information for specification of outcomes and design of intervention plans that are appropriate and relevant.

TABLE 9.5   Selected Resources on Parent-Infant Interaction

NAME	FORMAT	CONTENT	COMMENTS
Interactional Approach (Bromwich, 1981)	Book	Provides a description of the home-based model program. Focuses on mother-infant dyads, infants birth–3 years, original group was preterm infants. Provides assessment information using Parent Behavior Progression. Includes description of intervention strategies, focus on reciprocity, reading, and responding to infant's cues.	Book does not offer a single best way, but uses a problem-solving approach. Includes case studies.
My turn, your turn (Sandall, 1986)	Videotape	Demonstrates three strateiges for successful interventions: follow the child's lead, keep it going, & take it further.	Developed for parents and service providers. Incorporates features from MacDonald & Gillette, and Mahoney & Powell programs.
Relationship-Focused (Affleck, McGrade, McQueeney & Allen, 1982)	Program description	Describes home-based program. Focus on families with infants with biological risks or genetic disorders. Intervention strategies include emotional support, parent-infant reciprocity through reading and responding to infant's cues.	Home visits follow the parents lead. Incorporates problem-solving approach.
SIAI Model (McCollum 1984; McCollum & Stayton, 1985)	Research reports	Describes parent-infant assessment and intervention procedures used with infants with handicaps. Includes the Social Assessment Rating Scale and use of behavior counts.	Incorporates problem-solving approach. Specific intervention strategies are based on observation of interactions and parent/infant behaviors.
Supporting Parent-Child Interactions (Hanson & Krentz, 1986)	Program manual	Includes a rationale for the approach with theoretical bases, description of intervention framework, and strategies.	Includes case studies. Developed in a model program for infants and their families

(continued)

TABLE 9.5 (Continued)

NAME	FORMAT	CONTENT	COMMENTS
Transactional Intervention Program (TRIP) (Mahoney & Powell, 1986)	Teacher's Guide	Provides rationale and program description. Also includes a developmental profile. Provides descriptions of intervention strategies to facilitate turn-taking, interaction, and overall development (e.g., balancing turns, imitating, waiting)	Developed in a model program for infants and their families. Guide also includes program evaluation data.
Turntaking (ECO) (MacDonald & Gillette, 1989)	Kit includes training manuals, assessment materials (ECO scales).	Manuals provide background information and training materials. Designed for young children and families to facilitate social skills, play, turntaking, preverbal & nonverbal communication, language & conversation. Scales linked to intervention.	Based on clinical experience and research; includes information on use of materials in a variety of settings; videotapes available
Understanding my signals (Hussey, 1988)	Booklet	Booklet designed for parents of premature infants. Provides pictures of babies displaying approach signals, stress signals, and self-regulation signals.	Photographs help in recognizing and understanding the infant's behaviors.

Team planning and implementation ensures that an individual infant's posture and movement objectives are integrated into the infant's experiences and environments. For example, 14-month-old Tommy has increased muscle tone in his limbs, low muscle tone through the trunk, and limited ability to maintain postures against gravity. Outcomes in the motor area are aimed at normalizing his muscle tone, improving head control, and facilitating use of limbs. One of his stated objectives was that when placed in a side-lying position, Tommy would pat a switch with his hands and look at the activated toy. A special adaptive switch was constructed so that when Tommy touched it with his hands the toy (battery operated car, tape recorder) was activated. Learning to operate a switch allowed Tommy to play with toys. It may also be a preliminary step to further skills, such as operating a communication device.

Communication. Communication is "any overt conventional or nonconventional behavior, whether used intentionally or not, that has the effect of arousing in an onlooker a belief that the child is attempting to convey a message, make a demand or request, or is otherwise attempting to affect the behavior of the onlooker" (Dunst, 1978, p. 111). Infants communicate in a variety of ways such as crying, cooing, and kicking. Usually their parents and other caregivers respond to these prelinguistic behaviors as meaningful. Very simply, communication precedes linguistic expression.

Over the first two years of life, children whose communication skills are developing normally, move from use of prelinguistic, preintentional behaviors to the use of words and word combinations to express wants and needs, to comment on the world (including commenting on people and objects not immediately present), and to exchange information. That is, by age 2 the child is beginning to use language, a mutually understood symbol system, to communicate. Further, the child's understanding or comprehension of language has also grown remarkably. The 2-year-old understands many social conventions, directions, and words. The child continues to use a variety of contextual cues to support comprehension.

A large number of infants in early intervention programs will have communication needs. Communication and language development can be delayed or different for a variety of reasons. For example, the infant with a hearing loss experiences reduced sensory input, which interferes with output. The infant with Down syndrome may be significantly delayed in acquisition of communication and language skills. The infant with a motor impairment may be unable to produce gestures or vocalizations that are readily interpreted. Regardless of etiology, communication disorders can have pervasive effects on many features of the child's and family's life.

The field of communication and language development is characterized by changing, and sometimes conflicting, theories. Consequently, proposed intervention approaches are sometimes conflicting as well. Currently, much research and intervention with very young children takes an interactional approach (Warren & Kaiser, 1988). This approach emphasizes the social bases of language and assumes that language is based on social interactions and builds from the infant's early nonverbal exchanges with caregivers. Thus, early intervention in the communication domain is aimed at facilitating parent-infant interaction. The parent-infant interaction intervention strategies described previously are appropriate to the prelinguistic stage of communication intervention.

These and other intervention strategies are aimed at three broad goals, which are to foster the child's responsiveness to environmental stimuli in order to increase both the readability of the child's behavior and the probability that adults will interpret the behavior as meaningful, to foster the child's ability to initiate and sustain social interactions, and to foster the child's use of intentional communication (Holdgrafer & Dunst, 1986).

The speech therapist is the member of the team with professional training in speech and language development, disorders, and interventions. This individual collaborates with others on the team to plan intervention activities that support communication across all environmental settings. Whereas highly structured or isolated therapy settings may be needed occasionally, the bulk of communication interventions should take place in natural settings in which the infant needs to communicate.

The use of interactional or conversational approaches in natural settings is not meant to imply that intervention is unplanned. These children are not developing language naturally. They have difficulty with the basic language learning task, of learning the relationships between language content, form, and use (Fey, 1986). Their attempts and interactions may not be productive or sufficient. Their caregivers may find it difficult to interpret, respond, and extend the child's behavior to more advanced levels.

Planned, intentional intervention is needed. This process includes identification of the intervention objective(s). Appropriate communication objectives consider the child's interests, fit environmental requirements, and are just slightly above the child's current level. The intervention team then identifies potentially effective supports and strategies. One basic support is the use of a conversational format, which involves establishing a shared topic (often by following the child's lead) and taking turns. Changes in the physical environment may be effective. Other strategies require a more specific response by the conversational partner. Strategies include imitation of sounds, actions, or words to match the child's level (Mahoney & Powell, 1986; MacDonald & Gillette, 1989), using wait-time (Tronick, Als, Adamson, Wise, & Brazelton, 1978) or time delay (Halle, Baer, & Spradlin, 1981) to allow the child the opportunity to take turns, and using repetitions and expansions (Scherer & Olswang, 1984) to confirm and extend the child's utterance (Table 9.6). Interventions are then implemented in natural settings to allow multiple, dispersed learning opportunities. Interventions also incorporate natural consequences such as attention, continued interaction, and attainment of one's communicative intentions.

Augmentative communication is nonspeech communication. Examples include sign language, communication boards, and electronic devices. For some infants, preparation for and use of augmentative communication are important considerations in program planning. Resources on augmentative communication are provided at the end of this chapter.

Table 9.7 offers additional resources in the area of language and communication for the early intervention team.

Cognition. During infancy, children extend and integrate sensory and motor actions to produce adaptive responses to the environment. The development of symbolic thought to solve problems marks the end of infancy. Many infant curricula base the content of the cognitive domain on Piaget's descriptions of the sensorimotor period. These descriptions detail how the infant constructs

TABLE 9.6   Practical Strategies to Enhance Communication

STRATEGY	COMMENTS
Share a topic.	Follow the infant's interests. Use real objects and experiences.
Take turns.	Create a conversational atmosphere. Converse about the objects and experiences of interest.
Organize the environment.	Conversational partners need to be available. Provide toys and materials that do interesting things (roll, make noise, move). To encourage requests, toys can be in sight but out-of-reach.
Imitate.	Copy the infant's behavior. This helps keep the infant in the interaction. Children also seem to learn to imitate by having others imitate them.
Use wait time.	Take one turn and wait for the infant to take a turn. If necessary count silently to five before taking your next turn.
Use time delay.	Before reactivating a toy, or giving an object, wait 3–5 seconds. This encourages the intentional infant to request the object or your assistance.
Use repetitions.	Repeat or highlight your key words or phrases.
Use expansions.	Slightly increase the complexity of the infant's communication but maintain the intention. (e.g., if the child says "key," say "Mommy's keys."

reality through such behaviors as looking, listening, and manipulating objects. These early behaviors or schemes are modified, combined, and coordinated to create new schemes. A *scheme* can be thought of as a basic pattern of action, thought, or knowledge that is used to interact with the environment.

Piaget described six stages and six domains that make up the sensorimotor period. The domains are visual pursuit and permanence of objects, means-ends relationships, causality, construction of objects in space, imitation, and schemes relating to objects. Within each of these domains the infant moves from reflexive actions to stimuli, to voluntary sensory and motor skills to symbolic abilities. Making developmental progress involves building new schemes and combining schemes in new ways. For example, the 9-month-old, upon seeing cookies on the kitchen table, might vocalize and reach for the cookies, or might grab mother's leg and reach for the cookies. The 16-month-old might try vocalizing and reaching for the cookies, then try grabbing the table leg and shaking it, and then try pushing a chair to the table and climbing up to the cookies (trial and error). The 24-month-old might look at the cookies, look at the chair, push the chair to the table, climb up and grab the cookies (internal representation of problem and solution).

The goal of early intervention in the cognitive domain is to support and enhance the child's own capabilities to remember, gain information, and solve problems. Further, the goal is to support the use of increasingly more conven-

An effective early intervention program provides many opportunities for infants and toddlers to develop cognitive skills.

tional forms of those capabilities. That is, functional object use is more conventional than mouthing or poking, and talking is more conventional than vocalizing.

As noted in Chapter 7, a Piagetian approach provides a useful framework for assessing the cognitive abilities of handicapped and at-risk infants. Use of the Uzgiris and Hunt Scales (Uzgiris & Hunt, 1975) and the Dunst (1980) adaptations can lead the early intervention team to socially appropriate objectives and effective intervention strategies. If other assessments are used, the interventionists can analyze the assessment item (e.g., dangling a ring by string), and determine the sensorimotor domain and skill (i.e., imitation of unfamiliar gestures visible to the infant). Then, dependent on the child's response and need for intervention support, the interventionist can restate the item as an intervention objective (i.e., child will copy simple actions with objects that are performed by others). From this objective, a variety of activities can be formulated to provide experience, and opportunities to extend the child's skill in replicating an action. Planned opportunities can be integrated into daily routines and play activities. For example, during diaper changing, the child might imitate mother's action of pulling the cleaning tissue out of the container. During a music activity, the child might have the opportunity to imitate any of a variety of actions such as shaking bells or patting the drum.

Intervention strategies based on behavioral principles can be used to facilitate sensorimotor abilities (Bricker, 1986; Dunst, 1981). *Reinforcement* is any consequence that immediately follows a behavior and increases the likelihood the behavior will occur again. Potential reinforcers include smiles, attention, and praise. Contingent reinforcement means that the reinforcer is provided when and only when the behavior occurs. Many infant toys provide immediate and contingent reinforcement. For example, if the baby shakes the

TABLE 9.7   Selected Resources for the Communication Domain

NAME	FORMAT	CONTENT	COMMENTS
Child-Oriented Approach (Fey, 1986)	Book	Discusses the link between theory and practice; describes assessment, decision-making, and numerous intervention procedures.	Resource for language intervention.
Communication Training Program (Waryas & Stremel-Campbell, 1982)	Kit	Program includes assessment materials, objective cards with teaching instructions. Covers prelanguage functions, basic semantic relations and syntactic structures, and elaboration of grammatical constructions.	Comprehensive, systematic program that uses operant techniques to teach communication skills.
Developmental Interactive Approach (Bricker & Carlson, 1981; Bricker & Schiefelbusch, 1984)	Program description	Includes rationale & theoretical basis. Covers reciprocal action activities, social-communicative behaviors, comprehension, and production; also information on supporting parent-infant interaction.	Based on normal development and research/experience with children with handicaps. See also Evaluation and Programming for Infants and Young Children. (Bricker, Bailey, Gumerlock, Buhl, & Slentz, 1986).
INREAL (Weiss, 1981)	Research report, program description	Child-oriented approach that stresses communicative intent. Child's own play is basis. Natural environment is context for intervention. Includes specific adult strategies.	Additional training available at program development site.

(continued)

TABLE 9.7. (Continued)

NAME	FORMAT	CONTENT	COMMENTS
It Takes Two to Talk (Manolson, 1985)	Parent guidebook	Covers child initiations and creating opportunities for language learning. Includes intervention strategies, examples, parent tips, and tools for ongoing assessment.	Based on MacDonald & Gillette's conversational approach. Written for parents, useful for professionals as well.
Milieu Approach (Hart & Rogers-Warren, 1978; Warren & Rogers-Warren, 1985)	Program description, research reports	Program stresses the natural environment, significant others, functional language, generalization, and environmental arrangements. Specific teaching techniques include, models, mand-model, time-delay, and incidental teaching.	Incorporates social basis of language.
Parent-Infant Habilitation (Schuyler & Rushmer, 1987); Parent-Infant Communication (Infant Hearing Resource Staff, 1985)	Text plus curriculum guide.	Guide includes general information, development of auditory skills, development of presymbolic communication, receptive and expressive development, and numerous activities.	Designed for hearing impaired infants and their families.
Transactional Approach (McLean, Snyder-McLean & Sack, 1982)	Kit	Assessment and intervention materials cover content, form, and use. Other areas include joint action, joint attention, and communicative functions.	Based on normal development and research/experience with children with handicaps. Videotapes available.

TABLE 9.8   Intervention Guidelines

Be responsive.

Be consistent.

Teach through social experiences and play.

Take advantage of naturally occurring routines.

Provide varied experiences.

Integrate objectives from different developmental domains into the same activity or routine.

Have fun.

rattle it makes a noise; if the baby presses the buzzer on a busy box a figure pops up. As in the earlier example of Tommy, toys can be adapted based on the infant's response capabilities. Dunst, Cushing, and Vance (1985) provide examples of successful response-contingent learning by infants with profound handicaps.

Assistance provided by the adult before the infant responds is called a *prompt*. There are many types of prompts including gestural prompts (e.g., gesturing with hand while saying, "Find your coat"), verbal prompts (e.g., saying "Where's the ball?" to encourage crawling to find a hidden toy), and physical prompts (e.g., guiding at the infant's elbow to assist in reaching for a toy). *Modeling* is a procedure in which a demonstration of the desired behavior is provided by an adult or other child. For example, big brother shows Sarah how to hit the xylophone with a stick, then he gives the stick to Sarah.

Environmental support can also set the occasion for learning. Support includes using ongoing, naturalistic encounters, and providing predictability (e.g., storybooks can always be found in the basket next to the infant's crib).

General intervention guidelines are highlighted in Table 9.8. A responsive environment is the key. A responsive environment is one in which caregivers are sensitive to and responsive to babies' signals. Toys and materials are accessible and provide feedback as well. Learning objectives that are embedded within daily routines and play increase the functionality of objectives and probably increase the number of practice opportunities provided. Intervention across developmental domains is both expedient and fun. Crawling to get to an interesting toy is more fun and certainly more rewarding than simply crawling a distance of five feet; at the same time, the infant is practicing both motor and cognitive skills.

Self-Help. During the early childhood years, children master important skills and develop some measure of independence in the areas of toileting, feeding/eating, dressing, and grooming. For infants, independent feeding is a major accomplishment. Because handicapped and at-risk infants often demonstrate delays and difficulties in feeding, this area deserves special attention.

The newborn finds nourishment by using the rooting reflex and a suckling pattern to secure milk. As the sucking pattern improves and strengthens, a munching pattern begins, and hand-to-mouth skills are apparent by 4 to 6 months. Between 6 and 12 months, a number of new skills and refinements are added including rotary chewing, holding and bottle, reaching for the spoon, bringing bottle and food to the mouth, drinking from a cup, and spoon feeding.

It is apparent that accomplishment of these skills involves physiological maturation as well as learning. Further, there is overlap between feeding and social, communicative, cognitive, and motor functioning. Listing of major milestones does not always reveal this. For example, around 6 months of age an infant is introduced to finger foods. This is appropriately timed to beginning chewing movements, improved sitting posture, grasp, hand-to-mouth skills, and increased attention to others in the environment.

Most children with motor impairments will also have difficulties with feeding. Problems relate to abnormal muscle tone, retention of primitive reflexes, structural abnormalities, or abnormal movement; preterm infants often show feeding problems as well. Infants of less than 32 weeks gestational age can be expected to have poorly coordinated sucking and swallowing and thus are unable to nipple feed. Alternatives include intravenous feeding and gavage feeding. Careful attention must be given to provide the growing infant with opportunities to suck (finger or pacifier), and to make the transition to bottle or breast. Specialized techniques and lengthy feeding sessions may be required. However, some infants, particularly those who have had multiple intrusive treatments around the mouth, may become resistant to oral feeding. These babies present quite a challenge to their caregivers and may require specialized procedures (Bernbaum, Pereira, Watkins, & Peckham, 1983; Blackman & Nelson, 1985; Harris, 1986; and Palmer, Thompson, & Lindsheld, 1975).

Infants with feeding problems may require the assistance of a feeding specialist. This individual may be the occupational therapist, speech therapist, physical therapist, or other professional with specialized training or extensive experience with these children. A team approach through which the team members look at the whole child, not just the feeding skills and nutritional status, is most effective. Intervention may be long and involved and require multiple modifications to reach adaptive rather than "normal" eating patterns.

In designing and implementing interventions, the team should consider the whole child and how the child functions in the daily environment with other family members. In addition to where the child is fed and by whom, the parent should be asked what the normal feeding environment would be for a child this age. Intervention strategies should inhibit limiting patterns and promote more normal patterns. It is sometimes helpful for the interventionist to experience the skill involved, particularly to sense the differences in munching, chewing, and biting. These are new activities and sensations for young children, and as such caution, reluctance, curiosity, and play are all valid responses.

A variety of resources that provide assistance with feeding difficulties are included in the resource list at the end of the chapter.

CASE STUDY: JAMIE

Jamie was born at 26 weeks gestation, developed bronchopulmonary dysplasia, failed to gain weight, had a gastrostomy tube inserted, and remained hospitalized until shortly after his first birthday. At age 2 Jamie continued to receive most of his nutrition by gastrostomy tube feedings. His mother, responding to advice given separately by the pediatrician, nutritionist, physical therapist, and teacher, was attempting to feed Jamie by spoon and cup at meal times. Her attempts were not successful; meal times were unpleasant and her frustration level was high.

An arena assessment was done with the speech therapist in the role of feeder. When the speech therapist tried to feed Jamie, he pushed the spoon or cup away, arched his back, and screamed. But the team also wanted to know what Jamie would do with few demands. The therapist set up several situations—dry cereal bits and crackers on the high chair tray, partially filled bowls of mashed potatoes and applesauce, and a bowl and a spoon. The therapist sat nearby but gave no verbal directions. Jamie picked up and put some cereal in his mouth. Later, he stuck his fingers in the applesauce and rubbed his fingers on the tray. He banged the spoon on the tray, the bowl, and his face. After these activities, he even let the therapist put the cup to his lips while he tried to sip. In many ways, Jamie acted like a toddler. He wanted some control over the feeding situation, but he was also interested in learning new skills at his own pace.

A plan was developed that incorporated Jamie's perspective, his mother's time and emotional energy, as well as Jamie's need to orally feed. The plan included short sessions in the high chair just prior to family meals, time to investigate finger foods, and a few minutes of feeding with a spoon while giving Jamie another spoon to hold. The cup was offered and supported while drinking was attempted, as Jamie requested. Weekly sessions with the speech therapist were used to monitor Jamie's progress and to experiment with other feeding techniques. Gradually Jamie learned to eat, and eventually he was weaned from the gastrostomy tube.

Monitoring Progress

Much time and energy typically go into the identification of outcomes, the design of fun and interesting activities, and the implementation of those activities. A next step, and an important one, is monitoring the effects of the activities. With regular checks of the infant's progress, teachers, therapists, and parents can make accurate decisions as to continuing with an activity, providing additional practice opportunities, altering the activity, materials, or responses for likelier success, or moving on to a new objective. Regular monitoring is a test of whether methods and strategies are working.

There are a variety of ways in which teachers, therapists, and parents can keep track of progress. Some of the curriculum materials reviewed include this component. Ideally, early interventionists link assessment, intervention, and monitoring of progress. In selecting a monitoring technique, the team will consider the intervention objective and the activity, and then select a technique that is compatible with both. Possibilities include anecdotal records, developmental checklists, rating scales, permanent products, and performance data. All involve observation of the infant's behavior in relation to the identified intervention objectives.

Anecdotal records or diaries are written notes made by the teacher, therapist, or parents on events of interest. The notes may be primarily factual and include what the adult did and what the child did. It may also be important to include the situation or environment and the child's state. The notes may also include subjective or interpretive information. Many interventionists also use their note-making time to formulate plans for the next day, session, or activity.

Developmental checklists are lists of skills or behaviors that are of interest for an individual child or group of children. The skills may be arranged developmentally or in an alternative instructional sequence. These lists can be used to monitor changes over time, with the interventionist recording the child's performance next to the skill item usually by simply checking that item, or recording the date the skill was observed.

Rating scales are more often used to collect information on specific behaviors or sets of behaviors, or to rate the qualitative aspects of a behavior or interaction. For example, the interventionist might have a list of expected social behaviors during meal time. Then, upon observing the child during meal time, performance of those behaviors is rated on some scale (e.g., present-not present, always-sometimes-never).

Examples of permanent products are audiotapes or videotapes. These can be used to keep a record of changes. For example, a short videotape might be made at regular intervals to monitor progress in the infant's motor abilities. At point A, the infant moves across the floor by crawling on his or her belly. At point B, the videotape shows that the infant now moves on hands and knees. These permanent products can also be further examined using any of the other techniques. For example, using the same segment of videotape of the infant's motor abilities, the interventionist might use a rating scale to assess the quality of the infant's crawling movements.

Performance data refer to counts or timings of specified behaviors. Data may be gathered differently depending upon the behavior and the objective. Sometimes a *count* of the number of occurrences of the behavior is meaningful. Other times *rate* data or number of occurrences within a specified time period is the better method. For other behaviors or objectives *time* is the more critical element, and so the interventionist might record the time a behavior lasts (duration) or the elapsed time before the child responds (latency). An example of a data sheet is provided in Figure 9.1. In this example, the infant has achieved the objective of using a pointing gesture to respond to questions paired with

Child: Annie

Objective: Will point at desired object when asked a question with the object in view, at least five times during a 10-minute play session.

Time: 10:00–10:15

Notes: During Annie's scheduled time in free play area tally all questions asked. Circle if Annie responds by pointing.

Change Rules: 2 sessions of 5 pointing gestures or 2 sessions of fewer than 3 pointing gestures

Date 4/3

| / ① ① / / ① / / | 3/session |

Date 4/11

| ①① / ① / ① ① | 5/session |

Date 4/18

| ①① ① / ①① / ① | 6/session |

FIGURE 9.1.   Sample Performance Data Sheet

a desired object. Now, a decision must be made. In this case the decision was made to move to an initiating behavior. The new objective was, when a desired object is in view, Annie will point to the object at least 5 times during a 10-minute play session.

Further information on monitoring child change may be found in Bagnato and Neisworth, 1981; Bricker and Gumerlock, 1985; Thurman and Widerstrom, 1990; and Wolery, Bailey, and Sugai, 1988.

IMPLICATIONS FOR THE EARLY INTERVENTION TEAM

Planning, implementing, and monitoring child change require teamwork. Collaborative teamwork reduces the fragmentary effects of professionals working separately with infants and their families. It requires the pooling of expertise towards the goal of quality, integrated programming. For example, an outcome may be aimed at improving gestural communication. The physical therapist brings his or her knowledge of posture and movement and the functional use of movement. The speech therapist adds knowledge of the development of communication skills, particularly the use of gestures, and the functional use of movement to communicate. The teacher contributes knowledge of intervention methods, motivation, and the child's classroom environment. The parents bring their knowledge of the child's likes and dislikes and the child's usual environments and activities. Pooling of knowledge and expertise facilitates pinpointing appropriate objectives and the use of effective interventions, whether implemented by several individuals (interdisciplinary model) or a single facilitator (transdisciplinary model). Effective teamwork requires shared goals for the program, active participation by all team members, respect for the contributions of others, and leadership from one team member.

Suggestions for Further Reading

Intervention Content and Strategies

BAGNATO, S.J., NEISWORTH, J. T., & MUNSON, S. M. (1989). Linking developmental assessment and early intervention. Rockville, MD: Aspen.

BAILEY, D.B., & WOLERY, M. (1984). Teaching infants and preschoolers with handicaps. Columbus, OH: Charles Merrill.

BRICKER, D.D. (1986). Early education of at-risk and handicapped infants, toddlers, and preschool children. Glenview, IL: Scott, Foresman.

HANSON, M.J., & LYNCH, E.W. (1989). Early intervention. Austin, TX: Pro-Ed.

Adaptive Toys/Augmentative Communication

BLACKSTONE, S. (Ed.) (1986). Augmentative communication: An introduction. Rockville, MD: American, Speech, Hearing, and Language Association.

BRANDENBURG, S.A., BENGSTON, D.A., & VANDERHEIDEN, G.C. (1987). The rehab/education technology resourcebook series: Communication, control, and computer access for disabled individuals, 1986–1987. Madison, WI: Trace Research and Development Center, University of Wisconsin.

BURKHART, L.J. (1980). Homemade battery-powered toys and educational devices for severely handicapped children. (Available from L. Burkhart, 8503 Rhode Island Ave., College Park, MD 20740).

BURKHART, L.J. (1982). More handmade devices for severely handicapped children with suggested activities. Author.

BURKHART, L.J. (1987). Using computers and speech synthesizers to facilitate communicative interaction with young and/or severely handicapped children. Author.

VANDERHEIDEN, G.C., & KRAUSE, L.A. (Eds.) (1983). Non-vocal communication resource book. Baltimore: University Park Press.

Feeding

MORRIS, S.E., & KLEIN, M.D. (1987). Pre-feeding skills. Tucson, AZ: Therapy Skill Builders.

PIPES, P.L. (1985). Nutrition in infancy and childhood. St. Louis: Times Mirror/Mosby.

ZECHMAN, R., ROSS, A., & WATKINS, J. (1985). Pediatric adaptive technologies: Gastrostomy tube feedings. (Videotape). Seattle: University of Washington Press.

———— (1989). Feeding infants and young children with special needs. (Videotape). Lawrence, KS: Learner Managed Designs, Inc.

Motor

BRINSON, C.L. (Ed.) (1982). The helping hand: A manual describing methods for handling the young child with cerebral palsy. Charlottesville, VA: University of

Virginia. (Available from National Clearinghouse of Rehabilitative Material, 115 Old USDA Building, Oklahoma State University, Stillwater, OK 74078).

CAMPBELL, S.K. (Ed.) (1984). Pediatric neurologic physical therapy. New York: Churchill Livingstone.

FINNIE, N.R. (1975). Handling the young cerebral palsied child at home. New York: E.P. Dutton.

HANSON, M.J., & HARRIS, S.R. (1986). Teaching the young child with motor delays. Austin, TX: Pro-Ed.

JAEGER, L. (1987). Home program instruction sheets for infants and young children. Tucson, AZ: Therapy Skill Builders.

WILLIAMSON, G.G. (Ed.) (1987). Children with spina bifida. Baltimore: Paul Brookes.

_____ (1988). Positioning for infants and young children. (Videotape). Lawrence, KS: Learner Managed Designs.

Chapter 10

Early Intervention
Program Models

Programs for at-risk and handicapped infants and toddlers are not new, but they have become increasingly important with the passage of PL 99-457 (Lowenthal, 1988; Parson & McIntosh, 1987; Trohanis, 1988). The implementation of PL 99-457 has generated a number of program-related issues (Barnett, 1988; Garwood, Fewell, & Neisworth, 1988; Harbin, 1988; Smith & Strain, 1988) and implementation has taken a variety of forms (Walsh, Campbell, & McKenna, 1988). In their early stages of development, infant programs tended to focus exclusively on the infant, with a heavy orientation toward infant stimulation and medical interventions. Recently developed programs have moved toward a broader, more comprehensive orientation, incorporating and integrating educational, psychological, and medical perspectives, and including the families in program planning, development, and implementation.

In a review of 12 experimentally designed longitudinal studies of education programs for at-risk infants, Ramey and Bryant (1988) find that infant intervention programs vary in their form, duration, and content. The major distinctions they find in the programs are between home- or center-based programs and parent- or child-oriented curricula, but programs also vary along a number of other characteristics:

- The child's age during the intervention
- The intensity of the treatment program
- The number of children involved in the intervention program
- The primary target of the intervention (e.g., the child, one or both parents)
- The program's educational activities
- The site of the intervention (e.g., center, home, or a combination of center and home)

Therefore, programs vary according to program factors as well as additional variables such as funding, the nature of the population being served, the program's goals, personnel, and theoretical orientation, and prevailing social policy.

Odom, Yoder, and Hill (1988) note that there are typically three general early intervention program characteristics. The first is an orientation toward prevention of eventual developmental delay; many programs try to prevent or mediate the severity of factors thought to cause or exacerbate a handicapping condition. The second characteristic is an orientation toward change in the infant's behavior, development, or relations with caregivers. And, the third distinguishing aspect is a focus on change within the family system in order to foster positive changes in the infant.

Infant programs may be discussed and presented in a number of different ways. For the purpose of this chapter, preventive intervention programs, infant-focused intervention programs, and parent-infant programs are discussed first.

The chapter continues with infant program evaluation, a discussion of issues in infant intervention programming, and a summary of progress to date in infant program development.

PREVENTIVE INTERVENTION PROGRAMS

Preventive intervention programs are often difficult to describe and justify because they seek to avert a problem that has not yet occurred. Prevention programs, generically described, have three separate levels: primary, secondary, and tertiary (Felner, Jason, Moritsugu, & Farber, 1983). The goal of primary prevention is the reduction of new disorder cases and the building of skills and competencies as protection against the specified problem. Secondary prevention targets early identification and intervention for babies who are displaying initial signs of a disorder, but the difficulty is not yet established. And, tertiary prevention focuses on the individual with an established disorder, with the goal of reducing the effects of the disorder and rehabilitating the individual to a level at which there is an eventual adjustment to community life.

At-Risk Women and Infants

Early preventive intervention programs rarely specifically articulate the level at which they are focused. But, in general, they attempt to identify mothers who are at-risk due to environmental or physiological factors for delivering an at-risk or handicapped infant. In that sense, these programs tend to be primary prevention programs. Kopp (1987) identifies three groups of at-risk women: mothers with medical or biological difficulties (e.g., epilepsy, heart disease), mothers from low socioeconomic status groups, and adolescent mothers.

Mothers with Biological Difficulties. Programs oriented toward mothers with chronic health problems, a history of reproductive difficulties, or problematic genetic backgrounds, try to educate and inform the mother and lessen the effects of these factors on the infant (Leonard, 1987; Odom, Yoder & Hill, 1988; Steel, 1985). Program designs include educational instructional programs, nutrition guidance, and pre-pregnancy counseling. Direct medical intervention is also part of these programs, when the mother or developing infant's physical condition warrants it.

Mothers of Low Socioeconomic Status. Mothers from a low socioeconomic background traditionally have many difficulties, including becoming pregnant prematurely, having more children than they can manage, becoming pregnant again at too short an interval, and not having adequate prenatal/obstetrical care or adequate social support systems (Brody, 1988). They are also more likely, as mothers, to be exposed to hazardous experiences and materials during pregnancy, and more likely to have infants who are low birthweight or premature, than women from higher socioeconomic levels. For low socioeconomic status mothers, there are two major federal programs. The Special Supplemental Food Program for Women, Infants, and Children (WIC) (Chelimsky, 1984; Stockbauer, 1987) focuses on nutrition education and the provision of nutritionally strong supplemental foods to low-income women and children. The Maternal and Infant Care Programs (MIC) target medical services for low-income women and children with prenatal and postnatal followup examinations.

Pregnant Adolescent Women. Adolescent women who become pregnant typically have many birth-related difficulties, including delivery of low birthweight infants, increased levels of infant mortality, and premature delivery (Finkelstein, Finkelstein, Christie, Roden, & Shelton, 1982). In addition, pregnant adolescent women tend to come from low socioeconomic backgrounds and, therefore, have problems associated with mothers from difficult economic circumstances.

Programs for pregnant adolescents tend to provide child development education, health care, instruction on parenting skills, pregnancy and childbirth education, and social support (Anastasiow, 1983; Hardy, King, & Repke, 1987). In general, they seek to eliminate or minimize the negative consequences of early childbearing and child-rearing (McDonough, 1985). An important issue in working with adolescent parents is a sensitivity to their developmental level and how their needs change over time as their own skills develop and parenting issues change (Helm, 1988).

Program Settings

Programs targeting each of these groups of women are usually found in prenatal clinics and in agency, hospital, and school settings (Kopp, 1987). One of the largest issues with preventive approaches and programs is to reach the women and families who cannot or will not use the programs that exist to help them and their infants (Lourie, 1988). The perinatal period, for example, can be an opportunity for enhancing parent-infant communication by teaching parents interaction and communication skills with their infants and thereby preventing parental mistreatment of children (Helfer, 1987). In order to be effective, however, Brody (1988) asserts that prevention programs must view the woman's position within an ecological and social context, including the long-term institutionalized relations between the sexes, and between parents and their children. Because there are numerous factors influencing preventive intervention with infants and parents (Greenspan, 1987), long-term preventive programming needs to be viewed within a context larger than an agency, community, or governmental action.

INFANT-FOCUSED INTERVENTION PROGRAMS

Infant-focused intervention programs have the longest and most diverse history of all intervention programs in infant programming. Traditionally found in medical settings, many of these programs have come to be identified with the NICU. These programs historically tend to be heavily medically oriented, to a great extent overlooking the mother's and infant's many other needs. Currently, there is a vast range of infant-focused intervention programs, some found in NICUs, others located in other medical facilities, agency settings, educational facilities, and the home. The focus is as diverse as the locations in which these programs are found. Some are oriented toward a developmental care model, others on remediating perceived deficits, stimulating sensory modalities, teaching skills, or facilitating infant interactions. Examples of some infant-focused intervention programs follow.

Program Settings

Center-Based Programs. Tripp (1988) describes a model therapeutic school intervention program to treat emotionally disturbed children. The target population of children were exhibiting anxiety, behavioral difficulties, eating problems, phobias, and sleep disturbances. Interventions addressed their emotional needs and, to a great extent, enabled them to enter and continue in a regular school with a normal academic program.

There are many difficulties in setting up a center-based program and conducting this type of activity, but there are potentially significant rewards for children, parents, and staff. Indeed, Abroms and Bennett (1983) note that in

Center-based programs are popular with parents and infants alike.

addition to helping young children, center-based programs can help parents overcome their sense of aloneness and also facilitate their absorption of information related to their child's needs.

Combination Center- and Home-Based Programs. The San Francisco Infant Program (Hanson & Krentz, 1986) is a combination program, providing classroom and home educational components for at-risk and handicapped infants and toddlers. The focus is on cognitive development, communication skills, gross and fine motor development, self-help issues, and social development. In addition to the infant-focused portion of the program, the San Francisco Infant Program also includes parent training, preservice and in-service training for professionals, and ongoing research on infants. This program is based at San Francisco State University.

Home-Based Programs. An example of a home-based infant stimulation program is one carried out by a South Louisiana School District (Aprill & Schifani, 1983). In this program, home teachers helped parents implement an individualized curriculum for their children. In addition, physical therapists and speech therapists were available. The program focused on infant development in cognitive skills, language development, motor areas, self-help skills, and social development; in addition to the services provided children, a parent support group grew out of program efforts.

Other. In addition to the center-based, combination, and home-based approaches, a number of specific infant-focused programs have been developed, including, programmed instruction, the use of microcomputers, and networking strategies to provide services. A programmed instruction program specifically for blind and multiple handicapped infants focused on infant orientation and mobility. The program concentrated on cognitive development, movement, touch, motor development, and sound localization, and the infants demonstrated significant performance gains in the first three of these areas.

Behrmann and Lahm (1983) present an infant program utilizing microcomputers, which focuses on cognitive, language, and motor development. At-risk and handicapped infants were taught to interact with microcomputers in order to foster development in the targeted areas. Brinker (1982, 1984), also found that microcomputers have the potential to teach handicapped infants, as well as to examine infants' learning and response contingency styles.

Hulme's (1985) Iowa Program provides coordinated services for children needing technical medical care in their home and community. The Iowa Regional Child Health Centers provide services by physicians and pediatric nurse practitioners with a networking approach from a regional community perspective. The Tennessee Department of Health and Environment also is concerned about services for at-risk and handicapped infants and established a high-risk registry to enhance infant followup program efforts (Riggs, 1985).

Related Issues

Infant-focused intervention programs have been questioned along a number of grounds. For example, Russman (1986) questions whether children with biologically caused cognitive or motor impairments benefit from infant stimulation programs in the same manner as do children from environmentally deprived situations. Ferry (1986) echos many of these concerns and finds that in some cases (e.g., pediatric brain damage) there is a denial of the permanent, nonfixable nature of the problem. Her point is that the program focus should be directed toward helpful aspects of infant intervention, such as fostering ambulation, feeding, posturing, improving communication skills, and strengthening the parent-child relationship. Barnard, Booth, Mitchell, and Telzrow (1988) sum up many of the issues by stating that infant therapy and toddler play groups need to be used in conjunction with interventions directed at mothers if they are to be effective.

PARENT-FOCUSED INTERVENTION PROGRAMS

Programs have been developed to educate, support, and teach parents with special needs babies. Parents of handicapped children often face a great amount of stress; sometimes there is the loss of an ideal child who was not born, with the consequent difficulties of handling a new situation (Farran & Sparling, 1988). Trout (1983) cites the many factors that are involved, including the effects of frequent infant hospitalization, father's reactions to a sick youngster, feelings of parental ambivalence, infant-parent interactions, parental grief, sibling issues, and seeking the cause of illness.

Types of Programs

Counseling Programs. A parent-focused infant intervention program dealing with deaf infants was developed in which hearing parents of deaf children were counseled about deaf identity and the deaf community (Clark, 1983). Counseling groups focused on the cultural implications of deafness, implications of a child's deafness on parent issues, and understanding of issues related to deafness.

Parent Education Programs. Hedge and Johnson (1986) described an infant intervention program in Southeast Kansas which teaches parents to provide daily one-to-one therapy in gross and fine motor development, speech and language development, social adjustment, and behavior management. In general, the evidence on effective parenting is so compelling as to propose mandatory parent education programs (Anastasiow, 1988b). Anastasiow (1988a) finds that there is no question that infant cognitive development is facilitated by maternal warmth, responsiveness, low physical punishment, a push to achieve, verbalness, and appropriate toys and exploration.

Parent Interaction Skill Programs. Rosenberg and Robinson (1985) describe a project to enhance mothers' interactional skills in an infant education program. The focus of the training was on increasing mothers' skills in interacting with their handicapped infants or toddlers. Training involved teaching mothers strategies to enhance the quality of interaction with their infants. The results demonstrated that mothers made substantial gains in interaction during the course of the intervention program.

Consistent with this approach is the counseling intervention program described by Pulskamp (1987). She presents a program to train parents in specific positive skills of child-rearing, which included four meetings per week in a playroom setting where parents were taught increased interaction time, increased positive interactions, increased positive physical responses, and decreased directiveness.

Program Goals

In general, infant programs focusing on parents seek to improve parent skills in facilitating their infant's growth and development. Programs address different issues in parents' interaction with their children, but the assumption is that improved parent skills and parenting directly affect children's growth and development. Farran and Sparling (1988) find that parent-focused interventions need to anticipate times when parents will need help and to focus on the adaptive, changing capacity of parents.

PARENT-INFANT FOCUSED INTERVENTION PROGRAMS

One of the most striking changes in infant intervention programs in the past two decades has been in the role of parents (Guralnick & Bennett, 1987). Initially parents were asked to extend center-based activities into their homes; now, programs are focusing on family systems that emphasize the parent's role and the interaction between the infant and the infant's family. Kysela and Marfo (1983) remark on the changes in early intervention and they focus on a transactional model which emphasizes the child in the context of the parent-child relationship.

Much of the shift to a parent-infant program emphasis is due to the research findings in child development. Early research studies focused either on the parent or on the infant (Barnard, Booth, Mitchell, & Telzrow, 1988), but there is strong increasing evidence that early mutual adaptation between the infant and parents is important for long-range patterns of development and interaction (Bee et al.,

1982; Hammond, Bee, Barnard, & Eyres, 1983). Research findings strongly support the conclusion that desirable cognitive and social-emotional development is related to the quality of the parent-child interaction during infancy (Barnard et al., 1988).

Parent-Infant Interaction Models and Programs

A number of models of parent-infant interaction and intervention have been developed. The following are some recent examples of parent-infant interaction models and programs.

A Theoretical Model for Parent-Infant Reciprocity. Recently, Brazelton (1988) described a model for understanding and facilitating parent-infant reciprocity and fostering infant autonomy. According to the model, the parent initially approaches the infant in a specific and direct manner, which includes auditory, tactile, and visual stimulation. After the infant is oriented to the parent, the parent expands the affective and attentional ambience to maintain the infant's focused state. The infant begins to reciprocate with interaction; the parent maintains the interaction and builds on it, expanding it to include the next infant achievement. When the next achievement occurs, the parent profusely acknowledges it and allows time for the infant to recognize the achievement. This becomes integrated into the infant's sense of competence and leads to the infant's autonomy. By utilizing a model such as this, infant intervention programs can direct their efforts at one or many of the factors influencing the interaction.

Transactional Intervention Program. Mahoney and Powell (1988) describe the Transactional Intervention Program (TRIP), a program designed to modify patterns of interaction between parents and their infant handicapped children. They find that parents can be very successful at learning turn-taking and interactive match strategies, and parents' efforts at responsiveness, sensitivity, and directiveness increased. Further, they find that their work supports a shift in role for the child educator/therapist from that of a direct provider of services to a parent consultant role. Consistent with this approach is the Social Interaction Assessment/Intervention Model in which caregivers are helped to adjust their interactive styles to their particular infants (McCollum & Stayton, 1985).

Parent and Toddler Training Project. Klein, Van Hasselt, Trefelner, and Sandstrom (1988) describe the Parent and Toddler Training Project, an intervention program for visually impaired and blind multihandicapped infants, toddlers, and their families. The purposes of the program are striking in their focus on family intervention: to increase the social responsiveness of the program's handicapped infants, to implement a program to develop adequate parenting skills, to initiate treatment approaches with parents to reduce psychological distress and improve the family's quality of life, and to evaluate the progress of all participants in the program.

Medically Oriented Parent-Infant Interaction Programs

The Newborn Nursing Models Project (Barnard et al., 1988) is an empirically designed and tested nursing approach to facilitate parent-child adaptation and synchrony. Three nursing approaches were tested: the Nursing Parent and Child Environments (NPACE), the Nursing Support of Infants' Biobehavior (NSIBB), and the Nursing Standard Approach to Care (NSTAC). These programs had different foci; a comparison of approaches revealed that there were no significant treatment effects. The researchers found that the lack of differences between program groups may have been because all groups were to some extent effective: the NSIBB model works well for non-multiproblem families, the NPACE model is best used with multiproblem families, and the NSTAC model works well with specific family problems.

Related Issues

The physical and occupational therapy literature, as well as the diverse fields of psychiatric and psychological intervention and research on severely retarded infants, is calling for an emphasis on parent-infant interaction. For example, the physical and occupational therapy research finds that handicapped infants consistently demonstrate difficulties in signaling behaviors and are less engaged and engaging than normal infants in their interactions with their parents. Therefore, O'Sullivan (1985-86) stresses that early separation should be minimized and positive parent-infant interactions facilitated through intervention strategies.

In an analysis of psychiatric intervention in infancy, Minde and Minde (1982) conclude that treatment of infants must always focus primarily on improving the parent's interaction and childrearing techniques. Greenspan and Lourie (1981) concur and maintain that a preventive approach during infancy requires a four-way diagnostic or evaluation process, including assessment of the baby, the mother, the environment, and the cultural milieu of the baby and mother. Even early intervention programs for infants with severe retardation, when the issues include life-sustaining technology, susceptibility to disease, and combinations of handicapping conditions, stress the importance of social reciprocity and the need to increase interaction between children and their families (Calhoun & Rose, 1988). Stremel-Campbell and Rowland (1987) also assert that adaptive strategies for infants with severe cognitive, sensory, and motor impairment should focus on and incorporate the process of caregiver-child interactions.

Although the focus on parent-infant intervention is well supported by the research literature and programs are clearly moving in this direction, there is a need to caution parent-infant intervention program developers to capture the uniqueness of each parent-child dyad in order for program strategies to be effective (Guralnick & Bennett, 1987). In addition, Bailey (1987) maintains that interventionists should not attempt to force their values on families but to be sensitive and collaborative in setting goals. Several factors may help interventionists engage in collaborative efforts with families: effective interviewing and listening techniques, formally assessing family needs (e.g., Turnbull, 1988), using negotiation and case management skills, and viewing families from a systems perspective. The infant research literature and infant program development are moving in the direction of a strong emphasis on parent-infant interaction in infant intervention program models.

EVALUATION OF INTERVENTION PROGRAMS

Wolery (1987) finds that the multitude of infant program evaluation studies produce two consistent findings: numerous impact evaluation studies have occurred and the scientific merit of most of them is questionable. He maintains that evaluation studies of handicapped infants should be scientifically defensible, and he makes specific recommendations on the types of impact studies and specific issues to consider when evaluation studies are conducted. He goes further and describes a process for determining if programs meet their stated objectives:

1. Specify the purpose of the evaluation study.
2. Specify objectives of the program to be evaluated and develop goal attainment scales.
3. Generate questions and identify measurement sources related to the program's progress on each objective and suspected areas of need.
4. Develop multiple measurement strategies to answer each question.
5. Collect data from each measurement source.
6. Analyze and summarize data by objective.
7. Present a report of the evaluation study to the decision-makers of the program.

Problems with Evaluation Studies

Fewell and Vadasy (1987) review trends in the use of outcome measures in program evaluation efforts, including the use of IQ as a measure, as well as other child-oriented characteristics. They found problems with relying solely on child outcome measures to determine program efficacy and suggest measurement approaches that consider the transactional nature and impact of early interventions on the child and family system.

Fewell and Sandall (1986) found that program evaluation results vary with each different analysis and therefore lead to varying conclusions regarding program effectiveness. They point to problems with measurement, analysis, and methodologies and offer cautions in evaluating infant intervention programs. In particular, they recommend the use of alternative measures of child progress (e.g., multiple measures, expansion of assessed characteristics) in the evaluation of program effectiveness.

Evaluation Models

Bricker and Gumerlock (1988) describe a three-level model evaluation plan for monitoring child progress and program effects. The goals they describe include:

- To measure general program impact on participating children
- To monitor child progress toward acquisition of Individualized Education Plan (IEP) long-range goals and short-term objectives
- To gauge child progress toward specific instructional objectives to permit timely program modification (p. 68)

Consistent with the model, there are three different evaluation strategies, depending on the program goals and evaluation content. Despite being a helpful model to evaluate child progress, the plan fails to consider goals, evaluation content, and strategy with regard to families, which is a serious omission in view of the current thrust of embracing families as an integral part of program planning, implementation, and evaluation.

Dickin, McKim, and Kirkland (1983) are also concerned about suitable designs and evaluation frameworks for evaluating intervention programs for infants at risk. They suggest specific guidelines for the design, implementation and evaluation of infant intervention programs. The model, which serves as an aid to researchers, service providers, and administrators involved with high-risk infant programs, includes the following components:

- Policy and planning group formation
- Selection of program development model
- Needs assessment
- Literature review and consultation
- Determination of target population
- Selection of theoretical orientation(s)
- Specification of objectives
- Detailing operating components, evaluability assessment, and ethical, institutional, and legal requirements
- Financial viability

- Formal statement
- Community support assessment
- Funding

The implementation portion of the program includes a pilot project, sustaining project, process evaluation, and impact evaluation. They suggest this outline in assisting those interested in considering, implementing, and evaluating infant intervention programs.

Evaluation Study Findings

There have been numerous evaluation studies of infant programs. In general, interventions with more hours of child contact are related to more positive effects on the children, parents, and family circumstances (Bryant & Ramey, 1984).

In one study, Bailey and Bricker (1985) considered the effectiveness of a home- and center-based early intervention program for 36 handicapped infants and preschool children. The primary outcome variable was child change as measured by the Gesell Developmental Schedules and their own early evaluation and programming system. They found a positive impact on participating children and their parents. In another evaluation project, Bailey and Bricker (1984) analyzed 13 programs providing early intervention for severely handicapped infants and young children. Even though the programs varied in terms of population served, interventions delivered, and evaluation methodology, all reported some form of positive outcome data.

Casto and White (1984) examined the efficacy of early intervention programs for environmentally at-risk infants using meta-analytic techniques. Their results show some immediate positive effect, but their analysis failed to find long-term benefits and failed to relate the degree of parental involvement to intervention effectiveness. They found that the training of staff and the degree of program structure were positively related to program effectiveness.

In considering the long-term effects of infant stimulation programs for infants with Down syndrome, Sharav and Shlomo (1986) reported that such programs, along with home rearing and training, improved the children's functioning. In a larger project, Gibson and Fields (1984) reviewed the effectiveness of 11 early infant stimulation demonstration programs for children with Down syndrome over a 25-year period. They found there were gains in outcome measures—often at impressive levels—in the short term, but long-term investigations of the outcomes failed to support the gain. (The researchers explained the disparity by asserting that, if treatment was extended in time, intensified, or altered in content, the early gains would serve as building blocks for later cognitive development and academic achievement.) They conclude that future study of early intervention programs must address program definition and differentiation, the characteristics of Down syndrome children, and the durability of outcome gains.

Marfo and Kysela (1985) analyzed research on the impact of early intervention programs with mentally handicapped infants, young children, and their families. Their review of 20 studies in five countries from 1975 to 1983 revealed too much emphasis on child developmental progress to the neglect of parental and environmental variables, on which the child's ultimate progress depends.

Bricker (1984) complains that the program evaluation literature addresses issues apart from program impact and provides no objective evaluation outcomes. She finds that many variables, including population variability, inability to execute sound designs, and differences in dependent measures and equivalent outcomes, impede firm and generalizable conclusions regarding program effectiveness.

Increasingly, evaluation models will need to be developed which specifically address efficacy concerns related to specific program goals and objectives, infant interaction, and a family orientation. Already, scale development is occurring; for example, Seibert, Hogan, and Mundy (1987) describe scales designed to assess social and communication skills acquired in infancy. Increasingly, scale development of this type will become important.

ISSUES IN INFANT INTERVENTION PROGRAMS

There are many issues which emerge in the discussion of infant intervention programs. One of the most fundamental issues is that of definition at all levels of program development, implementation, and evaluation. Dickin, McKim, and Kirkland (1983) noted that definitions of risk vary from time to time and place to place, and they are influenced by political and bureaucratic decisions. Definitional issues lead to difficulties in classifying heterogeneous populations of infants and in drawing conclusions on infant interventions studies (Strauss & Brownell, 1984). Definitions, however, guide program development and evaluation and are critical to a discussion of infant programs (Graham & Scott, 1988).

Another obvious issue in infant programs is the increasing family focus. To some extent because program planning has been under the purview of professionals, models for including families in service delivery planning and implementation are in the developmental state. For example, family assessment strategies (e.g., Bailey & Simeonsson, 1988b) are just now emerging in the professional literature; the evaluation models incorporating family issues and perspectives have yet to be developed. Because of the increasing strong family focus in infant programs, professionals need to be sensitive to family issues, needs, and priorities. Moreover, a specific program orientation toward integral family involvement is needed in program planning, development, implementation, and evaluation.

This issue points to a real training need in the preparation of infant specialists and interventionists so that family dynamics and a relationship focus (Affleck, McGrade, McQueeney, & Allen, 1982a) become part of professionals' awareness, sensitivity, training, and service delivery. The specific family training needs for infant interventionists begs the question of the actual availability of trained personnel who can provide infant program services. Regardless, the preparation of qualified, well trained personnel for early intervention is critical to the accomplishment of the goals set forth in PL 99-457 (Gilkerson, Hilliard, Schrag, & Shonkoff, 1987).

The personnel shortages in working with at-risk and handicapped infants, toddlers, and their families leads to many concerns about the implementation of PL 99-457 (Burke, McLaughlin, & Valdivieso, 1988). Historically, in times of personnel shortages, state educators tend to lower or waive requirements for well trained professionals. Indeed, the training of well-qualified personnel to serve infants and their families was of high concern in the 1986 report accompanying the U.S. House of Representatives version of PL 99-457; this document specifically identified inadequate training standards for personnel as a major obstacle to implementing quality infant services under PL 99-457 (Campbell, Bellamy, & Bishop, 1988).

The issue of training is related to both preservice and in-service needs, and is found across educational, medical (Redditi, 1983), and psychological (Mowder, Widerstrom, & Sandall, 1989; Schrag, 1988) disciplines. *Preservice training* applies to the training of all infant specialists needed to carry out various infant and family services (Lourie, 1988). *In-service training* refers to updating the skills of professionals already delivering infant services. Stremel-Campbell and Rowland (1987), for example, find that there is a tremendous research knowledge base in communication intervention with infants, which needs to be part of the updated skills of those already providing infant services.

As the many infant specialists secure or update their training, there will need to be a sensitivity to multicultural considerations and to working with families from diverse cultural, racial, and socioeconomic backgrounds (Leung, 1987; Smith, 1987; Turner, 1987). A further issue of increasing concern, as professionals from many different specializations work together, will be liaison problems among infant service professionals (Bry, 1985; Early Intervention Project, 1987). Thus, training issues center on content and the process of training (McCollum & Thorp, 1988). For the present, commitment to the education of educators is key to an effective system of care for infants, toddlers, and their families (Iatrides, 1988), and properly preparing trained personnel to work in early intervention programs will be an essential issue for the future (Guralnick & Bennett, 1987).

There are numerous policy considerations in preparing professional personnel to serve at-risk and handicapped infants, toddlers, and their families (Burke, McLaughlin, & Valdivieso, 1988). The issue of trained personnel is not only an educational policy issue but leads to broader policy issues of who should be served, where, and on what basis (McNulty, Widerstrom, Goodwin, & Campbell, 1988), how societal resources are to be allocated (Garwood et al., 1988), and the role of research and policy formulation (Bricker, 1987). If infant and family needs are to be met in a quality fashion, their needs must be communicated to social planners, economic experts, national governments, and international decision-makers (Lourie, 1988). This is such a concern that Garwood (1987) wonders about the implementation of PL 99-457, given the perceived absence of leadership from the federal level. He would like to see a strategy in place that builds on the existing political culture and ensures that infant needs are met.

Beyond the key policy issues are specific concerns regarding issues such as the right to life and the treatment of handicapped infants (Shearer, 1985; Ellis & Luckasson, 1986; Smith, 1985; Stark, Menolascino, & McGee, 1984). Legal and ethical issues confront infant caregivers in a number of ways (Stark, Menolascino, & McGee, 1984), including the lengths to which programs are developed and delivered to meet the needs of severely impaired infants and the perceived cost effectiveness of these programs.

There are also the issues of mainstreaming handicapped and at-risk infants with nonhandicapped babies. Levine and McColoum (1983) examined this issue and the ways in which handicapped babies and toddlers can be mainstreamed with nonhandicapped children. They make a number of suggestions, including the physical placement of handicapped infants near nonhandicapped babies, matching younger nonhandicapped infants with older handicapped children and vice versa, according to their developmental levels and behavioral maturity, and using toys to enhance interactions between handicapped and nonhandicapped infants. Program guidelines for differing infant needs should be addressed (Dronek & Lundin, 1986).

Another issue is serving at-risk and handicapped infants, toddlers, and their families when the families reside in rural areas. Creative programs have been developed to serve those in rural areas, but providing services when distance and the availability of trained personnel are issues will continue to be a major concern (Gautt, 1986; Hutinger, 1986).

Gardner, Karmel, and Dowd (1984) are concerned with the risks involved in prescribing an intervention when it is not necessary; they maintain that interventions should only be attempted when the infant is at risk for poor outcome. Early stimulation as a means to enhance development may not always be beneficial for adaptive functioning at later ages.

General theoretical issues include questions about basic program assumptions (Ramey & Suarez, 1984), difficulties in classifying heterogeneous populations of infants, questions regarding the conceptual premise of infant stimulation and early intervention (Brownell & Strauss, 1984), the efficacy of stimulation programs, and the future directions for program implementation. Honig (1984a) is also concerned about issues regarding infant intervention programs and suggests that a clinical appraisal of model infant intervention projects can influence public policy regarding intervention efforts.

The issues that envelop infant intervention programs include the emerging, strong family orientation, multifaceted training issues, political questions regarding the use of resources, and legal and ethical concerns. Professionally, these issues need to be continuously addressed, cooperative professional models developed, and research on infant intervention programs rigorously and comprehensively conducted (Shonkoff, Hauser-Cram, Krauss, & Upshur, 1988).

Chapter 11

Future Trends
and Issues in
Early Intervention

As the 21st century approaches, predictions are inevitable about what life will be like during the next hundred years. The authors refrain from doing so, for with life already so fast-paced it seems difficult to even predict what events will take place within the next decade. Nevertheless, certain trends seem evident. In the following sections selected issues and future trends in the fields of health and human services are examined from an early intervention point of view.

AVAILABILITY OF HUMAN SERVICES

In the field of early intervention we face a paradox. Tremendous advances in technology during the past decade have made possible the prevention and remediation of disabilities that were previously untreatable. At the same time, funds for human services generally have become less available, particularly for low-income families. The lack of a universal health-care system in the United States has meant that many children and families are denied access to needed medical and other health-related services. In addition, critical educational and social service needs remain unmet. A well known example of this shortage is the fact that Head Start serves only one fifth of eligible children.

Future decades should see a redress of this situation. When problems become serious enough for citizens to demand that government take a more active role in funding health and human services, it is likely that a universal health-care plan will become a reality. Hopefully, this will mean more generally available prenatal care for all pregnant women, better access to family planning, birth control, and genetic counseling for all would-be parents, and the right to abortion for all women, regardless of income.

On this topic, a recent study published by the nonprofit Alan Guttmacher Institute in New York is of interest. In a study of unmarried young black women ages 17 or younger who were pregnant, it was found that teenagers who had abortions fared better economically, suffered less stress, and were more likely to graduate from high school than those who had their babies (Alan Guttmacher Institute, 1990). Researchers found that 82% of the young women who had abortions graduated from high school or remained in school 2 years after the procedure without falling behind, while only 63% of the women who gave birth completed high school or were still in school 2 years later. Additionally, women who had abortions were more economically secure after 2 years.

At the same time, it is generally recognized that adequate services for family planning and ready access to birth control methods for all citizens, particularly for young men and women in their teens, would go a long way toward prevention of unwanted pregnancies. This obviously is a more generally accepted solution than abortion. The lack of access to birth control information is illustrated by a group of interviews with teenagers who were experiencing unwanted pregnancies (Bode, 1980). Most of the young women stated that they did not use any method of birth control because either they or their partner were embarrassed or afraid to go through necessary parental permissions or other required steps. They also stated that they would have used birth control if they had realized what the consequences were.

In addition, the effectiveness of postnatal assistance programs has been well documented. One of the most successful is the federally funded Women, Infant and Children (WIC) program, which provides food supplements and nutrition information to pregnant women and women with young children as well as to their infants. This program has been credited with reducing risk and preventing disabilities among newborns and infants of low-income parents.

These studies and similar data illustrate the positive impact universally available services can have on preventing developmental problems for infants and their families. The general shortage of such preventive programs in the United States underscores the current and continuing need for addressing this issue.

At the same time, technology will undoubtedly continue to provide solutions and "cures" for diseases and conditions that were heretofore fatal or chronic. Daily newspaper accounts chronicle the progress that the medical and scientific communities make in extending life expectancy and lowering the neonatal mortality rate. As technology improves to maintain life, we in early intervention must grapple with how to improve the quality of life for those infants who are at risk or who have disabilities, and for their families.

SERVICE DELIVERY SYSTEMS

Because of declining revenues, service delivery will be quite different in the year 2000 from what it is today. At present it is an expensive, labor-intensive system dominated by professionals from various disciplines, with little input from consumers. Much of it, particularly in areas employing new technology, is hospital-based. NICUs, although very effective in saving the lives of preterm and low birthweight infants, are very expensive to maintain. Future service delivery systems will likely have the following characteristics:

1. *Service delivery systems will be less labor-intensive.* Several trends combine to predict that future service delivery must be less dependent on the availability of ample, highly trained professionals from numerous disciplines. First, special-needs populations are increasing, for reasons previously discussed. Second, training programs in health and human services fields are not significantly increasing the number of graduates they prepare (Hanson, 1990) and in some cases are facing serious funding cutbacks. Third, salaries in these fields, except for medicine, are generally not competitive with salaries available in the private sector. This implies a shortage of recruits for training, and the end result is more clients and fewer professionals to serve them.

2. *The consumer will have a larger, more responsible role.* In the case of early intervention, parents will have more responsibility, both in decision-

making and in carrying out those decisions. In fact, there is accumulating evidence that increasing family involvement in early intervention is not only cost-effective but more efficacious than in other models. In a recent research review illustrating some emerging trends in the field, Guralnick (1989) noted that there is strong potential for parent-mediated early intervention to yield clinically significant benefits. "By enhancing natural parenting skills and providing the conditions for families to become more competent and more confident in their unique relationships with their children, conditions for optimal child development may well be created" (p. 12). Guralnick further states that models which encourage optimal parent-child relationships and emphasize parent empowerment may prove to be more effective than the more traditional models with a didactic focus that require parents to carry out instructional activities.

Associated with this trend in infant intervention is the trend in preschool special education, that is, the emphasis on child-centered, child-directed educational models with roots in early childhood education. These models are based upon, and promote, spontaneous adult-child interactions similar to natural parent-child interactions.

In health-related fields the more active and assertive role of consumers is illustrated by the acknowledgment of infants' needs for social interactions, especially interactions with their parents, when they are confined to neonatal special care and followup programs in hospitals. Additionally, the new emphasis on allowing parents into the NICU on a regular basis, combined with a realization of the positive effect they have on their infant's development in that environment, represent steps forward for the medical and nursing professions.

3. *Public schools will become centers for comprehensive services in each community.* The services will most likely include education for all children from infancy, comprehensive child care from infancy, community health clinics including family planning clinics, well-baby clinics, teen pregnancy programs, early intervention/prevention programs, and social service programs for low-income families (Zigler, 1990). It is natural for the community public school to become the hub for community services, since it has taken on an increasingly broader and more comprehensive role in serving children and families in recent years, particularly in urban environments. Teen health clinics, parent/infant programs for teen parents, and after-school child care are examples of programs that are currently offered in many high schools. With the advent of PL 99-457 and its requirement for states to name a lead agency for implementation of the law, public schools in states where the Department of Education has been so designated have begun to take a larger role in serving infants and toddlers and their families.

Such a comprehensive community-based service delivery system has several obvious advantages. First, it ensures a wide distribution of service centers geographically within the community, making services readily available to those families without transportation. In many cases the comprehensive busing system in place in most public schools could be adapted to include these children and families. Second, it avoids duplication and promotes coordination of services by health, education, and social service providers when all available services are under one roof. Third, such a comprehensive setting allows for a truly multidisciplinary team concept in the delivery of services. Such a neighborhood-based network could result in a more personal and more humane service delivery system in which professionals and the families they serve would have the opportunity to develop mutually beneficial long-term relationships. And fourth, such services could be responsive to the special needs of varying cultural groups found in a community, while at the same time be tailored to the individual needs of a particular family.

Of course, there are potential disadvantages to such a system, too. Critics of public schools assert, with some justification, that in the past schools have not shown themselves to be very responsive to community needs. Some public schools, actively or by default, have discouraged parent participation, and many parents undoubtedly view their child's school as a place with which they have contact only in times of trouble. Although public schools and churches in this country have traditionally occupied the center of community life, that tradition is no longer as strong as it once was, particularly in urban communities. Some, therefore, question whether public schools in the present environment can introduce a service delivery system that is truly family-centered in the spirit of PL 99-457.

Additionally, with the disappearance of the neighborhood school concept in many communities, and the accompanying reliance on busing, most public schools no longer serve a geographically restricted community. This makes it more difficult to implement a neighborhood-based service system. These reservations are shared by many early intervention professionals and must be adequately addressed before a comprehensive, community-based system of human services can become a reality.

4. *Long-term intervention and care will be based in the home and community.* In realizing the goal of providing more comprehensive services with reduced revenues, these services will gradually move from expensive settings like hospitals and clinics to community-based and home-based settings. This will mean less reliance on hospitals for long-term care of infants and children, and a greater emphasis on parents carrying out intervention with the assistance of home visitors (paraprofessionals).

This trend is compatible with the renewed movement toward normalization that is currently influencing public schools to follow a policy of *full inclusion.* This means integrating all children, whatever their needs or abilities, into regular programs with typical children. This point of view emphasizes the community as the proper setting for all but the most technical service delivery.

Another aspect of the trend toward community-based care will be the growth and wider acceptance of the midwifery movement. Like most European countries today, it seems likely that the United States will join the movement toward births supervised by licensed midwives outside the hospital, rather than the expensive, labor-intensive hospital births currently the norm. Deliveries will increasingly occur at home or in community-based clinics if the mother is not at risk.

PARENT EDUCATION

In the years to come it seems certain that the critical need for parent education will become recognized, as policy makers are made aware of the research on the long-term effects of early family dynamics. The belief that preventive measures can reduce the need for later intervention services will hopefully gain support, with parent education seen as a major means for preventing problems in families. Despite the large body of research denoting the key role parents play in their children's development, few men and women in our affluent society receive adequate education to prepare them for their role as parents. In fact, they receive more education on almost any other topic one could mention.

This situation needs to change. There is ample evidence available from research and from professional experience that certain parenting dimensions, such as sensitivity, responsivity, and warmth, facilitate optimal development in infants and young children. But this information is not being conveyed to parents or prospective parents in any systematic fashion. Literature detailing positive practices written for parents is scarce, and few organized parenting programs exist. Just as health education, driver education, and sex education have been incorporated into public school curricula, so too this critical aspect of human development needs to become part of the adolescent educational program.

THE TRANSDISCIPLINARY TEAM

A continuing thread running through this book has been the role of the multidisciplinary team in providing early intervention to infants and toddlers. As we examine future trends, it seems probably that this emphasis will continue, and indeed is likely to intensify. Certainly the transdisciplinary approach to teams as described in Chapter 7, with its emphasis on role release and role-sharing, appears to be the most favored at present and is likely to continue so, given the current economic climate. The number of professionals working with any given infant or toddler may be fewer, but through transdisciplinary practice, the needed services will be provided.

Future service providers will also adopt the role of consultant in cases in which one professional can conduct the assessment or intervention by relying on specialized information from several experts. Of course, this model has implications for certification and credentialing. In the consultation model, services are provided in an indirect manner, in contrast to the medical model in which every professional involved with the patient has direct involvement in the prescribed treatment (Mowder, Willis & Widerstrom, 1985).

In short, teams will expand their scope, and the number of disciplines represented will increase. As early intervention becomes more community-based and more comprehensive, a combination of services from health, education, and social services individualized to each family's special needs will gradually become available in a single setting. This will certainly mean a more important role for talented case managers to act as liaison between professionals and families.

STAFF DEVELOPMENT

It seems likely that training for professionals to provide early intervention will be expanded in future years through both in-service and preservice activities. A major concern in the implementation of PL 99-457 has been the issue of personnel preparation to ensure an adequate supply of service providers of quality for infant and toddler programs. Universities must step up their efforts to prepare a new cadre of professionals for work on infant teams, and those already-existing team members must continually update their skills and knowledge.

Following a transdisciplinary model, training should be coordinated between disciplines, so that professionals in health, psychology, education, and speech/language, for example, share course work and internship experiences. In addition, training should also be coordinated within each discipline, so that professionals serving infants and toddlers have contact with those serving preschool and older children with disabilities. In this way, preparation for interagency coordination and interdisciplinary cooperation can begin at the initial level of training.

A related issue is the development of training materials for both in-service and preservice programs. The need is great for curriculum guides and instructional materials in both print and videotape formats for training of early interventionists. The need for training programs and instructional materials underlines the need for more research in early intervention.

RESEARCH IN EARLY INTERVENTION

Certainly the current trend toward more extensive research addressing early intervention issues will continue in the next decade. One hopes the emphasis will be to develop more refined research methods that offer better control of validity threats and improved designs for conducting longitudinal, multivariate research. The focus of research in the next decade will most likely be on technological advances, development of assessment models and techniques that have better predictive validity, examination and refinement of intervention models and techniques, and further examination of the role of the family in infant growth and development, including family-focused early intervention. For this to happen, however, far more resources need to be channeled into these areas of research.

With the emerging consensus on the validity of early intervention, much future research will take a longitudinal approach (e.g., questions will be developed on the long-term implications of varying intervention practices, the predictive validity of assessment measures, and the long-term outcomes of parenting variables). If the gap between research and practice can be more efficiently bridged than at present, the ultimate result should be more effectively trained professionals, more effective instructional materials, and more cost-effective programs.

PUBLIC POLICY AND EARLY INTERVENTION

It is possible that a policy shift at the federal level will mandate services for at-risk infants and toddlers and those with handicaps. PL 99-457 encourages, but does not mandate, services to handicapped infants, toddlers, and their families. Additionally, questions concerning what constitutes a state of risk, and which risk factors make an infant eligible for early intervention services under PL 99-457, have raised much controversy since passage of the law. Some states have adopted broad eligibility criteria while others have decided not to serve the at-risk population with their Part H funds. If early intervention efficacy data continue to impress policy makers, further laws will be adopted to ensure universal availability of services.

At the same time, there should emerge an emphasis on developing preventive educational programs to address the enormous problems of substance abuse, violent crime, and other social ills. Hopefully, policy makers will begin to recognize the cost benefits of prevention as opposed to treatment, whether it be in a drug rehabilitation clinic, hospital, or prison.

GLOBAL PERSPECTIVES

Currently the gap between rich and poor appears to be widening in the world as a whole, as well as in the United States. One need only look at the world today to confirm that this trend is unlikely to be reversed in the current decade. However, it is probable that some redistribution of wealth on a worldwide basis will occur during the next century. No matter how we view the division, as northern and southern hemispheres, First World and Third World, developed and developing countries, Caucasian people and people of color, the growing gap between those with adequate resources and those in need is apparent and well documented. In our own country this means that early intervention is at present much more comprehensive for some infants and families than for others. In a worldwide context, it means that hundreds of thousands of families receive no services whatsoever.

To consider problems with our own service delivery system without taking into account the wider global context seems short-sighted and insensitive. One hopes that as national barriers diminish, an international approach might be taken to solving problems related to infants and families; certainly these problems take a similar form worldwide. Perhaps reasserting our belief as educators that children and families, despite their special needs, share more similarities than differences may help all of us to adopt a more global perspective. Perhaps we can then provide some leadership in effecting a more equitable distribution of resources on a worldwide basis. Until there exists a mandate similar to PL 99-457 in every country, capable of being fully implemented with adequate funds, the task of providing adequate early intervention to infants and their families will remain unfinished.

References

ABROMS, K.I., & BENNETT, J.W. (1983). Current findings in Down syndrome. *Exceptional Children, 49*, 449–450.

ACREDOLO, L.P., & HAKE, J.L. (1982). Infant perception. In B.B. Wolman & G. Stricker, (Eds.), *Handbook of developmental psychology*. Englewood Cliffs, NJ: Prentice Hall.

ADAMS, J.A., & WEAVER, S.J. (1986). Self-esteem and perceived stress of young adolescents with chronic disease: Unexpected findings. *Journal of Adolescent Health and Care, 7*, 173–177.

ADELSON, E. & FRAIBERG, S. (1975). Gross motor development in infants blind from birth. In B.Z. Friedlander, G.M. Sterritt, & G.E. Kirk (Eds.), *Exceptional infant: Vol. 3, Assessment and intervention*. New York: Bruner/Mazel.

AFFHOLTER, D.P., CONNELL, D., & NAUTA, M.J. (1983). Evaluation of the child and family resource program: Early evidence of parent-child interaction effects. *Evaluation Review, 7*, 65–79.

AFFLECK, G., McGRADE, B.J., McQUEENEY, M., & ALLEN, D.A. (1982a). Relationship-focused early intervention in developmental disabilities. *Exceptional Children, 49*, 259–261.

AFFLECK, G., McGRADE, B.J., McQUEENEY, M., & ALLEN, D.A. (1982b). Promise of relationship-focused early intervention in developmental disabilities. *The Journal of Special Education, 16*, 413–430.

AINSWORTH, M.D.S. (1973). The development of infant-mother attachment. In B.M. Caldwell & H.N. Ricciuti (Eds.), *Review of child development research* (Vol. 3). Chicago: University of Chicago Press.

AINSWORTH, M.D.S. (1974). Infant-mother attachment and social development: Socialization as a product of reciprocal responsiveness to signals. In M. Edwards (Ed.), *The integration of the child into the social world*. Cambridge, England: Cambridge University Press.

AINSWORTH, M.D.S. (1979). Attachment as related to mother-infant interaction. In J.S. Rosenblatt, R.A. Hinde, C. Beer, & M. Busnal (Eds.), *Adavnces in the study of behavior* (Vol. 9). New York: Academic Press.

AINSWORTH, M.D.S. (1982). Attachment: Retrospect and prospect. In C.K. Parke & J. Stevenson-Hinde (Eds.), *The place of attachment in human behavior* (pp. 3–30). New York: Basic Books.

AINSWORTH, M.D.S., & BELL, S.M.V. (1969). Some contemporary patterns of mother-infant interaction in the feeding situation. In J.A. Ambrose (Ed.), *Stimulation in early infancy* (pp. 133–170). London: Academic.

AINSWORTH, M.D.S., BELL, S.M.V., & STAYTON, D.J. (1971). Individual differences in strange-situation behavior of one-year-olds. In H.R. Schaffer (Ed.), *The origins of human social relations* (pp. 17–52). New York: Academic.

AINSWORTH, M.D.S., BELL, S.M.V., & STAYTON, D.J. (1974). Infant mother attachment and social development: "Socialization" as a product of reciprocal responsiveness to signals. In M. Edwards (Ed.), *The integration of the child into the social world.* Cambridge, England: Cambridge University Press.

AINSWORTH, M.D.S., BLEHAR, M.C., WATERS, E., & WALL, S. (1978). *Patterns of attachment.* Hillsdale, NJ: Lawrence Erlbaum Associates.

ALAN GUTTMACHER INSTITUTE. (1990). When urban adolescents choose abortion. *Perspectives, 21*(6), 18–23.

ALBERMAN, E., BENSON, J., & MCDONALD, A. (1982). Cerebral palsy and severe educational subnormality in low-birthweight children: A comparison of births in 1951–53 and 1970–73. *Lancet, 1,* 606–608.

ALPERN, G., BOLL, T., & SHEARER, M. (1980). *Developmental profile II.* Aspen, CO: Psychological Development Publications.

ALS, H. (1983). Infant individuality: Assessing patterns of very early development. In J.D. Call, E. Galenson & R.L. Tyson (Eds.), *Frontiers in infant psychiatry* (pp. 363–378). New York: Basic Books.

ALS, H. (1984a). Manual for the naturalistic observation of newborn behavior (preterm and full term). Unpublished manuscript. Child Development Unit, Children's Hospital Medical Center, Boston.

ALS, H. (1984b). Preterm and low birthweight infants in the NICU environment. Presentation at the Second Biennial Training Institute, National Center for Clinical Infant Programs, Washington DC.

ALS, H. (1985). Patterns of infant behavior: Analogues of later organizational difficulties. In F.H. Duffy & N. Geschwind (Eds.), *Dyslexia* (pp. 67–92). Boston: Little, Brown, & Company.

ALS, H. (1986). Assessing the neurobehavioral development of the premature infant and the environment of the neonatal intensive care unit: A synactive model of neonatal behavioral organization. *Physical and Occupational Therapy in Pediatrics, 6,* 3–53.

ALS, H., & BRAZELTON, T.B. (1981). A new model of assessing the behavioral organization in preterm and full-term infants. *Journal of the American Academy of Child Psychiatry, 20,* 239–263.

ALS H., DUFFY, F.H., MCANULTY, G.B., & BADIAN, N. (1989). Continuity of neurobehavioral functioning in preterm and full-term newborns. In Bornstein, M.H., & Krasneger, N.A. (1989). *Stability and continuity in mental development: Behavioral and biological perspectives.* Hillsdale, NJ: Lawrence Erlbaum Associates.

ALS, H., LAWHORN, G., BROWN, E., GIBES, R., DUFFY, F.H., MCANULTY, G., & BLICKMAN, J.G. (1986). Individualized behavioral and environmental care for the very low birth weight preterm infant at high risk for bronchopulmonary dysplasia: Neonatal intensive care unit and developmental outcome. *Pediatrics, 78,* 1123–1132.

ALS, H., LESTER, B.M., TRONICK, E.C., BRAZELTON, T.B. (1982). Towards a research instrument for the assessment of preterm infants' behavior (APIB). In H.E. Fitzgerald, B.M. Lester, & M.W. Yogman (Eds.), *Theory and research in behavioral pediatrics* (Vol. 1, pp. 1–35). New York: Plenum.

ALS, H., LESTER, B.M., TRONICK, E.C., & BRAZELTON, T.B. (1984). Manual for the assessment of preterm infants' behavior (APIB). In H.E. Fitzgerald, B.M. Lester, & M.W. Yogman (Eds.), *Theory and research in behavioral pediatrics,* Vol. 1. New York: Plenum.

AMERICAN PSYCHOLOGICAL ASSOCIATION. (1981). Ethical principles of psychologists. *American Psychologist, 36*(6), 633–638.

AMIEL-TISON, C. (1968). Neurological evaluation of the maturity of newborn infants. *Archives of Disease in Childhood, 43,* 89–93.

AMIEL-TISON, C., & GRENIER, A. (1983). Neurological examination of the newborn and infant. New York: Masson.

ANASTASI, A. (1982). *Psychological testing* (5th ed.). New York: Macmillan.

ANASTASIOW, N.J. (1983). Adolescent pregnancy and special education. *Exceptional Children, 49,* 396–403.

ANASTASIOW, N.J. (1988a). Facilitating cognitive development. In E.D. Hibbs (Ed.), Children and families: *Studies in prevention and intervention.* Madison, WI: International Universities Press.

ANASTASIOW, N.J. (1988b). Should parenting education be mandatory? *Topics in Early Childhood Special Education, 8*(1), 60–72.

ANDERS, T.F. (1989). Clinical syndromes, relationship disturbances, and their assessment. In A.J. Sameroff & R.N. Emde (Eds.), *Relationship disturbances in early childhood: A developmental approach.* New York: Basic Books.

ANDERSON, C. (1983). An ecological developmental model for a family orientation in school psychology. *Journal of School Psychology, 21,* 179–189.

APGAR, V. (1953). A proposal for a new method of evaluation of the newborn infant. *Current Researches in Anesthesia and Analgesia, 32,* 260–267.

APPELBAUM, M.I., BURCHINAL, M.L., & TERRY, R.A. (1989). Quantification methods and the search for continuity. In P. Fedor-Freybergh & M.L.V. Vogel (Eds.), *Prenatal and perinatal psychology and medicine; Encounter with the unborn.* Lancaster, UK: Parthenon Publishing Group.

APRILL, K.H., & SCHIFANI, J. (1983). Innovative infant stimulation program as being executed by a South Louisiana School District. Paper presented at the Annual International Conference of the Council for Exceptional Children, Detroit, April.

AREND, R. (1984). Preschoolers' competence in a barrier situation: Patterns of adaptation and their precursors in infancy. Unpublished doctoral dissertation, University of Minnesota.

AREND, R., GOVE, F.L., & SROUFE, L.A. (1979). Continuity of individual adaptation from infancy to kindergarten: A predictive study of ego-resiliency and curiosity in preschoolers. *Child Development, 50,* 950–959.

AYRES, J. (1986). *Southern California Sensory Integration Tests* (Rev.) Los Angeles: Western Psychological Services.

BAGNATO, S.J., & NEISWORTH, J.T. (1981). *Linking developmental assessment and curricula.* Rockville, MD: Aspen.

BAGNATO, S.J., NEISWORTH, J.T., & MUNSON, S.M. (1989). *Linking developmental assessment and early intervention,* Rockville, MD: Aspen.

BAILEY, D.B. (1987). Colloborative goal-setting with families: Resolving differences in values and priorities for services. *Topics in Early Childhood Special Education, 7*(2), 59–71.

BAILEY, D.B. (1989). Case management in early intervention, *Journal of Early Intervention, 13,* 120–134.

BAILEY, D.B., & SIMEONSSON, R.J. (1985a). A functional model of social competence. *Topics in Early Childhood Special Education Quarterly, 4,* 20–31.

BAILEY, D.B., & SIMEONSSON, R.J. (1985b). *Family needs survey.* Chapel Hill, NC: Frank Porter Graham Child Development Center.

BAILEY, D.B., & SIMEONSON, R.J. (1988a). Assessing needs of families with handicapped infants. Special issue: Early intervention for infants with handicaps and their families. *Journal of Special Education, 22*(1), 117–127.

BAILEY, D.B., & SIMEONSSON, R.J. (1988b). *Family assessment in early intervention.* Columbus, OH: Charles E. Merrill.

BAILEY, D.B., SIMEONSSON, R.J., ISABELLE, P., HUNTINGTON, G.S., WINTON, P.J., COMFORT, M., & HELM, J. (1988). Inservice training in family assessment and goal-setting for early interventionists: Outcomes and issues. *Journal of the Division of Early Childhood, 12,* 126–136.

BAILEY, D.B., & WOLERY, M. (1984). *Teaching infants and preschoolers with handicaps.* Columbus, OH: Charles Merrill.

BAILEY, D.B., & WOLERY, M. (1989). *Assessing infants and preschoolers with handicaps.* Columbus: Merrill Publishing Company.

BAILEY, E.J., & BRICKER, D. (1984). The efficacy of early intervention for severely handicapped infants and young children. *Topics in Early Childhood Special Education, 4*(3), 30–51.

BAILEY, E.J., & BRICKER, D. (1985). Evaluation of a three-year early intervention demonstration project. *Topics in Early Childhood Education, 5*(2), 52–65.

BAIRD, A.S., & HEMMING, A.M. (1982). Neonatal vision screening. *Journal of Visual Impairment and Blindness, 76,* 182–185.

BAKEMAN, R., ADAMSON, L.B., BROWN, J.V. & ELDRIDGE, M. (1989). Can early interaction predict? How and how much? In P. Fedor-Freybergh & M.L.V. Vogel (Eds.), *Prenatal and perinatal psychology and medicine; Encounter with the unborn.* Lancaster, UK: Parthenon Publishing Group.

BALE, J.F., BLACKMAN, J.A., MURPH, J., & ANDERSEN, R.D. (1986). Congenital cytomegalovirus infection. *American Journal of Diseases of Children, 140,* 128–131.

BALOGH, R.S., & PORTER, R.H. (1986). Olfactory preferences resulting from mere exposure in human neonates. *Infant Behavior and Development, 9,* 395–401.

BANDURA, A. (1969). Social-learning theory of identificatory processes. In D.A. Goslin (Ed.), *Handbook of socialization theory and research* (Chap. 2). Chicago: Rand McNally.

BANDURA, A. (1977). *Social learning theory.* Engelwood Cliffs, NJ: Prentice Hall.

BANGS, T.E., & DODSON, S. (1979). *Birth to three developmental scale.* Allen, TX: DLM Teaching Resources.

BANKS, M.A., & SALAPATEK, P. (1983). Infant visual perception. In P.H. Mussen (Ed.), *Handbook of child psychology,* Vol. 2. New York: John Wiley & Sons.

BANKS, M.S., & GINSBURG, A.P. (1987). Early visual preferences: A review and a new theoretical treatment. In H.W. Reese (Ed.), *Advances in child development and behavior.* New York: Academic Press.

BARBER, B. (1976). Compassion in medicine: Toward new definitions and new institutions. *New England Journal of Medicine, 295,* 939–943.

BARNARD, K.E., & BEE, H.L. (1982). The assessment of parent-infant interaction by observation of feeding and teaching. In T.B. Brazelton & H. Als (Eds.), *Behavioral assessment of newborn infants.* Hillsdale, NJ: Lawrence Erlbaum Associates.

BARNARD, K.E., BOOTH, C.L., MITCHELL, S.K., & TELZROW, R.W. (1988). Newborn nursing models: A test of early intervention to high-risk infants and families. In E.D. Hibbs (Ed.), *Children and families: Studies in prevention and intervention.* Madison WI: International Universities Press.

BARNES, S., GULFREUND, M., SATTERLY, D., & WELLS, G. (1983). Characteristics of adult speech which predict children's language development. *Journal of Child Language, 10,* 65–84.

BARNETT, W.S. (1988). The economics of preschool special education under Public Law 99-457. *Topics in Early Childhood Special Education, 8,* 12–23.

BARRERA, M.E., ROSENBAUM, P.L., & CUNNINGHAM, C.E. (1986). Early home intervention with low-birth-weight infants and their parents. *Child Development, 57,* 20–33.

BATES, J.E., MASLIN, C.A., & FRANKEL, K.A. (1985). Attachment security, mother-child interaction, and temperament as predictors of behavior-problem ratings at age three years. In I. Bretherton & E. Waters (Eds.), Growing points of attachment, theory and research. *Monographs of the Society for Research in Child Development, 50* (2, Serial No. 209).

BATSHAW, M.L., & PERRET, Y.M. (1986). *Children with handicaps: A medical primer.* Baltimore: Brookes.

BAUMRIND, D. (1966). Effects of authoritative parental control on child behavior. *Child Development, 37,* 887–907.

BAUMRIND, D. (1967). Child care practices anteceding three patterns of preschool behavior. *Genetic Psychology Monographs, 75,* 43–88.

BAUMRIND, D. (1968). Authoritarian vs. authoritative parental control. *Adolescence, 3,* 256.

BAUMRIND, D. (1970). Socialization and instrumental competence in young children. *Young Children, 26*(2), 104–119.

BAUMRIND, D. (1971). Current patterns of parental authority. *Developmental Psychology Monographs, 4* (1, Pt.2).

BAUMRIND, D. (1979). Sex-related socialization effects. Paper presented at the meeting of the Society for Research in Child Development, San Francisco, CA.

BAUMRIND, D., & BLACK, A.E. (1967). Socialization practices associated with dimensions of competence in preschool boys and girls. *Child Development, 38,* 291–327.

BAYLEY, N. (1969). *Bayley scales of infant development.* New York: Psychological Development.

BECKMAN, P.J. (1983). Influence of selected child characteristics on stress in families of handicapped infants. *American Journal of Mental Deficiency, 88,* 150–156.

BECKMAN, P.J., & POKORNI, J.L. (1988). A longitudinal study of families of preterm infants: Changes in stress and support over the first two years. *Journal of Special Education, 22*(1), 55–65.

BECKWITH, L. (1979). The influence of caregiver-infant interaction on development. In E. Sell (Ed.), *Follow-up of the high-risk newborn: A practical approach.* Springfield, IL: C. Thomas.

BECKWITH, L. (1984). Parent interaction with their preterm infants and later mental development. *Early Child Development and Care, 16,* 27–40.

BECKWITH, L. (1988). Intervention with disadvantaged parents of sick preterm infants. *Psychiatry, 51,* 242–247.

BECKWITH, L., & PARMELEE, A.H. (1986). EEG patterns of preterm infants, home environment, and later IQ. *Child Development, 57,* 777–789.

BEE, H.L., BARNARD, K.E., EYRES, S.J., GRAY, C.A., HAMMOND, M.A., SPIETZ, A.L., SNYDER, C., & CLARK, B. (1982). Prediction of IQ and language skill from perinatal status, child performance, family characteristic, and mother-infant interaction. *Child Development, 53,* 1134–1156.

BEHRMANN, M., & LAHM, L. (1983). *Critical learning: Multiply handicapped babies get on-line.* Paper presented at the Council for Exceptional Children National Conference on the use of Microcomputers in Special Education, Hartford, CT.

BELSKY, J., LERNER, R., and SPANIER, G. (1985). *The child in the family.* Reading, MA: Addison-Wesley.

BELSKY, J., & ROVINE, M. (1987). Temperament and attachment security in the strange situation: An empirical repproachment. *Child Development, 58,* 787–795.

BELSKY, J., ROVINE, M., & TAYLOR, D. (1984). The Pennsylvania Infant and Family Development Project: III. The origins of individual differences in infant-mother attachment: Maternal and infant contributions. *Child Development, 55,* 718–728.

BENNETT, F.C. (1984). Neurodevelopmental outcome of low birthweight infants. In V.C. Kelly (Ed.), *Practice of pediatrics* (pp. 1–24). Philadelphia: Harper & Row.

BENNETT, F.C. (1987). Infants at biological risk. In M.J. Guralnick & F.C. Bennett (Eds.), *Effectiveness of early intervention for at-risk and handicapped children* (pp. 79–112). New York: Academic Press.

BENSON, H., & TURNBULL, A.P. (1986). Approaching families from an individualized perspective. In R.H. Horner, L.H. Meyer, & H.D. Fredericks (Eds.), *Education of learners with severe handicaps: Exemplary service strategies*. Baltimore: Paul H. Brookes.

BERNBAUM, J.C., PEREIRA, G.R., WATKINS, J.B., PECKHAM, G.J. (1983). Non-nutritive sucking during garage feeding enhances growth and maturation in premature infants. *Pediatrics, 71*(1), 41–45.

BERRY, J.O. (1987). A program for training teachers as counselors of parents of children with disabilities. *Journal of Counseling and Development, 65*, 508–509.

BERRY, P., GUNN, P., & ANDREWS, R. (1980). Behavior of Down's syndrome infants in a strange situation. *American Journal of Mental Deficiency, 85*, 213–218.

BIRNHOLZ, J.C., & BENECERRAF, B.R. (1983). The development of human fetal hearing. *Science, 222*, 516–518.

BLACHER, J., & MEYERS, C.E. (1983). A review of attachment formation and disorder of handicapped children. *American Journal of Mental Deficiency, 87*, 359–371.

BLACKBURN, S.T. (1986). Assessment of risk: Perinatal, family and environmental perspectives. *Physical and Occupational Therapy in Pediatrics, 6*, 105–120.

BLACKMAN, J.A. (1990). *Medical aspects of developmental disabilities in children birth to three* (2nd ed.) Rockville, MD: Aspen.

BLACKMAN, J.A., ANDERSEN, R.D., HEALY, A., & ZEHRBACH, R. (1985). Management of young children with recurrent herpes simplex skin lesions in special education programs. *Pediatric Infectious Disease, 4*(3), 221–224.

BLACKMAN, J.A. & NELSON, C.L.A. (1985). Reinstituting oral feeding in children fed by gastrostomy tube. *Clinical Pediatrics, 24*, 434–438.

BLANCHARD, M., & MAIN, M. (1979). Avoidance of the attachment figure and social-emotional adjustment in day care infants. *Developmental Psychology, 14*, 445–446.

BLAUCHER, J. (1984). Sequential stages of adjustment to the birth of a child with handicaps: Fact or artifact? *Mental Retardation, 22*, 55–68.

BLOOM, K., RUSSELL, A. & WASSENBERG, K. (1987). Turn taking affects the quality of infant vocalizations. *Journal of Child Language, 14*, 211–228.

BLOOM, L., BECKWITH, R., & CAPATIDES, J.B. (1988). Developments in the expression of affect. *Infant Behavior and Development, 11*, 169–186.

BLUMA, S.M., SHEARER, M.S., FROHMAN, A.H., & HILLIARD, J.M. (1976). *Portage guide to early education*. Portage, WI: CESA 5.

BOBATH, K., & BOBATH, B. (1964). The facilitation of normal postural reactions and movements in the treatment of cerebral palsy. *Physiotherapy, 50*, 246–252.

BOBATH, K., & BOBATH, B. (1972). Cerebral palsy. In P.H. Pearson & C. Williams (Eds.), *Physical therapy services in the developmental disabilities* (pp. 31–185). Springfield, IL: Thomas.

BOCHNER, S. (1983). The infant hospital as a setting for language acquisition in the handicapped. *Australia and New Zealand Journal of Developmental Disabilities, 9*(2), 65–73.

BODE, J. (1980). *Kids having kids: The unwed teenage parent*. New York: Franklin Watts.

BOHLIN, G., HAGEKULL, B., GERMER, M., ANDERSSON, K., & LINDBERG, L. (1989). Avoidant and resistant reunion behaviors as predicted by maternal interactive behavior and infant temperament. *Infant Behavior and Development, 12*, 105–117.

BOONE, H.A., SANDALL, S.R., LOUGHRY, A., & FREDERICK, L.L. (1990). An informed, family-centered approach to Public Law 99–457: Parental views. *Topics in Early Childhood Special Education, 10*(1), 100–111.

BOOTH, C.L., MITCHELL, S.K., BARNARD, K.E., & SPIEKER, S.J. (1989). Development of maternal social skills in multiproblem families: Effects on the mother-child relationship. *Developmental Psychology, 25*, 403–412.

BOPP, J. (1985). Protection of disabled newborns: Are there constitutional limitations? *Issues in Law and Medicine, 1*(3), 173–200.

BORNSTEIN, M.H. (1989). Stability in early mental development: From attention and information processing in infancy to language and cognition in childhood. In P. Fedor-Freybergh & M.L.V. Vogel (Eds.), *Prenatal and perinatal psychology and medicine; Encounter with the unborn.* Lancaster, UK: Parthenon Publishing Group.

BORNSTEIN, M.H., & BENASICH, A.A. (1986). Infant habituation: Assessments of short-term reliability and individual differences at 5 months. *Child Development, 57*, 87–89.

BORNSTEIN, M.H. & KRASNEGOR, N.A. (1989). *Stability and continuity in mental development: Behavioral and biological perspectives.* Hillsdale, NJ: Lawrence Erlbaum Associates.

BORNSTEIN, M.H., PECHEUX, M.G., & LECUYER, R. (1988). Visual habituation in human infants: Development and rearing circumstances. *Psychological Research, 50*, 130–133.

BORNSTEIN, M.H. & LAMB, M.E. (1988). *Developmental psychology: An advanced textbook* (2nd ed.) Hillsdale, NJ: Lawrence Erlbaum Associates.

BOSS, P.G. (1983). The marital relationship: Boundaries and ambiguities. In H.I. McCubbin & C.R. Figley (Eds.), *Stress and the family, Vol. I:* Coping with normative transitions.

BOWEN, M. (1978). *Family therapy in clinical practice.* New York: J. Aronson.

BOWLBY, J. (1951). *Maternal care and mental health.* Geneva: World Health Organization.

BOWLBY, J. (1969). *Attachment and loss:* Vol. 1. Attachment. New York: Basic Books.

BOWLBY, J. (1973). *Attachment and loss:* Vol. 2. Separation: Anxiety and anger. New York: Basic Books.

BOWLBY, J. (1980). *Attachment and loss:* Vol. 3. Loss, sadness and depression. New York: Basic Books.

BRADLEY, R.H. (1989). The use of the Home Inventory in longitudinal studies of child development. In P. Fedor-Freybergh & M.L.V. Vogel (Eds.), *Prenatal and perinatal psychology and medicine; Encounter with the unborn.* Lancaster, UK: Parthenon Publishing Group.

BRADLEY, R.M., & STERN, L.B. (1967). The development of the human taste bud during the fetal period. *Journal of Anatomy, 101*, 743–752.

BRADSHAW, D.L., GOLDSMITH, H.H., & CAMPOS, J.J. (1987). Attachment, temperament, and social referencing: Interrelationships among three domains of infant affective behavior. *Infant Behavior and Development, 10*, 223–231.

BRANN, A.W. (1985). Neonatal hypoxic-ischemic encephalopathy. In S. Harel & N.J. Anastasiow (Eds.), *The at-risk infant: Psycho/socio/medical aspects.* Baltimore: Paul H. Brookes.

BRAZELTON, T.B. (1973). *Neonatal behavioral assessment scale.* Philadelphia: J.B. Lippincott.

BRAZELTON, T.B. (1984). *Neonatal behavioral assessment scale* (2nd ed.). Clinics in Developmental Medicine, No. 88. Philadelphia: J.B. Lippincott.

BRAZELTON, T.B. (1988). Importance of early intervention. In E.D. Hibbs (Ed.), *Children and families: Studies in prevention and intervention.* Madison, WI: International Universities Press.

BRAZELTON, T.B., & YOGMAN, M.W. (1986). Reciprocity, attachment and effectance: Anlage in early infancy. In T.B. Brazelton & M.W. Yogman (Eds.), *Affective development in infancy*. Norwood, NJ: Ablex Publishing Corporation.

BREMNER, J.G. (1988). *Infancy*. Oxford: Blackwell.

BREWER, E.J., MCPHESON, M., MAGRAB, P., & HUTCHINS, V. (1989). Family centered, community-based, coordinated care for children with special health care needs. *Pediatrics, 83* (6), 1055–1060.

BRICKER, D.D. (1984). The effectiveness of early intervention with handicapped and at-risk infants. *Journal of the Child in Contemporary Society, 17*(1), 51–65.

BRICKER, D.D. (1986). *Early education of at-risk and handicapped infants, toddlers, and preschool children*. Glenview, IL: Scott, Foresman.

BRICKER, D.D. (1987). Impact of research on social policy for handicapped infants and children. *Journal of the Division for Early Childhood, 11*, 98–105.

BRICKER, D., BAILEY, E., & BRUDER, M.B. (1984). The efficacy of early intervention and the handicapped infant: A wise or wasted resource. In M. Wolraich & D.K. Routh (Eds.), *Advances in developmental and behavioral pediatrics* (Vol. 5, pp. 373–423). Greenwich, CT: JAI Press.

BRICKER, D.D., BAILEY, E.J., GUMERLOCK, S., BUHL, M., & SLENTZ, K. (1986). *Evaluation and programming system for infants and young children*. Eugene, OR: University of Oregon.

BRICKER, D.D., & CARLSON, L. (1981). Issues in early language intervention. In R.L. Schiefelbusch & D. Bricker (Eds.), *Early language: Acquisition and intervention*. Baltimore: University Park Press.

BRICKER, D., & GUMERLOCK, S. (1985). A three-level strategy. In J. Danaher (Ed.), *Assessment of child progress* (pp. 7–18). Chapel Hill, NC: TADS.

BRICKER, D., & GUMERLOCK, S. (1988). Application of a three-level evaluation plan for monitoring child progress and program effects. *Journal of Special Education, 22*(1), 55–65.

BRICKER, D., & SCHIEFELBUSCH, R.L. (1984). Infants at risk. In L. McCormick & R.L. Schiefelbusch (Eds)., *Early language intervention* (pp. 244–265). Columbus, OH: Charles Merrill.

BRIGANCE, A.H. (1978). *Brigance diagnostic inventory of early development*. Worcester, MA: Curriculum Associates.

BRINKER, R.P. (1982). Contigency intervention with the help of microcompters. *Journal of Special Education Technology, 5*, 37–39.

BRINKER, R.P. (1984). The microcomputer as a perceptual tool: Searching for systematic learning strategies with handicapped infants. *Special Services in the Schools, 1*, 21–36.

BRINKER, R.P., & LEWIS, M. (1982). Making the world work with microcomputers: A learning prosthesis for handicapped infants. *Exceptional Children, 49*, 163–170.

BROCK, D.J.H. (1983). Amniotic fluid tests for neural tube defects. *British Medical Bulletin, 39*, 373.

BRODY, E.B. (1988). Advocacy for healthy infancy—Prenatal intervention. In E.D. Hibbs (Ed.), *Children and families; Studies in prevention and intervention*. Madison, WI: International Universities Press.

BROFENBRENNER, U. (1977). Toward an experimental ecology of human development. *American Psychologist, 32*, 513–531.

BROFENBRENNER, U. (1986). Ecology of the family as a context for human development: Research perspective. *Developmental Psychology, 22*, 723–742.

BROMAN, S.H. (1989). Infant physical status and later cognitive development. In M.H. Bornstein, & N.A. Krasnegor (Eds.), *Stability and continuity in mental development: Behavioral and biological pespectives*. Hillsdale, N.J.: Lawrence Erlbaum Associates, Publishers.

BROMAN, S.H., NICHOLS, P.L., & KENNEDY, W.A. (1975). *Preschool IQ.: Prenatal and early development correlates.* Hillsdale, NJ: Lawrence Erlbaum, Associates.

BROMWICH, R. (1981). *Working with parents and infants: An interactional approach.* Baltimore: University Park Press.

BRONSON, W.C. (1974). Mother-toddler interaction: A perspective on studying the development of competence. *Merrill-Palmer Quarterly, 20,* 275–301.

BROOKHART, J., & HOCK, E. (1976). The effects of experimental context and experiential background on infants' behavior toward their mothers and a stranger. *Child Development, 47,* 333–340.

BROOKS-GUNN, J., & LEWIS, M. (1982). Temperament and affective interaction in handicapped infants. *Journal of the Division for Early Childhood, 5,* 31–41.

BROOKS-GUNN, J., & LEWIS, M. (1984). Maternal responsivity in interactions with handicapped infants. *Child Development, 55,* 782–793.

BROWN, J.V., & BAKEMAN, R. (1980). Relationships of human mothers with their infants during the first year of life: Effects of prematurity. In R.W. Bell & W.P. Smotherman (Eds.), *Maternal influences and early behavior.* Holliswood, NY: Spectrum.

BROWNELL, C.A., & STRAUSS, M.S. (1984). Infant stimulation and development: Conceptual and empirical considerations. *Journal of Children in Contemporary Society, 17,* 109–130.

BROWN-GORTON, R., & WOLERY, M. (1988). Teaching mothers to imitate their handicapped children: Effects on maternal mands. *Journal of Special Education, 22*(1), 97–107.

BRUCE, S.J., & KILADIS, P.A. (1986). Childbirth education. In R.F. Levant (Ed.), *Psychoeducational approaches to family therapy and counseling.* New York: Springer.

BRUNER, J.S. (1975). The ontogenesis of speech acts. *Journal of Child Language, 2,* 1–19.

BRUNER, J.S. (1983). *Child's talk: Learning to use language.* New York: Norton.

BRY, T. (1985). Liaison problems among infant psychiatry, psychology, pediatrics, nursing, and social work in infant mental health care. Paper presented at the Biennial meeting of the National Center for Clinical Infant Programs National Training Institute, Washington, DC.

BRYANT, D.M. & RAMEY, C.T. (1984). Prevention-oriented infant education programs. *Journal of Children in Contemporary Society, 17,* 17–35.

BUIUM, N., RYNDERS, J., & TURNURE, J. (1974). Early maternal linguistic environment of normal and Down's syndrome language learning children. *American Journal of Mental Deficiency, 79,* 52–58.

BURKE, P.J., MCLAUGHLIN, M.J., & VALDIVIESO, C.H. (1988). Preparing professionals to educate handicapped infants and young children: Some policy considerations. *Topics in Early Childhood Special Education, 8*(1), 73–80.

BUSSOD, N., & JACOBSON, N.S. (1986). Cognitive behavioral marital therapy. In R.F. Levant (Ed.), *Psychoeducational approaches to family therapy and counseling.* New York: Springer.

BUSTAN, D., & SAGI, A. (1984). Effects of early hospital-based intervention on mothers and their preterm infants. *Journal of Applied Developmental Psychology, 5,* 305–317.

BZOCH, K.R., & LEAGUE, R. (1971). *The Bzoch-League receptive-expressive language scale.* (REEL). Austin, TX: Pro Ed.

CADMAN, D., BOYLE, M.M., SZATMARI, P., & OFFORD, D.R. (1987). Chronic illness, disability and mental and social wellbeing: Findings of the Ontario Child Health Study. *Pediatrics, 79,* 805–813.

CALDWELL, B., & BRADLEY, R. (1984). *Home observation for measurement of the environment.* Little Rock: University of Arkansas.

CALHOUN, M.L., & ROSE, T.L. (1988). Early social reciprocity interventions for infants with severe retardation: Current findings and implications for the future. *Education and Training in Mental Retardation, 23*(4), 340–343.

CAMERON, J.R., & RICE, D.C. (1986). Developing anticipatory guidance programs based on early assessment of infant temperament: Two tests of a prevention model. *Journal of Pediatric Psychology, 11*(2), 221–234.

CAMPBELL, P.H., BELLAMY, G.T., & BISHOP, K.K. (1988). Statewide intervention systems: An overview of the new federal program for infants and toddlers with handicaps. *Journal of Special Education, 22*(1), 25–40.

CAMPBELL, S.K., SIEGEL, E., PARR, C.A., & RAMEY, C.T. (1986). Evidence for the need to renorm the Bayley Scales of Infant Development based on the performance of a population-based sample of 12-month-old infants. *Topics in Early Childhood Special Education, 6*(2), 83–96.

CAMPOS, J., BARRETT, K., LAMB, M., GOLDSMITH, H. & STENBERG, C. (1983). Socio-emotional development. In M. Haith & J. Campos (Eds.), Infancy and developmental psychobiology, Vol. II of P.H. Mussen, *Handbook of child psychology* (4th ed.). New York: Wiley.

CAMPOS, J.J., CAMPOS, R.G., & BARRETT, K.C. (1989). Emergent themes in the study of emotional development and emotion regulation. *Developmental Psychology, 25,* 394–402.

CANNELLA, G.S., BERKELEY, T.R., CONSTANS, T.M., & PARKHURST, S.A. (1987). Cognitive processes of at-risk and typically developing infants: Comparisons of exploration, play and problem solving. *Child Study Journal, 17,* 269–286.

CAPUTE, A.J., ACCARDO, P.J., VINING, E.P., RUBENSTEIN, J., & HARRYMAN, S. (1978). Primitive reflex profile. *Monographs in Developmental Pediatrics* (Vol. 1). Baltimore: University Park Press.

CAPUTE, A.J., PASQUALE, J.A., VINING, E.P., RUBENSTEIN, J.E., & HARRYMAN, S. (1978). *Primitive reflex profile.* Baltimore: University Park Press.

CAREY, W.B. (1979). Clinical appraisal of temperament. Paper presented at the symposium on developmental disabilities in the child, Chicago.

CAREY, W.B., & McDEVITT, S.C. (1978). Revision of the infant temperament questionnaire. *Pediatrics, 61,* 735–738.

CARLSON, V., CICCHETTI, D., BARNETT, D., & BRAUNWALD, K. (1989). Disorganized/disoriented attachment relationships in maltreated infants. *Developmental Psychology, 25,* 525–531.

CASATI, I., & LEZINE, I. (1968). *Les etapes de l'intelligence sensorimotrice.* Paris: Editions du Centre de Psychologie Appliquii.

CASTO, G., & MASTROPIERI, M. (1986). The efficacy of early intervention programs: A meta-analysis. *Exceptional Children, 52,* 417–424.

CASTO, G., & WHITE, K. (1984). The efficacy of early intervention programs with environmentally at-risk infants. *Journal of Children in Contemporary Society, 17,* 37–50.

CATTELL, P. (1940/1960). *Cattell Infant Intelligence Scale.* San Antonio: The Psychological Corporation.

CENTERS FOR DISEASE CONTROL. (1988, December 26). *AIDS Weekly Surveillance Report.* Atlanta.

CERNOCH, J.M. & PORTER, R.H. (1985). Recognition of maternal axillary odors by infants. *Child Development, 56,* 1593–1598.

CHAMBERLAIN, D.B. (1988). The mind of the newborn: Increasing evidence of competence. In P. Fedor-Freybergh & M.L.V. Vogel (Eds.), *Prenatal and perinatal psychology and medicine; Encounter with the unborn.* Lancaster, UK: Parthenon Publishing Group.

CHANDLER, L.S., ANDREWS, M.S., & SWANSON, M.W. (1980). *Movement assessment of infants: A manual*. Rolling Bay, WA: Authors.

CHASNOFF, I.J. (1986). *Drug use in pregnancy: Mother and child*. Lancaster: MTP Press Limited.

CHELIMSKY, E. (1984). Evaluation of the special supplemental program for women, infants, and children (WIC's) effectiveness. *Children and Youth Services Review, 6*, 219–226.

CHESS, S., & THOMAS, A. (1982). Infant bonding: Mystique and reality. *Journal of Orthopsychiatry, 52*, 213–222.

CHERVENAK, F.A., ISAACSON, C., & MAHONEY, M.J. (1986). Advances in the diagnosis of fetal defects. *New England Journal of Medicine, 315*, 305–307.

CICCHETTI, D. (1987). Developmental psychopathology in infancy: Illustrations from the study of maltreated youngsters. *Journal of Consulting and Clinical Psychology, 55*, 837–845.

CICCHETTI, D., & SCHNEIDER-ROSEN, K. (1984). Theoretical and empirical considerations in the investigation of the relationship between affect and cognition. In C. Izard, J. Kagan & R. Zajonc (Eds.), *Emotions, conditions and behavior* (pp. 366–406). New York: Cambridge University Press.

CICCHETTI, D., & TOTH, S. (1987). The application of a transactional risk model to intervention with multi-risk maltreating families. *Zero to Three, 7*, 1–8.

CLARK, G.N., & SEIFER, R. (1985). Assessment of parents' interactions with their developmentally delayed infants. *Infant Mental Health Journal, 6*, 214–225.

CLARK, S. (1983). Counseling hearing parents of deaf children about deaf identity and the deaf community. Paper presented at the Annual International Conference of the Council for Exceptional Children, Detroit, MI.

CLARKE-STEWART, K.A. (1973). Interactions between mothers and their young children: Characteristics and consequences. *Monographs of the Society for Research in Child Development, 36* (6, Serial No. 153).

CLARKE-STEWART, K.A., & HEVEY, C.M. (1981). Longitudinal relations in repeated observations of mother-child interactions from 1 to 2½ years. *Developmental Psychology, 17*, 127–145.

CLYMAN, R.B., EMDE, R.N., KEMPE, J.E., & HARMON, R.J. (1986). Social referencing and social looking among twelve-month-old infants. In T.B. Brazelton and M.W. Yogman (Eds.), *Affective development in infancy*. Norwood, NJ: Ablex.

COATES, D. & LEWIS, M. (1984). Early mother-infant interaction and infant cognitive status as predictors of school performance and cognitive behavior in six year olds. *Child Development, 55*, 1219–1230.

COLES, C.D., SMITH, I.E., & FALEK, A. (in press). Prenatal alcohol exposure and infant behavior: Immediate effects and implications for later development. *Advances in Alcohol and Substance Abuse*.

COLES, C.D., SMITH, I.E., FERNHOFF, P.M., & FALEK, A. (1985). Neonatal neurobehavioral characteristics as correlates of maternal alcohol use during gestation. *Alcoholism, 9*, 454–459.

COLES, C.D., SMITH, I.E., LANCASTER, J.S., & FALEK, A. (1987). Persistence over the first month of neurobehavioral differences in infants exposed to alcohol prenatally. *Infant Behavior and Development, 10*, 23–37.

COMPAS, B.E., HOWELL, D.C., PHARES, V., WILLIAMS, R.A., & LEDOUX, N. (1969). Parent and child stress and symptoms: An integrative analysis. *Developmental Psychology, 25*, 550–559.

CONNELL, J.P. & THOMPSON, R. (1986). Emotion and social interaction in the Strange Situation: Consistencies and asymmetric influences in the second year. *Child Development, 57*, 733–745.

COPLAN, J. (1982). Early language milestone scale. Austin, TX: Pro-Ed.

CORNELL, E.H., & GOTTFIED, A.W. (1976). Intervention with premature human infants. *Child Development, 47,* 32–39.

COTTON, E. (1970). Integration of treatment and education in cerebral palsy. *Physiotherapy, 4,* 143–147.

COTTON, E. (1975). *Conductive education and cerebral palsy.* London: Spastics Society.

COUNCIL FOR EXCEPTIONAL CHILDREN. (1983). Code of ethics and standards for professional practice. *Exceptional Children, 50*(3), 205–218.

CRAMER, B. (1986). Assessment of parent-infant relationships. In T.B. Brazelton & M.W. Yogman (Eds.), *Affective development in infancy.* Norwood, NJ: Ablex.

CRATTY, B.J. (1986). *Perceptual and motor development in infants and children.* Englewood Cliffs, NJ: Prentice Hall.

CRAWLEY, S.B., & Spiker, D. (1983). Mother-child interactions involving two year olds with Down Syndrome: A look at individual differences. *Child Development, 54,* 1312–1323.

CRNIC, K.A., GREENBERG, M.T., ROBINSON, N.M., & RAGOZIN, A.S. (1984). Maternal stress and social support: Effects on the mother-infant relationship from birth to eighteen months. *American Journal of Orthopsychiatry, 54*(2), 224–235.

CRNIC, K.A., GREENBERG, M.T., & SLOUGH, N.M. (1986). Early stress and social support influences on mothers' and high risk infants' functioning in late infancy. Special Issue: Social support, family functioning, and infant development. *Infant Mental Health Journal, 7*(1), 19–33.

CROCKENBERG, S.B. (1981). Infant's irritability, mother responsiveness, and social support influences on the security of infant-mother attachment. *Child Development, 52,* 857–865.

CROCKENBERG, S. (1985). Professional support and care of infants by adolescent mothers in England and the United States. *Journal of Pediatric Psychology, 10*(4), 413–428.

CULP, R.E., APPELBAUM, M.I., OSOFSKY, J.D., & LEVY, J.A. (1988). Adolescent and older mothers: Comparison between prenatal maternal variables and newborn interaction measures. *Infant Behavior and Development, 11*(3), 353–362.

CUNNINGHAM, C.E., REULER, E., BLACKWELL, J., & DECK, J. (1981). Behavioral and linguistic developments in the interactions of normal and retarded children with their mothers. *Child Development, 52,* 62–70.

DARLING, R.B. (1987). The economic and psychosocial consequences of disability: Family-society relationships. In M. Ferrari & M.B. Sussman (Eds.), *Childhood disability and family systems.* New York: Haworth Press.

DAWSON, G. (1983). Lateralization of brain function in autism. *Journal of Autism and Developmental Disorders, 13,*369–386.

DAY, P.S., & PREZIOSO, C. (1987). Anxious mothers and at-risk infants: The influence of mild hearing impairment on early interaction. Paper presented at the biennial meeting of the Society for Research in Child Development, Baltimore, MD.

DEAL, A.G., DUNST, C.J., & TRIVETTE, C.M. (1989). A flexible and functional approach to developing Individualized Family Support Plans. *Infants and Young Children, 1*(14), 32–43.

DE CHATEAU, P. (1980). Parent-neonate interaction and its long-term effects. In E.C. Simmel (Ed.), *Early experiences and early behavior: Implications for social development.* New York: Academic.

DEINER, P.L. (1987). Systems of care for disabled children and family members: New paradigms and alternatives. In M. Ferrari & M.B. Sussman (Eds.), *Childhood disability and family systems.* New York: Haworth Press.

DEINER, P.L., & WHITEHEAD, L.C. (1988). Delaware FIRST: Implementing handicapped infant/toddler curriculum through families and family day care providers. Paper presented at the annual conference of the Council for Exceptional Children, Washington, DC.

DeCasper, A. & Fifer, W. (1980). Of human bonding: Newborns prefer their mothers' voices. *Science, 208,* 1174–1176.

DeCasper, A. & Prescott, P.A. (1984). Human newborns' perception of male voices: Preference, discrimination, and reinforcing value. *Developmental Psychobiology, 17,* 481–491.

DeCasper, A.J., & Sigafoos, A.D. (1982). The intrauterine heartbeat: A potent reinforcer for newborns. *Infant Behavior and Development, 6,* 19–25.

DeCasper, A.J., & Spence, M.J. (1986). Prenatal maternal speech influences newborns' perceptions of speech sounds. *Infant Behavior and Development, 9,* 133–150.

De Mause, L. (1974). The evolution of childhood. In L. de Mause (Ed.), *The history of childhood.* New York: Psychohistory Press.

Demos, V. (1986). Crying in early infancy: An illustration of the motivational function of affect. In T.B. Brazelton & M.W. Yogman (Eds.), *Affective development in infancy.* Norwood, NJ: Ablex.

DeVries, J.I.P., Visser, G.H.A., & Prechtl, H.F.R. (1982). The emergence of fetal behaviour. I. Qualitative aspects. *Early Human Development, 7,* 301–322.

DeVries, J.I.P., Visser, G.H.A., & Prechtl, H.F.R. (1984). Fetal motility in the first half of pregnancy. In H.F.R. Prechtl (Ed.), Continuity of neural functions from prenatal to postnatal life. *Clinics in Developmental Medicine, 94,* 79–92.

DeVries, J.I.P., Visser, G.H.A., & Prechtl, H.F.R. (1985). The emergence of fetal behaviour. II. Quantitative Aspects. *Early Human Development, 12,* 99–120.

Diamond, K.E., & Reed, D.J. (1981). *Modifying parents' perceptions of their child's developmental progress: An approach to creating optimal learning environments.* Saratoga Springs, NY: Skidmore College.

Di Catherwood, B.C., & Freiberg, K. (1989). Infant response to stimuli of similar hue and dissimilar shape: Tracing the origins of the categorization of objects by hue. *Child Development, 60,* 752–762.

Dickin, K.L., McKim, M.K., & Kirkland, J. (1983). Designing intervention programs for infants at risk: Considerations, implementation, and evaluation. *Early Child Development and Care, 11,* 145–163.

Dixon, R.A., & Lerner, R.M. (1984). A history of systems in developmental psychology. In M.H. Bornstein & M.E. Lamb (Eds.), *Developmental Psychology: An advanced textbook.* Hillsdale, New York: Lawrence Erlbaum Associates.

Dixon, S. (1989). Effects of transplacental exposure to cocaine and methamphetamine on the neonate. *Western Journal of Medicine, 150,* 436–442.

Dodge, K.A. (1989). Coordinating responses to adverse stimuli: Introduction to a special section on the development of emotion regulation. *Developmental Psychology, 25,* 339–432.

Dokecki, P.R., Baumeister, A.A., & Kupstas, F.D. (1989). Biomedical and social aspects of pediatric AIDS. *Journal of Early Intervention, 13*(2), 99–113.

Dronek, M., & Lundin, J. (1986). *Program guidelines for hearing impaired individuals.* Sacramento, CA: California State Department of Education.

Drotar, D., Baskiewicz, B.A., Irvin, N., Kennell, J., & Klaus, M. (1975). The adaptation of parents to the birth of an infant with a congenital malformation: A hypothetical model. *Pediatrics, 56*(5), 710-717.

Drotar, D., & Bush, M. (1985). Mental health issues and services. In N. Hobbs & J.M. Perrin (Eds.), *Issues in the care of children with chronic illness: A source book on problems, services and policies.* San Francisco: Jossey-Bass.

Drotar, D., Crawford, T., & Bush, M. (1984). The family context of childhood chronic illness: Implications for psychosocial intervention. In M.G. Eisenberg, L.C.

Suttin, & M.A. Jansen (Eds.), *Chronic illness and disability through the lifespan: Effects on self and family* (pp. 103–129). New York: Springer.

DROTAR, D., & STURM, L. (1988). Parent-practitioner communication in the management of nonorganic failure to thrive. *Family Systems Medicine, 6,* 304–316.

DuBOSE, R.F. (1977). Predictive validity of infant intelligence scales with multiply handicapped children. *American Journal of Mental Deficiency, 81*(4), 388–390.

DuBOSE, R.F., & KELLY, J. (1981). *Curricula and instruction for young handicapped children: A guideline for selection and evaluation.* Monmouth, OR: Westar.

DUBOWITZ, L.M., & DUBOWITZ, V. (1981). *The neurological assessment of the preterm and full-term newborn infant.* Philadelphia: J.B. Lippincott.

DUBOWITZ, L.M., DUBOWITZ, V., & GOLDBERG, C. (1970). Clinical assessment of gestational age in the newborn infant. *Journal of Pediatrics, 77,* 1–10.

DUNST, C.J. (1978). A cognitive-social approach for assessment of early non-verbal communicative behavior. *Journal of Childhood Communicative Disorders, 2,* 110–123.

DUNST, C.J. (1980). *A clinical and educational manual for use with the Uzgiris and Hunt Scales of Infant Psychological Development.* Austin, TX: Pro-ed.

DUNST, C.J. (1981). *Infant learning: A cognitive-linguistic intervention strategy.* Allen, TX: DLM/Teaching Resources.

DUNST, C.J. (1985). Rethinking early intervention. *Analysis and Intervention in Developmental Disabilities, 5,* 165–201.

DUNST, C.J. (1989, October). Case management practices in early intervention. Presentation at International Conference on Children with Special Needs, Division for Early Childhood, Minneapolis.

DUNST, C.J., CUSHING, P.J., & VANCE, S. (1985). Response-contingent learning in profoundly handicapped infants: A social systems perspective. *Analysis and Intervention in Developmental Disabilities, 5,* 33–47.

DUNST, C.J., JENKINS, V., & TRIVETTE, C.M. (1984). Family support scale: Reliability and validity. *Journal of Individual, Family, and Community Wellness, 1*(4), 45–52.

DUNST, D.J., LEET, H., & TRIVETTE, C.M. (1988). Family resources, personal well-being, and early intervention. *Journal of Special Education, 22,* 108–116.

DUNST, C.J., LESKO, J.J., HOLBERT, K.A., WILSON, L.L., SHARPE, K.L., & LILES, R.F. (1987). A systematic approach to infant intervention. *Topics in Early Childhood Special Education, 7,* 19–37.

DUNST, C.J., RHEINGROVER, R.M. (1981). An analysis of the efficacy of infant intervention programs with organically handicapped children. *Evaluation and Program Planning, 4,* 287–323.

DUNST, C., & TRIVETTE, C. (1985). *A guide to measures of social support and family behaviors.* Chapel Hill, NC: TADS.

DUNST, C.J., & TRIVETTE, C.M. (1989). An enablement and empowerment perspective of case management. *Topics in Early Childhood Special Education, 8*(4), 87–102.

DUNST, C.J., TRIVETTE, C.M., & DEAL, A. (1988). *Enabling and empowering families: Principles and guidelines for practice.* Cambridge, MA: Brookline Books.

EARLY INTERVENTION PROJECT. (1987). Summary report, narrative report, and supplemental report. Augusta, ME: Maine State Department of Mental Health and Mental Retardation.

EATON, W.O., CHIPPERFIELD, J.G., & SINGBEIL, C.E. (1989). Birth order and activity level in children. *Developmental Psychology, 25,* 668–672.

EBRAHIM, J. (1989, March). Use of the kangaroo position to maintain stable body temperatures in Venezuelan neonates. Presentation at the Annual Conference on Perinatal Care Practices in Developing Countries, London.

EDWARDS, C.P., LOGUE, M.E., LOEHR, S., & ROTH, S. (1986). The influence of model infant-toddler group care on parent-child interaction at home. *Early Childhood Research Quarterly, 1,* 317–332.

EGELAND, B., & FARBER, E. (1984). Infant-mother attachment: Factors related to its development and changes over time. *Child Development, 55*(3), 753–771.

EGELAND, B., JACOBVITZ, D., & SROUFE, L.A. (1988). Breaking the cycle of abuse: Relationship predictors. *Child Development, 59*, 1080–1088.

EGELAND, B. & SROUFE, L.A. (1981). Attachment and early maltreatment. *Child Development, 52*, 44–52.

EHEART, B.K. (1981). Mother-child interactions with nonretarded and mentally retarded preschoolers. *American Journal of Mental Deficiency, 87*, 20–25.

ELLIS, E. (1967). Physical management of developmental disorders. *Clinics in developmental medicine* (No. 26). London: Heinemann.

ELLIS, J. W., & LUCKASSON, R. (1986). Denying treatment to infants with handicaps: A comment on Bowen V. American Hospital Association. *Mental Retardation, 24*(4), 237–240.

ELLISON, P.H., HORN, J.L., BROWNING, C.A. (1985). Construction of an infant neurological international battery (Infanib) for the assessment of neurological integrity in infancy. *Physical Therapy, 65*, 1326–1331.

EMBRY, L.H. (1980). Family support for handicapped preschool children at risk for abuse. In J.J. Gallagher (Ed.), *New directions for exceptional children* (pp. 29–57). San Francisco: Jossey-Bass.

EMDE, R. (1980). Emotional availability: A reciprocal reward system for infant and parents with implications for prevention of psychosocial disorders. In P. Taylor (Ed.), *Parent-infant relationships*. Orlando, FL: Grune & Stratton.

EMDE, R. (1983). The prerepresentation self and its affective core. *Psychoanalytic Study of the Child, 38*, 165–192.

EMDE, R. (1988). Development terminable and interminable: I. Innate and motivational factors from infancy. *International Journal of Psychoanalysis, 69*, 23–42.

EMDE, R. (1989). The infant's relationship experience: Developmental and affective aspects. In A.J. Sameroff & R.N. Emde (Eds.), *Relationship disturbances in early childhood: A developmental approach*. New York: Basic Books.

EMDE, R.N., & BROWN, C. (1978). Adaptation to the birth of a Down's syndrome infant: Grieving and maternal attachment. *Journal of the American Academy of Child Psychiatry*, 299–323.

EMDE, R.N., & SAMEROFF, A.J. (1989). Understanding early relationship disturbances. In A.J. Sameroff & R.N. Emde (Eds.), *Relationship disturbances in early childhood: A developmental approach*. New York: Basic Books.

EMPSON, J.V., et al. (1988). *An impact evaluation of the Resource Access Projects, 1986–1987*. Washington, DC: Littlejohn Associates.

ENHORNING, G., SHENNAN, A., POSSMAYER, F., et al. (1985). Prevention of respiratory distress syndrome by tracheal installation of surfactant: A randomized clinical trial. *Pediatrics, 76*, 145–153.

ENSHER, G.L., & CLARK, D.A. (1986). *Newborns at risk: Medical care and psychoeducational intervention*. Rockville, MD: Aspen.

EPSTEIN, N., SCHLESINGER, S.E., & DRYDEN, W. (1988). Concepts and methods of cognitive-behavioral family treatment. In N. Epstein, S.E. Schlesinger, & W. Dryden (Eds.), *Cognitive-behavioral therapy with families*. New York: Bruner/Mazel.

ERIKSON, E. (1950). *Childhood and society*. New York: Norton.

ESCALONA, S., & CORMAN, H. (1966). *The Albert Einstein Scales of Sensorimotor Development*. Unpublished papers. Department of Psychiatry, Albert Einstein College of Medicine, New York.

EVANS, E.D. (1975). *Contemporary influences in early childhood education* (2nd ed.) New York: Holt, Rinehart & Winston.

FAGAN, J.F. (1982). New evidence for the prediction of intelligence from infancy. *Infant Mental Health Journal, 3,* 219–228.

FAGAN, J.F. (1984). Recognition memory and intelligence. *Intelligence, 8,* 31–36.

FAGAN, J.F., & McGRATH, S.K. (1981). Infant recognition memory and later intelligence. *Intelligence, 5* 121–130.

FALLOON, J., EDDY, J., WIENER, L., & PIZZO, P. (1989). Human immunodeficiency virus infection in children. *Journal of Pediatrics, 114,* 1–30.

FANTZ, R. (1958). Pattern vision in young infants. *Psychological Review, 8,* 43–49.

FARRAN, D.C., KASARI, C., YODER, P., HARBER, L., HUNTINGTON, G.S., & COMFORT, M. (1987). Rating mother-child interaction in handicapped and at-risk infants. In T. Tamir (Ed.), *Stimulation and intervention in infant development.* London: Freund Publishing House.

FARRAN, D.C., & SPARLING, J. (1988). Coping styles in families of handicapped children. In E.D. Hibbs (Ed.), *Children and families: Studies in prevention and intervention.* Madison, WI: International Universities Press.

FEDERAL REGISTER. (June 22, 1989). *Early Intervention Program for Infants and Toddlers with Handicaps; Final Regulations,* Vol. 54, 119, pp. 26306–26348. Washington, DC: U.S. Government Printing Office.

FEIN, D., SKOFF, B. & MIRSKY, A.F. (1981). Clinical correlates of brainstem dysfunction in autistic children. *Journal of Autism and Developmental Disorders, 11,* 303–316.

FELDMAN, D.H. (1982). Transcending IQ in the definition of giftedness. *Early Childhood Review, 23,* 15–18.

FELDMAN, D.H. (1986). Giftedness as a developmentalist sees it. In R.J. Sternberg & J.E. Davidson (Eds.), *Conceptions of giftedness.* Cambridge: Cambridge University Press.

FELDMAN, D.H., & ADAMS, M.L. (1989). Intelligence, stability, and continuity: Changing conceptions. In P. Fedor-Freybergh and M.L.V. Vogel (Eds.), *Prenatal and perinatal psychology and medicine; Encounter with the unborn.* Lancaster, UK: Partheneon Publishing Group.

FELNER, R.D., JASON, L.A., MORITSUGU, J.N., & FARBER, S.S. (1983). Preventive psychology: Evolution and current status. In R.S. Felner, L.A. Jason, J.N. Moritsugu, & S.S. Farber (Eds.), *Preventive psychology: Theory, research and practice.* New York: Pergamon Press.

FERRELL, K.A. (1984). A second look at sensory aids in early childhood. *Education of the Visually Handicapped, 16*(3), 83–101.

FERRY, P.C. (1986). Infant stimulation programs: A neurologic shell game? *Archives of Neurology, 43*(3), 281–282.

FEWELL, R.R. (1986). The measurement of family functioning. In L. Bickman, & D.L. Weatherford (Ed), *Evaluating early intervention programs for severely handicapped children and their families* (pp. 263–307). Austin, TX: Pro-ed.

FEWELL, R.R., & KAMINSKI, R. (1988). Play skills development and instruction for young children with handicaps. In S.L. Odom & M.B. Karnes (Eds.), *Early intervention for infants and children with handicaps: An empirical base* (pp. 145–158). Baltimore: Paul H. Brookes.

FEWELL, R.R., & LANGLEY, M.B. (1984). *Developmental activities screening inventory—II.* Austin, TX: Pro-Ed.

FEWELL, R.R., & SANDALL, S.R. (1983). Curricular adaptations for young children: Visually handicapped, hearing impaired, and physically impaired. *Topics in Early Childhood Special Education, 2*(4), 51–66.

FEWELL, R.R., & SANDALL, S.R. (1986). Developmental testing of handicapped infants: A measurement dilemma. *Topics in Early Childhood Special Education, 6*(3), 86–99.

FEWELL, R.R., & VADASY, P.F. (1983). *Learning through play.* Allen, TX: DLM/Teaching Resources.

FEWELL, R.R., & VADASY, P.F. (1987). Measurement issues in studies of efficacy. *Topics in Early Childhood Special Education, 7*(2), 85–96.

FEY, M. (1986). *Language intervention with young children.* San Diego: College Hill Press.

FIELD, T. (1980). Supplemental stimulation of preterm neonates. *Early Human Development, 4,* 301–314.

FIELD, T. (1986). Affective responses to separation. In T.B. Brazelton & M.W. Yogman (Eds.), *Affective development in infancy.* Norwood, NJ: Ablex.

FIELD, T., & GOLDSON, E. (1984). Pacifying effects of nonnutritive sucking on term and preterm neonates during heelsticks. *Pediatrics, 74,* 1012–1015.

FIELD, T., VEGA-LAHR, N., GOLDSTEIN, S., SCAFIDI, F. (1987a). Face-to-face interaction behavior across early infancy. *Infant Behavior and Development, 10,* 111–116.

FIELD, T., VEGA-LAHR, N., GOLDSTEIN, S., & SCAFIDI, F. (1987b). Interaction behavior of infants and their dual-career parents. *Infant Behavior and Development, 10,* 371–378.

FIELD, T., VEGA-LAHR, N., SCAFIDI, F., & GOLDSTEIN, S. (1987). Reliability, stability, and relationships between infant and parent temperament. *Infant Behavior and Development, 10,* 117–122.

FIFER, W.P. (1987). Neonatal preference for mother's voice. In N.A. Krasnegor, E.M. Blass, M.A. Hofer, & W.P. Smotherman (Eds.), *Perinatal development: A psychobiological perspective.* Orlando: Academic Press.

FINEGAN, J.K., QUARRINGTON, B.J., HUGHES, H.E., & DORAN, T.A. (1987). Infant development following midtrimester amniocentesis. *Infant Behavior and Development, 10,* 379–383.

FINKELSTEIN, J.W., FINKELSTEIN, J.A., CHRISTIE, M., RODEN, M., & SHELTON, C. (1982). Teenage pregnancy and parenthood: Outcomes for mother and child. *Journal of Adolescent Health Care, 3,* 1–7.

FINN, D.M., & VADASY, P.F. (n.d.). *Prioritizing family needs scale.* Seattle, WA: University of Washington Experimental Education Unit.

FINNEGAN, L.P. (1985). Smoking and its effects on pregnancy and the newborn. In S. Harel & N.J. Anastasiow (Eds.), *The at-risk infant: Psycho/socio/medical aspects.* Baltimore: Paul H. Brookes.

FIORENTINO, M.R. (1973). *Reflex testing methods for evaluating C.N.S. development* (2nd ed.). Springfield, IL: Thomas.

FISHBEIN, H.D. (1984). *The psychology of infancy and childhood: Evolutionary and cross-cultural perspectives.* Hillsdale, NJ: Lawrence Erlbaum Associates.

FITZGERALD, I.M. (1987). Childhood disability: Prevalence and incidence. In M. Ferrari & M.B. Sussman (Eds.), *Childhood disability and family systems.* New York: Haworth Press.

FOLIO, R., & FEWELL, R.R. (1984). *Peabody developmental motor scales and activity cards.* Allen, TX: DLM/Teaching Resources.

FOX, N.A. (1989). Psychophysiological correlates of emotional reactivity during the first year of life. *Developmental Psychology, 24,* 364–372.

FRANKENBURG, W.K., DODDS, J., & FANDAL, A. (1975). *Denver developmental screening test.* Denver: LADOCA Project and Publishing.

FRASER, B.C. (1987). Child impairment and parent/infant communication. *Child-Care, Health and Development, 12,* 141–150.

FREEDMAN, D.G. (1971). Behavioral assessment in infancy. In G.A.B. Stoelinga & J.J. Van Der Werff Ten Bosch, (Eds.), *Normal and abnormal development of brain and behavior.* Leiden, The Netherlands: Leiden University Press.

FREEDMAN, S.A., REISS, J.G., & PIERCE, P.A. (1988). *Focus and functions of family centered case management.* Gainesville, FL: Institute for Child Health Policy.

FREEMAN, J. (1985). The early years: Preparation for creative thinking. *Gifted Education International, 3,* 100–104.

FREEMAN, J. (1983). Neonatal seizures. In F.E. Dreifuss (Ed.), *Pediatric epilestology: Classification and management of seizures in the child.* Boston: John Wright, P.S.G.

FREUD, S. (1917). *Psychopathology of everyday life.* New York; Macmillan.

FREUD, S. (1923/1962). *The ego and the id.* New York: Norton.

FREUD, S. (1940). *An outline of psychoanalysis.* New York: Norton.

FRIEDRICH, W.N., GREENBERG, M.T., & CRNIC, K. (1983). A short-form of the questionnaire on resources and stress. *American Journal of Mental Deficiency, 88,* 41–48.

FRODI, A.M. (1981). Contribution of infant characteristics to child abuse. *American Journal on Mental Deficiency, 85,* 341–349.

FRODI, A.M., & LAMB, M. (1978). Sex differences in responsiveness to infants: A developmental study of psychophysiological and behavioral responses. *Child Development, 49,* 1182–1188.

FRODI, A.M., & THOMPSON, R. (1985). Infants' affective responses in the strange situation: Effects of prematurity and of quality of attachment. *Child Development, 56,* 1280–1290.

FULLARD, W., McDEVITT, S.C., & CAREY, W.B. (1984). Assessing temperament in one-to-three year old children. *Journal of Pediatric Psychology, 9*(2), 205–217.

FURUNO, S., O'REILLY, K., HOSAKA, C., INATSUKA, T., ALLMAN, T., & ZEISLOFT, B. (1979). *Hawaii early learning profile.* Palo Alto, CA: Vort Corp.

GAITER, J. L. (1985). Nursery environments: The behavior and caregiving experiences of term and preterm newborns. In A.W. Gottfried & J.L. Gaiter (Eds.), *Infant stress under intensive care: Environmental neonatology.* Baltimore: University Park Press.

GALLAGHER, J.J., & GOWEN, J.W. (1982). *The Carolina Institute for Research on Early Education for the Handicapped, final report.* Chapel Hill, NC: Frank Porter Graham Center, North Carolina University.

GALLER, J.R. (1984). Behavioral consequences of malnutrition in early life. In J.R. Galler (Ed.), *Nutrition and behavior.* New York: Plenum Press.

GALLER, J.R., RAMSEY, F., & FORDE, V. (1986). A follow-up study of the influence of early malnutrition on subsequent development: 4. Intellectual performance during adolescence. *Nutrition Behavior, 3,* 211–222.

GARDNER, H. (1983). *Frames of mind: The theory of multiple intelligences.* New York: Basic Books.

GARDNER, H. (1984). Assessing intelligence: A comment on 'testing intelligence without IQ tests.' *Phi Delta Kappan, 65,* 699–700.

GARDNER, J.M. & KARMEL, B.Z. (1983). Attention and arousal in preterm and full-term neonates. In T. Field & A. Sostek (Eds.), *Infants born at risk: Physiological, perceptual and cognitive processes* (pp. 69–98). New York: Grune & Stratton.

GARDNER, J.M., KARMEL, B.Z., & DOWD, J.M. (1984). Relationship of psychological development to infant intervention. *Journal of the Child in Contemporary Society, 17*(1), 93–108.

GARDNER, W., LAMB, M.E., THOMPSON, R.A., & SAGI, A. (1986). On individual differences in strange situation behavior: Categorical and continuous measurement systems in a cross-cultural data set. *Infant Behavior and Development, 9,* 355–375.

GARLAND, C., WOODRUFF, G., & BUCK, D.M. (1988). Case management: Division for early childhood white paper. Washington, D.C. Council for Exceptional Children.

GARRITY, J., & MENGLE, H. (1983). Early identification of hearing loss: Practices and procedures. *American Annals of the Deaf, 128*(2), 99–106.

GARWOOD, S.G. (1987). Political, economic, and practical issues affecting the development of universal early intervention for handicapped infants. *Topics in Early Childhood Special Education, 7*(2), 6–18.

GARWOOD, S.G., FEWELL, R.R. & NEISWORTH, J.T. (1988). Public Law 99–457: You can get there from here! *Topics in Early Childhood Special Education, 8*(1), 1–11.

GAUTT, S.W. (1986). Community linkage development: Expanding services to developmentally delayed infants in rural areas. *Rural Special Education Quarterly, 7*, 17–19.

GERBER, M.A. & BERLINER, B.C. (1981). The child with a "simple" febrile seizure: Appropriate diagnostic evaluation. *American Journal of Diseases in Children, 135*, 431–433.

GERSTEN, M. COSTER, W., SCHNEIDER-ROSEN, K., CARLSON, V., & CICCHETTI, D. (1987). The socioemotional bases of communicative functioning: Quality of attachment, language development and early maltreatment. In M. Lamb, A.L. Brown, & B. Rozoff (Eds.), *Advances in developmental psychology* (pp. 306–322). New York: Academic Press.

GESELL, A. (1925). *The mental growth of the preschool child.* New York: Macmillan.

GESELL, A. (1940). *The first five years of life: A guide to the study of the preschool child.* New York: Harper & Brothers.

GESELL, A. (1945). *The embryology of behavior.* New York: Harper.

GESELL, A., & AMATRADA, C.S. (1947). *Developmental diagnosis.* New York: Paul B. Holden.

GETZ, H., & GUNN, W.B. (1988). Parent education from a family-systems perspective. *School Counselor, 35*, 331–336.

GIBBS, E.D., TETI, D.M., & BOND, L.A. (1987). Infant-sibling communication: Relationships to birth-spacing and cognitive and linguistic development. *Infant Behavior and Development, 10*(3), 307–323.

GIBSON, D., & FIELDS, D.L. (1984). Early infant stimulation programs for children with Down syndrome: A review of effectiveness. In M. Wolraich & D.K. Routh (Eds.), *Advances in Developmental and Behavioral Pediatrics, 5*, 331–371. Greenwich, CT: JAI Press.

GIBSON, E.J. (1988). Exploratory behavior in the development of perceiving, acting, and the acquiring of knowledge. *Annual Review of Psychology, 39*, 1–42.

GIL, L.L. (1984). *The integration of handicapped and nonhandicapped infants and toddlers: A guide for program development.* Seattle, WA: Northwest Center for Retarded.

GILKERSON, L., HILLIARD, A.G., SCHRAG, E., & SHONKOFF, J.P. (1987). Commenting on PL 99-457. *Zero-to Three, 7*(3), 13–17.

GINSBURG, G.P., & KILBORNE, B.K. (1988). The emergence of vocal alternation in mother-infant interchanges. *Journal of Child Language, 15*, 221–236.

GLOVER, E.M., PREMINGER, J., & SANFORD, A. (1978). *Early learning accomplishment profile.* Lewisville, NC: Kaplan School Supply.

GOLDBERG, S. (1977). Social competence in infancy: A model of parent-infant interaction. *Merrill-Palmer Quarterly, 23*, 163–177.

GOLDBERG, S. (1978). Prematurity: Effects on parent-child interaction. *Journal of Pediatric Psychology, 3*, 137–144.

GOLDBERG, S. (1983). Parent-to-infant bonding: Another look. *Child Development, 54*, 1355–1382.

GOLDBERGER, J. (1988). Infants and toddlers in hospitals: Addressing developmental risks. *Zero to Three, 3*(3), 1–6.

GOLDSTEIN, M. (1988). The family and psychopathology. *Annual Review of Psychology, 39*, 283–299.

GOODWIN, W.L. & DRISCOLL, L.A. (1980). *Handbook of measurement and evaluation in early childhood.* San Francisco: Jossey-Bass.

GOPNIK, A., & MELTZOFF, A. (1987). The development of categorization in the second year and its relation to other cognitive and linguistic developments. *Child Development, 58,* 1523–1531.

GORSKI, P.A. (1983). Premature infant behavioral and physiological responses to caregiving interventions in the intensive care nursery. In J.D. Call, E. Galenson, & R.L. Tyson (Eds.), *Frontiers in infant psychiatry* (pp. 256–263). New York: Basic Books.

GORSKI, P.A. (1984). Experience following premature birth: Stresses and opportunities for infants, parents, and professionals. In J.D. Call, E. Galenson, & P.L. Tyson (Eds.), *Frontiers of infant psychiatry* (pp. 145–151). New York: Basic Books.

GOTTFRIED, A.W. (1985). Environment of newborns in special care units. In A.W. Gottfried & J.L. Gaiter (Eds.), *Infant stress under intensive care: Environmental neonatology* (pp. 23–54). Baltimore: University Park Press.

GOTTFRIED, A.W. & GAITER, J.L. (1985). *Infant stress under intensive care: Environmental neonatology.* Baltimore: University Park Press.

GOTTFRIED, A.W., HODGMAN, J.E., & BROWN, K.W. (1984). How intensive is newborn intensive care? An environmental analysis. *Pediatrics, 72,* 198–202.

GOTTFRIED, A.W., WALLACE-LANDE, P., SHERMAN-BROWN, S., KING, J., COEN, C., & HODGMAN, J.E. (1981). Physical and social environment of newborn infants in special care units. *Science, 214,* 637–675.

GOTTMAN, J.M., & KATZ, L.F. (1989). Effects of marital discord on young children's peer interaction and health. *Developmental Psychology, 25,* 373–381.

GOTTWALD, S.R., & THURMAN, S.K. (1990). Parent-infant interaction in neonatal intensive care units: Implications for research and service delivery. *Infants and Young children, 2*(3), 1–10.

GRAHAM, M.A., & SCOTT, K.G. (1988). The impact of definitions of high risk on services to infants and toddlers. *Topics in Early Childhood Special Education, 8*(1), 23–38.

GRAZIANO, A.M. (1986). Behavioral approaches to child and family systems. In R.F. Levant (Ed.), *Psychoeducational approaches to family therapy and counseling.* New York: Springer.

GREENBERG, R., & FIELD, T. (1983). Temperament ratings of handicapped infants during classroom, mother, and teacher interactions. *Annual Progress in Child Psychiatry and Child Development,* 363–382.

GREENSPAN, S.I., & LOURIE, R.S. (1981). Developmental structuralistic approach to the classification of adaptive and pathologic personality organization. *Amerian Journal of Psychiatry, 138,* 728–735.

GREENSPAN, S.I., WEIDER, S., LIEBERMAN, A. NOVER, R. LOURIE, R. & ROBINSON, M. (Eds.). (1987). *Infants in multirisk families: Case studies in preventive intervention.* Madison, CT: International Universities Press.

GRIESER, D., & KUHL, P.K. (1989). Categorization of speech by infants: Support for speech-sound prototypes. *Developmental Psychology, 25,* 577–588.

GRIFFITH, D.R. (1988). The effects of perinatal cocaine exposure on infant neurobehavior and early maternal-infant interactions. In I.J. Chasnoff (Ed.), *Drugs, alcohol, pregnancy, and parenting.* Lancaster, UK: Kluwer.

GRIFFITHS, R. (1978). *Griffiths mental developmental scales.* Sarasota, FL: Test Center.

GROSSMAN, H.J. (1973). *Manual on terminology and classification in mental retardation.* Washington, D.C.: American Association on Mental Deficiency.

GROSSMAN, H.J. (1983). *Classification in mental retardation.* Washington, DC: American Association on Mental Deficiency.

GROSSMAN, K., GROSSMAN, K.E., SPANGLER, G., SUESS, G., & UNZER, L. (1985). Maternal sensitivity and newborns' orientation responses as related to quality of attachment in Northern Germany. In I. Bretherton & E. Waters (Eds.), *Growing points of attachment theory and research* (pp. 223–257). Monographs of the Society for Research in Child Development, 50 (1–2, Serial No. 209).

GUESS, D., HORNER, R., UTLEY, B., HOLVOET, J., MAXON, B., TUCKER, D., & WARREN, S. (1978). A functional curriculum sequencing model for teaching the severely handicapped. *AAESPH Review, 3,* 202–215.

GUNNAR, M.R., MANGELSDORF, LARSON, M., & HERTSGAARD, L. (1989). Attachment, temperament, and adrenocortical activity in infancy: A study of psychoendocrine regulation. *Developmental Psychology, 25,* 355–363.

GURALNICK, M.J. (1986). The peer relations of young handicapped and nonhandicapped children. In P.S. Strain, M.J. Guralnick, & H.M. Walker (Eds.), *Children's social behavior: Development, assessment, and modification* (pp. 93–140). New York: Academic Press.

GURALNICK, M.J. (1988). Efficacy research in early childhood intervention programs. In S.L. Odom & M.B. Karnes (Eds.), *Early intervention for infants and children with handicaps: An empirical base* (pp. 75–88). Baltimore: Paul H. Brookes.

GURALNICK, M.J. (1989). Recent developments in early intervention efficacy research: Implications for family involvement in PL 99-457. *Topics in Early Childhood Special Education, 9,* 1–17.

GURALNICK, M.J., & BENNETT, F.C. (1987a). *The effectiveness of early intervention for at-risk and handicapped children.* New York: Academic Press.

GURALNICK, M.J., & BENNETT, F.C. (1987b). Early intervention for at-risk and handicapped children: Current and future perspectives (pp. 365–382). In M.J. Guralnick & F.C. Bennett (Eds.), *The effectiveness of early intervention for at-risk and handicapped children.* New York: Academic Press.

GURALNICK, M.J., & BRICKER, D. (1987). The effectiveness of early intervention for children with cognitive and general developmental delays. In M.J. Guralnick & F.C. Bennett (Eds.), *The effectiveness of early intervention for at-risk and handicapped children* (pp. 115–173). New York: Academic Press.

GUTTMAN, A.J., & RONDAL, J.A. (1979). Verbal operants in mothers' speech to nonretarded and Down's syndrome children matched for linquistic level. *American Journal of Mental Deficiency, 83,* 446–452.

HAHN, P. (1979). Nutrition and metabolic development in mammals. In M. Winick (Ed.), *Nutrition: Pre- and postnatal development.* New York: Plenum Press.

HAITH, M.M. (1980). *Rules that babies look by.* Hillsdale, N.J.: Lawrence Erlbaum Associates.

HALL, G. (1891). Notes on the study of infants. *The Pedagogical Seminary, 1,* 127–138.

HALLAHAN, D.P. & KAUFMAN, J.M. (1982). *Exceptional children: Introduction to special education* (2nd ed.). Englewood Cliffs, NJ: Prentice Hall.

HALL, G.S. (1904). *Adolescence (Vols. I and II).* Englewood Cliffs, NJ: Prentice Hall.

HALLE, J.W., BAER, D.M., & SPRADLIN, J.E. (1981). Teachers' generalized use of delay as a stimulus control procedure to increase language in handicapped children. *Journal of Applied Behavior Analysis, 14,* 387–400.

HAMMOND, M., BEE, H.L., BARNARD, K.E., & EYRES, S.J. (1983). *Child health assessment. Part 4: Follow-up at second grade.* Final report of project supported by Grant No. R01-NU-00816, Division of Nursing, Bureau of Health Professions, Health Resources and Services Administration, U.S. Public Health Service.

HANNAN, T.E. (1987). A cross-sequential assessment of the occurrences of pointing in 3- to 12-month-old human infants. *Infant Behavior and Development, 10,* 11–22.

HANSON, M.J. (Ed.). (1984). *Atypical infant development.* Austin, TX: Pro-Ed.

HANSON, M.J. (1985). An analysis of the effects of early intervention services for infants and toddlers with moderate and severe handicaps. *Topics in Early Childhood Special Education, 5*(2), 36–51.

HANSON, M.J. (1987). *Teaching the infant with Down syndrome: A guide for parents and professionals* (2nd ed.). Austin, TX: Pro-Ed.

HANSON, M., (1990). *Final Report.* California Early Intervention Personnel Model, Personnel Standards, and Personnel Preparation Plan. Report prepared for the California Department of Developmental Services. California Early Intervention Personnel Study Project. Department of Special Education, San Francisco State University.

HANSON, M.J., & HARRIS, S.R. (1986). *Teaching the young child with motor delays: A guide for parents and professionals.* Austin, TX: Pro-Ed.

HANSON, M.J., & KRENTZ, M.K. (1986). *Supporting parent-child interactions: A guide for early intervention program personnel.* San Francisco: Department of Special Education, San Francisco State University.

HANSON, M.J., & LYNCH, E.W. (1989). *Early intervention: Implementing child and family services for infants and toddlers who are at-risk or disabled.* Austin, TX: Pro-Ed.

HARBIN, G.L. (1988). Implementation of P.L. 99-457: State technical assistance needs. *Topics in Early Childhood Special Education, 8,* 24–36.

HAREL, S., & ANASTASIOW, N. (Eds.) (1985). *The at-risk infant: Psycho/social/medical aspects.* Baltimore: Paul H. Brookes.

HARLEY, R.D. (Ed.). (1983). *Pediatric opthamology* (2nd ed.) Philadelphia: W.B. Saunders.

HARLEY, R.K., LONG, R.G., MERBLER, J.B., & WOOD, T.A. (1987). Orientation and mobility for the blind multiply handicapped young child. *Journal of Visual Impairment and Blindness, 81,* 377–381.

HARRIS, M.B. (1986). Oral-motor management of the high-risk neonate. In J.K. Sweeney (Ed.), *The high-risk neonate* (pp. 231–253). New York: Haworth Press.

HARRIS, S.L. (1987). The family crisis: Diagnosis of a severely disabled child. In M. Ferrari & M.B. Sussman (Eds.), *Childhood disability and family systems.* New York: Haworth Press.

HARRIS, S.R. (1981). Effects of neurodevelopmental therapy on improving motor performance in Down's syndrome infants. *Developmental Medicine and Child Neurology, 23,* 477–483.

HARRIS, S.R. (1987). Early intervention for children with motor handicaps. In M.J. Guralnick & F.C. Bennett (Eds.), *The effectiveness of early intervention for at-risk and handicapped children* (pp. 175–212). New York: Academic Press.

HARRIS, S.R. (1988). Neuromotor assessment for infants with Down syndrome. *Down syndrome: Papers and abstracts for professionals, 11*(1), 1–4.

HARRIS, S.R., & TADA, W.L. (1983). Providing developmental therapy services. In S.G. Garwood & R.R. Fewell (Eds.), *Educating handicapped infants* (pp. 343–368). Rockville, MD: Aspen.

HARRISON, L. (1985). Effects of early supplemental stimulation programs for premature infants: Review of the literature. *Maternal Child Nursing Journal, 14,* 69–90.

HARRISON, R., EDWARDS, J. (1983). *Child abuse.* Portland, OR: Ednick Publications.

HART, B., & ROGERS-WARREN, A. (1978). Milieu approach to teaching language. In R.L. Schiefelbusch (Ed.), *Language intervention strategies.* Baltimore: University Park Press.

HARVEY, C., JOHNS, N., WALKO, L., & GILBERT, P. (1988). Training parents for home care of babies who have bronchopulmonary dysplasia: The role of the parenting specialist. *Zero to Three, 3*(3), 19–22.

HATCH, O.G. (1984). Environmental constraints affecting services for the handicapped. *Topics in Early Childhood Special Education, 4*(1), 83–90.

HAYES, D. (1986). Audiological assessment. In D.L. Wodrich & J.E. Joy (Eds.), *Multidisciplinary assessment of children with learning disabilities and mental retardation*. Baltimore: Paul H. Brookes.

HEBER, R. (1961). A manual on terminology and classification in mental retardation (rev. ed.). *American Journal of Mental Deficiency Monograph* (Suppl. 64). New York: American Association on Mental Deficiency.

HEDGE, R., & JOHNSON, W. (1986, October). Serving rural families of developmentally disabled in a cost-effective manner. Paper presented at the annual conference of the National Rural and Small Schools Consortium, Bellingham, WA.

HEDLUND, R. (1989). Fostering positive social interactions between parents and infants. *Teaching Exceptional Children, 21*(4), 45–48.

HEINICKE, C., CARLIN, E., & GIVEN, K. (1984). Parent and mother-infant groups: Building a support system. *Young children, 39*, 21–27.

HEINICKE, C.M., DISKIN, S.D., RAMSEY-KLEE, D.M., & GIVEN, K. (1983). Pre-birth parent characteristics and family development in the first year of life. *Child Development, 54*, 194–208.

HEINICKE, C.M. & LAMPL, E. (1988). Pre- and post-birth antecedents of 3- and 4-year-old attention, IQ, verbal expressiveness, task orientation, and capacity for relationships. *Infant Behavior and Development, 11*, 381–410.

HELFER, R.E. (1987). The perinatal period, a window of opportunity for enhancing parent-infant communication: An approach to prevention. *Child Abuse and Neglect, 11*, 565–579.

HELM, J.M. (1988). Adolescent mothers of handicapped children: A challenge for interventionists. *Journal of the Division for Early Childhood, 12*, 311–319.

HENDRICK, D.L., PRATHER, E.M., & TOBIN, A.R. (1984). *Sequenced inventory of communication development* (rev. ed.). Seattle, WA: The University of Washington Press.

HERIZA, C.B., & SWEENEY, J.K. (1990). Effects of NICU intervention on preterm infants: Part 1: Implications for neonatal practice. *Infants and Young Children, 2*(3), 31–48.

HETHERINGTON, E.M. (1983). Socialization in the context of the family: Parent-child interaction. In P.H. Mussen (Ed.), *Handbook of child psychology:* Vol. IV. Socialization, pesonality, and social development. New York: John Wiley & Sons.

HIRTZ, D.G. ELLENBERG, J.H. & NELSON K.B. (1984). The risk of recurrence of nonfebrile seizures in children. *Neurology, 34*, 637–641.

HOFF-GINSBERG, E. (1986). Function and structure in maternal speech: Their relationship to the child's development of syntax. *Developmental Psychology, 22*, 155–163.

HOFFMAN, H.R. (1982). *The Bayley scales of infant development: Modifications for youngsters with handicapping conditions*. Commack, NY: United Cerebral Palsy Association of Greater Suffolk.

HOLADAY, B. (1987). Patterns of interaction between mothers and their chronically ill infants. *Maternal Child Nursing Journal, 16*(1), 29–45.

HOLDGRAFER, G., & DUNST, C. (1986). Communicative competence: From research to practice. *Topics in Early Childhood Special Education, 6*(3), 1–22.

HOLMES, D.L., REICH, J.N., & PASTERNAK, J.F. (1984). *The development of infants born at risk*. Hillsdale, NJ: Lawrence Erlbaum Associates.

HONIG, A.S. (1982). Evaluation of infant/toddler intervention programs. *Studies in Educational Evaluation, 8*, 305–316.

HONIG, A.S. (1984a). Reflections on infant intervention programs: What have we learned? *Journal of Children in Contemporary Society, 17*, 81–92.

HONIG, A.S. (1984b). Working partnership with parents of handicapped infants. *Early Child Development and Care, 14*, 13–36.

HONIG, A.S. (1987). Quality infant/toddler caregiving: Are there magic recipes? Paper presented at a teacher conference of the Lomas and Nettleton Child Care Center, Dallas, TX.

HOOKER, D. (1939). Fetal behavior. *Research Publications of the Association for Nervous and Mental Disorders, 19,* 237–243.

HOOKER, D. (1952). *The prenatal origin of behavior.* Lawrence: University of Kansas Press.

HOOKER, D. (1969). *The prenatal origin of behavior.* New York: Hafner.

HORBAR, J.D., PASNICK, M., & MCAULIFFE, T.L. et al. (1983). Obstetric events and risk of periventricular hemorrhage in premature infants. *American Journal of Diseases of Children, 137,* 678–681.

HOROWITZ, F.D., & LINN, P. (1984). Uses of the NBAS in research. In T.B. Brazelton (Ed.), *Neonatal behavioral assessment scale* (2nd ed., pp. 97–104). Philadelphia: J.B. Lippincott.

HOUSTON, J.P. (1986). *Learning and memory.* Orlando, FL: Harcourt Brace.

HOWARD, J. (1989, February). Developmental patterns for infants prenatally exposed to drugs. Presentation at Perinatal Substance Abuse Educational Forum, California Legislative Ways and Means Committee, Sacramento.

HOWARD, J., BECKWITH, L., RODNING, C., & KROPENSKE, V. (1989). The development of young children of substance-abusing parents: Insights from seven years of intervention and research. *Zero to Three, 9*(5), 8–12.

HRONSKY, S.L., & EMORY, E.K. (1987). Neurobehavioral effects of caffeine on the neonate. *Infant Behavior and Development, 10,* 61–80.

HUBERT, N.C. (1989). Parental subjective reactions to perceived temperament behavior in their 6- and 24-month-old children. *Infant Behavior and Development, 12,* 185–198.

HULME, T.S. (1985). *The Iowa program to provide coordinated services for children who need technical medical care in their home/community: A network approach.* Paper presented at the Biennial National Training Institute of the National Center for Clinical Infant Programs, Washington, DC.

HUNT, J.V. (1983). Environmental risks in fetal and neonatal life as biological determinants of infant intelligence. In M. Lewis (Ed.), *Origins of intelligence: Infancy and early childhood.* New York: Plenum Press.

HUNT, J.V. & COOPER, B.A.B. (1989). Differentiating the risk from high-risk preterm infants. In P. Fedor-Freybergh & M.L.V. Vogel (Eds.), *Prenatal and perinatal psychology and medicine; Encounter with the unborn.* Lancaster, UK: Parthenon Publishing Group.

HUSSEY, B. (1988). *Understanding my signals.* Palo Alto: VORT.

HUTINGER, P.L. (1986). Sharing centers for handicapped infants and toddlers: Settings for parent and child interaction and growth. *Rural Special Education Quarterly, 7,* 6–9.

HUTLINER, P. (1988). Stress: Is it an inevitable condition for families of children at risk? *Teaching Exceptional Children, 20,* 36–39.

IANNIRUBERTO, A., & TAJANI, E. (1981). Ultrasonographic study of fetal movements. *Seminars in Perinatology, 5,* 175–181.

IATRIDES, M. (1988). Educating the educators: Infant care-giving in early childhood education and the training of infant educators. In E.D. Hibbs (Ed.), *Children and families; Studies in prevention and intervention.* Madison, WI: International Universities Press.

ICN INTERACT OUTREACH PROJECT. *Final report, July 1, 1983–August 30, 1984.* Oakland, CA: Children's Hospital Medical Center of Northern California.

INTENT HEARING RESOURCE STAFF (1975). *Parent-infant communication.* Portland, OR: IHR Publications.

IRELAND, W.W. (1900). *The mental affections of children: Idiocy, imbecility and insanity.* Philadelphia: Balkiston.

IRETON, H., & THWING, E. (1979). *Minnesota child development inventory.* Minneapolis: Behavior Science Systems.

ITAGLIATA, J. (1982). Improving the quality of community care for the chronically mentally disabled: The role of case management. *Schizophrenia Bulletin,* 8(4), 12–19.

JACOBSON, J.W., et al. (1984). Factors and clusters for the Brazelton scale: An investigation of the dimensions of neonatal behavior. *Developmental Psychology,* 20(3), 339–353.

JACOBSON, S., FEIN, G., JACOBSON, J., SCHWARTZ, P., & DOWLER, J. (1984). Neonatal correlates of prenatal exposure to smoking, caffeine, and alcohol. *Infant Behavior and Development, 7,* 253–265.

JENKINS, J.P., FEWELL, R.R., & HARRIS, S.R. (1983). A comparison of sensory integration therapy and motor programming. *American Journal of Mental Deficiency, 88,* 221–224.

JOHNSON, B., MARTIN, N., JENS, K.G., & ATTERMEIER, S.M. (1986). *The Carolina curriculum for handicapped infants and infants at risk.* Baltimore: Paul H. Brookes.

JOHNSON, B., MCGONIGEL, M., & KAUFMANN, R. (Eds.) (1989). *Guidelines for recommended practices for the Individualized Family Service Plan.* Chapel Hill, NC: NECTAS.

JOHNSON, J.E., CHRISTIE, J.F., & YAWKEY, T.D. (1987). *Play and early childhood development.* Glenview, IL: Scott, Foresman, & Company.

JOHNSON-MARTIN, N., JENS, K.G., & ATTERMEIER, S. (1986). *Carolina curriculum for handicapped infants and infants at risk.* Baltimore: Paul H. Brookes.

JONES, C.L., & LOPEZ, R. (1988). Direct and indirect effects on the infant of maternal drug use. United States Department of Health and Human services/ National Institutes of Health.

JONES, K.L., SMITH, D.W., ULLELAND, L., & STREISSGUTH, A.P. (1973). Recognition of the fetal alcohol syndrome in early infancy. *Lancet, 2,* 99–100.

JONES, O.H.M. (1977). Mother-child communication with prelinguistic Down's Syndrome and normal infants. In H.R. Schaffer, (Ed.)., *Studies in mother-infant interaction* (pp. 379–401). New York: Academic Press.

JONES, O.H.M. (1980). Prelinguistic communication skills in Down's syndrome and normal infants. In T.M. Field, S. Goldberg, D.M. Stern, & A.M. Sostek (Eds), *High-risk infants and children: Adult and peer interactions* (pp. 205–225), New York: Academic Press.

KAGAN, J., KEARSLEY, R.B., & ZELAZO, P.R. (1978). *Infancy: It's place in human development.* Cambridge, MA: Harvard University Press.

KAGAN, J., REZNICK, J.S., & GIBBONS, J. (1989). Inhibited and uninhibited types of children. *Child Development, 60,* 838–845.

KAHN, J.V. (1976). Utility of the Uzgiris and Hunt scales of sensorimotor development with severely and profoundly retarded children. *American Journal of Mental Deficiency, 80,* 663–334.

KANNER, L. (1943). Autistic disturbances of affective contact. *Nervous child, 2,* 217–250.

KARNES, M.B. (1981). Small wonder. Circle Pines, MN: American Guidance Service.

KATZ, K.S., POKORNI, J.L., & LONG, T.M. (1989). *Chronically ill and at risk infants.* Palo Alto: VORT.

KAZAK, A.E. (1987). Professional helpers and families with disabled children: A social network perspective. In M. Ferrari and M.B. Sussman (Eds.), *Childhood disability and family systems.* New York: The Haworth Press.

KENNEL, J.H., VOOS, D.K., & KLAUS, M.H. (1979). Parent-infant bonding. In J.D. Osofsky (Ed.), *Handbook of infant development.* New York: John Wiley & Sons.

KEOGH, B.K., & KOPP, C.B. (1978). From assessment to intervention: An elusive bridge. In F.D. Minifie & L.L. Lloyd (Eds.), *Communicative and cognitive abilities—Early behavioral assessment* (pp. 523–547). Baltimore: University Park Press.

KEREN, B., & ROMMENS, J.M. (1990). Identification of the cystic fibrosis gene: Genetic analysis. *Science, 245* (4922), 1073.

KESSEN, W. (1965). *The child.* New York: John Wiley & Sons.

KITCHEN, W., FORD, G., ORGILL, A., et al. (1984). Outcome of infants with birthweights 500 to 999 gm: A regional study of 1979 and 1980 births. *Journal of Pediatrics, 104*, 921–927.

KLAUS, M.H., & FANAROFF, A.A. (1979). *Care of the high-risk neonate* (2nd. ed.). Philadelphia: W. B. Saunders.

KLAUS, M.H., & KENNELL, J. (1976). *Maternal-infant bonding*. St. Louis, MO: C.V. Mosby.

KLAUS, M.H., & KENNELL, J.H. (1981). *Parent-infant bonding*. St. Louis: C.V. Mosby.

KLAUS, M., & KENNEL, J. (1983). An evaluation in the premature nursery. In J. Davis, M. Richards, & N. Robertson (Eds.), *Parent-baby attachment in premature infants*. New York: St. Martin's Press.

KLEIN, B., VAN HASSELT, V. B., TREFELNER, M., & SANDSTROM, D.J. (1988). The parent and toddler training project for visually impaired and blind multihandicapped children. *Journal of Visual Impairment and Blindness, 82*(2), 59–64.

KLEIN, N.K. (1988). Children who were very low birthweight: Cognitive abilities and classroom behavior at five years of age. *Journal of Special Education, 22*(1), 41–54.

KLEIN, P.S., RAZIEL, P., BRISH, M., & BIRENBAUM, E. (1987). Cognitive performance of 3 year olds born at very low birth weight. *Journal of Psychosomatic Obstetrics and Gynaecology, 7*, 117–129.

KLINE, M., TSCHANN, J.M., JOHNSTON, J.R., & WALLERSTEIN, J.S. (1989). Children's adjustment in joint and sole physical custody families. *Developmental Psychology, 25*, 430–438.

KLINZING, D.G., & KLINZING, D.R. (1987). The hospitalization of a child and family responses. In M. Ferrari & M.B. Sussman (Eds.), *Childhood disability and family systems*. New York: Haworth Press.

KNOBLOCH, H., & PASAMANICK, B. (1974). *Developmental diagnosis*. Hagerstown, MD: Harper & Row.

KNOBLOCH, H., STEVENS, F., & MALONE, A.F. (1980). *The revised developmental screening inventory*. Houston, TX: Gesell Developmental Test Materials.

KOCHANEK, T.T. (1985). *Project access V: An investigation of the impact of P.L. 89-313 funds on early intervention programs: Summative evaluation reports 1984 and 1985*. Boston, MA: Massachusetts State Department of Public Health.

KOLB, B. & FANTIE, B. (1989). Development of the child's brain and behavior. In C.R. Reynolds & E. Fletcher-Janzen, *Handbook of clinical child neuropsychology*. New York: Plenum Press.

KONIAK-GRIFFIN, D., & LUDINGTON-HOE, S.M. (1987). Paradoxical effects of stimulation on normal neonates. *Infant Behavior and Development, 10*, 261–277.

KOPF, R.C., & MCFADDEN, E.L. (1974). Nursing intervention in the crisis of new born illness. *Journal of Nursing Midwifery, 16*, 629–636.

KOPP, C.B. (1987). Developmental risk: Historical reflections. In J.D. Osofsky (Ed.), *Handbook of infant development*, 2nd ed., (pp. 881–912). New York: John Wiley & Sons.

KOPP, C.B. (1989). Regulation of distress and negative emotions: A developmental view. *Developmental Psychology, 25*, 343–354.

KORNER, A.F. (1985, April). Effects of waterbeds on preterm infants. Paper presented at the biennial meeting of the Society for Research in Child Development, Toronto.

KORNER, A.F. (1988). Early intervention with preterm infants. In E.D. Hibbs (Ed.), *Children and families: Studies in prevention and intervention*. Madison, WI: International Universities Press.

KORNER, A.F., KRAEMER, H.C., HAFFNER, M.E., & COSPER, L.M. (1975). Effects of waterbed flotation on premature infants: A pilot study. *Pediatrics, 56*, 361–367.

KOTELCHUCK, M. (1976). The infant's relationship to the father: Experimental evidence. In M.E. Lamb (Ed.), *The role of the father in child development* (pp. 329–344). New York: John Wiley & Sons.

KRAMER, L.I., & PIERPONT, M.E. (1976). Rocking waterbeds and auditory stimuli to enhance growth of preterm infants. *Journal of Pediatrics, 88,* 297–299.

KREPPNER, K., PAULSE, S., SCHUETZE, Y. (1982). Infant and family development: From triads to tetrads. *Human Development, 25,* 373–391.

KRUGMAN, S., & GERSHON, A.A. (Eds.). (1975). *Infections of the fetus and the newborn infant: Proceedings.* New York: Symposium sponsored by the New York University Medical Center and the National Foundation of the March of Dimes.

KUHL, P.K. (1987a). Perception of speech and sound in early infancy. In P. Salapatek & L.B. Cohen (Eds.), *Handbook of infant perception: Vol. 2. From perception to cognition.* Orlando, FL: Academic Press.

KUHL, P.K. (1987b). The special-mechanisms debate in speech: Categorization tests on animals and infants. In S. Harnad (Ed.), *Categorical perception: The groundwork of cognition.* New York: Cambridge University Press.

KUHL, P.K. (1988). Auditory perception and the evolution of speech. *Human Evolution, 3,* 19–43.

KYSELA, G.M., & MARFO, K. (1983). Mother-child interactions and early intervention programs for handicapped infants and young children. *Educational Psychology, 3*(3–4), 201–212.

LACY, J.R. & PENRY, J.K. (1976). *Infantile spasms.* New York: Raven Press.

LAFRENIERE, P., & SROUFE, L.A. (1985). Profiles of peer competence in the preschool: Interrelations between measures, influence of social ecology, and relation to attachment history. *Developmental Psychology, 21,* 58–68.

LAMB, M.E. (1980). The development of parent-infant attachments in the first year of life. In F.A. Pedersen (Ed.), *The father-infant relationship observational studies in a family setting.* New York: Praeger Special Studies.

LAMB, M.E. (1982a). The bonding phenomenon: Misinterpretations and their implications. *Journal of Pediatrics, 101,* 555–557.

LAMB, M.E. (1982b). Early contact and mother-infant bonding: One decade later. *Pediatrics, 70,* 763–768.

LAMB, M.E. (1987). Predictive implications of individual differences in attachment. *Journal of Consulting and Clinical Psychology, 55,* 817–824.

LAMB, M.E. (1988). Social and emotional development in infancy. In M.H. Bornstein & M.E. Lamb (Eds.), *Developmental psychology: An advanced textbook.* Hillsdale, NJ: Lawrence Erlbaum Associates.

LAMB, M.E., & BORNSTEIN, M.H. (1987). *Development in infancy: An introduction.* New York: Random House.

LAMB, M.E., HOPPS, K., & ELSTER, A.B. (1987). Strange situation behavior of infants with adolescent mothers. *Infant Behavior and Development, 10,* 39–48.

LAMB, M.E., & HWANG, C.P. (1982). Maternal attachment and mother-neonate bonding: A critical review. In M.E. Lamb & A.L. Brown (Eds.), *Advances in developmental psychology* (Vol. 2). Hillsdale, NJ: Lawrence Erlbaum Associates.

LAMB, M.E., THOMPSON, R.A., GARDNER, W., & CHARNOV, E.L. (1985). *Infant-mother attachment: The origins and developmental significance of individual differences in strange situation behavior.* Hillsdale, N.J.: Lawrence Erlbaum Associates.

LAMB, W. (1986). Parent education. In R.F. Levant (Ed.), *Psychoeducational approaches to family therapy and counseling.* New York: Springer.

LAMM, N. & GREER, R.D. (1988). Induction and maintenance of swallowing responses in infants with dysphagia. *Journal of Applied Behavior Analysis, 21,* 143–156.

LANCASTER, J.S., COLES, C.D., PLATZMAN, K.A., SMITH, I.E., & FALEK, A. (in press). Contribution of maternal alcohol, caffeine, and cigarette use on prenatal growth and neonatal neurological states. *Neurobehavioral toxicology and teratology.*

LANGLEY, M.B. (1980). *Functional vision inventory for the multiple and severely handicapped.* Chicago: Stoelting.

LANGLEY, P. (1983). Exploring the space of cognitive architectures. *Behavior Research Methods and Instrumentation, 15,* 289–299.

LAZAR, I., DARLINGTON, R., MURRAY, H., ROYCE, J., & SNIPPER, A. (1982). Lasting effects of early intervention: A report from the Consortium for Longitudinal Studies. *Monographs of the Society for Research in Child Development, 47* (2–3, Serial No. 195).

LEGUM, C. (1985). Antenatal screening for fetal malformations and genetic disorders. In S. Harel & N. Anastasiow (Eds.), *The at-risk infant: Psycho/socio/medical aspects.* Baltimore: Paul H. Brookes.

LEIBSON, C., BROWN, M.S., & MOORE, L.G. (1986). Neonatal hyperbilirubinemia is more common at high than low altitude in Colorado. *American Journal of Physical Anthropology, 69,* 228.

LEIDERMAN, P.H. (1989). Relationship disturbances and development through the life cycle. In A.J. Sameroff & R.N. Emde (Eds.), *Relationship disturbances in early childhood: A developmental approach.* New York: Basic Books.

LeLAURIN, K. (1985). The experimental analysis of the effects of early intervention with normal, at-risk, and handicapped children under three. *Analysis and Intervention in Developmental Disabilities, 5,* 128–150.

LENNEBERG, E. (1967). *Biological foundations of language.* New York: John Wiley & Sons.

LEUNG, B. (1987). Cultural considerations in working with Asian parents. Paper presented at the conference of the National Center for Clinical Infant Programs, Los Angeles, February.

LEVANT, R.F. (1986). An overview of psychoeducational family programs. In R.F. Levant (Ed.), *Psychoeducational approaches to family therapy and counseling.* New York: Springer.

LEVANT, R.F. (1986). Client-centered skills-training programs for the family. In R.F. Levant (Ed.), *Psychoeducational approaches to family therapy and counseling.* New York: Springer.

LEVINE, M.H., & McCOLOUM, J.A. (1983). Peer play and toys: Key factors in mainstreaming infants. *Young Children, 38*(5), 22–26.

LEWIS, M. (1984). Developmental principles and their implications for at-risk and handicapped infants. In M.J. Hanson (Ed.), *Atypical infant development* (pp. 3–24). Austin, TX: Pro-Ed.

LEWIS, M., & FEIRING, C. (1989). Infant, mother, and mother-infant interaction behavior and subsequent attachment. *Child Development, 60,* 831–837.

LEWIS, M., FEIRING, C., McGUFFOG, C., & JASKIR, J. (1984). Predicting psychopathology in six-year-olds from early social relations. *Child Development, 55,* 123–136.

LIEBMAN, R., & ZIFFER, R.L. (1985). Case consultation within a family systems framework. In R.L. Ziffer (Ed.), *Adjunctive techniques in family therapy.* New York: Grune and Stratton.

LILLY, T.J., & SHOTEL, J.R. (1987). Legal issues and the handicapped infant: From policy to reality. *Journal of the Division for Early Childhood, 12,* 4–12.

LINDEMANN, J.E., & LINDEMANN, S.J. (1987). A typology of childhood disorders and related support services. In M. Ferrari and M.B. Sussman (Eds.), *Childhood disability and family systems.* New York: Haworth Press.

LINDER, T.W. (1982). Pleasurable play: Its value for handicapped infants and their parents. *Journal for Special Educators, 19,* 59–68.

LINDER, T.W. (1989). *Transdisciplinary play-based assessment.* Baltimore: Paul H. Brookes.

LING, D. (1984). *Early intervention for hearing impaired children: Total communication options.* New York: College Hill Press.

LIPPMAN, A., & EVANS, J. (1987). Screening for maternal serum of fetoprotein: What about the low side. *Canadian Medical Association Journal, 136,* 801.

LIPSITT, L.P. (1977). The study of sensory and learning processes of the newborn. Symposium on Neonatal Neurology. *Clinics in Perinatology, 4,* 163–186.

LITTMAN, G., & PARMELEE, A.H. (1978). Medical correlates of infant development. *Pediatrics, 61,* 470–474.

LONDON, R. (1982). Optokinetic nystagmus: A review of pathways, techniques, and selected diagnostic applications. *Journal of the American Optometric Association, 53,* 791–798.

LOU, H.C. (1985). Perinatal hypoxic-ischemic brain damage and periventricular hemorrhage: The pathogenic significance of arterial pressure changes. In S. Harel & N.J. Anastasiow (Eds.), *The at-risk infant: Psycho/socio/medical aspects.* Baltimore: Paul H. Brookes.

LOURIE, R.S. (1988). Implications for intervention and service delivery: Cross-cultural considerations. In E.D. Hibbs (Ed.), *Children and families: Studies in prevention and intervention.* Madison, WI: International Universities Press.

LOWENTHAL, B. (1987). Stress factors and their alleviation in parents of high risk preterm infants. *Exceptional Child, 34,* 21–30.

LOWENTHAL, B. (1988). United States Public Law 99–457: An ounce of prevention. *Exceptional Child, 35,* 57–60.

LUTKENHAUS, P., GROSSMAN, E.E., & GROSSMAN, K. (1985). Infant-mother attachment at twelve months and style of interaction with a stranger at the age of three years. *Child Development, 56,* 1538–1542.

LYDIC, J.S., & NUGENT, J.K. (1982). Theoretical background and uses of the Brazelton neonatal assessment scale. *Physical and Occupational Therapy in Pediatrics, 2*(2–3), 117–131.

MACCOBY, E.E., & JACKLIN, C.N. (1983). The "person" characteristics of children and the family as environment. In D. Magnusson & V.L. Allen (Eds.), *Human development: An interactional perspective.* New York: Academic Press.

MACCOBY, E.E., & MARTIN, J.A. (1983). Socialization in the context of the family: Parent-child interaction. In P.M. Mussen (Ed.), *Handbook of Child Psychology: Vol. IV. Socialization, personality, and social development.* New York: John Wiley & Sons.

MACDONALD, J.D., & GILLETTE, Y. (1989). *Eco: A Partnership Program* (kit). San Antonio, Tx. Special Press, Inc.

MACEY, T.J., HARMON, R.J., & EASTERBROOKS, M.A. (1987). Impact of premature birth on the development of the infant in the family. *Journal of Consulting and Clinical Psychology, 55,* 846–852.

MAHONEY, G., FINGER, I., & POWELL, A. (1985). The relationship of maternal behavioral style to the developmental status of organically impaired mentally retarded infants. *American Journal of Mental Deficiency, 90,* 296–302.

MAHONEY, G., & POWELL, A. (1986). *Transactional intervention program: A child centered approach to developmental intervention with young handicapped children.* (Monograph No. 1). Farmington, CT: Pediatric Research and Training Center, University of Connecticut School of Medicine.

MAHONEY, G., & POWELL, A. (1988). Modifying parent-child interactions: Enhancing the development of handicapped children. *Journal of Special Education, 22*(1), 82–96.

MAHONEY, G., POWELL, A., & FINGER, I. (1986). The maternal behavior rating scale. *Topics in Early Childhood Special Education, 6*(2), 44–56.

MAHONEY, G., & ROBENALT, K. (1986). A comparison of conversational patterns between mothers and their Down syndrome and normal infants. *Journal of the Division for Early Childhood, 10,* 172–180.

MAIN, M. & CASSIDY, J. (1988). Categories of response to reunion with the parent at age 6: Predictable from infant attachment classifications and stable over a 1-month period. *Developmental Psychology, 24,* 15–26.

MAIN, M., KAPLAN, N., & CASSIDY, J. (1985). Security in infancy, childhood and adulthood: A move to the level of representation. In I. Bretherton & E. Waters (Eds.), Growing points of attachment theory and research. *Monographs of the Society for Research in Child Development, 50* (1-2, Serial No. 209).

MAIN, M., & SOLOMON, J. (1986). Discovery of an insecure-disorganized/disoriented attachment pattern. In T.B. Brazelton and M.W. Yogman (Eds.), *Affective development in infancy*. Norwood, NJ: Ablex.

Maine Interdepartmental Coordinating Committee for Preschool Handicapped Children. (1987). *Early intervention project. Summary report, narrative report, and supplemental report*. Maine State Department of Mental Health and Mental Retardation, Augusta, ME.

MANOLSON, A. (1985). *It takes two to talk*. Toronto: Hanen Early Language Resource Center.

MARFO, K. (1988). *Parent-child interaction and developmental disabilities: Theory, research, and intervention*. New York: Praeger Publishers.

MARFO, K., & KYSELA, G.M. (1985). Early intervention with mentally handicapped children. A critical appraisal of applied research. *Journal of Pediatric Psychology, 10*(3), 305-324.

MARSHALL, N.R., HEGRENES, J.R., & GOLDSTEIN, S. (1973). Verbal interactions: Mothers and their retarded children vs. mothers and their non-retarded children. *American Journal of Mental Deficiency, 77*, 415-419.

MARTIN, J.A. (1981). A longitudinal study of the consequences of early mother-infant interaction: A microanalytic approach. *Monographs of the Society for Research in Child Development, 46*(3, Serial NO. 190).

MATAS, L., AREND, R., & SROUFE, L.A. (1978). Continuity of adaptation in the second year. The relationship between quality of attachment and later competent functioning. *Child Development, 49*, 547-555.

MATHER, J. & WEINSTEIN, E. (1988). Teachers and therapists: Evolution of a partnership in early intervention. *Topics in Early Childhood Special Education, 7*, 1-9.

MATIAS, R., COHN, J.F., & ROSS, S. (1989). A comparison of two systems that code infant affective expression. *Developmental Psychology, 25*, 483-489.

McADOO, H.P. (1983). Societal stress: The black family. In H.I. McCubbin & C.R. Figley (Eds.), *Stress and the family: Vol. I. Coping with normative transitions*. St. Paul, MN: Family Stress Project, University of Minnesota.

McCALL, R. (1971). New directions in psychological assessment of infants. *Proceedings of the Royal Society of Medicine, 64*, 465-467.

McCALL, R.B. (1979). The development of intellectual functioning in infancy and the prediction of later IQ. In J.D. Osofsky (Ed.), *Handbook of infant development*. New York: John Wiley & Sons.

McCALL, R.B. (1981). Predicting developmental outcome: Resume and redirection. In C.C. Brown (Ed.), *Infants at risk: Assessment and intervention* (pp. 57-69). Palm Beach, FL: Johnson and Johnson.

McCALL, R.B. (1982). A conceptual approach to early mental development. In M. Lewis (Ed.), *Origins of intelligence* (2nd ed.). New York: Plenum.

McCOLLUM, J.A. (1984). Social interaction between parents and babies: Validation of an intervention procedure. *Child: Care, Health, and Development, 10*, 301-315.

McCOLLUM, J.A. (1986). Charting different types of social interaction objectives in parent-infant dyads. *Journal of the Division for Early Childhood, 11*, 28-45.

McCOLLUM, J.A., & STAYTON, V.D. (1985). Infant/parent interaction: Studies and intervention guidelines based on the S1A1 model. *Journal of the Division for Early Childhood, 9*(2), 125-135.

McCOLLUM, J.A., & THORP, E.K. (1988). Training of infant specialists: A look to the future. *Infants and Young Children, 1*, 55-65.

McCUBBIN, H.I., COMEAU, J., & HANKINS, J. (1981). Family inventory of resources for management. In H.I. McCubbin & J. Patterson (Eds.), *Family stress, resources, and coping: Tools for research education and clinical intervention.* St. Paul, MN: Family Stress Project, University of Minnesota.

McCUBBIN, H.I., & PATTERSON, J.M. (1983). Family transitions: Adaptation to stress. In H.I. McCubbin and C.R. Figley (Eds.), *Stress and the family: Vol. I. Coping with normative transitions.* St. Paul, MN: Family Stress Project, University of Minnesota.

McCUNE-NICOLICH, L. (1980). A manual for analyzing free play. New Brunswick: Douglas College, Rutgers University.

McCUNE—NICOLICH, L., & RUFF, H.A. (1985). Infant special education: Interactions with objects. *Topics in Early Childhood Special Education, 5,* 59–67.

McDEVITT, S.C. (1986). Continuity and discontinuity of temperament in infancy and early childhood: A psychometric perspective. In R. Plomin & J. Dunn (Eds.), *The study of temperament: Changes, continuities and challenges.* Hillsdale, NJ: Lawrence Erlbaum Associates.

McDEVITT, S.C. (1988). Assessment of temperament in developmentally disabled infants and preschoolers. In T. Wachs & R. Sheehan (Eds.), *Assessment of young developmentally disabled children* (pp. 255–265). New York: Plenum.

McDONOUGH, S.C. (1984). Intervention programs for adolescent mothers and their offspring. *Journal of Children in Contemporary Society, 17,* 67–78.

McGONIGEL, M.J. & GARLAND, C.W. (1988). The individualized family service plan and the early intervention team: Team and family issues and recommended practices. *Infants and Young Children, 1*(1), 10–21.

McHALE, S.M. & GAMBLE, W.C. (1989). Sibling relationships of children with disabled and nondisabled brothers and sisters. *Developmental Psychology, 25,* 421–429.

McKUSICK, V. (1988). *Mendelian inheritance in man* (8th ed.) Baltimore: Johns Hopkins Press.

McLEAN, J.E., SNYDER-McLEAN, L.K., & SACK, S. (1982). *A transactional approach to early language training: A mediated program for inservice professionals.* Columbus, OH: Charles Merrill.

McNULTY, B.A., WIDERSTROM, A., GOODWIN, L., & CAMPBELL, S. (1988). Who should be served, where, and why: Local special education administrators' views. *Topics in Early Childhood Special Education, 8,* 51–60.

MEDNICK, S.A., & MEDNICK, B. (1984). A brief history of North American longitudinal research. In S.A. Mednick, M. Harway, & K.M. Finello (Eds.), *Handbook of longitudinal research.* New York: Praeger.

MEISELS, S.J. (1984). The efficacy of early intevention: Why are we still asking this question? *Topics in Early Childhood Special Education, 5*(2), 1–11.

MEREDITH, H.V. (1978). *Human body growth in the first ten years of life.* Columbia, SC: State Printing Company.

MESSER, D.J., & VIETZE, P.M. (1988). Does mutual influence occur during mother-infant social gaze? *Infant Behavior and Development, 11,* 97–110.

MEYER, D.J. (1982). Involving fathers of handicapped infants: Translating research into program goals. *Journal of the Division of Early Childhood, 5,* 64–72.

MILLER, B.C., & MYERS-WALLS, J.A. (1983). Parenthood: Stresses and coping strategies. In H.I. McCubbin and C.R. Figley (Eds.), *Stress and the family: Vol. I. Coping with normative transitions.* St. Paul, MN: Family Stress Project, University of Minnesota.

MILLER, G. (1989a). Addicted infants and their mothers. *Zero to Three, 9*(5), 20–23.

MILLER, G. (1989b). *Giving children a chance: The case for more effective neonatal policies.* Lanham, MD: University Press of America.

MILLER, P.H. (1989). *Theories of developmental psychology.* New York: W.H. Freeman and Company.

MILLER, S.A. (1987). *Developmental research methods.* Englewood Cliffs, NJ: Prentice Hall.

MINDE, K.K., & MINDE, R. (1982). Psychiatric intervention in infancy: A review. *Annual Progress in Child Psychiatry and Child Development, Vol. 2*, 463–483.

MINDE, K.K., PERROTTA, M., & MARTON, P. (1985). Maternal caretaking and play with full-term and premature infants. *Journal of Child Psychology and Psychiatry and Allied Disciplines, 26*, 231–244.

MINDE, K., SHOSENBERG, N., THOMPSON, J., & MARTON, P. (1983). Self-help groups in a premature nursery: Follow-up at one year. In J.D. Call, E. Galenson, & R.L. Tyson (Eds.), *Frontiers in infant psychiatry* (pp. 363–378). New York: Basic Books.

MINUCHIN, P. (1985). Families and individual development: Provocations from the field of family therapy. *Child Development, 56*, 289–302.

MINUCHIN, S. (1974). *Families and family therapy.* Cambridge, MA: Harvard University Press.

MINUCHIN, S. (1980). *Structural family therapy: Activating alternatives within a therapeutic system.* Philadelphia: Smith, Kline & French Laboratories Report #3.

MINUCHIN, S., & FISHMAN, H.C. (1981). *Family therapy techniques.* Cambridge, MA: Harvard University Press.

MINUCHIN, S., MONTALVO, B., GUERNEY, B., ROSMAN, B., & SCHUMER, F. (1967). *Families of the slums.* New York: Basic Books.

MINUCHIN, S., ROSMAN, B.L., BAKER, L., & LIEBMAN, R. (1978). *Psychosomatic families: Anorexia nervosa in context.* Cambridge, MA: Harvard University Press.

MIRANDA, S., HACK, M., FANTZ, R., FANAROFF, A., & KLAUS, M. (1977). Neonatal pattern vision: A predictor of future mental performance? *Pediatrics, 91*, 642–647.

MISTRETTA, C.M. & BRADLEY, R.M. (1977). Taste in utero: Theoretical considerations. In J.M. Weiffenbach (Ed.), *Taste and development: The genesis of sweet preference.* Washington, DC: U.S. Government Printing Office.

MOFFAT, R.J., & HACKEL, A. (1985). Thermal aspects of neonatal care. In A.W. Gottfried & J.L. Gaiter (Eds.), *Infant stress under intensive care: Environmental neonatalogy* (pp. 171–198). Baltimore: University Park Press.

MOLFESE, M.J. (1989). *Perinatal risk and infant development: Assessment and prediction.* New York: Guilford Press.

MOORE, L.G., NEWBERRY, M.A., FREEBY, G.M., & CRNIC, L.S. (1984). Increased incidence of neonatal hyperbilirubinemia at 3,100 m in Colorado. *American Journal of Diseases of Children, 138*, 157–161.

MOORE, L.G., & REEVES, J.T. (1983, December). Maternal arterial oxygenation is a determinant of infant birth weight at high altitude (3,100 m). In *Adjustment to high altitude.* Proceedings of the International Symposium on Acclimatization, Adaptation and Tolerance to High Altitude, National Institutes of Health, Washington, DC.

MOORE, L.G., & REGENSTEINER, J.G. (1983). Adaptation to high altitude. *Annual Reviews of Anthropology, 12*, 285–304.

MOORE, S. (1984). The need for programs and services for visually handicapped infants. *Education of the Visually Handicapped, 16*, 48–57.

MOOS, R.H. (1974). *Family environment scale.* Palo Alto, CA: Consulting Psychologists Press.

MORSE, M.T. (1983). The MICE Project: An innovative service delivery system for visually handicapped children. *Journal of Visual Impairment and Blindness, 77*, 52–55.

MOWDER, B.A., WIDERSTROM, A.H., & SANDALL, S.R. (1989). School psychologists serving at-risk and handicapped infants, toddlers and their families. *Professional School Psychology, 4*(3), 159–171.

MOWDER, B.A., WILLIS, W.G., & WIDERSTROM, A.H. (1985). Consultation with parents of handicapped infants: A model for practice. Paper presented at the annual meeting of National Association of School Psychologists, Las Vegas.

MOYERS, A.J. (1989). *Parents as case managers.* Albuquerque, NM: New Ways Publishing.

MUELLER, H.A. (1972). Facilitating feeding and prespeech. In P.H. Pearson & C.E. Williams (Eds.), *Physical therapy services in the developmental disabilities* (pp. 283–310). Springfield, IL: Charles Thomas.

MUSICK, J.S., & HOUSEHOLDER, J. (1986). *Infant development: From theory to practice.* Belmont, CA: Wadsworth Publishing Company.

MUSSELWHITE, C.R. (1986). *Adaptive play for special needs children: Strategies to enhance communication and learning.* San Diego: College-Hill Press.

MYERS, B.J. (1987). Mother-infant bonding: The status of this critical-period hypothesis. In M.H. Bornstein (Ed.), *Sensitive periods in development: Interdisciplinary perspectives.* Hillsdale, NJ: Lawrence Erlbaum Associates.

NARAYANAN, I., DUA, K., GUJRAL, V., MEHTA, D.K., MATTHEW, M., & PRABHAKAR, A. (1982). A simple method for assessment of gestational age in newborn infants. *Pediatrics, 69,* 27–32.

National Center for Health Statistics. (1978). Hospital handbook on birth registration and fetal death reports. Hyattsville, MD: United States Department of Health, Education, and Welfare.

NEISWORTH, J.T., & BAGNATO, S.J. (1988). Assessment in early childhood special education: A typology of dependent measures. In S.L. Odom & M.B. Karnes (Eds.), *Early intervention for infants and children with handicaps* (pp. 23–49). Baltimore: Paul H. Brookes.

NELSON, B. (1989). A comprehensive program for pregnant adolescents: Parenting and prevention. *Child Welfare, 68*(1), 57–60.

NELSON, C.L., & HALLGREN, R.A. (1989). Gastrostomies: Indications, management, and weaning. *Infants and Young Children, 2*(1), 66–74.

NELSON, K.B. & ELLENBERG, J.H. (Eds.) (1981). *Febrile seizures.* New York: Raven Press.

NELSON, K.E. (1987). Some observations from the perspective of the rare event cognitive comparison theory of language acquisition. In K.E. Nelson & A. Van Kleek (Eds.), *Children's language* (Vol. 6, pp. 289–331). Hillsdale, NJ: Lawrence Erlbaum Associates.

NEWBORG, J., STOCK, J.R., WNEK, L., GUIDUBALDI, J., & SVINICKI, J. (1984). *Battelle developmental inventory.* Allen, TX: Teaching Resources.

NEWMAN, J. (1987). Background forces in policies for care and treatment of disability. In M. Ferrari & M.B. Sussman (Eds.), *Childhood disability and family systems.* New York: Haworth Press.

NICOL, A.R. (Ed.). (1985). *Longitudinal studies in child psychology and psychiatry.* New York: John Wiley & Sons.

NOBLE, J.H., JR. (1987). Ethical considerations facing society in rehabilitating severely disabled persons. In M. Ferrari & M.B. Sussman (Eds.), *Childhood disability and family systems.* New York: Haworth Press.

NORA, J.J., & FRASER, F.C. (1989). Medical genetics: Principles and practice. Philadelphia: Lea & Febiger.

NUGENT, J.K. (1985). *Using the NBAS with infants and their families.* White Plains, NY: March of Dimes.

ODOM, S.L. (1985). Early intervention for handicapped children in Germany and the United States: A comparative view. *Journal of the Division for Early Childhood, 9,* 215–218.

ODOM, S.L., & WARREN, S.F. (1987). Early childhood special education in the year 2000. Paper presented at the annual conference of the Division for Early Childhood, Denver, CO.

ODOM, S.L., YODER, P., & HILL, G. (1988). Developmental intervention for infants with handicaps: Purposes and programs. *Journal of Special Education, 22*(1), 11–24.

OLSEN-FULERO, L. (1982). Style and stability in mother conversational behaviour: A study of individual differences. *Journal of Child Language, 9*, 543–564.

OLSON, S.L., BATES, J.E., & BAYLES, K. (1984). Mother-infant interaction and the development of individual differences in children's cognitive competence. *Developmental Psychology, 20*, 166–179.

OLSWANG, L., STOEL-GAMMON, C., COGGINS, T., & CARPENTER, R. (1987). *Assessing prelinguistic and early linguistic behaviors in developmentally young children.* Seattle: University of Washington Press.

ORENSTEIN, S.R., WHITINGTON, P.F., & ORENSTEIN, D.M. (1983). The infant seat as treatment for gastroesophageal reflux. *New England Journal of Medicine, 309*, 760–763.

ORNITZ, E.M. & RITVO, E.R. (1977). The syndrome of autism: A critical review. In S. Chess & A. Thomas (Eds.), *Annual progress in psychiatry and child development.* New York: Brunner/Mazel.

O'SULLIVAN, S.B. (1985–86). Infant-caregiver interaction and the social development of handicapped infants. *Physical and Occupational Therapy in Pediatrics, 5*(4), 1–12.

OSWALD, I. (1969). Human brain protein, drugs and dreams. *Nature, 233*, 893.

PALKOVITZ, R., & WOLFE, C.B. (1987). Rights of children born with disabilities: Issues, inconsistencies, and recommendations for advocacy. In M. Ferrari & M.B. Sussman (Eds.), *Childhood disability and family systems.* New York: Haworth Press.

PALMER, S. THOMPSON, R.J., & LINSHELD, T.R. (1975). Applied behavior analysis in the treatment of children's feeding problems. *Developmental Medicine and Child Neurology, 17*, 333.

PAPIERNIK, E. (1984). Proposals for a programmed prevention policy of preterm birth. *Clinical Obstetrics and Gynecology, 27*(3), 614–635.

PARKE, R.D., & O'LEARY, S.E. (1976). Family interaction in the newborn period: Some findings, some observations and some unresolved issues. In K.F. Riegel & J.A. Meacham (Eds.), *The developing individual in a changing world: Vol. 2. Social and environmental issues* (pp. 653–663). The Hague: Mouton.

PARKE, R.D. & TINSLEY, B.R. (1981). The father's role in infancy: Determinants of involvement in caregiving and play. In M.E. Lamb (Ed.), *The role of the father in child development (2nd ed.).* New York: Wiley.

PARKER, S., GREER, S., & ZUCKERMAN, B. (1988). Double jeopardy: The impact of poverty on early child development. In B. Zuckerman, M. Weitzman, & J. Alpert (Eds.), *Children at risk. Pediatric Clinics of North America, 35*, 1227–1240. Philadelphia: W.B. Saunders.

PARMELEE, A.H. (1963). The hand-mouth reflex of Babkin in premature infants. *Pediatrics, 31*, 734–740.

PARMELEE, A.H. (1979). Assessment of the infant at risk during the first year. In E. Sell (Ed.), *Follow-up of the high-risk newborn: A practical approach.* Springfield, IL: C. Thomas.

PARMELEE, A.H. (1981). Auditory function and neurological maturation in preterm infants. In S. Friedman & M. Sigman (Eds.), *Preterm birth and psychological development* (pp. 227–250). New York: Academic Press.

PARMELEE, A.H. (1989). The child's physical health and the development of relationships. In A.J. Sameroff & R.N. Emde (Eds.), *Relationship disturbances in early childhood: A developmental approach.* New York: Basic Books.

PARMELEE, A.H., BECKWITH, L., COHEN, S.E., & SIGMAN, M. (1983). Social influences on infants at medical risk. In J.D. Call, E. Galenson, & R.L. Tyson (Eds.), *Frontiers of infant psychiatry* (pp. 247–263). New York: Basic Books.

PARMELEE, A.H., & SIGMAN, M.D. (1983). Perinatal brain development and behavior.

In P.H. Mussen (Ed.), *Handbook of child psychology: Vol. 2. Infancy and developmental psychobiology* (4th ed., pp. 95–155). New York: John Wiley & Sons.

PARSON, A.S., & MCINTOSH, D.K. (1987). Serving handicapped infants and toddlers in rural areas: Impact of PL 99–457. *Journal of Rural and Small Schools, 2,* 2–7.

PATRICK, J., CAMPBELL, K., CARMICHAEL, L., & PROBERT, C. (1982). Patterns of gross fetal body movements over 24-hour observation intervals during the last 10 weeks of pregnancy. *American Journal of Obstetrics and Gynecology, 142,* 363.

PATTERSON, G.R. (1982). *Coercive family process.* Eugene, OR: Castalia Publishing.

PATTON, J.R., PAYNE, J.S., & BIERNE-SMITH, M. (1986). *Mental retardation* (2nd ed.) Columbus, OH: Charles E. Merrill.

PEABODY, J.L., & LEWIS, K. (1985). Consequences of newborn intensive care. In A.W. Gottfried & J.L. Gaiter (Eds.), *Infant stress under intensive care: Environmental neonatalogy* (pp. 199–226). Baltimore: University Park Press.

PEDERSEN, F.A. (1975). Mother, father, and infant as an interactive system. In J. Belsky (Ed.), *In the beginning: Readings on infancy.* New York: Columbia University Press.

PEDERSEN, F.A., & ROBSON, K.S. (1969). Father participation in infancy. *American Journal of Orthopsychiatry, 39,* 466–472.

PELLEGRINI, D.S., & NOTARIUS, C.I. (1988). Marital processes as childhood risk factors: Implications for intervention and prevention. In E.D. Hibbs (Ed.), *Children and families; Studies in prevention and intervention.* Madison, WI: International Universities Press.

PENROSE, L.S. (1949). *The biology of mental defect.* New York: Grune & Stratton.

PETTIT, G.S., & BATES, J.E. (1989). Family interaction patterns and children's behavior problems from infancy to 4 years. *Developmental Psychology, 25,* 413–420.

PFEIFFER, S., & TITTLER, B.I. (1983). Utilizing the multidisciplinary team to facilitate a school-family systems orientation. *School Psychology Review, 12,* 168–173.

PIAGET, J. (1929). *The child's conception of the world.* New York: Harcourt & Brace.

PIAGET, J. (1951). *Play, dreams and imitation in childhood.* New York: Norton.

PIAGET, J. (1952). *The origins of intelligence in children.* (M. Cook, Translator). New York: International Universities Press.

PIAGET, J. (1954). *The construction of reality in the child.* New York: Basic Books.

PIAGET, J. (1970). Piaget's theory. In P.H. Mussen (Ed.), *Carmichael's manual of child psychology* (3rd ed., pp. 703–732). New York: John Wiley & Sons.

PINKER, S. (1984). *Language development and language learnability.* Cambridge, MA: Harvard University Press.

PLOMIN, R. (1989). Developmental behavior genetics: Stability and instability. In M.H. Bornstein & N.A. Krasnegor (Eds.), *Stability and continuity in mental development: Behavioral and biological perspectives.* Hillsdale, NJ: Lawrence Erlbaum Associates.

PLUNKETT, J.W., KLEIN, T., & MEISELS, S.J. (1988). The relationship of preterm infant-mother attachment to stranger sociability at 3 years. *Infant Behavior and Development, 11,* 83–96.

POLLOCK, L. (1983). *Forgotten children: Parent-child relations from 1500–1900.* Cambridge, London: Cambridge University Press.

PORGES, S.W. (1983). Heart rate patterns in neonates. In T. Fields & A. Sostek (Eds.), *Infants born at risk: Physiological, perceptual and cognitive processes* (pp. 3–22). New York: Grune & Stratton.

POWELL, T.H., & HECIMOVIC, A. (1985). Baby Doe and the search for a quality life. *Exceptional Children, 51,* 315–323.

PRECHTL, H.F. (1958). The direct headturning response and allied movements of the human baby. *Behavior, 13,* 212–242.

PRECHTL, H.F. (1977). The neurological examination of the full-term newborn infant. *Clinics in Developmental Medicine* (No. 63). Philadelphia: J.B. Lippincott.

PRECHTL, H.F. (1981). The study of neural development as perspective of clinical problems. In K.J. Connolly & H.F. Prechtl (Eds.), *Maturation and development: Biological and psychological perspectives* (pp. 198–216). Philadelphia: J.B. Lippincott.

PRECHTL, H.F. (1987). Prenatal development of postnatal behaviour. In H. Rauh & H.C. Steinhausen (Eds.), *Psychobiology and early development*. Amsterdam: North-Holland.

PRECHTL, H.F., & BEINTEMA, D. (1964). The neurological examination of the full-term newborn infant. *Clinics in Developmental Medicine* (No. 12). Philadelphia: J.B. Lippincott (Spastics International Medicine Publications).

President's Commission for the Study of Ethical Problems in Medicine and Biomedical and Behavioral Research. (1983). Seriously ill newborns. In *Deciding to forego life-sustaining treatment*. Washington, DC: U.S. Government Printing Office.

Pueblo Infant Parent Education Project (PIPE Project). Final Report. Western Illinois University, Macomb College of Education.

PULSKAMP, B. (1987). *A model for mother and child counseling intervention.* Paper presented at the National Center for Clinical Infant Programs, Los Angeles.

PYE, C., INGRAM, D., & LIST, H. (1987). A comparison of initial consonant acquisition in English and Quiche. In K.E. Nelson & A. Van Kleek (Eds.), *Children's language* (vol. 6, pp. 175–190). Hillsdale, NJ: Lawrence Erlbaum Associates.

RABINOWITZ, F.M., GRANT, M.J., & DINGLEY, H.L. (1987). Computer simulation, cognition, and development: An introduction. In J. Bisanz, C.J. Brainerd, & R. Kail (Eds.), *Formal methods in developmental psychology: Progress in cognitive development research.* New York: Springer-Verlag.

RADKE-YARROW, M. (1986). Affective development in young children. In T.B. Brazelton & M.W. Yogman (Eds.), *Affective development in infancy.* Norwood, NJ: Ablex.

RADKE-YARROW, M., & KUCZYNSKI, L. (1983). Conceptions of environment in childbearing interactions. In D. Magnusson & V.L. Allen (Eds.), *Human development: An interactional perspective.* New York: Academic Press.

RAMEY, C.T., & BRYANT, D.M. (1988). Prevention-oriented infant education programs. In E.D. Hibbs (Ed.), *Children and families; Studies in prevention and intervention.* Madison, WI: International Universities Press.

RAMEY, C.T., LEE, M.W., & BURCHINAL, M.R. (1989). Development plasticity and predictability: Consequences of ecological change. In M.H. Bornstein & N.A. Krasnegor (Eds.), *Stability and continuity in mental development: Behavioral and biological perspectives.* Hillsdale, NJ: Lawrence Erlbaum Associates.

RAMEY, C.T., STEDMAN, D.J., BORDERS-PATTERSON, A. & MENGEL, W. (1978). Predicting school failure from information available at birth. *American Journal of Mental Deficiency, 82*(6), 525–534.

RAMEY, C.T., & SUAREZ, T.M. (1984). Early intervention and the early experience paradigm: Toward a better framework for social policy. *Journal of Children in Contemporary society, 17,* 3–13.

RAYE, J.R., & HEALEY, J.M. (1984). The neonatal intensive-care unit: Developing an acceptable public policy. *Topics in Early Childhood Special Education, 4*(1), 71–82.

REARDON, P., & BUSHNELL, W.Q. (1988). Infants' sensitivity to arbitrary pairings of color and taste. *Infant Behavior and Development, 11,* 245–250.

REDDING, R.E., MORGAN, G.A., & HARMON, R.J. (1988). Mastery motivation in infants and toddlers: Is it greatest when tasks are moderately challenging? *Infant Behavior and Development, 11,* 419–430.

REDDITI, J.S. (1983). Occupational and physical therapy treatment components for infant intervention programs. *Physical and Occupational Therapy in Pediatrics, 3,* 33–44.

REISS, D. (1989). The represented and practicing family: Contrasting visions of family continuity. In A.J. Sameroff & R.N. Emde (Eds.), *Relationship disturbances in early childhood: A developmental approach.* New York: Basic Books.

RESNICK, M.B., ARMSTRONG, S., & CARTER, R.L. (1988). Developmental intervention program for high-risk premature infants: Effects on development and parent-infant interactions. *Journal of Developmental and Behavioral Pediatrics, 9,* 73–78.

REUTER, J.M., & BICKETT, L. (1985). *Kent infant development scale manual.* Kent, OH: Kent Developmental Metrics.

RICKS, M.H. (1985). The social transmission of parental behavior: Attachment across generations. In I. Bretherton & E. Waters (Eds.), Growing points of attachment theory and research (pp. 211–227). *Monographs of the Society for Research in Child Development, 50* (1–2, Serial No. 209).

RIEDER, C., & CICCHETTI, D. (1989). Organizational perspective on cognitive control functioning and cognitive-affective balance in maltreated children. *Developmental Psychology, 25,* 382–393.

RIESER, J., YONAS, A., & WILKNER, K. (1976). Radical localization of odors by human newborns. *Child Development, 47,* 856–859.

RIGGS, K.M. (1985). *HCI-IFU: Infant follow-up services offered by the Tennessee Department of Health and Environment.* Paper presented at the National Center for Clinical Infant Programs, Biennial National Training Institute, Washington, DC.

ROBINSON, C.C., ROSE, J., & JACKSON, B. (1986). Multidomain assessment instruments. *Diagnostique, 11,* 180–192.

ROGERS, S.J. (1982). Techniques of infant assessment. In Ulrey, G., & Rogers, S.J. (Eds.), *Psychological assessment of handicapped infants and young children* (pp. 59–64). New York: Thieme-Stratton.

ROGERS, S.J., D'EUGENIO, D.B., BROWN, S.L., DONOVAN, C.M., & LYNCH, E.W. (1981). *Early intervention developmental profile.* Ann Arbor: University of Michigan Press.

ROGERS, S.J., HERBISON, J.M., LEWIS, H.C., PANTONE, J., & REIS, K. (1986). An approach for enhancing the symbolic, communicative and iterpersonal functioning of young children with autism and severe emotional handicaps. *Journal of the Division for Early Childhood, 10,* 135–148.

ROGGMAN, L.A., LANGLOIS, J.H., & HUBBS-TAIT, L. (1987). Mothers, infants, and toys: Social play correlates of attachment. *Infant Behavior and Development, 10,* 233–237.

ROSE, S.A. (1989). Measuring infant intelligence: New perspectives. In M.H. Bornstein & N.A. Krasnegor (Eds.), *Stability and continuity in mental development: Behavioral and biological perspectives.* Hillsdale, NJ: Lawrence Erlbaum Associates.

ROSE, S.A., FELDMAN, J.F., WALLACE, I.F., & McCARTON, C. (1989). Infant visual attention: Relation to birth status and developmental outcome during the first 5 years. *Developmental Psychology, 25,* 560–576.

ROSE, S.A., & RUFF, H. (1987). Cross modal abilities in human infants. In J. Osofsky (Ed.), *Handbook of infant development* (2nd ed., pp. 318–362). New York: John Wiley & Sons.

ROSENBERG, S., & ROBINSON, C. (1985). Enhancement of mothers' interactional, skills in an infant education program. *Education and Training of the Mentally Retarded, 20*(2), 163–169.

ROSENBERG, S., ROBINSON, C., & BECKMAN, P. (1984). Teaching skills inventory: A measure of parent performance. *Journal of the Division for Early Childhood, 8,* 107–113.

ROSENBERG, S.A., ROBINSON, C.C., & BECKMAN, P.J. (1986). Measures of parent-infant interaction: An overview. *Topics in Early Childhood Special Education, 6*(2), 32–43.

ROSENBLITH, J.F., & SIMS-KNIGHT, J.E. (1985). *In the beginning: Development in the first two years.* Monterey, CA: Brooks/Cole.

ROSS, R., MIMOUNI, F., & TSANG, R.C. (1988). Fetal and neonatal skeletal growth and mineralization. In B.S. Linblad (Ed.), *Perinatal nutrition.* New York: Academic Press.

ROSSETTI, L.M. (1986). *High risk infants: Identification, assessment, and intervention.* London: Taylor & Francis.

RUBENSTEIN, A., & BERNSTEIN, L. (1986). The epidemiology of pediatric acquired immunodeficiency syndrome. *Clinical Immunology and Immunopathology, 40,* 115-121.

RUSSMAN, B.S. (1986). Are infant stimulation programs useful? *Archives of Neurology, 43*(3), 282-283.

RUTTER, M. (1984). Issues and prospects in developmental neuropsychiatry. In M. Rutter (Ed.), *Developmental neuropsychiatry* (pp. 577-598). New York: Guilford.

RUTTER, M. (1985). Infantile autism and other pervasive developmental disorders. In M. Rutter & L. Hersov (Eds.), *Child and adolescent psychiatry: Modern approaches* (2nd ed., pp. 545-566). Oxford: Blackwell.

RUTTER, M. (1986). Infantile autism: Assessment, differential diagnosis and treatment. In D. Shaffer, A. Erhardt & L. Greenhill (Eds.), *A clinical guide to child psychiatry* (pp. 314-332). New York: Free Press.

SAIGAL, S., ROSENBAUM, P., STOSKOPF, B., & MILNER, R. (1982). Follow-up of infants 501-1500 grams birthweight delivered to residents of a geographically defined region with perinatal intensive care facilities. *Journal of Pediatrics, 100,* 606-613.

SAMEROFF, A.J. (1989). Principles of development and psychopathology. In A.J. Sameroff & R.N. Emde (Eds.), *Relationship disturbances in early childhood: A developmental approach.* New York: Basic Books.

SAMEROFF, A., & CHANDLER, M. (1975). Reproductive risk and the continuum of caretaking causalty. In F.D. Horowitz, M. Hetherington, S. Scarr-Salapatek, & M. Siegel (Eds.), *Review of child development research,* (Vol. 4, pp. 187-244) Chicago: University of Chicago Press.

SAMEROFF, A.J., & EMDE, R.N. (1989). Relationship disturbances in context. In A.J. Sameroff & R.N. Emde (Eds.), *Relationship disturbances in early childhood: A developmental approach.* New York: Basic Books.

SANDALL, S. (1986). *Turntaking: Strategies for enhancing adult-child interactions.* Unpublished dissertation, University of Washington, Seattle.

SANDERS-PHILLIPS, K., STRAUSS, M.E., & GUTBERLET, R.L. (1988). The effect of obstetric medication on newborn infant feeding behavior. *Infant Behavior and Development, 11,* 251-263.

SANFORD, A. (1981). *Learning Accomplishment Profile for Infants* (Early LAP). Winston Salem, NC: Kaplan School Supply.

San Francisco Infant Program. (1982). *Final progress report, July 1, 1981-June 30, 1982.* San Francisco State University and California Department of Special Education.

SATTERFIELD, M.J., & YASUMURA, K. (1987). Facilitating the high risk neonate's head control: Effect of teaching method on mother's performance. *International Journal of Rehabilitation Research, 10*(1), 55-62.

SAYLOR, C.F., LEVKOFF, A.N., & ELKSNIN, N. (1989). Premature infants with intraventricular hemorrhage: A need for early intervention. *Topics in Early Childhood Special Education, 9*(3), 86-99.

SCHAFER, D.S., & MOERSCH, M.S. (Eds.) (1981). *Developmental programming for infants and young children.* Ann Arbor: University of Michigan Press.

SCHAFER, D.S., & MOERSCH, M.S. (Eds.) (1981). *Early intervention developmental profile.* Ann Arbor, MI: University of Michigan Press.

SCHAFER, M., HATCHER, R.P., & BARGLOW, P.D. (1980). Prematurity and infant stimulation: A review of research. *Child Psychiatry and Human Development, 10,* 199–212.

SCHAFFER, H.R. (Ed.). (1977). *Studies of mother-infant interaction.* New York: Academic press.

SCHAFFER, H.R. (1984). *The child's entry into a social world.* London: Academic Press.

SCHAFFER, H.R., & EMERSON, P.E. (1964). The development of social attachments in infancy. *Monographs of the Society for Research in Child Development, 29* (e, Serial No. 94).

SCHERER, N., & OLSWANG, L. (1984). Role of mothers' expansions in stimulating childrens' language production. *Journal of Speech and Hearing Research, 27,* 387–396.

SCHNEIDER, J.W., GRIFFITH, D.R., & CHASNOFF, I.J. (1989). Infants exposed to cocaine in utero: Implications for developmental assessment and intervention. *Infants and Young Children, 2*(1), 25–36.

SCHOPLER, E. & MESIBOV, G.B. (1986). Introduction to social behavior in autism. In E. Schopler & G.B. Mesibov (Eds.) *Social behavior in autism* (pp. 1–14). New York: Plenum.

SCHRAG, E. (1988). *Sensitivities, skills, and services: Mental health roles in the implementation of Part H of PL 99-457 the Education of the Handicapped Act Amendments of 1986.* Washington, DC: National Center for Clinical Infant Programs.

SCHUYLER, V. & RUSHMER, N. (1987). *Parent-infant habilitation.* Portland, OR: IHR Publications.

SCHWARTZ, S.R., GOLDMAN, H.H., & CHURGIN, S. (1982). Case management for the chronically mentally ill: Models and dimensions. *Hospital and Community Psychiatry, 33* (12), 1006–1009.

SEIBERT, J.M., HOGAN, A.E., & MUNDY, P.C. (1987). Assessing social and communication skills in infancy. *Topics in Early Childhood Special Education, 7*(2), 38–48.

SEITZ, V. (1988). Methodology. In M.H. Bornstein & M.E. Lamb (Eds.), *Developmental psychology: An advanced textbook* (2nd ed.). Hillsdale, N.J.: Lawrence Erlbaum Associates.

SELF., P.A., & HOROWITZ, F.D. (1979). The behavioral assessment of the neonate: An overview. In J.D. Osofsky, (Ed.), *Handbook of infant development,* New York: John Wiley & Sons.

SHARAV, T., & SHLOMO, L. (1986). Stimulation of infants with Down syndrome: Long-term effects. *Mental Retardation, 24*(2), 81–86.

SHATZ, M. (1987). Bootstrapping operations in child language. In K.E. Nelson & A. Van Kleek (Eds.), *Children's language* (Vol. 6, pp. 1–22). Hillsdale, NJ: Lawrence Erlbaum Associates.

SHAYWITZ, S.E., COHEN, D.J., & SHAYWITZ, B.A. (1978). The expanded fetal alcohol syndrome (EFAS): Behavioral and learning deficits in children with normal intelligence. *Pediatric Research, 12,* 375.

SHEARER, A. (1985). Everybody's ethics: What future for handicapped babies? *Early Child Development and Care, 18*(3–4), 189–216.

SHEARER, D.E., & SHEARER, M.S. (1976). The Portage Project: A model for early childhood intervention. In T. Tjossem (Ed.), *Intervention strategies for high risk infants and young children* (pp. 335–350). Austin, TX: Pro-Ed.

SHELTON, T.L., JEPPSON, E.S., & JOHNSON, B.H. (1987). *Family-centered care for children with special health-care needs.* Washington, D.C.: Association for the Care of Children's Health.

SHIPE, D., VANDENBERG, S., & WILLIAMS, R.D.B. (1968). Neonatal Apgar ratings as related to intelligence and behavior in preschool children. *Child Development, 39,* 861–866.

SHONKOFF, J.P., HAUSER-CRAM, P., KRAUSS, M.W., & UPSHUR, C.C. (1988). Early intervention efficacy research: What have we learned and where do we go from here? *Topics in Early Childhood Special Education, 8,* 81–93.

SHULMAN, V.L. (1985). *The future of Piagetian theory: The neo-Piagetians.* New York: Plenum Press.

SIEGEL, L. (1985). Biological and environmental variables as predictors of intellectual functioning at 6 years of age. In S. Harel & N.J. Anastasiow (Eds.), *The at-risk infant: Psycho/socio/medical aspects.* Baltimore: Paul H. Brookes.

SIEGEL, L.S. (1989). A reconceptualization of prediction from infant test scores. In P. Fedor-Freybergh & M.L.V. Vogel (Eds.), *Prenatal and perinatal psychology and medicine; Encounter with the unborn.* Lancaster, UK: Parthenon Publishing Group.

SIGMAN, M. & UNGERER, J.A. (1984). Attachment behaviors in autistic children. *Journal of Autism and Developmental Disorders, 14,* 231–244.

SIMEONSSON, R.J., BAILEY, D.B., HUNTINGTON, G.S., & COMFORT, M. (1986). Testing the concept of goodness of fit in early intervention. Special issue: Social support, family functioning, and infant development. *Infant Mental Health Journal, 7(1),* 81–94.

SIMEONSSON, R.J., HUNTINGTON, G.S., & PARSE, S. (1980). Expanding the developmental assessment of young handicapped children. In J.J. Gallagher (Ed.), *New directions for exceptional children: Young exceptional children* (No. 3., pp. 51–74). San Francisco: Jossey-Bass.

SIMEONSSON, R.J., HUNTINGTON, G.S., & SHORT, R.J. (1982). Individual differences and goals: An approach to the evaluation of child progress. *Topics in Early Childhood Special Education, 1(4),* 71–80.

SIMEONSSON, R.J., HUNTINGTON, G.S., SHORT, R.J., & WARE, W.B. (1982). The Carolina record of infant behavior: Characteristics of handicapped infants and children. *Topics in Early Childhood Special Education, 2(2),* 43–55.

SIMMONS, F.B. (1977). Automated screening test for newborns: The Crib-O-Gram. In B.F. Jaffe (Ed.), *Hearing loss in children.* Baltimore: University Park Press.

SIMONS, C.J.R., RITCHIE, S.K., MULLETT, M.D., & MINGARELLE, C.C. (1989). Subject loss and its implications for a high-risk population. *Infant Behavior and Development, 12,* 139–146.

SKEELS, H.M., & DYE, H.B. (1939). A study of the effects of differential stimulation on mentally retarded children. *Proceedings and Addresses of the American Association on Mental Deficiency, 44,* 114–136.

SKINNER, B.F. (1957). *Verbal behavior.* New York: Appleton-Century-Crofts.

SKINNER, B.F. (1966). *The behavior of organisms: An experimental analysis.* New York: Appleton-Century-Crofts.

SKINNER, B.F. (1972). *Cumulative record: A selection of papers* (3rd ed.). New York: Appleton-Century-Crofts.

SKINNER, B.F. (1976). *About behaviorism.* New York: Vintage Books.

SLADE, C.I., REDL, O.J., & MANGUTEN, H.H. (1977). Working with parents of high-risk newborns. *Journal of Obstetric and Gynecologic Nursing, 6,* 21–26.

SLUCKIN, W. & HERBERT, M. (1986). *Parental behaviour.* Oxford: Blackwell.

SMETANA, J.G. (1989). Toddlers' social interactions in the context of moral and conventional transgression in the home. *Development Psychology, 25,* 499–508.

SMITH, B.J. (1988). Early intervention public policy: Past, present, and future. In J.B. Jordan, J. Gallagher, P.L. Hutinger, & M.B. Karnes (Eds.), *Early childhood special education: Birth to three* (pp. 213–229). Reston, VA: Council for Exceptional Children.

SMITH, B.J., & STRAIN, P.S. (1988). Early childhood special education in the next decade: Implementing and expanding P.L. 99–457. *Topics in Early Childhood Special Education, 8,* 37–47.

SMITH, D.W. (1988). *Recognizable patterns of human malformations* (4th ed.) Philadelphia: W.B. Saunders.

SMITH, J.D. (1985). Handicapped infants and euthanasia: A challenge to our advocacy. *Expectional Children, 51(4),* 335–338.

SMITH, P.D. (1989). Assessing motor skills. In D.B. Bailey & M. Wolery (Eds.), *Assessing infants and preschoolers with handicaps* (pp. 301–338). Columbus, OH: Merrill.

SMITH, R.D. (1987). Multicultural considerations: Working with families of developmentally disabled and high risk children. The Hispanic perspective. Paper presented at the conference of the National Center for Clinical Infant Programs, Los Angeles, CA.

SMOTHERMAN, W.P. & ROBINSON, S.R. (1987). Psychobiology of fetal experience in the rat. In N.A. Krasnegor, E.M. Blass, M.A. Hofer, & W.P. Smotherman (Eds.), *Perinatal development: A psychobiological perspective.* New York: Harcourt Brace Jovanovich.

SNEAD, O.C., BENTON, J.W., and MYERS, G.J. (1983). ACTH and prednisone in childhood seizure disorders. *Neurology, 33,* 966–970.

SNOW, C.W. (1989). *Infant development.* Englewood Cliffs, N.J.: Prentice Hall.

SNOW, C.E., PERLMAN, R., & NATHAN, D. (1987). Why routines are different: Toward a multiple-factors model of the relation between input and language acquisition. In K.E. Nelson & A. Van Kleek (Eds.), *Children's language* (Vol. 6, pp. 65–98). Hillsdale, NJ: Lawrence Erlbaum Associates.

SNYDER-McLEAN, L. (1986). Forword. In L.M. Rossetti, *High risk infants: Identification, assessment and intervention.* (pp. xi–xiii). London: Taylor & Francis.

SOLOMON, M.A. (1985). How do we really empower families? New strategies for social work practitioners. *Family Resource Coalition Report, 3,* 2–3.

SOSTEK, A.M. (1978). Annotated bibliography of research using the neonatal behavioral assessment scale. *Monographs of the Society for Research in Child Development, 43,* 124–135.

SPENCE, M.J., & DeCASPER, A.J. (1987). Prenatal experience with low frequency maternal-voice sounds influence neonatal perception of maternal voice samples. *Infant Behavior and Development, 10,* 133–142.

SPUNGEN, L.B., & FARRAN, A.C. (1986). Effect of intensive care unit exposure on temperament in low birth weight preterm infants. *Journal of Developmental and Behavioral Pediatrics, 7,* 288–292.

SROUFE, L.A. (1983). Infant-caregiver attachment and adaptation in the preschool: The roots of competence and maladaptation. In M. Perlmutter (Ed.), *Development of cognition, affect, and social relations* (pp. 41–81). Hillsdale, NJ: Lawrence Erlbaum Associates.

SROUFE, L.A. (1985). Attachment classification from the perspective of infant-caregiver relationship and infant temperament. *Child Development, 56,* 1–14.

SROUFE, L.A. (1988). The role of infant-caregiver attachment in development. In J. Belsky & T. Nexworski (Eds.), *Clinical implications of attachment.* Hillsdale, N.J.: Lawrence Erlbaum Associates.

SROUFE, L.A. (1989a). Relationships and relationship disturbances. In A.J. Sameroff & R.N. Emde (Eds.), *Relationship disturbances in early childhood: A developmental approach.* New York: Basic Books.

SROUFE, L.A. (1989b). Relationships, self, and individual adaptation. In A.J. Sameroff & R.N. Emde (Eds.), *Relationship disturbances in early childhood: A developmental approach.* New York: Basic Books.

SROUFE, L.A., COOPER, R.G., & MARSHALL, M.E. (1988). *Child development: Its nature and course.* New York: Alfred A. Knopf.

SROUFE, L.A., & FLEESON, J. (1986). Attachment and the construction of relationships. In W. Hartup & Z. Rubin (Eds.), *Relationships and development.* Hillsdale, NJ: Lawrence Erlbaum Associates.

SROUFE, L.A., & ROSENBERG, D. (1980, March). *Coherence of individual adaptation in lower SES infants and toddlers.* Paper presented at the International Conference on Infant Studies, Providence, RI.

SROUFE, L.A., & WATERS, E. (1977). Attachment as an organizational construct. *Child Development, 48,* 1184–1199.

STARK, J.S., MENOLASCINO, F.J., & MCGEE, J.J. (1984). Major legal/ethical challenges in the care and treatment of the mentally retarded. *Psychiatric Medicine, 2*(3), 295–304.

STEEL, K.O. (1985). The satellite clinic: A model for the treatment of handicapped children in towns and rural areas. *Developmental Medicine and Child Neurology, 27,* 355–363.

STEIN, L., & PIEN, D. (1982). *A model program for hearing handicapped infants providing medical, academic, and psychological services (HI-MAPS).* Final Report, July 1979–June, 1982. Chicago, IL: Michael Reese Hospital and Medical Center.

STEINBERG, R.M., & CARTER, G.M. (1983). *Case management and the elderly.* Lexington, Mass: Lexington Books.

STEINER, J. (1977). Facial expressions of the neonate indicating the hedonics of food related chemical stimuli. In J. Wiffenbach (Ed.), *Taste and development: The genesis of sweet preference* (pp. 173–204). Bethesda, MD: National Institute of Health (DHEW Pub. No. NIH 77-1068).

STERN, D.N. (1974). Mother and infant at play: The dyadic interaction involving facial, vocal and gaze behaviors. In M. Lewis & L.A. Rosenblum (Eds.), *The effect of the infant on its caregiver.* New York: John Wiley & Sons.

STERN, D.N. (1989). The representation of relational patterns: Developmental considerations. In A.J. Sameroff & R.N. Emde (Eds.), *Relationship disturbances in early childhood: A developmental approach.* New York: Basic Books.

STERN, D.N., BEEBE, B., JAFFE, J., & BENNETT, S.L. (1977). The infant's stimulus world during social interaction: A study of caregiver behaviors with particular reference to repetition and timing. In H.R. Schaffer (Ed.), *Studies in mother-infant interaction.* London: Academic Press.

STERNBERG, R.J. (1984). Testing intelligence without IQ tests. *Phi Delta Kappan, 65,* 694–698.

STERNBERG, R.J. (1986). *Intelligence applied: Understanding and increasing your intellectual skills.* San Diego: Harcourt Brace Jovanovich.

STERNBERG, R.J. (1987). Implicit theories: An alternative to modeling cognition and its development. In. J. Bisanz, C.J. Brainerd, & R. Kail (Eds.), *Formal methods in developmental psychology: Progress in cognitive development research.* New York: Springer-Verlag.

STEVENSON, M.B., LEAVITT, L.A., THOMPSON, R.H., & ROACH, M.A. (1988). A social relations model analysis of parent and child play. *Developmental Psychology, 24*(1), 101–107.

STEVENSON, M.B., VER HOEVE, J.N., ROACH, M.A., & LEAVITT, L.A. (1986). The beginning of conversation: Early patterns of mother-infant vocal responsiveness. *Infant Behavior and Development, 9,* 423–440.

STEWART, R.B. (1983). Sibling interaction: The role of the older child as teacher for the younger. *Merrill Palmer Quarterly, 29*(1), 47–68.

STEWART, R.B., & MARVIN, R.S. (1984). Sibling relations: The role of conceptual perspective-taking in the ontogeny of sibling caregiving. *Child Development, 55*(4), 1322–1332.

STIFTER, C.A., FOX, N.A., & PORGES, S.W. (1989). Facial expressivity and vagal tone in 5- and 10-month-old infants. *Infant Behavior and Development, 12,* 127–137.

STILLMAN, R. (Ed.), (1978). *The Callier Azusa scale.* Dallas: The University of Texas at Dallas.

STOCKBAUER, J.W. (1987). WIC prenatal participation and its relation to pregnancy outcomes in Missouri: A second look. *American Journal of Public Health, 77,* 813–818.

STONE, L.J., & CHURCH, J. (1984). *Childhood and adolescence; A psychology of the growing person.* New York: Random House.

STRAIN, P. & SMITH, B. (1986). A counter-interpretation of early intervention effects: A response to Casto and Mastropieri. *Exceptional Children, 53,* 260–265.

STRAUSS, M.S., & BROWNELL, C.A. (1984). A commentary on infant stimulation and intervention. *Journal of Children in Contemporary Society, 17,* 133–139.

STREISSGUTH, A.P., BARR, H.M., SAMPSON, P.D., DARBY, B.L., & MARTIN, D.C. (1989). IQ at age 4 in relation to maternal alcohol use and smoking during pregnancy. *Developmental Psychology, 25,* 3–11.

STREISSGUTH, A.P., MARTIN, D.C., BARR, H.M. & SANDMAN, B. (1984). Intrauterine alcohol and nicotine exposure: Attention and reaction time in 4-year-old children. *Developmental Psychology, 20,* 533–541.

STREMEL-CAMPBELL, K., & ROWLAND, C. (1987). Prelinguistic communication intervention: Birth-to-2. *Topics in Early Childhood Special Education, 7*(2), 49–58.

STROM, R.D., BERNARD, H.W., & STROM, S.K. (1987). *Human development and learning.* New York: Human Sciences Press.

SUBER, C.F. (1987). Formal representation of qualitative and quantitative reversible operations. In J. Bisanz, C.J. Brainerd, & R. Kail (Eds.), *Formal methods in developmental psychology: Progress in cognitive development research.* New York: Springer-Verlag.

SULLIVAN, M.W., & LEWIS, M. (1988). Facial expressions during learning in 1-year-old infants. *Human Behavior and Development, 11,* 369-373.

SUTTON, E.H. (1975). *An introduction to human genetics.* New York: Holt, Rinehart & Winston.

SZAJNBERG, N., WARD, M.J., KRAUSS, A.,& KESSLER, D.B. (1987). Low birth-weight prematures: Preventive intervention and maternal attitude. *Child Psychiatry and Human Development, 17*(3), 152–165.

TAMIS-LeMONDA, C.S., & BORNSTEIN, M.H. (1989). Habituation and maternal encouragement of attention in infancy as predictors of toddler language, play, and representational competence. *Child development, 60,* 738–751.

TELLER, D.Y., McDONALD, M., PRESTON, K., SEBRIS, S.L., & DOBSON, V. (1986). Assessment of visual acuity in infants and children: The acuity card procedure. *Developmental Medicine and Child Neurology, 28,* 779–789.

TERKELSON, K.G. (1980). Toward a theory of family life cycle. In E. Carter & M. McGoldrick (Eds.), *The family life cycle: A framework of family therapy* (pp. 21–52). New York: Gardner Press.

TETI, D.M., BOND, L.A., & GIBBS, E.D. (1986). Sibling-created experiences: Relationships to birth-spacing and infant cognitive development. *Infant Behavior and Development, 9,* 27–42.

THOMAN, E.B. (1981). Affective communication as the prelude and context for language learning. In R.L. Schiefelbusch & D. Bricker (Eds.), *Early language: Acquisition and intervention.* Baltimore: University Park Press.

THOMAS, A., & CHESS, S. (1977). *Temperament and development.* New York: Bruner-Mazel.

THOMAS, A., & CHESS, S. (1980). *The dynamics of psychological development.* New York: Bruner-Mazel.

THOMAS, A., CHESS, S., & BIRCH, H.G. (1968). *Temperament and behavior disorders in children.* New York: New York University Press.

THOMPSON, G., & WILSON, W. (1984). Clinical application of visual reinforcement audiometry. In J. Northern & W. Perkins (Eds.), *Seminars in hearing: Early identification of hearing loss in infants* (Vol. 5(1), pp. 85–99). New York: Thieme-Stratton.

THOMPSON, J.S. & THOMPSON, M.W. (1986). *Genetics in medicine* (2nd Ed.). Philadelphia: W.B. Saunders.

THOMPSON, R.A., LAMB, M.E., & ESTES, D. (1982). Stability of infant-mother attachment and its relationship to changing life circumstances in an unselected middle class sample. *Child Development, 53,* 144–148.

THOMPSON, E.J. (1989). A genetics primer for early service providers. *Infants and Young Children, 2*(1), 37–48.

THURMAN, S.K., & WIDERSTROM, A.H. (1990). *Infants and young children with special needs: A developmental and ecological approach* (2nd ed.). Baltimore: Paul H. Brookes.

TINSLEY, B.R., & ROSS, D.P. (1983). The person-environment relationship: Lessons from families with preterm infants. In D. Magnusson & V.L. Allen (Eds.), *Human development: An interactional perspective.* New York: Academic Press.

TITTLE, B., & ST. CLAIRE, N. (1989). Promoting the health and development of drug-exposed infants through a comprehensive clinic model. *Zero to Three, 9*(5), 18–20.

TOUWEN, B.C. (1978). Variability and sterotype in normal and deviant development. *Clinics in developmental medicine* (No. 67). Philadelphia: J.B. Lippincott.

TREGOLD, A.F. (1908). *Mental deficiency.* London: Bailliera, Tindall, and Fox.

TREVARTHEN, C. (1977). Descriptive analyses of infant communicative behavior. In H.R. Schaffer (Ed.), *Studies in mother-infant interaction.* New York: Academic Press.

TRAVERS, J. (1982). *The effects of social programs: Final report of the child and family resource programs' infant-toddler component.* Washington, DC: Administration for Children, Youth, and Families (DHHS).

TRIPP, E.D. (1988). Perivolaki: A model therapeutic nursery school. In E.D. Hibbs (Ed.), *Children and families: Studies in prevention and intervention.* Madison, WI: International Universities Press.

TRIVETTE, C.M., DEAL, A., & DUNST, C.J. (1986). Family needs, sources of support, and professional roles: Critical elements of family systems assessment and intervention. *Diagnostique, 11,* 246–267.

TROHANIS, P.L. (1988). Public Law 99-457: New programs for infants, toddlers, and preschoolers. *School Law Bulletin, 19,* 7–12.

TRONICK, E., ALS, H., & BRAZELTON, T.B. (1980). Monadic phases: A structural descriptive analysis of infant-mother face to face interaction. *Merrill-Palmer Quarterly, 26,* 3–24.

TRONICK, E., RICKS, M., & COHN, J. (1982). Maternal and infant affective exchange: Patterns of adaptation. In T. Fields & A. Fogel (Eds.), *Emotion and interaction: Normal and high-risk infants* (pp. 83–100). Hillsdale, NJ: Lawrence Erlbaum Associates.

TROUT, M.D. (1983). Birth of a sick or handicapped infant: Impact on the family. *Child Welfare, 62,* 337–348.

TURNBULL, A.P. (1988). The challenge of providing comprehensive support to families. *Education and Training in Mental Retardation, 23*(4), 261–272.

TURNBULL, A.P., SUMMERS, J.A., & BROTHERSON, M.J. (1984). *Working with families with disabled members: A family systems approach.* Lawrence, KS: Kansas University Affiliated Facility, University of Kansas.

TURNBULL, A.P., SUMMERS, J.A., & BROTHERSON, M.J. (1986). Family life cycle: Theoretical and empirical implications and future directions for families with mentally retarded members. In J.J. Gallagher & P.M. Vietze (Eds.), *Families of handicapped persons: Research, programs, and policy issues* (pp. 45–65). Baltimore: Paul H. Brookes.

TURNBULL, A., & TURNBULL, H.R. III. (1986). *Families, professionals, and exceptionality: A special partnership.* Columbus, OH: Merrill.

TURNER, A. (1987). *Multicultural considerations: Working with families of developmentally disabled and high-risk children. The Black perspective.* Paper presented at the conference of the National Center for Clinical Infant Programs, Los Angeles.

TYLER, C.W. (1982). Assessment of visual function in infants by evoked potentials. *Developmental Medicine and Child Neurology, 24,* 853–856.

UZGIRIS, I.C. (1989). Transformations and continuities: Intellectual functioning in infancy and beyond. In P. Fedor-Freybergh & M.L.V. Vogel (Eds.), *Prenatal and perinatal psychology and medicine; Encounter with the unborn.* Lancaster, UK: Parthenon Publishing Group.

UZGIRIS, I., & HUNT, J.M. (1975). *Assessment in infancy: Ordinal scales of psychological development.* Urbana: University of Illinois Press.

UZGIRIS, I., & HUNT, J.M. (Eds.), (1987). *Infant performance and experience: New findings with the ordinal scales.* Urbana: University of Illinois Press.

VANDELL, D.L., & WILSON, K.S. (1987). Infant's interactions with mother, sibling, and peer: Contrasts and relations between interaction systems. *Child Development, 58*(1), 176–186.

VANDENBERG, K. (1985). Revising the traditional model: An individualized approach to developmental interventions in the intensive care nursery. *Neonatal Network, 3*(5), 4–9.

VAN SERVELLEN, G.M. (1984). *Group and family therapy: A model for psychotherapeutic nursing practice.* St. Louis: C.V. Mosby.

VAUGHN, B.E., EGELAND, B., SROUFE, L.A., & WATERS, E. (1979). Individual differences in infant-mother attachment at 12 and 18 months: Stability and change in families under stress. *Child development, 50,* 971–975.

VAUGHN, B.E., GOVE, F.L., & EGELAND, B. (1980). The relationship between out-of-home care and the quality of infant-mother attachment in an economically disadvantaged population. *Child Development, 51,* 1203–1214.

VAUGHN, B.E., LEFEVER, G.B., SEIFER, R., & BARGLOW, P. (1989). Attachment behavior, attachment security, and temperament during infancy. *Child Development, 60,* 728–737.

VAUGHN, B.E., TARALDSON, B., CRICHTON, L., & EGELAND, B. (1980). Relationships between neonatal behavioral organization and infant behavior during the first year of life. *Infant Behavior and Development, 3,* 47–66.

VIBBERT, M., & BORNSTEIN, M.H. (1989). Specific associations between domains of mother-child interaction and toddler referential language and pretense play. *Infant Behavior and Development, 12,* 163–184.

VIETZE, P.M., & COATES, D.L. (1986). Using information processing strategies for early identification of mental retardation. *Topics in Early Childhood Special Education, 6*(3), 72–85.

VOHS, J.R. (1988). *What families need to know about case management.* Boston: Federation for Children with Special Needs.

VULPE, S.G., POLLINS, E.I., & WILSON, J. (1979). *Vulpe assessment battery.* Toronto, Ontario: Canadian Association for the Mentally Retarded.

WALLERSTEIN, J.S., & KELLY, J.B. (1975). The effects of parental divorce: Experiences of the preschool child. *Journal of the American Academy of Child Psychiatry, 14,* 600–616.

WALLERSTEIN, J.S., & KELLY, J.B. (1976). The effects of parental divorce: Experiences of the child in later latency. *American Journal of Orthopsychiatry, 46,* 256–269.

WALSH, S., CAMPBELL, P.H., & McKENNA, P. (1988). First-year implementation of the federal program for infants and toddlers with handicaps: A view from the states. *Topics in Early Childhood Special Education, 8,* 1–22.

WARREN, S.F., ALPERT, C.L., & KAISER, A.P. (1986). An optimal learning environment for infants and toddlers with severe handicaps. *Focus on Exceptional Children, 18*(8), 1–11.

WARREN, S.F., & KAISER, A.P. (1988). Research in early language intervention. In. S.L. Ocom & M.B. Kaines (Eds.), *Early intervention for infants and children with handicaps.* (pp. 89–108). Baltimore: Paul Brookes.

WARREN, S.F., & ROGERS-WARREN, A.K. (Eds.) (1985). *Teaching functional language.* Austin, TX: Pro-Ed.

WARYAS, C.L., & STREMEL-CAMPBELL, E.K. (1982). *Communication training program: Levels 1, 2, and 3.* Allen, Tx: DLM/Teaching Resources.

WASSERMAN, G.A. (1986). Affective expression in normal and physically handicapped infants: Situational and developmental effects. *Journal of the American Academy of Child Psychiatry, 25*(3), 393–399.

WASSERMAN, G.A., LENNON, M.C., ALLEN, R., & SHILANSKY, M. (1987). Contributors to attachment in normal and physically handicapped infants. *Journal of the American Academy of Child and Adolescent Psychiatry, 26*(1), 9–15.

WATERS, E., WIPPMAN, J., & SROUFE, L.A. (1979). Attachment, positive affect, and competence in the peer group: Two studies in construct validation. *Child Development, 50,* 821–829.

WATKINS, K.P. (1987). *Parent-child attachment: A guide to research.* New York: Garland.

WATSON, J.B. (1924). *Behaviorism.* New York: Norton.

WATSON, J.B. (1928). *Psychological care of infant and child.* New York: Norton.

WATSON, J.B. (1930). *Behaviorism.* Chicago: University of Chicago Press.

WEIL, M., & KARLS, J.M. (1985). *Case management in human service practice.* San Francisco: Jossey-Bass.

WEINER, R., & HUME, M. (1987). . . . *And education for all—Public policy and handicapped children* (2nd ed.). Alexandria, VA: Capitol Publications.

WEINER, R., & KOPPELMAN, J. (1987). *From birth to 5: Serving the youngest handicapped children.* Alexandria, VA: Capitol Publications.

WEINRAUB, M., & WOLF, B.M. (1983). Effects of stress and social support on mother-child interactions in single-parent and two-parent families. *Child Development, 54,* 1297–1311.

WEISS, R. (1981). INREAL intervention for language handicapped and bilingual children. *Journal of the Division for Early Childhood, 4,* 40–51.

WENDT, R.N., & ZAKE, J. (1984). Family systems theory and school psychology: Implications for training and practice. *Psychology in the Schools, 21,* 204–210.

WESTBY, C.E. (1980). Assessment of cognitive and language abilities through play. *Language, Speech, and Hearing Services in Schools, 11,* 154–168.

WESTON, D.R., IVINS, B., ZUCKERMAN, B., JONES, C., & LOPEZ, R. (1989). Drug-exposed babies: Research and clinical issues. *Zero to Three, 9*(5), 1–7.

WIDERSTROM, A.H., & DUDLEY-MARLING, C. (1986). Living with a handicapped child: Myth and reality. *Childhood Education, 62,* 359–367.

WIDERSTROM, A.H., & GOODWIN, L.D. (1987). Effects of an infant stimulation program on the child and family. *Journal of Division for Early Childhood, 11,* 143–153.

WIDMAYER, S., & FIELD, T. (1981). Effects of Brazelton demonstrations for mothers on the development of preterm infants. *Pediatrics, 67,* 711–714.

WIKLER, L., WASOW, M., & HATFIELD, E. (1981). Chronic sorrow revisited: Parents vs. professional depiction of the adjustment of parents of mentally retarded children. *American Journal of Orthopsychiatry, 51,* 63–70.

WILKENSON, A.C., & HAINES, B.A. (1987). Learning a cognitive skill and its components. In J. Bisanz, C.J. Brainerd, & R. Kail (Eds.), *Formal methods in developmental psychology: Progress in cognitive developmental research.* New York: Springer-Verlag.

WILLIAMS, P.D., WILLIAMS, A.R., & DIAL, M.N (1986). Children at risk: Perinatal events, developmental delays and the effects of a developmental stimulation program. *International Journal of Nursing Studies, 23,* 21–38.

WILLIS, W.G., & WIDERSTROM, A.H. (1986). Structure and function in prenatal and postnatal neuropsychological development: A dynamic interaction. In J.E. Obrzut & G.W. Hynd (Eds.), *Child neuropsychology: Vol. 1. Theory and research* (pp. 13–53). New York: Academic Press.

WILLOUGHBY-HERB, S.J., & NEISWORTH, J.T. (1983). *HICOMP Curriculum.* San Antonio, TX: Psychological Corporation.

WILLS, D.M. (1979). The ordinary devoted mother and her blind baby. *Psychoanalytic Study of the Child, 34,* 31–49.

WINICK, M. (1979). *Nutrition: Pre- and postnatal development.* New York: Plenum Press.

WINTON, P.J., & BAILEY, D.B. (1988). The family focused interview: A collaborative mechanism for family assessment and goal-setting. *Journal of the Division for Early Childhood, 12*(3), 195–207.

WOLERY, M. (1983). Evaluating curricula: Purposes and strategies. *Topics in Early Childhood Special Education, 2*(4), 15–24.

WOLERY, M. (1987). Program evaluation at the local level: Recommendations for improving services. *Topics in Early Childhood Special Education, 7*(2), 111–123.

WOLERY, M., BAILEY, D.B., & SUGAI, G.M. (1988). *Effective Teaching.* Boston: Allyn and Bacon.

WOLERY, M., & DYK, L. (1984). Arena assessment: Description and preliminary social validity data. *Journal of the Association for the Severely Handicapped, 9,* 231–235.

WOLFF, P.H. (1987). *The development of behavioral states and the expression of emotions in early infancy: New proposals for investigation.* Chicago: University of Chicago Press.

WOODRUFF, G., STERZIN, E.D., & HANSON, C. (1989). Serving drug-involved families with HIV infection in the community: A case report. *Zero to Three, 9*(5), 12–17.

WOOLRIDGE, M.W., & BAUM, J.D. (1988). The regulation of human milk flow. In B.S. Lindblad (Ed.), *Perinatal nutrition.* New York: Academic Press.

WOROBEY, J. (1986). Convergence among assessments of temperament in the first month. *Child Development, 57,* 47–55.

WOREBEY, J., & BLAJDA, V.M. (1989). Temperament ratings at 2 weeks, 2 months, and 1 year: Differential stability of activity and emotionality. *Developmental Psychology, 25,* 257–263.

WOROBEY, J., & BRAZELTON, T.B. (1986). Experimenting with the family in the newborn period: A commentary. *Child Development, 57,* 1298–1300.

WOREBEY, J. & LEWIS, M. (1989). Individual differences in the reactivity of young infants. *Developmental Psychology, 25,* 663–667.

WYSOCKI, T. (1987). Training pediatric residents in early intervention with handicapped children. *Journal of Medical Education, 62,* 47–52.

YODER, P. (1986). Clarifying the relation between degree of infant handicaps and maternal responsivity to infant communicative cues: Measurement issues. *Infant Mental Health Journal, 7,* 281–293.

YODER, P.J. (1987). Relationship between degree of infant handicap and clarity of infant cues. *American Journal of Mental Deficiency, 91*(6), 639–641.

YODER, P.J., & FARRAN, D.C. (1986). Mother-infant engagements in dyads with handicapped and nonhandicapped infants: A pilot study. *Applied Research in Mental Retardation, 7*(1), 51–58.

YODER, P.J., & FEAGANS, L. (1988). Mothers' attributions of communication to prelinguistic behavior of developmentally delayed and mentally retarded infants. *American Journal on Mental Retardation, 93*(1), 36–43.

YODER, P.J., & KAISER, A.P. (1989). Alternative explanations for the relationship between maternal verbal interaction style and child development. *Journal of Child Language, 16,* 141–160.

YOGMAN, M.W. (1982). Development of the father-infant relationship. In H.E. Fitzgerald, B.M. Lester, & M.W. Yogman (Eds.), *Theory and research in behavioral pediatrics* (Vol. 1, pp. 221–279). New York & London: Plenum.

YURA, M.T. (1987). Family subsystem functions and disabled children: Some conceptual issues. In M. Ferrari & M.B. Sussman (Eds.), *Childhood disability and family systems.* New York: Haworth Press.

ZELAZO, P.R. (1976). From reflexive to instrumental behavior. In L.P. Lipsitt (Ed.), *Developmental psychobiology* (pp. 87–108). Hillsdale, NJ: Lawrence Erlbaum Associates.

ZELAZO, P.R. (1979). Reactivity to perceptual-cognitive events: Applications for infant assessment. In R.B. Kearsley & I.B. Sigel (Eds.), *Infants at risk: Assessment of cognitive functioning* (pp. 112–128). Hillsdale, NJ: Lawrence Erlbaum Associates.

ZESKIND, P.S. (1983). Production and spectral analysis of neonatal crying and its relation to other behavioral systems in the infant at risk. In T. Field & A. Sostek (Eds.), *Infants born at risk: Physiological, perceptual and cognitive processes* (pp. 23–44). New York: Grune & Stratton.

ZESKIND, P.S., & IACINO, R. (1984). Effects of maternal visitation to preterm infants in the neonatal intensive care unit, *Child Development, 55,* 1887–1893.

ZESKIND, P.S., & IACINO, R. (1987). The relation between length of hospitalization and the mental and physical development of preterm infants. *Infant Behavior and Development, 10,* 217–221.

ZIGLER, E. (January, 1990). Child care and children at risk. Keynote address at the annual Queens College School Psychology Conference, Queens, NY.

ZUCKERMAN, B., FRANK, D., HINGSON, R., et al. (1989). Effects of maternal marijuana and cocaine use on fetal growth. *New England Journal of Medicine, 320,* 762–768.

Index

Page numbers followed by t and f indicate tables and figures, respectively.